John Hill Burton

The History of Scotland

From Agricola's invasion to the revolution of 1688

John Hill Burton

The History of Scotland

From Agricola's invasion to the revolution of 1688

ISBN/EAN: 9783337227999

Printed in Europe, USA, Canada, Australia, Japan

Cover: Foto ©ninafisch / pixelio.de

More available books at **www.hansebooks.com**

THE

HISTORY OF SCOTLAND

FROM AGRICOLA'S INVASION TO THE
REVOLUTION OF 1688

BY

JOHN HILL BURTON

VOL. IV.

CONTENTS OF FOURTH VOLUME.

CHAPTER XXXVII.

The Reformation.

PAGE

GOVERNMENT OF MARY OF LORRAINE—HER INABILITY TO UNDERSTAND THE CONSTITUTION OF SCOTLAND—FRENCH PRACTICES—FRENCHMEN PROMOTED TO HIGH OFFICES—ATTEMPT TO PUT THE FORTRESSES IN THEIR HANDS—PROPOSAL OF A STANDING ARMY, AND ITS RECEPTION—QUEEN MARY'S MARRIAGE TO THE DAUPHIN—HIS ACCESSION TO THE CROWN OF FRANCE.—THE COUNTRY ALARMED BY PROJECTS OF ANNEXATION TO THE CROWN OF FRANCE — RISE OF SUSPICION AND DISLIKE OF FRANCE AND THE FRENCH ALLIANCE—THE ALIEN CHARACTER OF THE CHURCH IN SCOTLAND—HOW FAR THE DOCTRINES OF THE REFORMERS WERE SPREADING—SECULAR CAUSES OF ENMITY TO THE CHURCH—WEALTH AND LUXURIOUSNESS OF THE CHURCHMEN — THEIR MORAL CONDITION — THEIR TEMPORAL POWER AS ADMINISTRATORS OF THE LAW—THE POWER OF EXCOMMUNICATION OR CURSING—ITS USE FOR LEVYING DEBTS AND FOR ACTS OF PERSONAL OPPRESSION—SPECIMEN OF A CURSING—THE CHURCH CONSCIOUS OF ITS OWN DEFECTS—INTERNAL EFFORTS AT REFORMATION—REFORMING COUNCILS — ARCHBISHOP HAMILTON'S CATECHISM — THE TWOPENNY FAITH, ... 1-47

CHAPTER XXXVIII.

The Reformation.

(Continued.)

POLITICAL POSITION OF THE REFORMATION QUESTION IN EUROPEAN POLITICS—ARRIVAL OF KNOX—CHARACTERISTICS OF HIS NATURE AND INFLUENCE—HIS COADJUTORS AND THEIR MOTIVES — MAITLAND OF LETHINGTON — THE FIRST BAND OR COVENANT—THE LORDS OF THE CONGREGATION EMBODIED—PRESSURE ON THE QUEEN-REGENT — HER DUPLICITY — THE FIRST OUTBREAK—ATTACKS ON THE SYMBOLS OF POPISH WORSHIP AND THE BUILDINGS OF THE RELIGIOUS ORDERS—CONSIDERATION HOW FAR THE CONDITION OF OLD ECCLESIASTICAL BUILDINGS IN SCOTLAND DUE TO THE REFORMERS—THE CONGREGATION AT PERTH—DEALINGS WITH THE REGENT—OCCUPATION OF EDINBURGH—CONDITION AND DANGERS OF ENGLAND — QUEEN ELIZABETH — KNOX AND THE "BLAST" AGAINST FEMALE RULE—CECIL AND KNOX IN TREATY—DIFFICULTY OF FINDING A LEGITIMATE HEAD TO TREAT WITH IN SCOTLAND—TREATY OF BERWICK—WAR—SIEGE OF LEITH—DEATH OF THE REGENT—DEPARTURE OF THE FRENCH, AND TREATY OF EDINBURGH—REFORMATION STATUTES, . . 48-89

CHAPTER XXXIX.

Condition of the Nation from the War of Independence to the Reformation.

THE CONSTITUTION OF SCOTLAND—THE POWER OF THE ESTATES OF PARLIAMENT—THEIR EXERCISE OF THE EXECUTIVE—LORDS OF THE ARTICLES—THE ESTATES AS A FINAL COURT OF LAW—LORDS AUDITORS—DAILY COUNCIL—ESTABLISHMENT OF THE COURT OF SESSION ON THE MODEL OF THE PARLIAMENT OF PARIS—INFLUENCE OF THIS IMITATION—CHARACTER OF THE INSTITUTIONS—ADAPTATION OF THE CIVIL LAW—ABSENCE OF THE PREROGATIVE OR INVIDIOUS RIGHTS WHICH SET CLASS AGAINST CLASS—CONSTITUTIONAL AND HISTORICAL RESULTS—POPULARITY OF THE NATIONAL INSTITUTIONS—PROVISIONS FOR THE EDUCATION OF THE PEOPLE—GRAMMAR-SCHOOLS—UNIVERSITIES—THEIR TESTIMONY TO AN ELEMENT OF ENLIGHT-

ENED LIBERALITY IN THE CHURCH—THEIR MODEL BROUGHT
FROM FRANCE—VESTIGES OF THIS INFLUENCE IN UNIVERSITY
CONSTITUTION AND PRACTICE, . . . 90-116

CHAPTER XL.

Condition of the Nation from the War of Independence to the Reformation.

(Continued.)

SCOTTISH SCHOLARS—THEIR EARLY FAME ABROAD—COMMENCEMENT OF NATIONAL LITERATURE—THOMAS OF ERCILDOUN—RISE AND PECULIAR CONDITIONS OF A PATRIOTIC LITERATURE—BARBOUR, BLIND HARRY, WYNTOUN, FORDUN, BOWER, BOECE, MAJOR, BUCHANAN, LESLIE—'THE COMPLAYNT OF SCOTLAND'—INFLUENCE OF THE PATRIOTIC LITERATURE—DUNBAR, MONTGOMERY, AND THE OTHER POETS—LANGUAGE OF SCOTTISH LITERATURE—VESTIGES OF CELTIC LITERATURE—PRINTING—THE ARTS—SIGNIFICANCE OF THE ECCLESIASTICAL AND BARONIAL REMAINS—SHOW THE POVERTY FOLLOWING THE WAR, AND THE INFLUENCE OF FRANCE—MATERIAL CONDITION OF THE COUNTRY—EXPORTS AND IMPORTS—MINING—GOLD, SILVER, LEAD, AND COAL—A SPANISH AMBASSADOR'S ACCOUNT OF SCOTLAND IN THE FIFTEENTH CENTURY, . . 117-164

CHAPTER XLI.

Queen Mary.

DEATH OF THE KING OF FRANCE—VISITORS TO THE YOUNG QUEEN—HER BROTHER, AFTERWARDS EARL OF MURRAY—EMBASSY FROM HUNTLY AND THE ROMISH PARTY—PERTINACIOUS DEALING OF QUEEN ELIZABETH'S AMBASSADORS IN FRANCE—QUEEN MARY'S RETURN—HER COMPANIONS—HER RECEPTION—HER PAST AND FUTURE POSITION COMPARED—A PAGEANT—THE RELIGIOUS DIFFICULTY—THE QUESTION OF TOLERATING IDOLATRY—CALVIN CONSULTED—METHODS OF REVILING THE OLD CREED AND CEREMONIES—INTERVIEWS WITH JOHN KNOX—THE FIRST BOOK OF DISCIPLINE—FAILURE OF THE CLERGY TO GET IT CONFIRMED BY PARLIAMENT—REASONS FOR THE LAY MEMBERS OF THE CONGREGATION DISLIKING IT—CONTAINS PROVISIONS FOR APPROPRIATING THE TEMPORALITIES OF THE

CHURCH—WOULD THUS TAKE THEM FROM THE LAY LORDS WHO HAD SECURED THEM—INSTANCES OF THE METHOD OF GETTING AT THEM—ROASTING A COMMENDATOR—KNOX'S WRATH—THE COMPROMISE—MURRAY'S MARRIAGE AND ELEVATION—A CLEARING AMONG THE BORDER THIEVES, . 165-198

CHAPTER XLII.

Queen Mary.

(Continued.)

DANGERS IN THE NORTH—POSITION OF HUNTLY AS LEADER OF THE ROMANIST PARTY—MURRAY'S DESIGNS—A ROYAL PROGRESS—HUNTLY'S FEARS FROM IT—HE ARMS—BATTLE OF CORRICHIE—RUIN OF THE HOUSE OF HUNTLY—QUEEN MARY'S POLICY IN ASSISTING IN THE RUIN OF HER FRIENDS—POSITION OF MARY'S GOVERNMENT—ASPECT OF FIRMNESS AND MODERATION—HER HOME-LIFE AND AMUSEMENTS—HER POPULARITY—FURTHER DIALOGUES WITH KNOX—QUESTION AS TO WHAT LANGUAGE THEY WERE HELD IN?—PROSECUTIONS OF ROMANIST PRIESTS—ARCHBISHOP HAMILTON—THE QUEEN'S DEVOTEDNESS TO HER CHURCH—HER FOREIGN COMMUNICATIONS—ASSASSINATION OF HER UNCLE—PARLIAMENT—TENDENCY TO A REACTION AGAINST THE PROTESTANT PARTY—FURTHER ALTERCATIONS BETWEEN THE QUEEN AND KNOX—RIOTOUS ATTACK ON OFFICIATING PRIESTS—THE RIOTERS BROUGHT TO TASK—FEELING AMONG THE PROTESTANT CLERGY, . 199-235

CHAPTER XLIII.

Queen Mary.

(Continued.)

THE QUEEN AND HER ADMIRERS—MYSTERIOUS STORY OF THE PROJECT OF ARRAN AND BOTHWELL—BOTHWELL INDICTED FOR IT—HISTORY OF CHATELAR—HIS ADVENTURES—HIS FATE—POLITICAL IMPORTANCE OF THE QUEEN'S MARRIAGE—THE PROJECTS OF THE HOUSE OF GUISE—QUEEN MARY'S OWN VIEWS—PROJECT FOR UNION WITH THE HEIR OF THE SPANISH MONARCHY—POLITICAL PROSPECTS OF SUCH A UNION—MARY'S FOREIGN CORRESPONDENCE ABOUT IT—HER SCHEMES TRAVERSED BY CATHERINE OF MEDICI—OTHER PROJECTS—QUEEN

ELIZABETH—HER ESCAPADES ABOUT LEICESTER—PROPOSED MEETING OF MARY AND ELIZABETH—MARY MEETS HENRY STEWART, LORD DARNLEY—MARY'S SECRET EMISSARIES—DAVID RIZZIO—REACTION IN FAVOUR OF THE ROMANIST PARTY—GLOOM AND DIFFICULTIES OF THE REFORMERS—PROTESTANT RIOT SUPPRESSED—QUESTION OF CONSULTING THE ESTATES ABOUT THE MARRIAGE—MARRIAGE OF MARY AND DARNLEY, ... 236-277

CHAPTER XLIV.

Queen Mary.

(*Continued.*)

A STRONG GOVERNMENT—DARNLEY GETS THE TITLE OF KING—PARLIAMENTARY DISPLEASURE WITH THE ASSUMPTION—ARMING OF MURRAY AND HIS SUPPORTERS—THEIR DISPERSAL—PRESENT THEMSELVES TO ELIZABETH—HOW TREATED BY HER—DANGER OF ELIZABETH AND THE PROTESTANT CAUSE—PROJECTS OF THE ROMANIST POWERS—CONFERENCE AT BAYONNE—PHILIP, CATHERINE OF MEDICI, AND ALVA—DARNLEY'S CHARACTER DEVELOPS ITSELF—ODIOUS AMONG THE COURTIERS—HIS WIFE'S APPRECIATION OF HIM—PROGRESS OF RIZZIO'S INFLUENCE—PROJECT FOR PUTTING HIM OUT OF THE WAY—THE BAND FOR HIS SLAUGHTER—ARRANGEMENTS FOR EFFECTING IT—THE SUPPER-PARTY—RIZZIO DRAGGED OUT AND SLAIN—INQUIRY WHEN THE QUEEN KNEW OF HIS DEATH?—HER CONDUCT BEFORE AND AFTER THAT KNOWLEDGE—LURES BACK HER HUSBAND—RETURN OF MURRAY AND HIS FOLLOWERS FROM ENGLAND—MURRAY MAKES PEACE—SECRET ARRANGEMENT OF THE QUEEN AND HER HUSBAND—THEIR ESCAPE TO DUNBAR, . . . 278-316

CHAPTER XLV.

Queen Mary.

(*Continued.*)

THE CONFEDERATE LORDS AND THEIR DANGER—PROJECTS OF RETALIATION—THE SLAYERS OF RIZZIO SEEK REFUGE IN ENGLAND—A PARLIAMENT—THE FIT OF CONJUGAL ATTACHMENT PASSES—SYMPTOMS OF MARY'S FEELING TOWARDS HER HUS-

THE

HISTORY OF SCOTLAND.

CHAPTER XXXVII.

The Reformation.

GOVERNMENT OF MARY OF LORRAINE—HER INABILITY TO UNDERSTAND THE CONSTITUTION OF SCOTLAND—FRENCH PRACTICES—FRENCHMEN PROMOTED TO HIGH OFFICES—ATTEMPT TO PUT THE FORTRESSES IN THEIR HANDS—PROPOSAL OF A STANDING ARMY, AND ITS RECEPTION—QUEEN MARY'S MARRIAGE TO THE DAUPHIN—HIS ACCESSION TO THE CROWN OF FRANCE—THE COUNTRY ALARMED BY PROJECTS OF ANNEXATION TO THE CROWN OF FRANCE—RISE OF SUSPICION AND DISLIKE OF FRANCE AND THE FRENCH ALLIANCE—THE ALIEN CHARACTER OF THE CHURCH IN SCOTLAND—HOW FAR THE DOCTRINES OF THE REFORMERS WERE SPREADING—SECULAR CAUSES OF ENMITY TO THE CHURCH—WEALTH AND LUXURIOUSNESS OF THE CHURCHMEN — THEIR MORAL CONDITION—THEIR TEMPORAL POWER AS ADMINISTRATORS OF THE LAW—THE POWER OF EXCOMMUNICATION OR CURSING—ITS USE FOR LEVYING DEBTS AND FOR ACTS OF PERSONAL OPPRESSION—SPECIMEN OF A CURSING—THE CHURCH CONSCIOUS OF ITS OWN DEFECTS—INTERNAL EFFORTS AT REFORMATION — REFORMING COUNCILS — ARCHBISHOP HAMILTON'S CATECHISM—THE TWOPENNY FAITH.

MARY of Lorraine, the queen-mother, when in 1554 she entered on her acknowledged power as regent, had been sixteen years in Scotland. In these years, however, she had not so sufficiently read the character of the people as to be able to avoid cause of mortal offence. She might have seen how the interference of England was detested, and thus have judged that, when France interfered in Scotland, the old ally would get no better toleration than the old enemy. It was to be in the arrangement of events that France was to interfere, and in a vital and unpardonable shape. But even before such projects were ripened, the queen-regent, as if she had intended to awaken all suspicions, tampered where she might easily have let alone. The Scots could never be brought to tolerate foreigners, English or Continental, in political offices of trust or power. We have seen how poor De la Bastie's elevation ended. There was the unpopular history of the other French friends of Albany, and their holding of Dumbarton Castle—national offences to the country, only mitigated by the preponderance of the offences committed by England. There never appears a foreigner on the lists of the holders of high political office in Scotland down to this time; and that there were few foreigners promoted in the Church, we may gather from the notoriety surrounding one instance in which a foreigner got promotion. His name was Damien. He was made Abbot of Tongueland; and because he, a Frenchman, obtained this Scots benefice, he was the object of the satirical lash of the poet Dunbar.

The office of chancellor was held by the Earl of Huntly, perhaps the greatest territorial lord of the day. A deputy or vice-chancellor was appointed, who did the work of the office and held the power, and the person so appointed was a Frenchman named De Roubay. For some cause not fully cleared up, and only known to be connected with his intervention in Highland quarrels, Huntly came under the letter of the treason law, and had to compound with the crown by a money payment. His humiliation was doubly coupled with favour to Frenchmen. He held a lucrative office, connected apparently with the collection of the revenue in Orkney, whence he is called Governor of Orkney. This office, whatever may have been its exact name, was given to a Frenchman, M. Boutot. On the list of comptrollers of the exchequer, too, there appears the name of the famous De Roubay, and, as his successor, Bartholomew Villemore. Another Frenchman, D'Oysel, though not endowed with office, was supposed to have such influence in the counsels of the regent as none but a native Scot ought to exercise.

The regent remembered how convenient it was to France to hold a real position in the soil of Scotland, by having Dunbar Castle garrisoned and governed by Frenchmen. She would have done well, too, to remember how offensive that was to the people, and how it imperilled the French alliance. At Eyemouth, to the south of Dunbar, a fort was built on the new method of fortification adopted abroad—a step towards the Vauban type of fortresses. It was garrisoned by French troops. She pondered how she might, one by one, pick the strongholds of the great barons out of their hands and make them royal fortresses. Of these, old Angus's Castle of Tantallon was the most tempting; and she began to ply its owner with hints, which drew from him, according to tradition, a celebrated answer, marked by his own peculiar cast of grim derision. Yes, his castle and all he had were at her grace's command; but before God he vowed that he must himself be the governor, for no other person could hold it so well.

The Scots monarchs had not only no standing army, but they had scarcely a guard for the protection of the royal person and residence. When Henry VIII. supplied his sister with money to support two hundred men for her son's protection, it was a material boon, though one dangerous to accept, as suspiciously eyed. The only force the monarch could bring into the field was the feudal array, and it was a self-willed force, given to stand upon limitations and privileges, as we have often seen. The queen-regent saw a different sight when she visited the French Court. It had long been surrounded by troops of armed protectors, conspicuous and supreme among whom was that picked body of men, the Scots Guard. Beyond these, too, the monarch had a considerable standing army, supported by taxes and feudal dues. The queen-regent thought it would be an improvement on the institutions of Scotland to have a standing army, so that the Government might no longer be left in absolute dependence on that capricious institution, the feudal array. It was represented that the nation would thus be greatly strengthened against their old enemies of England. A force might be always kept on the border, so as to save the country from the sudden surprises and raids from which it had suffered so vitally for several generations. The project required a new tax. An act for raising it passed the Lords of the Articles. It authorised a minute inquiry into the possessions of every subject —lord, landowner, farmer, merchant, and craftsman. The "inquisition" was to be made by a parochial organisation under the sheriff of each county; and the whole arrangements are so stringent that the act might be supposed to have been prepared by some one anxious to make it seem as offensive as he could.[1]

By a contemporary noticer of events we are told that discontent at this project broke out through the country in many "privy assemblies and conventions." These tokens of discontent concentrated themselves into a meeting in the Abbey of Holyrood, where some three hundred of the principal territorial magnates assembled. They sent a deputation to the regent and her Council, " desiring most humbly not to alter the ancient custom, laws, and liberty of the realm, in putting them to such charges of payment, and sums of money, affirming that their forefathers and predecessors had defended the same many hundred years valiantly with their own hands." They maintained that the present inhabitants of the realm were " of as good courage and hardiment, able and valiant to defend their realm, as others their forebears have been in times past; and therefor would fecht with their own hands, and defend the same with their bodies, for they could not trust any waged man that he wad so faithfully defend their liberty, wifes, bairns, lands, and possessions." They held next that there was not such " substance" in the country, " as to sustain so many idle men as were necessary for the defence of the borders," meaning that a force was idle when not actually fighting or employed against an enemy. But they had a conclusive reason for protesting—trusting to mercenaries, the country would lose its old strength. As it is put by Leslie, "that the same should cause the lords, barons, gentlemen, fall into sic idleness and unskilfulness through lack of use of bearing and exercising their armour, that they

[1] Act. Parl., ii. 604.

should become an easy prey to whatsoever nation that would invade the realm." In this protestation there stands a curious little constitutional definition. It is noted that the monarch is not king or queen of Scotland, but of the Scots. "In that respect the king has been called at all times King of Scots—that is, rather in respect of men, nor of money and substance of the country."[1] The obnoxious tax and its occasion—the standing army—were together abandoned. Since she could not get an army at the absolute disposal of the crown, the regent endeavoured to get the feudal force committed to the policy of France by an invasion of England. As their old troubles on the borders were breaking out, and there was possible danger from England, an army assembled for the defence of Scotland, but its leaders refused to invade England.

Thus there were symptoms of variance between the queen-dowager, as a sort of representative of French interests and principles, on the one hand, and the Scots people on the other. Some great events, however, came to pass, which seemed to remove all discordant influences, and bring the two nations into closer union than ever. In the winter of 1557 the Estates were reminded by the King of France that the proper time had come for completing the promised marriage between his son and the Queen of Scots. A commission was appointed to go to France and represent Scotland on the occasion. It consisted of six persons, among whom was Beaton, the Archbishop of Glasgow. There were two others, whose appointment to such a purpose was significant—James Stewart, Prior of St Andrews, the queen's illegitimate brother, and

[1] History, Scots version, 255.

Erskine, the Laird of Dun; these, as we shall presently see, became the leaders of the Reformation party.

The marriage was celebrated with due splendour on the 24th of April 1558. Stipulations, in all forms deemed necessary for the purpose, were made for the maintenance of the Scots nationality and the independent privileges of the people. If there were a son of the marriage, he was to succeed to both thrones; if there were but daughters—excluded from the French succession—the eldest was to reign in Scotland: such were the public and ostensible conditions of the marriage. There is little doubt, however, of the fact that, some days before the ceremony, the queen signed three papers, the object and intent of which was to convey her kingdom, as if it were her private property, to the house of Valois. The documents were drawn on the principle so common in all attempts to dispose of governments on parchment. One of them contained the conveyance; another, in case this should be inefficient, pledged the country for a million of gold pieces, or any other sum that might be claimed as due by the queen for her entertainment in France; the third nullified any deeds signed by her, under the instructions of her Parliament, of a tenor inconsistent with those now executed: so was one worthless document to prop up another. It is not clear whether these documents were procured merely by the private dealing of her uncles the Guises, or were sanctioned by the King of France himself or by his other advisers.

It was agreed that the Dauphin should have the distinction, as it was termed, of being called King of Scots. The Scots commissioners were required to send for the honours of Scotland, as they were termed—

the crown, the sceptre, and the other decorations which had been used in the coronation of a king of Scots. The commissioners would do nothing to commit themselves to compliance with this request. Had they represented, however urgently, the propriety of sending these precious articles to France, the Estates certainly would not have permitted them to leave the country. The demanding of them was eminently suspicious. It betokened that the house of Valois wanted to have something more than the nominal or honorary title of king for the Dauphin; and if the honours once left the country, it was very unlikely that they would ever be brought back.

A mysterious calamity gave a sinister meaning to the rumours about this and some other matters, calculated to raise suspicion among the Scots. When the six commissioners reached Dieppe on their way home, three of them—the Lords Rothes and Cassilis, and Reid, Bishop of Orkney—sickened and died suddenly. It was held that things had been said to these men in France which it was very undesirable that they should repeat in Scotland, and so they were poisoned out of the way. At that time, in France, such an act was quite within the bounds of likelihood; and instead of rejecting the suspicion as ungenerous, one is inclined to be surprised that it was not pressed more strongly, and that no investigations or explanations were demanded regarding the cause of so remarkable a fatality.

The surviving commissioners, on reporting the completion of their important business to the Estates, which met in November, tendered to them a request, in the name of the queen, which was and has continued to be a cause of much discussion. It was, that the

Crown Matrimonial might be conferred on her husband. This involved an actual ceremony of coronation, with a crown made for the purpose, and sent over in charge of a special embassy. The commissioners, in putting the request to the Estates, said that it was to be " by way of gratification during the marriage, without any manner of prejudice to her highness's self, the succession of her body, or lawful succession of her blood whatsomever ;" and it was authorised by the Estates, with this limitation, and a declaration that the distinction was to last " during the marriage allenarly."[1]

It was said, however, that there was a deep meaning in this device. It came from the Guises, and it was believed that they were prepared to interpret its true meaning from certain precedents, when the right time came. The meaning of the term was much pondered on the occasion of Queen Mary's second marriage, and it was believed that it meant a complete partnership, in the crown ; so that, in default of children, it would go to the survivor and the survivor's heirs. On that principle, if Queen Mary died childless before the Dauphin, the crown of Scotland was transferred to the house of Valois.[2]

Among those Scots who still held by the French

[1] Act. Parl., ii. 506.
[2] Some hints dropped by the Cardinal of Lorraine are thus noted : " Monsieur le Cardinal me respondit, selon que jà il m'en avoit fait le discours une fois au commenchement de mars passé, que les commis d'Escosse au fait dudict mariaige, entre lesquels estoit le duc de Chastellerault, père du conte d'Haran, firent instance au feu roy Henry que le royaulme d'Escosse, dès lors pour tousjours, fut adjoinct à celluy de France, y enst enffans dudict mariaige ou non, et que la couronne d'Escosse fut incontinent transportée à St Denys, afin que, couronnant le Roy de celle de France, il fût aussi couronné de celle d'Escosse, et vonloient que les escussons de France fussent escartelez de France et Escosse."—4th May 1560, M. de Chantonay ; Teulet, i. 536.

alliance, throughout France, and over great part of Europe, the marriage was hailed as an event full of splendid promises for the future. It was celebrated in verse and prose by countless pens, conspicuous among whom was the greatest Latin poet of the day, Buchanan, and the French chancellor, L'Hôpital, whose literary genius would have been more renowned had it not been overshadowed by his more illustrious fame as a jurist, who, in the comprehensiveness of his survey and his accurate sense of true justice, was centuries beyond his age.[1]

Within a few months the greatness that was in store for Scotland seemed to be perfected. In a tournament with the Sieur de Montgomery, Henry II. of France got a wound in the face which proved mortal, and he died on the 10th of July 1559, making Catherine de Medici a widow, and the young beauty whom she hated Queen of France. Yet were there already symptoms that all this grandeur was not to be to the profit of Scotland. The tone held by the Court of France towards Scotland had changed, becoming patronising, if not domineering. Complete rights of citizenship were exchanged between

[1] As being less known, at least in this country, than Buchanan's Epithalamium, I take from L'Hôpital the following laudatory reference to the services of the Scots in France:—

"Parvum (inquis) parvum fateor, componimus illud
Si nostro. Sed cujus opem sensitque paratum
Non semel auxilium labefactis Gallia rebus,
Cum bellum gererent nostris in finibus Angli,
Desertam illorum patriam simul agmine facto
Scoti incursabant. Metus hic sua protinus illos
Respicere, et nostris cogebat cedere terris.
Quinetiam Tellus his tam fœcunda virorum,
Tamque ardens animus bellique incensus amore.
Ut cuum alius premeret vicinum exercitus hostem
Suppetias alius nobis laturus eodem
Tempore, cœrulei transmitteret æquora ponti."
—Hospitalii Epistol., lib. iv.

the two countries; but even in the Lettres de Grande Naturalisation, in which the Scots were in all courtesy received as citizens of France, there was perceptible a tone of superiority and condescension—as where the citizenship of France is compared with that of Rome, sought after by all nations, and the presence of King David at the battle of Poictiers is spoken of as one might praise the conduct of a faithful dependant.[1] It was known that the government of Scotland was discussed in French councils as if it were a French affair,

[1] Lettres de Grande Naturalisation accordées par Henri II. aux Ecossais, à l'occasion du Mariage de Marie Stuart avec le Dauphin; Teulet, Pièces, i. 303. The letters have all that prolixity for which the French offices of the crown were remarkable, though other government offices kept up with them as well as they could in tediousness of detail. The letters were registered by the Parliament of Paris, with the commentary referred to in the text. The *precis* of the substance of the letters is commendable: "Veult et statue que les Escossois puissent tenir offices et bénéfices en ce royaulme, y puissent acquérir biens, disposer d'iceulx et les transmettre à leur postérité, ainsy que s'ils estoient originaires, nez natifs et habitans perpétuels de ce royaulme, sans pour ce obtenir lettres de naturalité, payer finance ny estre subjectz à aultre particulière dispense."—P. 307.

After recording this neat abstract of the letters, the Parliament compares them with the early Roman extension of citizenship, and does so with a distinct hint that, as the Romans were in early times parsimonious in conferring such distinguished boons, they ought not to be lavishly bestowed by the great monarchy of France. In this the draftsmen of the Parliament are not so concise as in their abridgment of the royal letters. They begin thus: "Ces lettres sont pleines de tesmoignages de la grandeur de ceste monarchie de France *a qua jus civium postulatur, sicut antiquitus a populo Romano jura Quiritum, jus Latii veteris, jus Latinitatis, jus Italicum, jus civitatis peti solébat et magni beneficii loco concedi.* De ce furent du commencement fort espargnans les anciens Romains, tellement que *non nisi authoritate senatus et rogatione populi tale jus donabatur, etc.*" It is observable that the royal letters, in all their pomposity, give courtesy to Scotland, as a country whose sovereign belongs to the royal house of France; but the Parliament's registration interprets them as a gracious concession to a community favoured at court.—Vérification par le Parlement de Paris des Lettres Patentes du Mois de Juin en faveur des Ecossois, 307.

and it was even officially suggested that this part of the King of France's dominions might make a suitable appanage for a second son of the house of Valois. The Lords of the Congregation in Scotland were not far in the wrong when they complained that projects were afoot for converting Scotland into a province of France.¹

Without any absolute public acts tending to annexation or domination, many incidents gradually dropped into the minds of the Scots the impression that the independence of the country was endangered by France; and such impressions were strengthened by the conduct of the regent and her friends. The quartering of arms, for instance, which we shall find offensive to England, had something to awaken the suspicions of the Scots, who asserted that the manner of the quartering rather represented the annexation to the crown of the province of Scotland, than the personal union between the house of Valois and the house of Stewart; and whatever offence might thus be given was not in the mere pedantic manipulation of the heralds, but was matter of state policy.² In recent times, too, documents have turned up, which, had they been known to the Scots statesmen of the time, might well have fed their suspicions. One of these is a state paper, by the Parliament of Paris, on the government of Scotland in 1552,

¹ In a letter of M. de Chantonay to the Bishop of Arras, dated 4th May 1560 (Teulet, i. 536), there are remarks which may interest heraldic students on the question whether after all the quartering of Scotland with France as a united kingdom is the correct one, and hinting a preference for something that would show more distinctly how Scotland is at the disposal of the house of Valois. As King Henry put it, "Que ledict royaulme demeura à la disposition du Roy son filz et de sa femme pour en faire le partaige d'ung segond filz."
² See above note.

while yet Queen Mary was in her twelfth year.[1] It has all the external character of a piece of puerile pedantry, the fruit of the propensity of the civilians to draw subtle distinctions and adjust theoretical difficulties. The question is, whether Queen Mary, when she was eleven years old, had reached the age of puberty. At that period of life, by the civil law, young persons took a step towards self-government, by the choice of curators, who were to supersede those tutors who, appointed in infancy, were not of their own selection. The age of male puberty was fourteen; of female, twelve. The question here was, whether, in the case of sovereigns, it came at the beginning, instead of waiting till the completion of the year, so as to entitle Queen Mary to choose her curators when she had completed her eleventh year. There is no reference in the document to the peculiar government of Scotland, or to the all-powerful Estates. Precedents are called up from French history, as if the matter concerned Touraine, Aquitaine, or any other province of France.[2] So little

---

[1] Déclaration du Parlement de Paris sur le Gouvernement de l'Ecosse; Teulet, Pièces et Documents, i. 261.

[2] " A sçavoir que, pour la puberté des rois de France, pour les continuer et administrer, l'on n'a point attendu que les xiv ans soient complets, combien que, en tutelles privées, la perfection soit requise, car les lois ne sont contreins à la loy positive;

" Mais, pour le bien des royaulmes, avant les xiv ans accomplis out esté couronnés et ont administré le royaulme. Charlemagne, vivant le roy Pépin, fut couronné roi; et après fist couronner Louis dit le Débonnaire son filz, en berceau, qu'il fist porter en litière jusques à Rome où il fut couronné. Charles, dit le Simple, avant les xiv ans, administra; le roy Robert filz de Hue Capet, le roy Philippes Ier. de ce nom, le roy Louis dit le Gros, le roy Philipes-Auguste, avant les xiv ans administra, le roy sainct Louis avant ledict temps.

" Le roy Charles V. ordonna que Charles VI. son filz auroit gouverneurs jusques à ce qu'il eust xiv ans accomplis; toutefois, après son trespas, et après plusieurs remonstrances faictes par un advocat du roy

does the document carry the tenor of a practical policy, that it is difficult to realise the natural supposition, that the discussion must have arisen in the contemplation of a plan for governing Scotland by curators appointed in Paris by the young queen.

Let us now turn to other events as momentous as these, with which they will be found ultimately combining in the development of great historical conclusions. On the 17th of November 1558, the death of Mary, the Popish Queen of England, opened the succession there to her sister Elizabeth. By the same event, Philip of Spain ceased to be King of England. The effects that were to come of this change were not immediately visible. Philip was dreaming of, and aiming at, universal dominion—the restoration of the old Roman Empire over the world, to act in unity with the spiritual empire of the Popedom. The loss of his hold on England might, to a less sanguine and trusting aspirant, have seemed to weaken his chances of success; for, while he was the husband of Queen Mary, he supposed himself to be absolute master of that kingdom, and believed that, next to his own peninsula, it was the most devoted among the European powers to the support of the Popedom in all its spiritual supremacy. In this dutiful course, he had no doubt England would continue gratefully accepting of his

en Parlement, nommé Desmarets, fut conclu par le trois Estats du royaulme qu'il seroit couronné avant ledict temps et que le royaulme seroit administré soubz son nom, et receveroit en sa personne les hommages des vassaux.

"Le semblable fut conclu par le roy Charles VIII.; et encor, du temps du feu Roy, fut faict ordonnance, luy estant en Espagne, que Monseigneur le Dauphin son filz, non ayant encore xiv ans, seroit couronné roy de France, vivant son père, qui fut vérifiée en la cour du Parlement."—Teulet, i. 263, 264.

guidance. He was hard of belief when rumours reached him of the heretical propensities of the young queen. It was for his consideration whether he ought, for the sake of the good cause, to marry Queen Elizabeth. Looking to the object of such a union, the Pope would not, of course, hesitate to give a dispensation. Influenced by such ideas, he continued to dictate and advise about the conducting of the English Government much as he used to do when he styled himself King of England.

When Elizabeth's heresy was put beyond question, consolation came from another quarter;—she was not the rightful heiress to the English throne. A king of Spain should be the last man to overlook what led to that conclusion. Her father's marriage to his own collateral ancestress, Catherine, was not legally dissolved when Elizabeth was born; and Mary of Scotland, the Dauphiness of France, was the rightful Queen of England. As Europe stood at that time, the assertion of this right was a very formidable thing for Elizabeth and her advisers to look at. The title of Queen of England was taken by the Court of France for Queen Mary in a quiet, off-hand way, that was almost more provoking than a loud proclamation, because it was not so easily answered. The arms of France and Scotland were quartered with those of England, and the English ambassador in France complained that the offence was thrust under his very eyes and nostrils, for the quartered coat was emblazoned on the dishes set before him at royal entertainments. A claim that might bring Spain, France, and Scotland all at once down on England was truly formidable; and there was a great Romish party in England, whose consciences would compel them to co-operate with invaders coming under the banner of the Pope.

The great chance of safety was to detach Scotland from such a combination. It was known that the country was not keen for Romanism, since subjects of England, during the late persecuting reign, had found refuge there. This was a good sign, and Elizabeth's great adviser, Cecil, resolved to make of it what he could; for never had an alliance with France been more imminently sought for the safety of Scotland than an alliance with Scotland now was for the safety of England. The negotiations for the great European treaty of Château Cambresis were hastening to an end; they were finished on the 2d of April 1559. There were two things for which England fought hard in that diplomatic discussion—the restoration of Calais, which had just been taken from England by the Duke of Guise, Queen Mary's uncle, and a peace with Scotland. In the matter of Calais, some arguments were used on the part of France which cut far deeper than the question at issue. Suppose that France were in any way bound to make the restoration, to whom was it to be made? If rendered up to the person who now called herself Queen of England, the duty would not be discharged; for what if the rightful heiress, their own Dauphin's wife, were to claim it as hers? Calais had to be abandoned in the mean time, if the other alternative were to be pushed; and the English representative at the conference got instructions, if necessary—but only if it were so found at the last moment—to give up every other claim, provided Scotland should be included in the peace. This was done; but it was a step only to the end. The sensitiveness of the Scots had, on other occasions, made them restive when France professed to treat for them. France, on the face of the transaction, and in form, got the peace extended to Scotland, her ally; but Cecil laboured at the same time, and under great difficulties, to contract a separate alliance with Scotland.

These affairs brought a political crisis there. We have seen how, in 1543, there was a like critical period in the nation's destiny. Sixteen years had passed the boys of that day into manhood, and many other things had occurred to change the tenor of the opinions and predilections of the people. It is at this juncture that we must count the Reformation as a power in the state. As in almost all other nations, so in Scotland, its operations were fashioned, not according to the quiet course of internal changes in the religious opinions of one after another of the people, but by conjunction with great external political movements. There has been a natural enough disinclination to see this; and the tenor of history has been swayed at least, if not absolutely perverted, by a tendency to trace to the impulse of religious zeal events and actions prompted by motives of a more secular character.[1]

[1] Our own confidence in the absolute soundness of our own religious persuasions, deceives us into a reliance on any histories which show our special creed advancing and prevailing through the force of absolute conclusiveness and truth. When we boast of the power of resistance to the invasion of other faiths, we are more likely to be accurate. Converts crossing the great gulfs—such as that between Popery and Protestantism—are very rare in quiet times. They are apt to make a noise, and produce on the timid the effect of numbers, usually creating among the old steady members of the creed they join even more alarm than they have left among the faithful whom they have deserted; for they are restless creatures—they are on the move, and though they may have reached the ultimate temple in the line of their changes, and can go no further, they are apt to move about very rest-

A period of many years had now passed over, in which there had been at intervals several persons put to death for what the Church counted heresy. We must not suppose that in their own day these victims were treated as illustrious martyrs. For that crown their memory had to wait until Protestantism became triumphant. The executions were disagreeable affairs connected with church matters, and the laity in general kept as well aloof from them as they could. Even the death of Wishart, with its picturesquely tragical retribution, was an isolated matter. The party in favour of the French alliance—or, it would be more explicit to say, the party determined to resist English domination—swept all before them, and the affair had really very little visible influence. In 1550 there was another victim of the fire, named and described by Knox as "Adam Wallace, *alias* Fian, a simple man,

lessly and troublesomely to their new neighbours, in that abode which they have chosen as the only refuge from doubts and difficulties. Thus individual conversions make a noise; but at any time the number of persons who have changed faith through calm conviction is very small. Such a process has contributed very little to the distribution of the religious persuasions among the European nations. The Romish and the Protestant communities stand as they were left by the great struggle of the sixteenth century as modified in some measure by the Thirty Years' War. There are millions of tolerably accurate practisers of the requirements of the Church of Rome who would have been good Protestants had they been born and brought up in the Protestant communities; just as, on the other hand, there are millions of sound Protestants who would have been faithful observers of the Romish formularies had they been born and brought up in any of the states which held by the old Church. The boundaries of the Romish and Protestant states have not varied to any perceptible effect for two hundred years; some of them are as they were three hundred years ago. The Netherlands are Romish up to the boundary where Spain held dominion over them—Protestant beyond. The old decayed city of Nuremberg early put in its lot with the Reformation; and the city of Nuremberg is Protestant, though surrounded by communities which still hold by the old Church.

without great learning, but one that was zealous in godliness, and of an upright life."[1] In 1558 Walter Mill was burned in St Andrews. His fate created more real excitement than all the others that had gone before. He was a man past eighty years of age, a quiet country priest, of blameless life. Incidents were told about his burning which showed that such scenes were becoming odious. There was difficulty, it was said, in getting the necessary intervention of the civil power, and in securing persons to undertake the executioner's work. It was further said that the people piled stones to make a cairn on the place where he suffered, and ever as they were removed they were replaced. This execution was at St Andrews, and it recalled the death of Wishart there fourteen years earlier, with its wonderful retribution. A horror of such events was creeping into the people's minds. The like had not been known in Scotland in days of old. To the clergy, they were deeds of duty and humanity. What was the extinction of a life or two to the spread of heresy, which would ruin millions of souls? And as to the victims themselves, their torture in this world was short, and would expiate for them an infinitely greater amount of torture in the next. In such views the lay population could not sympathise. About other matters, more closely connected with the vulgar routine and objects of life, the two classes were drawing off from each other. The ecclesiastics were becoming peculiar, as a rich and luxurious class. The estates conferred on the prelacies and monastic houses centuries before had come, from being almost worthless, to produce great revenues. While there was a continual shifting in the possessions

[1] History, i. 237.

of the lay barons, the ecclesiastical estates remained unchanged, and ever grew in fertility and value.

There were two social specialties in the clergy apt to be irritating to a poor and homely landed gentry. They were rich, and they were aliens in taste and training, spending their affluence in conformity with foreign and luxurious fashions. Among the many Scots who sought a foreign education, those training themselves for the Church predominated. They were thus initiated into foreign tastes and connections, which fitted only too well into their foreign allegiance to the hierarchy of Rome. There were in this widened intercourse liberalising and humanising influences, but those of another kind prevailed. On the one side we may see the rich accomplished scholar and French courtier Elphinstone munificently endowing a university after the model of the University of Paris; but a type of the other and prevalent side is Beaton, audacious in his profuseness and profligacy.[1]

For all that the Scots had a rooted prejudice against any precedents coming from England, the revelations made by Henry VIII.'s raid on the monastic houses cannot but have caused a deep impression, and made thinking men ask whether it might be that like conditions were to be found in the noble clusters of buildings which lodged the Regular fraternities and sisterhoods in their own country. Henry's commission

[1] "For my maist princely prodigality
  Among prelates in France I bore the prise.
  I schew my lordly liberality
  In banqueting, playing at cards and dyce.
  Into such wisdom I was halden wise,
  And sparit not to play with king or knight
  Three thousand crowns of gold upon a night."
      —Sir David Lindsay, The Tragedy of the Cardinal.

of inquiry was a marvellous success. The designs and motives by which it was inspired had no claim to approval, but the result put to silence all that could be said against them. Public rumour, too, and the exaggeration of the designing, deepened the darkness of the revelation. Worse things than those that were done could not be invented by malicious tale-tellers; but the rare or solitary crime was spread over a wide area, and from an individuality became a generality. The whole story was told in the coarsest and broadest terms to the Government of Scotland by Sir Ralph Sadler, and by others who desired the English precedent to be followed there. Enumerating a loathsome and unrepeatable catalogue of vices, we find Sir Ralph telling King James V. that the same will be found in his own dominions, "unless your monks be more holy in Scotland than ours are in England." The king did not stand up for their purity; but there was no pressure on him to follow an English example, and the disappointed ambassador has to relate, "'Oh,' quoth the king, 'God forbid that if a few be not good, for them all the rest should be destroyed. Though some be not,' quoth he, 'there be a great many good; and the good may be suffered, and the evil must be reformed; as ye shall hear,' quoth he, 'that I shall help to see it redressed in Scotland, by God's grace, if I brook life.'"[1]

Some families of the poorer landed gentry held in relation to churchmen a position that could not but subject them to humiliation. Their sisters or daughters were the known concubines of rich priests, and held rank accordingly. For many of the clergy who lived in concubinage according to the letter of the law, there

[1] Sadler State Papers, i. 31.

was doubtless the plea that morally they led a life of married domesticity. They were dissenters or schismatics, rather than sinners. They repudiated the doctrine of clerical celibacy; and, holding that the clergy ought to be permitted to marry like other men, they took to their homes women who held the same view, and lived with them in soberness and constancy, regretting that perverse laws denied them the legal privileges of wedlock, but with consciences void of offence, doing what seemed to them right amid the difficulties by which they were surrounded. Whole branches of the Church had acted on this principle, and given to it the respectability of an established institution. So we have seen it among the old Culdees, and perhaps its spirit lingered in Scotland down to the Reformation. At the best, however, it was a lax and dangerous system. Every man who practised it was a law unto himself. There was no distinct sanction drawing, as the law of marriage draws, an obvious unmistakable line between domesticity and profligacy.

And of many of the great rich churchmen, such as Cardinal Beaton and his successor, it was known that they did not profess these humble domestic views, or place themselves in the position of dissenters from the Church, by affecting the life of married persons. They flared their amours in the face of the world, as if proud of the soundness of their taste for beauty, and the rank and birth that had become prostrate to their solicitations. It seemed as if their very greatness as temporal grandees enabled them to defy the ordinary laws of decorum, while their spiritual rank secured to them immunity from that clerical punishment which it was their duty to pronounce against less gifted sinners.

This blot upon the Romish establishment was not a matter of debate, like the soundness of its doctrines. The proceedings of ecclesiastical councils, and other documents having to deal with discipline and conduct, are profuse in wailings and denunciations of the ever-pervading irregularities. In Scotland they are denounced in the earliest ecclesiastical canons—those of the thirteenth century—and they are denounced with increased emphasis in the proceedings of the latest provincial council held by the Romish clergy. These denunciations make no distinction between those unions which were a virtual protest against the laws of celibacy, and the others which testified to defiant profligacy. Probably the more decorous kind were considered the more dangerous, as a following up of their principles by serious men professing to walk uprightly according to their false lights. But, taken in any way, the protestations and lamentations of the Church itself proclaimed within it a sore which centuries of endeavour had not cured — which had rooted itself all the deeper through all the efforts to eradicate it. We can only know the extent and influence of this social specialty by familiar acquaintance with contemporary documents. Those who, at a later period, interpreted the history of the times, when they found that some eminent person who had got a good start in life, and pursued the advantage into a career of eminence, was the son of a Popish clergyman, thought they had traced him to an origin more infamous than ordinary illegitimacy. It was, in his own days, actually more respectable, as coming of a usage countenanced by a party. This unconformity between the spirit of the age and the spirit of the writer dealing with it is productive occasionally of indistinctness.[1]

The result in the social condition of the country was that the rule of celibacy, though observed in law, was abrogated in practice among those of the clergy who were rich enough to support households. This was so much of an acknowledged system that, when there was moderation and constancy, the union was deemed respectable. The concubines of the dignified clergy and their illegitimate children had a fixed place in society. Such connection and parentage, instead of being huddled into obscurity, was expressly and definitely set forth in public documents and the title-deeds of estates. But nothing could remove a certain degree of stigma from the class of persons thus marked off. It was felt that what they got from society was bought by sheer wealth, not given by gratuitous social respect. The worshipful houses which had to submit to such alliances felt the humiliation of them, and were led to ponder on the problem whether the wealth of the clergy could not be got at in some more direct and less unpleasant way.

King James V. did his best to foster the alienation of the laity from the clergy, by distrusting the heads of

---

[1] Of the excellent Bishop Elphinstone of Aberdeen, one of the most enlightened of the patrons and advocates of the higher reaches of education, we are told that "there is no doubt that he was, like so many well-educated men of his time, the offspring of a churchman who could not legally marry, but whose connection and family, in violation of his vows, were then tolerated by society, and almost sanctioned by the practice of the highest of his order." As appropriate to the remark made above, it is stated in a note to this how two writers of the eighteenth century—Crawfurd and Keith—have covered this disgrace under the convenient and pious fiction that the bishop's father took orders after he became a widower.—Innes's Sketches, 260.

the feudal houses and taking counsel of the churchmen. We have seen how hard he pressed upon the aristocracy with forfeitures and penalties. These enabled him to enrich his favourites among the clergy, and the landed gentry felt as if their property and power were gradually dropping away from them to enrich their rivals. The two Beatons kept up a magnificence which none of the nobles, except perhaps Arran, could rival. It was said that the elder had prepared a list of forfeitures, and that King James V., taking note of the sum total represented by it as a conclusion, was, by a gradual process of suction, to draw the land away from its lay owners for the enrichment of his clerical advisers.

Such rumours, well or ill founded, led men to familiarity with the converse of the process. Long before the crisis of Elizabeth's accession, the lay gentry of Scotland had their eyes pretty steadily fixed on the estates of the Church and clergy. When a set of teachers arose whose doctrine pointed to the conclusion, that these clergy were false prophets who had no title to their position, and consequently no just right to the wealth it brought to them, there was a disposition to listen. The new doctrines, as presented to these greedy laymen, were expressed, after Knox's peculiar method, in the most abrupt and emphatic words, and in the most startling contrast to old received opinions. But if they were thus likely rather to shock and alarm than to conciliate the cautious and selfish, there was in the end a little sentence concerning the things of this world carrying compensation for novel and unusual doctrines bearing on the next—it announced that the tithes did not by God's law belong to the churchmen. Perhaps Knox regretted that he had put this view too generally when the lay impropriators interpreted it for themselves, and acted on their interpretation in such manner as to make him call down the divine vengeance on "the merciless devourers of the patronage of the Kirk."[1]

In later times it has been acknowledged that the race of churchmen who lived in the fifteenth century had left to the world a noble legacy in the establishment of universities, and in other efforts for the promotion of learning and the education of the people.

[1] The articles are announced by Knox himself in thorough character. The date is 1547.

"The bastard bischope, who yit was not execrated (consecrated thei call it), wrait to the Suppriour of Sanctandrois, who (*sede vacante*) was vicare-generall, 'That he wondered that he suffered sic hereticall and schismaticall doctrin to be tawght, and nott to oppone himself to the same.' Upoun this rebuck, was a conventioun of Grey Freiris and Black Feindis appointed, with the said suppriour, Dean Johnne Wynrame, in Sanct Leonardis yardis, whareunto was first called Johne Rowght, and certane articles redd unto him ; and thairafter was Johnne Knox called for. The caus of thare conventioun, and why that thei war called, was exponed ; and the articles war read, which war these :—

"I. No mortall man can be the head of the Church.

"II. The Pape is ane Antichrist, and so is no member of Christis misticall body.

"III. Man may nether maik nor devise a religioun that is acceptable to God ; butt man is bound to observe and keap the religioun that fra God is receaved, without chopping or changeing thairof.

"IV. The sacramentis of the New Testament aucht to be ministred as thei war institut by Christ Jesus and practised by His apostles ; nothing awght to be added unto thame ; nothing awght to be diminished from thame.

"V. The messe is abominable idolatrie, blasphemous to the death of Christ, and a prophanatioun of the Lordis Suppar.

"VI. Thare is no purgatorie, in the which the saules of men can eyther be pyned or purged after this lyef ; butt heavin restis to the faythfull, and hell to the reprobat and unthankfull.

"VII. Praying for the dead is vain, and to the dead is idolatrie.

"VIII. Thare is no bischoppes, except thei preach evin by thameselfis, without any substitut.

"IX. The teindis by Goddis law do not apperteane of necessitie to the kirkmen."—History, i. 193.

But the contemporaries whose ignorance prompted the clergy to this work were not likely to appreciate it. On the contrary, they felt invidiously the power which these churchmen were gathering to themselves through their superior learning. It enabled them to consolidate and strengthen their ever-accumulating estates. They were helped towards this end, and towards the oppression of the laity, by becoming the administrators of the law. There was no obdurate conglomerate of local customs, like the common law in England, to bid defiance by its bulk and weight to the subtle influence of the civilians and canonists. The Scots, indeed, when their lot was severed from that of their English fellow-Saxons, avowedly adopted the two foreign systems from their allies of France. The canon law, the child of the civil law, was part of the professional training of the churchman; and having the key to both systems, he had many chances beyond the layman of rendering himself a dexterous adept, and monopolising the administration of justice.

The office of Chancellor was nearest to the throne, and its holder was the head of the law. When the chief of any great house was aggrandising it into supremacy over all others, he would take this office to himself. So it had been held by Crichton, by Boyd the favourite of James III., and by Angus. Gradually, however, the office became absorbed in the Church, and no layman had held it since the beginning of the century. When the Court of Session was established, it was to consist half of clergy, half of laymen; but its first president was the Abbot of Cambuskenneth.

There was, at the same time, a large department in the administration of justice over which the Church arrogated entire management and control as a matter vitally connected with its spiritual functions. After centuries of pressure, the Church had been able to establish in practice throughout Christendom, that her sacrament was necessary to the estate of matrimony and the legitimacy of offspring. The Church could not trust it to the lay authorities to ascertain and determine whether the sacred mystery had been duly performed, and the corresponding privileges acquired. Questions of the validity of marriages, of their dissolution, and of the legitimacy of offspring, were consequently retained by the Church. This made churchmen the arbiters of succession. The feudal law was so far a barrier that they could carry their ecclesiastical law no farther than to separate those who, by illegitimacy, were excluded from its benefits. But the law of succession to other property was entirely worked by them. Where there were settlements, their interpretation, and where there were no settlements, the distribution of the estate among the next of kin, were business all managed by the bishop's consistory. The working of the system was all the more amenable to suspicion, that the Church or individual churchmen were often party claimants in the distribution of a dead man's goods.

To all these legitimate judicial services, the Church was enabled, by a very curious process, to add a large portion in the coercive functions of the common law. It became a practice, when any person undertook an obligation, that he should make a vow or oath to perform it, and that oath was put on record. Now the breaking of an oath was an ecclesiastical offence, for which a man became liable to Excommunication, or to Cursing, as it was aptly called in Scotland. Exacting

the oath was an established practice of the money-
lenders, and the borrowers, with the proverbial thought-
lessness of their class, took it with other risks. It was
not the spiritual influence of excommunication that was
the temptation for this use of the oath. Persons under
process of cursing were subjected to legal execution
against person and property. It was the preliminary
step of a warrant for arrest and imprisonment, and for
the impounding and seizure of goods. Hence "letters
of cursing" were as much the usual order in debit and
credit transactions as any common writ of later times
for seizing the person and distraining the goods.[1] Scotland had by no means reached that stage in the development of social science, in which those concerned in
executing the severities of the law are to be revered
as a terror to evildoers, and a praise and protection to
them that do well. From the burning of the heretic
down to the troubling of the poor debtor, the Church
was monopolising all this unpopular business to itself
—it was inquisitor, hangman, and bailiff. It was ever
endeavouring to widen its powers, even when they were
of this unenviable kind. For instance, it had become a
practice for the ecclesiastical authorities to curse the executive officers of the civil courts for giving effect to their
decisions. So early as the year 1484, we find steps taken
against this aggression. It was adjudged by the Lords

[1] This anomalous process became, in the course of events, the parent
of one of the most useful and effective means for obtaining rapid justice
known in modern legal practice. When the great change came, as a
substitute for the oath and the consequent cursing, came the "clause of
registration," a clause binding the parties to any deed or contract, on its
being recorded in the roll of a court, to submit to its terms as if a judgment of the court to that effect had passed against them. It has gone
into England in an imperfect shape, as the "warrant to confess judgment."

of Council that, for any such wrongous and inorderly cursing of the king's officer in the performance of his duty, by any bishop or other ecclesiastical person, "the said bishop or other ecclesiastical person may be corrected and punished by the king's highness, that the same may be an example to others to abstain from all such doings in time to come."[1]

This process, as well as many others of the old ecclesiastical tribunals, has excited considerable ungratified curiosity. It is observable that, while we have in abundance the title-deeds and other documents of ecclesiastical bodies which connected them with the outer world, we have very few vestiges of their judicial and executive proceedings, whether for the suppression of heresy or for other purposes.[2] The disappearance of all such records may be likened to what is said about the general burning of private letters in government departments when a change of ministry is undoubted. It hence happens that a very magnificent specimen of letters of cursing found lately among the English state papers is all the more curious. It was transmitted in 1525 by Magnus, an emissary in Scotland, to Cardinal Wolsey, as a document worthy of notice.[3]

[1] Balfour's Practiks, 565.

[2] We have the form of an excommunication, or cursing in the vernacular, to be read to the people four times a-year. It enumerates the various sins supposed chiefly to beset the community, and dooms those who remain in them unrepentant to perdition, by the symbol of extinguishing a lighted candle by dashing it down. The expressions of this document are pretty strong, and not unlike those in use on ceremonial occasions in some Protestant communities. But, issued as it is against hypothetical offenders, it has not that direct impulsive vehemence which seems to have been inspired by the realisation of the offences committed and the persons committing them. The form will be found in the Statuta Ecclesiæ Scoticanæ, 6.

[3] Of Magnus, see above, chap. xxxii.

AN ECCLESIASTICAL CURSING, 1550-60.

The occasion was one of public importance—an attempt, through this kind of spiritual warfare with its civil consequences, to subdue the border rievers, and make them give up their evil ways. The document may have risen to the occasion. It is called by Magnus "a terrible cursing," and may be, perhaps, an exaggeration on the chastisement administered to the swindler or defaulting debtor. It is certain that, as concerning this document, the usual charges against the Church of Rome regarding unknown tongues, and obscure and ambiguous phraseology, do not apply. After a preamble the cursing comes forth as follows :—

"I denounce, proclaim, and declare all and sundry the committers of the said sackless murders, slaughters, burnings, heirschippes, reiffes, thefts, and spulies, openly upon daylight, and under silence of the night, as well within temporal lands as kirklands ; together with their part-takers, assistars, suppliars, wittanlie resetters of their persons, the goods reft and stolen by them, art or part thereof, and their counsellors and defenders of their evil deeds;—generally cursed, waried, aggregate, and re-aggregate, with The Great Cursing. I curse their head and all the hairs of their head ; I curse their face, their eyes, their mouth, their nose, their tongue, their teeth, their crag, their shoulders, their breast, their heart, their stomach, their back, their waime, their arms, their legs, their hands, their feet, and every ilk part of their body, from the top of their head to the sole of their feet, behind and before, within and without. I curse them going, I curse them riding ; I curse them eating, I curse them drinking ; I curse them waking, I curse them sleeping ; I curse them rising, I curse them lying ; I curse them at home, I curse them from home ; I curse them within the house, I curse them without the house; I curse their wives, their bairns, and their servants participant with them in their deeds. I warie their corn, their cattle, their wool, their sheep, their horse, their swine, their hens, and all their quick goods. I curse their halls, their chambers, their kitchens, their stables, their barns, their byres, their barnyards, their kailyards, their ploughs, their harrows, and the goods and houses that is necessary for their sustentation and welfare. All the malisons and waresouns that ever gat worldly creature since the beginning of the world to this hour, mot light upon them. The malediction of God that lighted upon Lucifer and all his fellows, that struck them from the high heaven to the deep hell, mot light upon them. The fire and sword that stopped Adam from the yetts of paradise, mot stop them from the glory of heaven, till they forbear and make amends. The malison that lighted on cursed Cain, when he slew his brother just Abel without cause, mot light upon them for the saikless slaughter that they commit daily. The malediction that lighted upon all the world, man and beast, and all that ever took life, when all was drowned by the flood of Noah, except Noah and his ark, mot light upon them, and drown them, man and beast, and make this realm cumberless of them for their wicked sins. The thunder and lightning that went down as rain upon the cities of Sodom and Gomorrah, with all the lands about, and burnt them for their vile sins, mot rain upon them, and burn them for open sins. The malison and confusion that lighted on the giants for their oppression and pride, building the tower of Babel, mot confound them and all their works, for their open robberies and oppression. All the plagues that fell

AN ECCLESIASTICAL CURSING, 1550-60. 33

upon Pharaoh and his people of Egypt, their lands, corn, and cattle, mot fall upon them, their tacks, rowmes, and steadings, corn, and beasts. The water of Tweed, and other waters where they ride, mot drown them as the Red Sea drowned King Pharaoh and the people of Egypt pursuing God's people of Israel. The earth mot open, rive, and cleave, and swallow them quick to hell, as it swallowed cursed Dathan and Abiram that gainsaid Moses and the command of God. The wild fire that burned Korah and his fellows to the number of two hundred and fifty, and others 14,000 and 700 at once, usurping against Moses and Aaron, servants of God, mot suddenly burn and consume them daily gainsaying the commands of God and holy Kirk. The malediction that lighted suddenly upon fair Absalom, riding against his father King David, servant of God, through the wood, when the branches of a tree freed him of his horse and hanged him by the hair, mot light upon them riding against true Scottishmen, and hang them siclike that all the world may see. The malediction that lighted upon Holofernes, lieutenant to Nebuchadnezzar, making war and heirschippis upon true Christian men; the malediction that lighted upon Judas, Pilate, Herod, and the Jews that crucified our Lord, and all the plagues and troubles that lighted on the city of Jerusalem therefor and upon Simon Magus for his simony, bloody Nero, cursed Decius, Maxentius, Olybrius, Julianus Apostata, and the lave of the cruel tyrants that slew and murdered Christ's holy servants, mot light upon them for their cruel tyranny and murtherdom of Christian people. And all the vengeance that ever was taken since the world began for open sins, and all the plagues and pestilences that ever fell on man or beast, mot fall on them for their open robbery, saikless slaughter, and shedding of innocent blood. I dissever and part them from the Kirk of God, and deliver them quick to the devil of hell, as the apostle St Paul delivered Corinthion. I interdict the places they come in from divine service, ministration of the sacraments of holy Kirk, except the sacrament of baptism only; and forbid all kirkmen to shrive or absolve them of their sins, till they be first absolved of this cursing. I forbid all Christian man or woman to have any company with them, eating, drinking, speaking, praying, lying, going, standing, or in any other deed doing, under the pain of deadly sin. I discharge all bands, acts, contracts, oaths, and obligations made to them by any persons, either of lawte kindness or manrent, so long as they sustain this cursing; so that no man be bounden to them, and that they be bounden to all men. I take from them, and cry down all the good deeds that ever they did or shall do, till they rise from this cursing. I declare them partless of all matins, masses, even-songs, dirges, or other prayers, on book or bead; of all pilgrimages and almous deeds done or to be done in holy Kirk, or by Christian people, enduring this cursing. And, finally, I condemn them perpetually to the deep pit of hell, to remain with Lucifer and all his fellows, and their bodies to the gallows of the Boroughmuir, first to be hanged, syne riven and rugged with dogs, swine, and other wild beasts, abominable to all the world. And as their candles go from your sight, so may their souls go from the visage of God, and their good fame from the world, till they forbear their open sins aforesaid, and rise from this terrible cursing, and make satisfaction and penance."[1]

We can suppose all this to have had a very terrifying effect, so long as it was believed that the curses proclaimed by man were sure to be ratified by God. But if doubts and questions arose on this point, then would the whole resolve itself into wild ribaldry, and the cause of ribaldry in others. The practice came to be ridiculed by the satirists. About the beginning of the sixteenth century, a poet named Rowl—a priest, as it would appear—issued a rhyming cursing against persons who had robbed his poultry-yard and his garden.[2] In 1535 an act was passed for rendering more effective and severe the civil execution to follow upon cursing; and the reason assigned for this was, "because

[1] State Papers (Henry VIII.), iv. 418, 419.
[2] Reprinted in Laing's Select Remains of the Ancient Popular Poetry of Scotland:—

"Here followis
The cursing of Sir John Rowlis
Upoun the steilaris of his fowlis.

"Devyne power of michtis maist
Of Fadir, Sone, and Haly Ghaist,
Jesu Chryst and His appostellis,
Peter, Paul, and His discipillis,
And all the power under God ;
And now of Rome that beiris the rod
Under the hevin to loose and bind,
Paip Alexander that we do fynd,
With that power that Peter gaif.
God's braid malison next they haif,
And all the blude about their heart.
Black be their hour—black be their part,
For five fat geese of Sir John Rowlis,
With capons, hens, and uthir fowlis,
Baith the holders and concealers,
Resetters and the proved stealers,
And he that sauls, seizes, and damns,
Beteich the devil, their guts and gammis,
Their tongue, their teeth, their hands, their feet,
And all their body haill complete,
That brak his yaird and stole his frute."

the damnable persuasions of heretics and their perverse doctrine gives occasion to lightly the process of cursing and other censures of holy Kirk," &c.[1]

John Knox tells us of a friar named Arth who, in the year 1534, preached at St Andrews, and in the presence of several dignified clergymen, a sermon in which he attacked some usages in high favour with the Church, and that in such manner that only great skill could have prevented him from falling into the terrible pitfall of provable heresy. He said of cursing, that, " if it were rightly used, it was the most fearful thing upon the face of the earth, for it was the very separation of man from God; but that it should not be used lightly, or for very slight cause, but only against open and incorrigible sinners." And he continued to say, " But now the avarice of priests and their ignorance of their office have caused it altogether to be vilipended; for the priest, whose duty and office it is to pray for the people, stands up on Sunday and cries, ' Ane has tynt a spurtle. There is ane flail stolen from them beyond the burn. The goodwife on the other side of the gait has tynt ane horn spoon. God's malison and mine I give to them that knows of this geere, and restores it not;'" and he followed up with further illustrations " of how the people mocked their cursing."[2]

This process of excommunication or cursing had an ugly alliance with another fertile source of quarrel between clergy and laity—the levying of tithes, or, as the equivalent word stood in Scotland, teinds. A tithe uncommuted to a fixed payment becomes a tax increasing in its pressure with the productive industry of the people. Whatever it had been in early times, it

[1] Act. Parl., ii. 342.   [2] History, i. 39.

was felt in the sixteenth century to be heavily pressing on a number of small agriculturists or cottars who were rising into a class respectable and collectively powerful, but individually so little above poverty that a careful parsimony was necessary to the preservation of the self-supporting independence which they loved. The tithe, which this class felt as an oppressive impost, was levied on them, like other debts, through the process of cursing and the civil execution following on it; and naturally they felt that the clergy, by secular inflictions and spiritual anathemas, extracted from them— poor, and hard workers—the fruit of their industry, to swell their own wealth and minister to their pampered appetites. There were a quantity of other established dues exacted by the Church, the most offensive of which appear to have been made conditional on the rite of burial, which brought them on families in the time of affliction, and often when they were stricken with sudden poverty. Among these exactions we find "the kirk cow" and the "upmost cloth" recurring in the documents and the popular literature of the day as grievances keeping the common people in continual irritation.[1]

[1] Sir David Lindsay, in the Satire of the Three Estates, puts the incidents of such an extortion into the words of the mendicant who breaks in upon the performance. It is a highly-coloured illustration of the grievance. His father and mother have died, leaving him a small agricultural stock—" a mare that carried salt and coal, and three kye baith fat and fair," of the purest Ayrshire breed, then as now celebrated. The misfortunes begin with a feudal exaction :—

> "Our gude grey mare was bating on the field,
> Our land's laird took her for his haregeld.
> The vicar took the best cow by the head,
> Incontinent, when my father was dead.
> And when the vicar heard how that my mother
> Was deed, fra hand he took fra me ane uther.
> Then Meg my wife did mourn baith even and morrow,
> Till at the last she deit for very sorrow ;

All these transactions, in which the clergy gave offence to the people in matters affecting their secular affairs or interests, had much more influence on the coming change than any differences regarding matters of doctrine. It no doubt aggravated all these matters of offence, that the persons who had so much of the country's wealth and power, and had so much influence over the fate of the private citizen, took their instructions from and held themselves responsible to a foreign potentate. In other shapes, too, foreign influences and ties were strengthening their hold upon the Church. Its head was not only cardinal *a latere* from Rome, but was Bishop of Mirepoix, in France; and there was a busy intercourse between the Scots clergy and those of the great Continental despotisms.

The internal condition of the Church was not, like many other matters of accusation and defence connected with the times, a question on which there were two sides. The worldliness of the churchmen, regular and secular, their luxurious and profligate living, their neglect of their sacred functions, and their unscrupulous dealings with the property of the Church—even the offensive usages which made the clergy the instruments

> And when the vicar heard tell my wife was dead,
> The third cow then he cleiket by the head.
> Their upmost claithes, whilk was of raploch grey,
> The vicar gart his clerk bear them away.
> When that was gane, I micht make na debate,
> But with my bairnis part for to beg my meat.
> Now have I told you the black verity,
> How I am brocht into this misery.
> *Diligence.*—How did the parson? was he not thy gude friend?
> *Poor man.*—The devil stick him!—he cursed me for my teind."
> —Act ii. Scene 1.

To feel the significance of this, one must remember that it belongs to a piece which was eminently popular through the country several years before the Reformation, and while the Romish hierarchy was in the full flush of the powers and prerogatives against which its satire was levelled.

of secular oppression, were objects of continued alarm and reprehension within the Church itself, and of censure from its best friends without. There was much internal disquiet from the same cause in the several branches of the Church throughout Europe; but in Scotland it appears to have been excessive. Indeed, from the time of the great Catholic revival under the sons of St Margaret in the twelfth century, the Church's self-reproaches seem to have run on as if the leaven of the old disreputable Culdees still remained in it. In the year 1424 the Estates recorded among their acts a solemn admonition, addressed in the king's name, to the heads of the Benedictine and Austine houses, lamenting their irregularities, and sternly calling them to better order if they would save their establishments from ruin.[1]

Leslie, Bishop of Ross, an ardent partisan of the old Church, attributed its abuses to the influence of the crown at the Court of Rome overshadowing that of the local Church. Whatever may be said of his skill in pointing to the cause, his description of the effect is brief and emphatic. "The abbeys came to secular abuses, the abbots and priors being promovit furth of the Court, wha lived court-like, secularly, and voluptuously. And there ceased all religious and godly minds and deeds, wherewith the seculars and temporal men, being slandered with their evil example, fell fra all devotion and godlyness to the works of wickedness, whereof daily mikel evil did increase."[2]

[1] Act. Parl., ii. 25. Statuta Ecclesiæ Scoticanæ, Int., lxxxiv.
[2] History, 40. A generation earlier, another eminent ecclesiastic, Archdeacon Bellenden, had expressed himself to a like effect at greater length (Chronicles, xii. 17). A portion of the passage has been already cited, as questioning the policy of the profuse establishing of religious houses in King David's reign (see chap. xiii.) The archdeacon's reproof

In 1541 the Estates resumed consideration of the abuses of the clergy, and passed a second and broader censure, to be issued in the name of the king, calling on the prelates, "and every kirkman in his own degree, to reform themselves, their obedienciaries and kirkmen under them, in habit and manners to God and man." This injunction, expanding into particulars was inspired by no Calvinistic teaching; for among the abuses which it denounces as scandals to the Church is a lapsing from the proper observances to "the Virgin Mary and all holy saints."[1]

But the censures coming from external authority were gentle in comparison with those uttered by the Church against its own unworthy members. A provincial council, held in 1549, before the Reformation was yet a visible power in the state, resolved upon a sweeping reform, and in the remedies it enacted, echoed the depth of the abuses it laid open. A writer of our own day has furnished a narrative of the doings of that council, at once so full, so brief, and so distinct, that any attempt to recast it would be injustice to the reader. The injunctions on the clergy were: "To put away their concubines, under pain of deprivation of their benefices, to dismiss from their houses the children born to them in concubinage, not to promote such children to benefices, nor to enrich them—the daughters with dowries, the sons with baronies—from the patrimony of the Church. Prelates were admonished not to keep in their households manifest drunkards, gamblers, whore-

is the more emphatic that he went out of his way to render it. His book professes to be a translation of Boece's History; but this passage is an addition of his own.

[1] Act. Parl., ii. 370.

mongers, brawlers, night-walkers, buffoons, blasphemers, profane swearers. The clergy, in general, were exhorted to amend their lives and manners, to dress modestly and gravely, to keep their faces shaven and their heads tonsured, to live soberly and frugally, so as to have more to spare for the poor, to abstain from secular pursuits, especially trading.

"Provision was made for preaching to the people; for teaching grammar, divinity, and canon law in cathedrals and abbeys; for visiting and reforming monasteries, nunneries, and hospitals; for recalling fugitives and apostates, whether monks or nuns, to their cloisters; for sending from every monastery one or more monks to a university; for preventing unqualified persons from receiving orders, and from holding cure of souls; for enforcing residence, and for restraining pluralities; for preventing the evasion of spiritual censures by bribes or fines; for silencing pardoners, or itinerant hawkers of indulgences and relics; for compelling parish clerks to do their duty in person, or to find sufficient substitutes; for registering the testaments and inventories of persons deceased, and for securing faithful administration of their estates, by bringing their executors to yearly account and reckoning; for suspending unfit notaries, and for preserving the protocols of notaries deceased; for reforming the abuses of the consistorial courts."

That in all this there was no intention of a surrender to the new doctrines is shown in the tenor of the further reformatory injunctions, as follows: "Strict inquest for heresy was ordered to be made by every ordinary in his diocese, by every abbot or prior in his convent. That the inquest might be the more effectual, the inquisitors were supplied with a schedule of the chief points of heresy. These were—speaking against the rights and sacraments of the Church, especially the sacrifice of the mass, the sacraments of baptism, confirmation, extreme unction, penance; contempt of the censures of the Church; denial of the reign of the souls of saints with Christ in glory; denial of the immortality of the soul; denial of recompense for works of faith and charity; denial of purgatory; denial of prayer and intercession of the saints; denial of the lawfulness of images in Christian churches; denial of the authority of general councils in controversies of faith; neglect of the fasts and festivals of the Church. Heretical books, especially poems and ballads against the Church or clergy, were to be diligently sought after, and burned."[1]

This national ecclesiastical council was held while the Council of Trent was in the middle of its work. There had been some intention that Scotland should send representatives to that memorable assemblage, since funds were provided to pay the costs of their mission, but none went.[2] Towards the conclusion of its long sittings that council adopted, in the issuing of its celebrated catechism, a cautious and restricted precept to give the laity religious instruction in their vernacular tongue. The curious in the minor religious literature of the period are aware that books of devotion were at

[1] Joseph Robertson, Preface to Statuta Ecclesiæ Scoticanæ, cxlix. cl.

[2] There seems at all times to have been little interest in Scotland in the proceedings of councils-general. From foreign authorities we know that at the Council of Basle, in the fifteenth century, a certain Thomas, Abbot of Dundrennan, was a distinguished and leading member; but his eminence there has no echo at home, and nothing is said about him in the chronicles and the other sources of history. The fullest inquiry after traces of him will be found in the Preface to the Statuta, xcviii.

that time published for popular use in several parts of
Europe, with the sanction of the local Church while
still adhering to Rome. One of the most remarkable
of these was sanctioned in 1551 by a Scots provincial
council. It is known as Archbishop Hamilton's Catechism; but its authorship has been attributed to him
on account of the conspicuous way in which his name
and style appear in front, as conferring on the work
the sanction of the Church.[1]

The catechism is a fine piece of composition, full of a
spirit of charity and gentleness. It so carefully avoids
whatever might irritate those who have a remnant of the
old faith by which they may still be drawn back, that
Protestants not gifted with a powerful instinct for the
discovery of heterodoxies might read much of it without finding cause of offence. It exhorts the world to
peace and concord: "Since so it is, as St Paul says, that
we are all regenerate in Christ with ane baptism—all
oblaissed to have ane faith—all redeemed with ane
blood and dede of our Mediator Jesus Christ—all
livand in ane hope of the eternal glory—all subjectet
to the service of ane Lord—all guidet by the direction
of the Haly Spirit, whilk is ane daily teacher and
governour of the haill universal Kirk,—what can be
mair convenient, yea, mair necessarie, than that we al,
baith prelates and subjects, superiours and inferiours,

---

[1] "The catechisme—That is to say, ane commone and catholick instruc-
tioun of the Christin people in materis of our catholick faith and religioun, quhilk na gud Christin man or woman suld misknaw: set furth
be the maist reverend father in God, Johne, Archbischop of Sanct
Androus, Legatnait and Prymat of the Kirk of Scotland, in his provincial counsale haldin at Edinburgh the xxvi day of Januarie, the yeir of
our Lord 1551, with the advise and counsale of the bischoppis and uthir
prelatis, with doctouris of theologie and canon law of the said realme of
Scotland present for the tyme."

always agree and concord together in the brute of ane catholic doctrine concerning all points belonging to our Christian religion?"

Even so critical an injunction as the denial of the right of private judgment is uttered with somewhat of persuasive gentleness, thus :—

"Seek not to understand thay things that is above thy intelligence; seek naught to ken thay things whilk are above thy capacity; but evermair remember of thay things that God has commanded thee to do, and be not curious to understand the marks of God whilk is naught necessary or profitable to thee to knaw for thy salvatioun."

The authors of this manual of religious instruction to the laity had no benefit from the celebrated catechism of the Council of Trent, which was not issued until a later time.[1] The Scottish work had the advantage of itself appearing in a shape to be read by the people, instead of affording a mere aid to the clergy in the expositions they were told to make in the vernacular. But throughout its whole tone and tendency one would pronounce the Scottish catechism as the much more skilfully adjusted of the two, both for baffling and appeasing the common enemy.

The Church seems to have been less fortunate in another vernacular exposition, avowedly intended for the laity, and written down to their capacity. It

---

[1] The committee to adjust the catechism, the breviary, the missal, and the list of prohibited books, was appointed in the second session of Pius IV., or 1562 ("Sess. xxv. de Indice Librorum et Catechismo"). The object was to afford a manual whence the clergy might give instruction in the vernacular to prepare those coming to the sacraments. "Quam episcopi in vulgarem linguam fideliter verti, atque a parochis omnibus populo exponi curabunt."—Sess. xxiv. ch. vii.

was a brief exhortation issued by the national provincial council of 1559. Its immediate object brought it at once to a point of hostility with the new doctrines. It was to be read as a preparation for receiving the sacrament of the Eucharist, supplying what in later times has been called " A Companion to the Altar." Hence it begins with an exposition of the dogma of the real presence.[1] It was received with much scorn by the Reformers, and is spoken of by Knox in one of his exulting sneers as " the Twopenny Faith."[2]

The occasion of this hapless effort to meet one of the popular cries of the day, was a meeting of the clergy in provincial council, to make a last effort at internal reform. Meeting in the spring of 1559, while the existence of the Church itself stood at issue, the deliberations of this body got so little attention that they have almost dropped out of history. The business of the

[1] " Devote Christian men and women, wha at this present time are to resave the blysset sacrament of the altar, wyt ye perfectly and believe ye firmly, that under the form of bread, whilk I am now presently to minister to you, is containet treuly and really our Salvior Jesus Christ, heale in Godhead and manhead—that is, baith His body and blood and saule conjoinit with His Godhead, wha in His mortal life offeret Himself upon the croce to the Father of heaven ane acceptable sacrafice for our redemption fra the devil, sin, eternal dede, and hell ; and now, in His immortal life, sits at the richt hand of the Eternal Father in hevin, whom in this blisset sacrament, invisibly containit under the form of bread, I am to minister to you."

[2] Mr Laing says it has often been confounded with Hamilton's Catechism, and that " of the Twopenny Faith printed in 1559 no copy is known to be preserved."—Note to Knox's History, i. 291. The editor of the Statuta Ecclesiæ (p. 177) identifies it with a paper which he prints as part of the proceedings of the council, with the title, ' Ane Godly Exhortation made and set forth be the maist reverend father in God, John, Archbishop of St Andrews, Primate of Scotland, Legate, &c., with the avice of the provincial counsale halden, &c., to all vicars, curates, and others, consecrate priests, lawful ministers of the sacrament of the altar, to be read and shawn by them to the Christian people when any are to recave the said blessed sacrament.'

council was to consider certain suggestions by a body of gentlemen well affected to the Catholic establishment, remitted by the regent to the consideration of the council.[1]

These men had no sympathy with the new doctrines—on the contrary, the maintenance of Catholic orthodoxy, and the suppression of heresy within the Church, were among the objects desired by them. The changes they sought were in discipline and conduct. They pressed obedience to the injunctions of 1549 against the profligacy, the extravagance, and the idleness of the clergy. They had several proposals for the extended use of the vernacular tongue in church services and devotion. The most important portion of their original suggestions, however, bore on the strictly secular functions of the Church—looking to the shortening and simplifying of procedure in the ecclesiastical courts, and to the abolition or commutation of the odious taxes on the burial of the dead, and other ecclesiastical services.

The dealing of the council with these suggestions loses nearly all its importance, as being virtually an unheard voice in the tumult. The proposals for vernacular services were discountenanced, though, as we have seen, one little morsel in native Scots, not of a hopeful tenor, was issued. Something was passed towards checking ecclesiastical exactions. The most effective part of the resolutions of the council, however, went to the preservation of internal discipline among

[1] Articles proponit to the Queen-Regent of Scotland by some temporal lords and barons, and sent by her grace to the haill prelates and principals of the clergy convened in their provincial council in Edinburgh.—Statuta Ecclesiæ Scoticanæ, ii. 146.

the clergy; and we are told that the efficiency of these was of a kind so little contemplated by the framers, that they served by their strictness to drive many of the churchmen over to the Reformers.[1]

[1] Bishop Leslie calls these "sharp statutes," "whilk was the principal cause that a great number of young abbots, priors, deans, and beneficed men assisted to the enterprise and practice devised for the overthrow of the Catholic religion, and tumult against the queen and Frenchmen, fearing themselves to be put at according to the laws and statutes."—History, 271. A little more particularity as to a matter so curious would have been desirable.

CHAPTER XXXVIII.

The Reformation.

(*Continued.*)

POLITICAL POSITION OF THE REFORMATION QUESTION IN EUROPEAN POLITICS—ARRIVAL OF KNOX—CHARACTERISTICS OF HIS NATURE AND INFLUENCE—HIS COADJUTORS AND THEIR MOTIVES—MAITLAND OF LETHINGTON—THE FIRST BAND OR COVENANT—THE LORDS OF THE CONGREGATION EMBODIED—PRESSURE ON THE QUEEN-REGENT—HER DUPLICITY—THE FIRST OUTBREAK—ATTACKS ON THE SYMBOLS OF POPISH WORSHIP AND THE BUILDINGS OF THE RELIGIOUS ORDERS—CONSIDERATION HOW FAR THE CONDITION OF OLD ECCLESIASTICAL BUILDINGS IN SCOTLAND DUE TO THE REFORMERS—THE CONGREGATION AT PERTH—DEALINGS WITH THE REGENT—OCCUPATION OF EDINBURGH—CONDITION AND DANGERS OF ENGLAND—QUEEN ELIZABETH—KNOX AND THE "BLAST" AGAINST FEMALE RULE—CECIL AND KNOX IN TREATY—DIFFICULTY OF FINDING A LEGITIMATE HEAD TO TREAT WITH IN SCOTLAND—TREATY OF BERWICK—WAR—SIEGE OF LEITH—DEATH OF THE REGENT—DEPARTURE OF THE FRENCH, AND TREATY OF EDINBURGH—REFORMATION STATUTES.

THERE were early symptoms that Scotland would not struggle hard for the old religion. In 1542 a project already referred to was laid before the Estates, as a bill is now read in Parliament, authorising the common reading of the Scriptures, "baith the New Testament and the Auld, in the vulgar tongue, in Inglis or Scottis, of ane good and true translation."[1] The Archbishop of Glasgow, on behalf of the clerical estate, protested against this measure until the question should be discussed at a general council; but it was adopted by the Estates. From 1554 to 1558—that is, during the reign of Queen Mary in England—many English converts to the doctrines of the Reformation thought it prudent to seek refuge in Scotland, where anything that had in it an element of opposition to the ruling power in England was still sure to find welcome. Among these was a distinguished preacher named Willock. John Knox, too, was virtually a fugitive from the same danger. He went first from England to France; but in 1555 he returned to Scotland, and there taught for a time, until, for reasons about which there has been much dispute, he went to take charge of the English congregation at Geneva. There was nothing in Scotland parallel to the English persecutions under Philip and Mary. The Scots looked upon the troubles there as on the sufferings of their enemies, and would readily listen to Knox's sonorous denunciations of that wicked woman of Spanish blood who was persecuting the faithful.

It is of great importance, in understanding how the spirit of the Reformation was silently consolidating itself in Scotland, to keep in view that as yet the French connection, however distasteful it was becoming otherwise, did not of necessity involve hostility to the new doctrines. France, indeed, was that enemy, or at all events unsatisfactory servant, of the Popedom which the Empire, Spain, and England had been united in holy league to bring to reason. Their religion hung

[1] Act. Parl., ii. 415.

lightly on the people, especially those of the higher and educated classes. The doctrines of the more moderate Reformers, which oozed into the northern provinces from England and Germany, were gaining on them before the cause was injured by the fiery and sanguinary zealots of the south. As yet the great discovery had not been made, that disloyalty to the Church was the partner of disloyalty to the Crown. This was a very significant discovery, for it involved the fate of France, and almost of Europe, for half a century. It was the stock in trade with which the great house of Guise worked. It enabled the head of that house to defy the sovereign, and almost drive him from the throne, the house of Guise being more loyal to Church and king than the house of Valois itself. The conspiracy of Ambois may be dealt with as the turning-point at which the party of the league and of the Huguenots appear to have taken up their respective positions, and this event dates in 1560. During the time of the persecution in England, therefore, the queen-regent had not received the hint from her brothers that the enemies of the Church of Rome were to be dealt with as enemies of the state. Indeed there is strong reason to believe that the information she gave of her own experience in Scotland in the years 1559 and 1560, helped her brothers to that important conclusion. So little hostility did she at first show to the preachers of the Reformation, that she was supposed privately to favour them; and this supposition reacted on her, by deepening the charges of treachery to which she became amenable afterwards.

Queen Elizabeth had been scarce half a year on the throne when, on "the 2d of May 1559, arrived

John Knox from France."[1] Such are the words in which he enters the event in his own chronicle. Henceforth for a time we live in the broad clear light of that wonderful book. There certainly is in the English language no other parallel to it in the clearness, vigour, and picturesqueness with which it renders the history of a stirring period. Whoever would see and feel the spirit of the Reformation in Scotland—and in England too, for that matter—must needs read and study it. The reader who may happen not to be a zealous Calvinist will deal with it as the work of a partisan. From first to last there is no mistaking it for anything else. It is throughout the living spirit of partisanship—strong, resolute, and intolerant. But, for all that, it is full of truth. In fact the author had achieved a perfection of positivism which is incompatible with dissimulation and concealment. Whatever is done by him and his is so absolutely right, and so valuable as an example and encouragement to others, that the more loudly and fully it is proclaimed to the world the better.

Of all the revelations in this book, none is more remarkable than its writer's own character. His arrival in Scotland is an important event—all his doings are important in his own eyes, as well as in those of others. Whether it be for the adoration of the just or the malignity of the wicked, "John Knox" is ever the conspicuous figure in John Knox's book. When the regent, Mary of Lorraine, is seized with a fit of untimely exultation, it is against him that she flings. "She burst forth in her blasphemous railing, and said, 'Where is now John Knox his God? My God is now stronger than his, yea, even in Fife.'"[2] Speaking of the last ecclesias-

[1] History, i. 318.   [2] Ibid., ii. 8.

tical council which attempted the internal reform of the Church, he says, " The bishops continued in their provincial council until that day that John Knox arrived in Scotland," as if this conjunction aggravated the audacity of their doings.[1]

The way in which he thus sets forth his motions, as if he were writing the biography of some great man whose deeds he had the good fortune to witness, might be called egotism or vanity in one less in earnest. But it all comes of natural impulse, and reads naturally. All the world is astir, and he, John Knox, is the centre of its motion. He was a man of thorough practical experience, who had seen life in all grades—from the court to the galley-slave's bench. He was signally acute in penetrating political mysteries, and unfolding the designs of men when these were hostile; but he was as signally blind to the true character of compliant or perfidious partisans. Working with greedy selfish men intent on their own aggrandisement, he deemed them to be as completely as himself under the influence of an unselfish religious spirit; and when the evidence of sordidness was all too flagrant, he turned his honest eyes on it with surprise, like one who beholds his sober sedate friend take suddenly to drinking, or go off in a fit of acute madness.

Although the spirit of the Reformation in Scotland cannot be felt without a full study of the works of Knox, yet his testimony must be limited to the part of the field of battle in which he acted. He viewed the whole conflict as a triumph of the pure faith through its sole purity and acceptance with the Deity, and took little heed of the political and personal forces

[1] History, i. 191.

at work. Of these we form a livelier notion from the works of Sir David Lindsay, of which note is taken elsewhere. His attacks on the Church were earlier than Knox's, and indeed belong to a time when there was great danger for those who came within the ban of heresy. That this bold satirist and denouncer should have been spared when others less conspicuous and far less formidable suffered death may at first sight be hard to account for, but is in reality very simple. In attacking the clergy for licentiousness, greed, and cruelty, he was but repeating what the authorities of the realm asserted and the Church itself mournfully confessed. Anything might be said to this purport, if he who said it were so skilful as to avoid points of heresy—such as the denial of purgatory, the real presence, and the intermediating power of the saints. To justify his burning, the heretic must have committed the sin which could only be expiated for his soul in the next world by the burning of his body in this.

When Knox arrived in Scotland, it was to take up the work where he had left it in 1554. It was scarcely then of sufficiently conspicuous magnitude to affect the tenor of history. It influenced private conferences, and sometimes broke out into polemical discussion. But it is in connection with the public influence of his return that these earlier doings become significant.

We have one of his earliest triumphs among the politicians of his country told by himself, and in the full spirit of his own temper and character. It is in the year 1555, when the Reformers, far from supremacy, have not even achieved toleration—when everything tended towards the supremacy of the Romish power, and the Protestant party in Scotland were coming to an understanding with each other in quiet secrecy, doing the while all they could through their external conduct to evade inquiry and notice. Among these Knox naturally found " divers who had a zeal to godliness make small scruple to go to the mass, or to communicate with the abused sacraments in the papistical manner." The singleness of purpose that belonged to his infallibility rendered this intolerable, and he began, " as well in privy conference as in doctrine, to show the impiety of the mass, and how dangerous a thing it was to communicate in any sort with idolatry." His political coadjutors, who understood his vehement, intractable zeal much better than he understood their selfish aims, were disturbed by this. A conference was held at a supper in the house of Erskine of Dun, one of the few among the landed adherents of the Reformation who seems to have had religion at heart.

Knox had the advantage which the headstrong and single-purposed often have—the others must break with him, or submit. "The question was proposed, and it was answered by the said John, that nowise it was lawful to a Christian to present himself to that idol." He admits that there was much ingenious pleading for the " temporisers," and that especially they put forward very plausibly the precedent "that Paul, at the commandment of James and of the elders of Jerusalem, passed to the temple and feigned to pay his vow with others."[1] But Knox repudiated the precedent. Pay-

[1] This refers to the narrative in the latter portion of the twenty-first chapter of the Acts. When Paul, having come to Jerusalem, is told that a great crowd of Jews will gather, knowing of his arrival, and that from

ing vows and attending mass were not the same thing. Then he greatly doubted "whether either James's commandment or Paul's obedience proceeded from the Holy Ghost." But his most telling point was, that the incident was recorded for a warning rather than an example; for, in reality, it preceded and was probably the source of St Paul's danger and calamities. Both in broad determination of purpose and in skilful biblical criticism, he was master of the situation; and he tells, with his usual chuckling exultation, how young William Maitland of Lethington, "a man of good learning, and of sharp wit and reasoning," admitted himself to be utterly defeated by Knox's reasoning, saying, "I see perfectly that our shifts will serve nothing before God, seeing that they stand us in so small stead before men."[1] He, and deeper men than he was, found that, if they were to get service from Knox to their cause at that juncture, they must go with him as far as he would drag them. In such times of revolution, the man who in quiet times would be counted an obstinate and troublesome enthusiast, taxing the dexterity of people to keep out of his way, if he is anything at all in the councils of his party, is its leader.

Few things have perhaps ever been said more insincere than the admission which thus imposed on a man whose sagacity in some directions was marvellous.

what they have heard of his attacks on the observances of the law they may be dangerous, the brethren recommend to him an act of conformity calculated for the time to disarm suspicion. "Do therefore this that we say to thee: We have four men which have a vow on them; them take, and purify thyself with them, and be at charges with them, that they may shave their heads: and all may know that those things, whereof they were informed concerning thee, are nothing; but that thou thyself also walkest orderly, and keepest the law."

[1] History, i. 247, 248.

The statesman found that at this time he must go with the stream of their absolute opinions, if he were to make a political use of Knox and his followers. They had other contests of wit, in which Maitland found it more suitable to cast a sneer at the absolute zeal of the polemical leader than to follow his dictation; and then he would be commemorated, not in praise of his piety and docility, but in fierce rebuke for his worldliness and profanity. This young Maitland, also, had a character and a sphere of his own. He is well known in history simply as "Lethington," the name of his paternal estate. He was deep in all the political doings of that busy time, and perhaps knew more of its bloody mysteries than any other man. His name was a byword for subtlety and statecraft. Yet, though it ever comes up in connection with events as that of one supposed to pull the hidden strings, if we look at his life and doings, we do not find that he was one of those who have left the mark of their influence upon their age. He appears to have been too artificial and technically subtle to have great weight. He was an accomplished scholar, and bethought himself to draw on the resources of his reading for political influence—to bring the sagacity of the whole world of political authors and actors to aid his own. But if it succeed elsewhere, that is not the teaching that makes strong-handed statesmen in this country. Craft and sagacity did much in Maitland's day; but it was the craft and sagacity of those who were familiar with the political forces close at hand, and all the craft and wisdom of Machiavelli or Aristotle would have added little to their resources. Among men like these, the avowed scientific politician, whose intellect was stuffed with foreign subtleties, was a man to be feared and suspected. He was like an actor among men who seemed to follow where truth and nature led them; and he was consequently more easily seen through than those who had not a like reputation for subtlety. Withal, he had great abilities, but they were rather those of the wit and rhetorician than of the practical man. He had marvellous and dangerous powers of repartee, and, like others so gifted, let fly the shaft when he had better have reserved it. We can see, in occasional growls of pain and wrath, how Knox himself winced under such punctures, and repaid them with solid blows.

Knox, on his second coming, was not uninvited. His presence, indeed, was urgently demanded, as that of one who had for a time deserted his post of honour and danger. There were several preachers dispersed over the country who were in use to gather the people and read to them the English service-book of King Edward. A considerable body of the landed gentry had an understanding with one another, as friends of the new religion. They soon saw that an ecclesiastical revolution would set free a great stretch of land for new owners. This, too, made a common interest, which held them firmly together when they professed a union for purely religious objects. In the winter of 1557 they adopted a plan which we have seen in practice in Scotland from a very early day. Many of them signed a band or bond to co-operate with each other for the purposes set forth in the document. This was termed the First Covenant; and as it is a short, expressive enunciation, it may be allowed to explain its own object :—

"We, perceiving how Satan, in his members, the Antichrists of our time, cruelly doth rage, seeking to overthrow and to destroy the evangel of Christ and His Congregation, ought, according to our bounden duty, to strive in our Master's cause even unto the death, being certain of the victory in Him. The which our duty being well considered, we do promise, before the majesty of God and His Congregation, that we (by His grace) shall with all diligence continually apply our whole power, substance, and our very lives, to maintain, set forward, and establish the most blessed Word of God and His Congregation; and shall labour at our possibility to have faithful ministers purely and truly to minister Christ's evangel and sacraments to His people. We shall maintain them, nourish them, and defend them, the whole Congregation of Christ, and every member thereof, at our whole powers and wearing of our lives, against Satan, and all wicked power that does intend tyranny or trouble against the foresaid Congregation. Unto the which Holy Word and Congregation we do join us, and also do forsake and renounce the congregation of Satan, with all the superstitious abomination and idolatry thereof: and moreover, shall declare ourselves manifestly enemies thereto, by this our faithful promise before God, testified to His Congregation, by our subscriptions at these presents. At Edinburgh, the 3d day of December 1557 years."

Having met to subscribe this document, they passed two resolutions, in these terms:—

"First, It is thought expedient, devised, and ordained, that in all parishes of this realm the Common Prayer be read weekly on Sunday, and other festival days, publicly in the parish churches, with the lessons of the

Old and New Testament, conform to the order of the Book of Common Prayer. And if the curates of the parishes be qualified, to cause them to read the same; and if they be not, or if they refuse, that the most qualified in the parish use and read the same.

"Secondly, It is thought necessary that doctrine, preaching, and interpretation of Scriptures be had and used privately in quiet houses, without great conventions of the people thereto; while afterward that God move the prince to grant public preaching by faithful and true ministers."

The first occasion on which the Protestants came forth as a public power in the state, and had anything resembling a contest with their natural enemies, was in 1558. The affair is thus narrated by Knox :—

"They kept their conventions, and held councils with such gravity and closeness, that the enemies trembled. The images were stolen away in all parts of the country; and in Edinburgh was that great idol called St Giles first drowned in the North Loch, after burnt, which raised no small trouble in the town. For the friars rowping like ravens upon the bishops, the bishops ran upon the queen, who to them was favourable enough, but that she thought it could not stand with her advantage to offend such a multitude as then took upon them the defence of the evangel, and the name of Protestants. And yet consented she to summon the preachers; whereat the Protestants, neither offended, nor yet thereof afraid, determined to keep the day of summons, as that they did. Which perceived by the prelates and priests, they procured a proclamation to be publicly made, 'That all men that were come to the town without commandment of the authority, should with all diligence repair to the borders, and there remain fifteen days;' for the Bishop of Galloway, in this manner of rhyme, said to the queen, 'Madam,

> 'Because they are come without order,
> I rede ye, send them to the border.'

Now so had God provided that the quarter of the West-land (into the which were many faithful men) was that same day returned from the border, who, understanding the matter to proceed from the malice of the priests, assembled themselves together, and made passage to themselves, till they came to the very privy-chamber, where the queen-regent and the bishops were. The gentlemen began to complain upon their strange entertainment, considering that her grace had found into them so faithful obedience in all things lawful. While that the queen began to craft, a zealous and a bold man, James Chalmer of Gadgirth, said, 'Madam, we know that this is the malice and devise of the jefwellis, and of that bastard (meaning the Bishop) of St Andrews) that stands by you. We avow to God we shall make ane day of it. They oppress us and our tenants for feeding of their idle bellies; they trouble our preachers, and would murder them and us. Shall we suffer this any longer? No, madam; it shall not be.' And therewith every man put on his steel bonnet. There was heard nothing of the queen's part but 'My joys, my hearts, what ails you? Me means no evil to you nor to your preachers. The bishops shall do you no wrong. Ye are all my loving subjects. Me knew nothing of this proclamation. The day of your preachers shall be discharged, and me will hear the controversy that is betwixt the bishops and you. They shall do you no wrong. My lords,' said she to the bishops, 'I forbid you either to trouble them or their preachers.' And unto the gentlemen, who were wondrously commoved, she turned again, and said, 'O my hearts, should ye not love the Lord your God with all your heart, with all your mind? and should ye not love your neighbours as yourselves?' With these and the like fair words she kept the bishops from buffets at that time."[1]

The burning of Walter Mill was a sort of declaration of war, rousing the Protestant party to wrath and action. The leaders now called themselves "the Lords of the Congregation," and in that capacity laid a remonstrance before the regent charging the Church with cruelty. "There abideth," they said, "nothing for us but faggot, fire, and sword, by the which many of our brethren most cruelly and most unjustly have been stricken of late years within this realm, which now we find to trouble and wound our consciences; for we acknowledge it to have been our bounden duties before God, either to have defended our brethren from these cruel murders, seeing we are a part of that power which God hath established in this realm, or else to have given open satisfaction of our faith with them, which now we offer ourselves to do, lest that by our continual silence we shall seem to justify their cruel tyranny." They then demanded a reformation of abuses, and the establishment of religion on the basis of their bond and resolutions.[2] The queen-regent received this and other remonstrances respectfully, and pressed nothing against them but moderation and delay. Her winning

[1] History, i. 256-58. [2] History, 302. Calendar of State Papers, 7.

pleasant manner had great influence over those she spoke to; and it was chiefly owing to a reliance on her good feeling that the meeting of the Estates, in the winter of 1558, passed over without a fierce discussion of the great question. Knox even was won by the gentleness of her dealing and its tone of sincerity. "In public letters," he says, "to that excellent servant of God, John Calvin, we did praise and commend her for her excellent knowledge of God's Word, and goodwill towards the advancement of His glory, requiring of him that, by his grave counsel and godly exhortation, he would animate her grace constantly to follow that which godly she had begun." It was to his after mortification that he went still farther, and did "sharply rebuke both by word and writing all those who appeared to suspect in her any venom of hypocrisy, or were contrary to that opinion which we had conceived of her godly mind."[1]

De Béthencourt soon afterwards arrived as ambassador from France, now closely knit to Scotland by the recent marriage; and it is supposed that he expounded to the queen-regent the policy of her brothers, which was to be war—a deadly unsparing war—with the propagators of the new opinions. In the words of Knox, "Then began she to frown, and to look frowardly to all such as she knew did favour the evangel of Jesus Christ. She commanded her household to use all abominations at Pasche; and she herself, to give example to others, did communicate with that idol in open audience. She comptrolled her household, and would know where that every ane received their sacrament. And it is supposed that after that day the

[1] History, i. 315.

devil took more violent and strong possession in her than he had before; for, from that day forward, she appeared altogether altered, insomuch that her countenances and facts did declare the venom of her heart."[1] It is just at the same time — in January 1559 — that we find the suggestions of an alliance with England taking shape.

Arran, now called Duke of Chatelherault, or "The Duke," had a meeting with Sir Henry Percy, in which the position of England and Scotland was discussed. The duke admitted that the connection with France was becoming oppressive to Scotland. He said the old enmity to England was dying out; and he mentioned, as an instance of this, how the queen-regent had lately ordered a Scots army to invade England, but that, acting otherwise in all duty, they had refused to cross the border, as not a service demanded by their feudal duty. Sir Henry Percy spoke of the favour which England bore to the right-thinking portion of the Scots. The realm was suffering too much, however, from the consequences of the late reign to offer any assistance in the mean time, and nothing was concluded between the two representatives.[2] The old project for a marriage of Queen Elizabeth to the duke's son, now Earl of Arran, was renewed. The father was not a man likely to press such a matter, or plot ingeniously in its favour. The proposition was simply made, and courteously declined by the queen.

That ecclesiastical council of 1559 which attempted the adjustment of projects of internal reformation in the Church was then assembled in the hall of the

---

[1] History, i. 315.
[2] Calendar of State Papers (Foreign), 1559, 98.

Dominican monastery at Edinburgh.[1] It rose on the 10th of April, and adjourned until Septuagesima Sunday of the year 1560; but never met again. The projects entertained and those adopted, with their relations to each other, might have become an important chapter in ecclesiastical history; but all was swept away by the torrent from without. It has been generally understood that the regent laid the demands of the Reformers before this council.[2] We have seen that there came before the council certain propositions, offered by those well affected to the Church, who pleaded for internal reformation. These are respectfully recorded; but the proceedings of the council bear no reference to any proposals by a hostile body.[3] Hence it would appear either that the regent did not, in an official form and from authority, desire the attention of the council to the demands of the Protestants, or that, if she did so, the council took no formal notice of the document laid before them.

They knew that she was prepared to back them in resistance to the new force, and it was during the sitting of the council that she was observed to take an attitude of distinct hostility to the Reformers. A deputation from the Congregation touched on the symptoms of her change of policy, and reminded her of the encouragement which she had given to the cause of the Reformation. It was to these visitors that she was accused of making the too characteristic remark, that "it became not subjects to burden their princes with promises further than it pleaseth them to

---

[1] See above, p. 45.
[2] M'Crie's Knox, Works, i. 123. Grub, Ecclesiastical History.
[3] See the Record in Statuta Ecclesiæ Scoticanæ, ii. 146 et seq.

keep the same." She was about to give a still clearer example of her opinions on this head. She cited certain of the preachers to appear before the Privy Council at Stirling, to answer for their conduct. A large body of men of influence were prepared to accompany them, and assembled at Perth for the purpose. The regent begged that they would abandon their project, and return home; and to induce them to do so, she promised to withdraw the citations. They dispersed accordingly, but she had no intention of keeping her promise. The names of the ministers cited were called in court in the usual manner; and as they did not appear, they were treated as fugitives from justice, and in common form outlawed and proclaimed as rebels. News of this came to Perth, where still there was a remnant of the gathering, who were hearing John Knox preach and exhort; and here came the first outbreak of popular reforming zeal into actual violence. The scene may best be told in Knox's own words:—

"The manner whereof was this: the preachers before had declared how odious was idolatry in God's presence; what commandment He had given for the destruction of the monuments thereof; what idolatry and what abomination was in the mass. It chanced that the next day, which was the 11th of May, after that the preachers were exiled, that after the sermon, which was vehement against idolatry, that a priest in contempt would go to the mass; and to declare his malapert presumption, he would open up ane glorious tabernacle which stood upon the high altar. There stood beside certain godly men, and amongst others a young boy, who cried with a loud voice, 'This is intolerable, that when God by His Word hath plainly damned idolatry, we shall stand and see it used in despite.' The priest, hereat offended, gave the child a great blow, who in anger took up a stone, and, casting at the priest, did hit the tabernacle, and broke down ane image; and immediately the whole multitude that were about cast stones, and put hands to the said tabernacle, and to all other monuments of idolatry, which they despatched before the tentmen in the town were advertised (for the most part were gone to dinner), which noised abroad, the whole multitude convened, not of the gentlemen, neither of them that were earnest professors, but of the rascal multitude, who, finding nothing to do in that church, did run without deliberation to the Grey and Black Friars', and, notwithstanding that they had within them very strong guards kept for their defence, yet were their gates incontinent burst up. The first invasion was upon the idolatry, and thereafter the common people began to seek some spoil; and in very deed the Grey Friars' was a place so well provided, that unless honest men had seen the same, we would have feared to have reported what provision they had. Their sheets, blankets, beds, and coverlets were such as no earl in Scotland hath the better; their napery was fine. There were but eight persons in convent, yet had eight puncheons of salt beef (consider the time of the year, the 11th day of May), wine, beer, and ale, besides store of victuals effeiring thereto. The like abundance was not in the Black Friars', and yet there was more than became men professing poverty. The spoil was permitted to the poor; for so had the preachers before threatened all men, that for covetousness' sake none should put their hand to such a reformation, that no honest man was enriched thereby the value of a groat. Their conscience so moved them that they suffered those hypocrites take away what they could of that which was in their places. The Prior of Charterhouse was permitted to take away with him even so much gold and silver as he was well able to carry. So was men's consciences before beaten with the Word that they had no respect to their own particular profit, but only to abolish idolatry, the places and monuments thereof, in which they were so busy and so laborious that within two days these three great places, monuments of idolatry — to wit, the Grey and Black thieves, and Charterhouse monks (a building of a wondrous cost and greatness) — was so destroyed that the walls only did remain of all these great edifications."[1]

This passage introduces us to a notorious feature of the Scottish Reformation—the destruction that befell the monuments of early ecclesiastical architecture throughout the country. Two conditions are apt to give an exaggerated notion of the destruction perpetrated by these Reformers. One is the frank admission of Knox, that his followers heartily set their hands to demolition. The other is the total disappearance of many ecclesiastical buildings, and the mere ruinous shreds which show where others existed. Tradition, too, has joined to swell the charge against the iconoclasts, or to enhance their glory as it may be otherwise put. Round the ruins of multitudes of Gothic churches there crowd traditions of the righteous Reformers destroying the citadels of superstition and infamy. Even in far Iona we are asked to believe that a mob tore to

[1] History, i. 320.

pieces great masses of Norman masonry, and that they even carried off some hundred or so of monuments.

But there were other elements of destruction. The most merciless has been mere neglect. In England, the Reformation was not antagonistic to the old buildings and the old forms; in Scotland it was. Ecclesiastical architecture came to a stand in 1560. It seemed as if necessity only would make people submit to worship in the fanes of the old religion, and they raised no new buildings after the same model. The churches thus fell to pieces from exposure and neglect. The several stages of destruction from this cause passed unnoticed. After many years perhaps the roof would give way, then the wet getting into the chinks of the stones the walls would fall piecemeal, so the pillars, and in the end all would be a heap of rubbish, becoming more and more chaotic, until, on the revival of the love of Gothic architecture, within the memory of the present generation, the Government Board of Works would make an effort to preserve such fragments as could be saved. Among all the great churches of Scotland the most nearly obliterated is that of Elgin. Yet we know from old prints that about the time of the Revolution its walls were complete, and the progress it had made towards destruction went no farther than the falling-in of the roof.

The Reformation mobs, in their destruction of everything savouring of idolatry, destroyed not merely the gaudy and valueless symbols by which the Church of Rome strove to impress the minds of the ignorant, but a deal of the fine interior decorative masonry of the first pointed and the flamboyant styles, which are now so much prized. But beyond things thus savouring of

MISCHIEF TO RELIGIOUS HOUSES, 1559. 69

idolatry, the fabric of the churches did not excite their destructive indignation. The cloisters and other dwelling-places of the regulars, however, did. These were, in a manner, fortresses of the enemy. Hence we must believe in the destruction of the monasteries at St Andrews and at Perth as described by Knox, as well as of many others.[1] It is noticeable at the present day that, even where the churches of the monastic houses still exist, the remnants of the cloisters and other domestic buildings which had surrounded them are extremely scanty.

We have, in one instance at least, the formal instruction under which the sweepers-away of the matter of offence did their work. It refers to the Cathedral of Dunkeld. That building as it now stands, no doubt, bears mark of rough handling; but it probably suffered more injury in standing a siege of Highland Jacobites after the Revolution than it received from the Reformers. At all events, the Directions, while they contain a full and hearty licence for the destruction of images, altars, and all monuments of idolatry, profess carefully to guard against any injury either to the stone or wood work of the fabric of the church.[2]

In the history of the invasions directed by King

---

[1] Sadler, on the 29th of September 1559, when he announces the arming of the Lords of the Congregation and his information on the matter from his spy, says, " He told us also that they had suppressed the Abbeys of Paisley, Kilwinning, and Dunfermline, and burned all the images, idols, and Popish stuff in the same."—State Papers, i. 468.

[2] The authority subscribed by Argyle and Ruthven on 12th August 1560, requires the Lairds of Arntully and Kinvaid " to pass incontinent to the Kirk of Dunkeld, and tak doun the haill images thereof, and bring furth to the kirkyard, and burn them openly. And siclyke cast doun the altars, and purge the kirk of all kinds of monuments of idolatry; and this ye fail not to do as ye will do us singular empleasure, and so com-

Henry and Somerset, we have seen enough to account for large items in the ruin that overcame ecclesiastical buildings in Scotland. For Melrose, Kelso, Jedburgh, and the many other buildings torn down in these inroads, the Scots Reformers have no censure to incur beyond that of neutrality or passiveness. The ruined edifices were not restored, as they naturally would have been had the old Church remained predominant.

Knox, and those who followed him for conscience' sake, had not intended that their followers should perpetrate even what mischief befell; but once done, and done in the cause, they were not to disavow it or abandon those coadjutors whose only defect was a superabundance of zeal. And, besides, might not the finger of God have been shown in the method of the destruction of idolatry? and was it for them to question His will, or the method in which He fulfilled it? They issued several manifestoes—to the regent, to the French commanders, and to others—all casting defiance, and standing on the argument, which never can be refuted, that their work was sanctified, and that they must continue to serve God rather than man. The briefest and perhaps the most characteristic of these documents was the following :—

"To the generation of Antichrist, the pestilent prelates and their shavelings within Scotland, the Congregation of Christ Jesus within the same sayeth—

"To the end that ye shall not be abused, thinking to escape just punishment, after ye in your blind fury have caused the blood of many to be shed, this we

mits to the protection of God. Fail not but ye tak good heed that neither the desks, windocks, nor doors be onyways hurt or broken, either glassin work or iron work."—Statistical Account of Scotland, x. 976.

notify and declare unto you, that if ye proceed in this your malicious cruelty, ye shall be entreated, wheresoever ye shall be apprehended, as murderers and open enemies to God and unto mankind; and therefore betimes cease from this blind rage. Remove first from yourselves your bands of bloody men of war, and reform yourselves to a more quiet life; and thereafter mitigate ye the authority which, without crime committed upon our part, ye have inflamed against us; or else be ye assured that, with the same measure that ye have measured against us, and yet intend to measure to others, it shall be measured unto you—that is, as ye by tyranny intend not only to destroy our bodies, but also by the same to hold our souls in bondage of the devil subject to idolatry, so shall we, with all force and power which God shall grant unto us, execute first vengeance and punishment upon you; yea, we shall begin that same war which God commandeth Israel to execute against the Canaanites—that is, contract of peace shall never be made till that ye desist from your open idolatry, and persecution of God's children. And this we signify unto you, in the name of the Eternal God, and of His Son Christ Jesus—whose verity we profess, and gospel we have preached, and holy sacraments rightly administered—so long as God will assist us to gainstand your idolatry. Take this for advertisement, and be not deceived."[1]

This was the critical point in the contest, and it may safely be said that, if the queen-regent had kept her promises, and had not attempted to carry her point by French money and French troops, the Reformation in Scotland would have borne a character different from

[1] Printed in Keith, 87; Knox (History), i. 335; and elsewhere.

what it actually took. Argyle, the Lord James Stewart, afterwards Earl of Murray, Lord Semple, and other men of mark of the party of the Congregation, joined the regent, to show their respect for law and order; and had they found her faithful to the moderate courses which she readily promised, they might have remained by her side. The Congregation strengthened themselves in Perth, and a French force marched to Auchterarder, fifteen miles southward of them. A battle was imminent. Argyle, the Lord James, and Semple went to commune with the Protestants, and had much talk with Knox, in which they found that the yielding of any point on that side was a hopeless expectation. Towards the maintaining of moderation on the other side, however, there came to their assistance an unanswerable argument in a small army of two thousand five hundred men, brought to the aid of the Congregation by Lord Glencairn. The enemy now came to terms, which were a distinct triumph to the Congregation. They were that—

" 1. Both the armies shall be disbanded, and the town left open to the queen.

" 2. None of the inhabitants shall be molested on account of the late alteration in religion.

" 3. No Frenchmen shall enter the town, nor come within three miles of it; and when the queen retires, no French garrison shall be left in the town.

" 4. That all other controversies be left to the next Parliament."[1]

The Congregation dispersed from Perth; but ere they went, Knox preached a sermon, in which he said, " I am assured that no part of this promise made shall

[1] Keith, 89.

be longer kept than till the queen and her Frenchmen have the upper hand." He was quite right—the articles were preadjusted, with a defect which gave the means of discarding them. The Congregation knew that the regent could not levy a feudal force for her purposes, and they thought themselves safe if no French force could be brought against them. But the regent had French money, and with that she hired a native force to garrison Perth, and went thither with a French force under D'Oysel—they were her body-guard, and not a garrison. The Congregation counted that the stipulation not to "molest" the inhabitants was grossly violated.

This affair gave sudden strength to the Reformers, like a rush of new blood. The influential men who had departed from them for a while came back, and multitudes flocked to them from distant places. They invaded St Andrews. The archbishop threatened a vigorous resistance, but found it hopeless. Knox preached, and his sermon was followed by the usual demonstration against idolatry, and the wrecking of the religious houses. The queen's army marched from Linlithgow to sweep them away, but St Andrews was found to be well fortified and strongly garrisoned. Again there was treaty and stipulations. No Frenchmen were to remain in Fifeshire, and certain commissioners were to be appointed by the regent to adjust finally with the leaders of the Congregation. No such commissioners were appointed, however, and it became clear that the regent was working for delay up to the time when a fresh force should arrive from France. On the 29th of June 1559, the Congregation made a decisive stroke by marching on and occupying Edinburgh, whence the Court and the French had to retire.

It was charged against the new occupants that here they took on themselves to perform some of the functions of a government; for instance, that they took and used the coining irons, or the dies of the national mint. They had, doubtless, done enough to cost them all their heads, if their enemies had power to work their will on them. But there was more yet to come. On the 23d of October 1559, a solemn proclamation professed to depose the regent. It was issued with the nearest practicable approach to Parliamentary form. The spiritual lords of the Estates were not parties to it, but the burghs were represented, and the whole body set forth that they acted in "our sovereign lord and lady's name," "whose council we are of native birth in the affairs of this our common weal."

The regent and her party took no notice of this document. In the quietness of inaction, some of the Protestants repented of their course and dropped off. Most conspicuous among these was the wavering duke. Yet the moment should have been one to excite his interest. The driving forth of the Jezebels, mother and daughter, and a change in the succession of the crown, were freely talked of. The natural channel to shift the succession into was the house of Hamilton. Young Arran, the heir of that house, was then in France. It was deemed of moment that he should make his appearance in Scotland, and he escaped from France and wandered northward through England in disguise. There is a romantic legend that he thus providentially preserved his life, for the Guises had resolved to strike some distinguished members of the Reform party, and he was selected as the first victim.

It was evident, however, that, when a French army

arrived, the cause would be lost unless England came to the rescue. In existing conditions, the policy of that step was undoubted ; but for the same reason, interference at the present stage would be the admission of principles against which Queen Elizabeth had a horror. She was a champion of the divine right of sovereigns. She felt that her own right required every sanction she could get, and it might be a precedent to react on herself were she to countenance subjects in opposing their sovereign. It might be otherwise if there were disputed claims, and a legitimate leader to be acknowledged. We shall see how far these demands were supplied by the ingenuity of English statesmen ; but to the end the countenancing of opposition to a crowned and anointed queen was a difficulty.

Cecil set his wisdom to work upon the difficulty in "a short discussion of the weighty matter of Scotland," dated in August 1559. In his perplexity he had recourse to some views which at this day sound grotesquely when connected with so great a name for sagacity. He proposed to set to work the claim of feudal superiority over Scotland, but after a quite original plan. It was not for the purpose of subjugating the country to a foreign yoke, after the example of King Edward, but that the people might be relieved by the masterful exercise of English power from the foreign yoke now holding them, and might be restored to their native customs and their liberties. But after all, perhaps, looking at it from Cecil's side, the scheme was not so mad as it appears. He, no doubt, seriously believed in the superiority; for being, as he was, a busy man, if he looked into the documents relating to the matter, he would find at that time the whole story in a very complete form, and supported by abundance of records which he would have no reason to distrust, though they have been since denounced as forgeries.[1] After he had got some experience of the country he was dealing with, Cecil was wise enough to keep silence on the question of the superiority. Intercourse with practical Scotsmen made him better acquainted with the political conditions. Early in the year we find him in communication with Kirkcaldy of Grange. That ardent and ambitious young man is among the first to strike the key-note of the great change in the

[1] "The crown of England hath a just and unfeigned title, of longer continuance than the friendship betwixt Scotland and France, unto the superiority of Scotland; and for the right thereof, it is as good, and in some respect better, than the right of the French queen to the realm of Scotland, as hereafter shall appear. To prove the antiquity and continuance of the right of this superiority, remain good, ancient, and abundant stories; and which is the best proof, the authentic and manifest writings under the seals of Scotland, declaring from age to age, from king to king, from parliament to parliament, the homages done to the kings of England by the kings of Scots; coming sometimes to York, sometime to London, sometime to Lincoln, sometime to Canterbury. By which title of superiority, the crown of England hath upon differences decided the controversies, and appointed the crown of Scotland as to it was thought fit. And by this title and dignity doth the French queen, as Queen of Scots, owe homage to the crown of England; and so consequently ought the crown of England to defend the liberties, the laws, the baronage, and people of Scotland, from oppression, and that in honour and conscience, no less than the emperor ought to defend the state of Milan, or the kingdom of Bohemia, being vassals to the empire. And therefore, if it may appear that the French king, by pretence of the marriage of an heir of Scotland, will alter the laws, liberties, and customs of Scotland, and will subvert the lawful heirs of the Scottish blood to the crown, and deprive the barons and states of the realm of their inheritance, whereby the French nation and blood may possess that land; then the crown of England is bound in honour and conscience to defend and protect the realm of Scotland against the French. And so doth the first question alter in the most principal point; for then is not the case betwixt subjects and a natural prince, but betwixt a superior king and a realm of the one part, and an inferior king alone joining with strangers on the other part."—Sadler State Papers, i. 378, 379.

national sentiments—terror of France, and a desire for
common cause with England. We find the Scotsman
pressing on the English statesman the danger of both
countries, and the infinite importance of England
securing the aid of a people who had heretofore been
true to themselves, and would be true to their ally in
the hour of danger.[1]

There was one thing of vital importance to the
views of Cecil and his fellow-statesmen of England—
they must secure the hearty co-operation of John Knox.
His own temper and capacity, working under peculiar
political conditions, had raised up the preacher to be
one of the dictators of the political movements of
Europe. Environed by perils as Elizabeth's Government was, to secure the help of Scotland was an object
almost vital. The new party there were influenced by
many motives arising from selfish hate and greed; but
the cry which united them as a power was the "evangel"
of the Reformation, and of that Knox was master. If
the self-seeking aristocracy did not satisfy him that
their zeal in this cause was orthodox and sufficient, he
could break up their power; and nothing would prevent
him from doing so, if he so willed. He must, if possible,
be made to see, then, that his own cause and that of
England were one. It would not suffice to show him
that worldly prudence suggested this union of forces—
worldly prudence might go to the winds; but he might
be made to see that a junction of forces between
the English Government and the Scots Reformers was
the shape which the ways of Providence were taking
towards the blessed result.

To deal with one so absolute in his own spiritual

[1] Calendar of State Papers, 1558-59, 385.

empire demanded caution and patience. Cecil seems to have required all the training to the ways of a pliant statesman, which his experience of Henry and his daughter had given him, to endure arrogance and dictation from so unwonted a quarter. He got a scolding, after Knox's peculiar manner, to begin with. It has generally been thought that Cecil behaved with unexpected spirit when he retired from Court during the reign of Mary Tudor, carrying with him the avowal of Protestantism. This did not satisfy Knox; he should have lifted his testimony against the Jezebel, and he is told, "As the benefit which ye have received is great, so must God's justice require of you a thankful heart; for seeing that His mercy hath spared you being traitor to his majesty — seeing, further, that amangs your enemies He hath preserved you—and last, seeing, although worthy of hell, He hath promoted you to honour and dignity,—of you must He require, because He is just, earnest repentance for your former defection, a heart mindful of His merciful providence, and a will so ready to advance His glory, that evidently it may appear that in vain ye have not received these graces of God to performance whereof, of necessity it is, that carnal wisdom and worldly policy—to the which both ye are bruited too much inclined—give place to God's simple and naked truth."[1]

Whatever of this kind, however, Cecil had to bear was a trifle to another difficulty. His wilful mistress hated Knox for that book of his against the right and the capacity of women to govern. It was necessary that he should do something to appease her on this point, but would he do it? To men with ordinary motives

[1] History, ii 17, 18.

the opportunity was a brilliant one; the denouncer of feminine rule had only to say that he had drawn his philosophy from bad examples—he was fallible, like all men—he had now seen a brilliant reverse of the wretched experience on which he had drawn, and must recant his broad conclusions. It soon became apparent that anything like this was hopeless. The Reformer had many times to admit, with due sorrow, that he had been deceived in the character of individual men who had professed zeal in the great cause and afterwards abandoned it. But that he, John Knox, should admit himself to have been fallible in a broad declaration of doctrine—as soon expect the holy Court of Rome to drop the keys of St Peter, and recant its whole traditions as wretched fallacies! He stood by what he maintained to the utmost. He heard that a refutation of his doctrine was to appear: let the author of such an attempt beware, lest it call forth a more conclusive denunciation, for he must stand by the truth.

Yet he could not but feel that it was through Elizabeth that his great cause could triumph—that it could even escape destruction; and that no other power seemed destined for its work save this which he had denounced as a kind contrary to the Word of God. He had a remedy, however, and it was as strange and original as everything about the man. It was, in a manner, breaking through the difficulty instead of solving it. He offered to the queen, in his own fervent style, such devotion as is due to a beneficent and powerful human being. He admitted that she was the chosen instrument for the work of the gospel. But it was a special act of Providence—a sort of miracle—accomplishing a great end by the smallest and basest of human means.

All would go well, if she would feel the due humility of one selected for her nothingness rather than her eminence. So it behoved her to remember that it was not her Tudor descent, nor yet her wisdom or ability, that had any concern with the exalted work on hand, and to demean herself with a humility befitting the occasion. At least this appears to be the tenor of his explanation to Cecil, and of a letter to the queen herself.[1]

In this latter document he put the hardest pressure

[1] "The wreitting of that booke I will nott deny, but to prove it treassonable I think it salbe hard. For, sir, no more do I doubt of the treuth of my principall propositioun, then that I doubt that was the voce of God which first did pronunce this penaltie aganis woman, 'In douloure sall thou beare thy chyldrein.' It is bruitted that my booke is or salbe writtin against. If so be, sir, I greatlie feare that flattereris sall rather hurte nor mend the mater, which thei wald seame to mainteine; for, except that my error be plainlie schawin and confuted be better authoritie then by suche lawis as frome yeir to yeir may and do change, I dar nott promitt silence in so weehtie a besines, leist that in so doing I sall appear to betray the verretie whiche is not subjected to the mutabilitie of tyme. And if ony think me ather ennemye to the persone or yet to the regiment of her whome God hath now promoted, thei are utterlie deceived of me. For the miraculouse wark of God, conforting His afflicted by ane infirme veschell, I do acknawledge, and the power of His most potent hand (raiseing up quhome best pleiseit His mercie to suppresse such as fecht aganis His glorie) I will obey, albeit that boyth nature and Goddis most perfyt ordinance repugne to suche regiment. Moir plainlie to speik, if Quene Elizabeth sall confesse that the extraordinarie dispensatioun of Goddis great mercie macketh that lauchfull unto her whiche boyth nature and Goddis law do deny to all women, then sall non in England be more willing to mainteine her lauchfull authoritie then I salbe; but if (Goddis wonderouse werk sett asyd) scho ground (as God forbid) the justnes of her title upoun consuetude, lawis, or ordinances of men, then I am assured that, as suche foolishe presumpcioun doeth heyghlie offende Goddis supreame majesty, so do I greatlie feare that her ingratitude sall nocht lang lack punishement. And this in the name of the Eternall God, and of His Sone Jesus Chryst (befoire quhome boyth you and I sall stand, to mak accomptes of all counsall we geve), I require you to signifie unto her grace in my name; adding, that onlie humilitie and dejectioun of herself before God salbe the firmitie and stabilitie of her throne, quhilk I knaw sall be assaulted mo wayis then one."—History, ii. 20, 21.

on his nature, to draw from it something soothing and
satisfactory; and when we consider that nature, he was
wonderfully successful. He cheers her with the expectation that all shall go well if, forgetting her birth,
and "all title which therefrom doth hang," she, with
due humility, remember that her power is held of special dispensation, " which only maketh lawful to your
grace what nature and law denieth to all women."[1]

Cecil managed in the end that Knox should be pro-
pitiated, and even that attention should be shown to
his wife on her way through England from France to
Scotland. It was proposed that there should be an
interview between the two great powers at the minister's country mansion of Hatton, in the very centre of
England. Whether there was danger, or other reason
against it, no such meeting could be held. It had to
suffice that Knox should meet the Governor of Berwick
on Holy Island. There they had an instructive conference. Knox did not enlarge on the topics which
charmed his audiences from the pulpit; but put it
plainly, that Scotland wanted men and money from
England, with the assistance, if possible, of a fleet.

Cecil, and other advisers of Queen Elizabeth, strongly
pushed this policy. They represented that the opportunity for severing Scotland from France, and securing
as a friend the worst enemy of England, had now at
last come, and might pass. It was an object on which
money ought not to be spared. The queen, who was
keenest of all for setting this barrier against France,
yet was, from her odd contradictory nature, the impediment to any fair, open-handed help to the Scots in
their extremity. She suggested many things that her

[1] History, ii. 29, 30.

advisers might do as "from themselves." Among these was the advancing of the money; it would come better from them as private persons having sympathy with the Scots, than if it came from the English Government. But they knew that not only were they unlikely to be repaid their advances, but if matters took an awkward turn, they might be delivered over, without remorse or hesitation, to be dealt with by the English treason laws. Among other clumsy pieces of trickery suggested, one was that an army should assemble in the north, and, without instructions from the English Government, cross the border as sympathisers with the Scots cause. They would then be proclaimed traitors for attacking a state at peace with England, and, unable to return, would have nothing for it but to fight out a position for themselves in Scotland; but no body of men thought proper to put themselves in this complex and peculiar position.

At length, on the 20th of August, Sir Ralph Sadler was sent to the borders to hold communication with the Lords of the Congregation. He was intrusted with three thousand pounds, but he represented that this would merely be so much money wasted if more were not sent. A larger sum was afterwards sent, but the bearer of it fell into the hands of the notorious Bothwell, who had much occasion for such a fund for his own uses. Sadler found political conditions directly the reverse of those he had seen sixteen years earlier. Then, there was dread of England, and the French alliance was all popular; now, the current was running rapidly the other way, and he found some politicians helping it onwards. "It seemeth," he says, "they make little or no account of the French power, which is looked for out of France, willing that the same should rather come than not; for, as the number cannot be great, so think they that the same should so stir and irritate the hearts of all Scotsmen as they would wholly and firmly adhere and stick together, whereby their power should so increase as they should be well able both to expel the French out of Scotland and also better achieve the rest of their whole purpose."[1] If this was the view held by the Scots Protestants, it is certain that they were far less frightened than Queen Elizabeth's Privy Council. Their view of the prospects of both countries is set forth with gloomy brevity. "They think that the French mean, after their forces are brought into Scotland, first, to conquer it—which will be neither hard or long to do—and next, that they and the Scots will invade this realm, principally upon the north parts."[2]

Meanwhile the Lords of the Congregation, their people dropping off from time to time, found themselves too weak to hold Edinburgh against such a force as the queen-regent could bring against it. Again there was treating, but with merely temporary aims, and charges that promises were not kept. The Lords of the Congregation retired westward. There came then an addition of a thousand troops to the French force, and a fortress or intrenched camp of great strength was constructed by them at Leith. There the regent, with her army, held out, abiding events, vainly besieged by the Congregation. These noticed, and reported to their friends in England, some very menacing specialties of the new influx of French troops. They seemed to come, not for a campaign, and its mere fighting-work,

---

[1] Sadler State Papers, i. 400.
[2] Privy Council to Queen Elizabeth, 24th Dec. 1559; Calendar of State Papers (Foreign), 221.

but for permanent establishment in the country. These features were described as "the inbringing of soldiers, with their wives, bairns, and instruments for manuring the ground, such as ploughs and suchlike, and for assaulting strengths, such as mattocks, spades, &c."[1]

The Congregation were joined, at this emergency, by an important deserter or refugee—Maitland of Lethington—whose character has been already discussed. Young as he then was, he was deemed a match for Cecil, as a sagacious, long-headed politician. He had given, he said, unpalatable advice to the queen-regent, to whom he was secretary of state, and he considered himself no longer safe in the camp at Leith. He undertook to do the business of the Congregation in England; and one like him, who had held high office in Scotland, was likely to have double influence.

In January 1560 a treaty was adjusted between Queen Elizabeth and the Congregation, called the treaty of Berwick. In a thing so unprecedented as combining with England against France, the Scots felt something like the misgiving that attends great changes of policy; and they showed their jealousy to the last in the punctiliousness with which they insisted on their dignity and equality. They would not go to England, but met the English on benches erected in the middle of the Tweed, where it was the national boundary; and the English complained that from one cause or another, and especially the excessive vigilance of the Scots in guarding their punctilios, they were at last taken over to treat on Scots ground.

This treaty of Berwick required very subtle diplomatic handling. It was, in reality, an arrangement to which the parties were—on the one side, the English

[1] Calendar of State Papers (Foreign), 1559, p. 225.

emissaries, sent to watch the affairs of Scotland; and, on the other, that body called the Lords of the Congregation, who were at war with the representative of their sovereign. But if it were a treaty, it must be between royalties; and how were they to be brought into it? Queen Elizabeth was to be the one party—but where was the other party to be found? The treaty on the English side was ratified by the Duke of Norfolk "in the name and behalf of her highness;" but on the other side there was no authorised representative of royalty, and though a body of commissioners acted, they were accepted neither by the young queen in France nor her mother the regent. The best that could be done was to make the commissioners act "in the name and behalf of the noble and mighty prince, James Duke of Chatelherault, second person of the realm of Scotland; and the remanent lords of his party joined with him in this cause for the maintenance and defence of the ancient rights and liberties of their country." To bring the duke a step still nearer to royalty, it is set forth that he is "declared by Act of Parliament in Scotland to be heir-apparent to the crown thereof." We learn the significance of the phraseology of this part of the treaty by the correspondence of the time, in which Queen Elizabeth's advisers are at their wits' end to find a political head with whom it might become her, as a crowned and anointed queen, to communicate. It is evident that what they most desired was that some one whose position fitted him for such a project should aspire to the throne. Queen Elizabeth would then be supporting the cause of the right sovereign, at least of the side she thought proper to adopt in a disputed succession. The head of the house of Hamilton was, of course, looked to; but he was not the man to play so bold a game. Hints were given to the Lord James; he was the son of the late king, and though he was illegitimate, that was a difficulty that had often been overcome in other instances. Whatever his conscience may have said, however, his prudence was sufficient to keep him from so perilous a project.[1]

These difficulties adjusted as best they might be, the treaty goes into thorough business. Queen Elizabeth's object is the preservation of the realm of Scotland in its old freedoms and liberties during a dangerous crisis, and the expulsion from it of the foreign troops, who are virtually foreign invaders. The imminence of the occasion comes out. Her majesty is certain, from the information received by her, and the career of the French troops in Scotland, "that they intend to conquer the realm of Scotland, suppress the liberties thereof, and unite the same unto the crown of France perpetually." Then comes the practical stipulation for averting this catastrophe, or "for expelling out of the same realm such as presently and apparently goeth about to practise the said conquest;" that "her majesty shall, with all speed, send unto Scotland a convenient aid of men of war on horse and foot, to join the powers of Scotsmen, with artillery, munition, and all other instruments of war meet for the purpose, as well by sea as by land, not only to expel the present power of France within that realm oppressing the same, but also to stop, as far as conveniently may be, all greater force of French to enter therein for the like purpose." There was a clause coming after these substantial undertakings, which served better than the preliminaries to save Queen Elizabeth from the scandal of treating with subjects.

[1] Calendar of State Papers, 404, 461, &c.

Her aid is to be given to the Lords "as long as they shall acknowledge their sovereign lady and queen, and shall endure themselves to maintain the liberty of their country and the estate of the crown of Scotland."

There is a provision which, if it do not hint suspicion, yet shows precaution bred of old jealousy of England. Whenever the English force take fortified places from the French, they are either to be demolished at the hand of the Scots or given over to the duke and his party, and the English auxiliaries are not to fortify themselves anywhere in Scotland without the permission of the duke and his followers.[1]

This arduous piece of diplomacy accomplished, it was resolved at last to send hearty aid. The French army, under D'Oysel, made a progress along the coast of Fife, plundering and burning, and purchasing undying enmity among the people, as English armies had done some ten or twenty years earlier. They beheld strange sails in the Firth, which they believed to be a reinforcement from France; but they were undeceived when they saw the strangers seize their own transports. The new vessels, in fact, brought an English force of six thousand men. There was now a scene, new and interesting—Scots and English fighting together against foreigners. But the French, and those who stood by them, held the new fortress at Leith with great firmness. There was, evidently, far more engineering science within the walls than without. The attacks were disastrous, and repeatedly driven back; and so far as the position of the two forces was concerned, it seemed likely that the fortress might remain permanently with its holders. Affairs, however, were working elsewhere towards changes. In March 1560 the conspiracy of

[1] Fœdera, xv. 569.

Ambois made a crisis in France. If it rendered the retention of Scotland to France and the Church of Rome all the more desirable, yet on the other hand it called for the return of all available troops to France. After a conference, it was agreed that the French troops should return home, and that no foreigners should be employed in Scotland without the consent of the Estates. The adjustment in which this and other matters were arranged was called "the treaty of Edinburgh." One important stipulation in it—afterwards the cause of much curious discussion—was a condition that the young queen and her husband acknowledged Elizabeth as Queen of England, and were to be bound not only to abstain from any pretences on England by the blazon of arms or otherwise, but to do their best to suppress any such attempts when made by others.[1]

The queen-dowager, sick and wearied with anxieties, was taken when the siege of Leith began to the Castle of Edinburgh. She died there on the 10th of June 1560. On her deathbed she showed that air of magnanimity and high generous feeling which her remarkable race could assume on all fitting occasions, insomuch so that she left a profound impression even on the hard minds of the sturdiest of the Reformers. She sent for the Lord James, and spoke regretfully, and almost as if penitently, of the past; and suffered Willock, the preacher, without interruption, to deliver some of the exhortations which his own order deemed good for such occasions. The cause of the Congregation was now triumphant, and about finally and emphatically to express itself.

The Estates convened in August. On the 17th the Confession of Faith, containing a rendering, in English

[1] Fœdera, xv. 593.

or Scots, of the principles of the Geneva Church, was approved of as "hailsom and sound doctrine, grounded upon the infallible truth of God's Word." At the same time there was a general repeal or revocation of all acts authorising any other form of belief or worship, and the authority of the Bishop of Rome was abjured. It was provided that the administering, or being present at the administration, of the mass, should be punishable—for the first offence, by forfeiture of goods, and corporal infliction at the discretion of the magistrate; for the second, by banishment from the realm; for the third, by "justifying to the deid," or death. These Acts were passed on the 25th of August. They have little organisation or legislative detail for the purpose of practical application, and may be held, as many Scots Acts then were, to be rather a resolution and declaration of opinion by the triumphant party in the States, than Acts of Parliament in the present constitutional meaning of the term.[1] It will be observed, in what has hereafter to be said, and makes a very significant point in the character and policy of Queen Mary, that these Acts never got the royal assent.

On the face of the parliamentary record it would seem as if the Reformation in Scotland were the work of one day. On the morning of the 25th of August 1560, the Romish hierarchy was supreme; in the evening of the same day, Calvinistic Protestantism was established in its stead. But the departure of the French and the treaty of Edinburgh were the conclusion of past events; and as to the Acts of Parliament, whether they were of any avail or not depended on events yet to come.

[1] Act. Parl., ii. 526 *et seq.*

CHAPTER XXXIX.

Condition of the Nation from the War of Independence to the Reformation.

THE CONSTITUTION OF SCOTLAND—THE POWER OF THE ESTATES OF PARLIAMENT—THEIR EXERCISE OF THE EXECUTIVE—LORDS OF THE ARTICLES—THE ESTATES AS A FINAL COURT OF LAW—LORDS AUDITORS—DAILY COUNCIL—ESTABLISHMENT OF THE COURT OF SESSION ON THE MODEL OF THE PARLIAMENT OF PARIS—INFLUENCE OF THIS IMITATION—CHARACTER OF THE INSTITUTIONS—ADAPTATION OF THE CIVIL LAW—ABSENCE OF THE PREROGATIVE OR INVIDIOUS RIGHTS WHICH SET CLASS AGAINST CLASS—CONSTITUTIONAL AND HISTORICAL RESULTS—POPULARITY OF THE NATIONAL INSTITUTIONS—PROVISIONS FOR THE EDUCATION OF THE PEOPLE—GRAMMAR-SCHOOLS—UNIVERSITIES—THEIR TESTIMONY TO AN ELEMENT OF ENLIGHTENED LIBERALITY IN THE CHURCH—THEIR MODEL BROUGHT FROM FRANCE—VESTIGES OF THIS INFLUENCE IN UNIVERSITY CONSTITUTION AND PRACTICE.

It is now proposed to pause for a while in the narrative, and look back upon such isolated occurrences or established facts as are suggestive about the progress of the nation in wealth, civilisation, literature, the administration of justice, and other matters coming within the compass of a country's social condition. In the similar retrospect of progress before the War of Independence, the materials for distinct knowledge were so

meagre that every trifle had to be seized with avidity.
The materials, too, for the succession of historical
events were too scanty to supply the significant specialties which enable us to see the manners and conditions of a people in the mere telling of the narrative.
The fuller particulars of the later periods ought of
themselves to tell about the social condition of the
several actors who come forward, more expressively
than a general dissertation can. On this occasion,
then, nothing seems to be appropriate or required
beyond a rapid grouping of such specialties as narrative does not naturally carry with its current.

The reasons have been given for supposing that there
was much comfort, if not affluence, in Scotland when
the War of Independence broke out.

In the earlier summary of national progress we find
traces of laws, which had grown up no one knew how,
older than the traces of the existence of a parliamentary body. We have seen how, through the feudal
institutions moulded by the spirit of the people, a
parliament gradually grew, under the title of the
Estates of the Realm; and we have seen that in the
reign of Robert the Bruce, if not earlier, the citizens of
the burghs were represented in that body. During
the period now referred to, the Estates continued to
exist, and to act as a constitutional establishment of
the nation. We have had many opportunities of noticing the laws passed by the Estates, and the other
transactions in which they were concerned. In some
of these instances it may have been observed that the
Estates interfered with transactions which, according
to modern English constitutional notions, belong to
the executive; and from this it would be inferred,

by many practical politicians, that the Estates of Scotland were not a properly constitutional parliament.

There can be no doubt of the superiority of the practice of the present British Parliament on all points in which it differs from the practice of the Scots Estates anterior to the Reformation. But may we not find that the perfection of the British system has grown with the other political conditions surrounding it, and that it is as vain to seek it in the Scotland of the sixteenth century, as to seek the peace, the security, and the other blessings of our civilisation in the same conditions of time and place?

Take, for instance, two features in which the British Constitution has gone far beyond any other human institution in the way to perfection, by affecting the rapid action of a despotism without weakening or checking the influence of popular control and responsibility. The one is the sacredness of the sovereign from personal responsibility, while every act of government must pass under the hand of some minister of the crown, who is personally responsible for what is done; the other is, that it lies with the sovereign to make peace and war, Parliament only having the power of reviewing the conduct of the ministers who have made themselves responsible for the line of policy adopted in each instance. But these principles were not adjusted by the political skill of wise lawgivers. They were the offspring of strife and bitter enmity. Parliament never conceded the inviolability of the royal person. All the world has heard of the conflict, designed to extinguish in blood that slavish doctrine, when it was resuscitated by the civilians from the maxims which the Roman Empire had taken from Eastern nations.

Nor, on the other hand, did the crown advisedly give up to Parliament the power of controlling the conduct of the sovereign's servants. Every devise of the constitution has a complex and contradictory shape, because it has been a remedy found in the period of power, for something that has been lost in the period of weakness. Thus every specialty in the constitution was either the fruit of some victory gained, or the result of a compromise and treaty between two hostile powers. The purport of what was so gained or lost was recorded with scrupulous exactness, and hence came that precision in the working of the machinery of the constitution which is so infinitely valuable in the present day.

In this view the English Constitution survived memorable perils, and it is no matter of wonder that a neighbouring constitution should avoid the risk of abandoning the holds it already had, with the dubious prospect of recovering them in a more perfect shape. The Scots Estates did not admit the irresponsibility of the sovereign. We have seen them bringing King James III. to task, and the precedent was made all the more emphatic by the attempt of the lawyers of the seventeenth century to conceal it by mutilating the record in which it is set forth. The punishment of bad sovereigns is a thing in which the literature of the country deals in a tone evidently directed towards practice. We find the Estates of Scotland dealing with many things now deemed the peculiar function of the executive. They kept in their own hands the power of making peace and war. We repeatedly find ambassadors receiving special instructions from the Estates; and there was a political crisis about the great question of marrying Queen Mary to the Prince of England, because a treaty had been negotiated under instructions from an imperfectly constituted parliament.[1] While the power of Rome yet existed, the Estates had made visible progress in establishing such a lay headship over the Church as the crown acquired in England by a sudden stroke. We shall find that at the time we have reached, a critical question was standing over, Whether the crown had a veto on the acts of the Estates? in other words, Whether the consent of the sovereign was necessary to an Act of Parliament? and down to the union with England this question was not decided. In forming the constitution of the Scots Estates, there was an element never felt by the English Parliament. There, throughout, the enemy was at home—it was the prerogative. The vigilance of the Scots Estates was ever exercised against the conquering encroachments of England. There are scarcely any traces of a conflict between the crown of Scotland and the Estates. These, in fact, were the careful guardians of the crown against peril from subjugation by the common enemy. Such faint traces as we have of the Estates coming in conflict with the crown are when there is suspicion that the sovereign is in too close amity with the enemy of England to be trusted with the keeping of the independence of Scotland.

[1] In the close discussions with France, at the time of Queen Mary's marriage, the power and functions of the Scots Estates puzzled the French courtiers. When Montluc, Bishop of Valence, had a discussion with the Lords of the Congregation, and put the point of loyalty to them, he says, " Ils répliquèrent, que le royaulme d'Escosse est gouverné aultrement que ne sont les aultres, et que s'il y a différends entre le Roy et les subjects, il faut qu'il soit débatu et décidé par les Estats ; et mesmes que les roys n'ont puissance de faire ligue ni ordonner la guerre sans leur consentement."—Teulet, Pièces, i. 593.

The many calamities of the royal family gave the Estates the opportunity of independent action, and made it a great national duty. From the death of Alexander III. to the majority of James VI. there is a period of 300 years. If we count in these the years when there was a minor king, and the period of the absence in England of King David, we shall have to deduct 134 years from the 300, leaving 166 years during which the kingdom was ruled by an adult monarch. It is less to be wondered at that, with such opportunities, the Estates should have acquired functions unsuited to a representative body, than that the monarchy should have been strictly preserved, and that it should have kept the exact course of hereditary descent unvaried, save by a slight oscillation from the shock of the great War of Independence.

This precise observance in Scotland of the strict rule of descent is all the more remarkable from the chaos of the Wars of the Roses in England. Perhaps it may be said that this was because Scotland did not happen, like England, to be afflicted by royal collaterals, whose power enabled them to break in upon any abstract principle, such as that of hereditary descent; but at least it is due to the Estates of Scotland that they took up the true rule of descent, and were careful that there should never be a deviation from it.

The Estates were not divided into two Houses, like the English Parliament, but transacted their business in one place of meeting. We have nothing to help us to the method in which this business was transacted, like the precise record of the votes and proceedings of the English Parliament; but, again, this precision was the growth of contest, everything done by either House, with the method of doing it, being recorded as a precedent for after reference, in case it should come to be impugned either by the crown or by the other House of Parliament.

The practice of passing projects of law from one House to another has been a great protection against impulsive legislation, by requiring that every measure should be reconsidered, even after it seems finally matured; and this, like the other specialties, was in England the growth of contest. The Scots Estates did the best they could towards the same end, by working through permanent committees, having, after their appointment, the character for the time of separate legislative chambers. We find the appointment of such a legislative committee in the reign of David II.—there are marks in the wording of the appointment which show that the institution was then a novelty. In the first parliament of the reign of James I., we find that such a committee had gradually become a permanent institution, under the name of the "Committee of Articles," or the "Lords of the Articles." It would appear that from that time the legitimate method of transacting the legislative business of Parliament was that, on the assembling of the Estates, they decided on the tenor of the measures which it was desirable to pass. Certain persons were then chosen from each Estate to be the Committee on the Articles. To them the preparation and maturing of each measure was confided, somewhat after the method in which, at the present day, a committee of the whole House deals with a bill referred to it after the second reading. The Estates stood adjourned while this committee was at work. When the several projects of law were matured, the Estates reassembled. The committee reported to the meeting the bills matured, and they were then put finally to the vote for adoption or rejection. In later times this, the legitimate form of action, was sometimes invaded or perverted. The courtiers of the later reigns, when they desired to influence the proceedings of the Estates, found the delegation of business to this committee to be the weakest part of the organisation of the legislature, and they accomplished their ends by corrupting its constitution.

The Estates, in their jealousy of all prerogative powers exercised by the crown, strove against its monopolising the administration of justice. While the king's chancellor, justiciars, and sheriffs exercised their remedial jurisdiction, the Estates or high court of Parliament professed to administer justice, or give "remeid of law" to those who might apply to them. For this branch of work a separate committee was appointed, called the Lords Auditors of Complaints. The proceedings of this committee, from 1466 to 1494, have been printed by the Record Commission, and are a substantial contribution to our means of becoming acquainted with the early law and forensic practice of the country. A like contribution is afforded in the proceedings of the Lords of Council from 1478 to 1495.[1]

This tribunal was recast in the year 1503, by an act of the Estates. The lords were to be appointed by the crown, and to "sit continually in Edinburgh, or where the king makes residence, or where he pleases."[2] One reason for establishing such a court was that

[1] 'Acta Dominorum ad Causas et Querelas Audiendas Electorum,' and 'Acta Dominorum Concilii,' both printed by the Record Commission in 1839.

[2] Act. Parl., ii. 241.

the Lords Auditors had authority only during the sitting of Parliament, so that the procedure before them stopped when Parliament rose. It became the practice to hand the unfinished litigations before the Auditors, at the end of a session, over to the Lords of Council. The jurisdiction of both was alike. The same men often served on both, and the staff of officers seems to have been common to both.[1]

We find that the sheriffs, as representing the crown, occasionally resist the orders of the Auditors, or fail in due compliance, and then orders are issued for their "warding" or imprisonment, raising contests about "privilege," resembling in some measure those which have so often disturbed the equanimity of the English Houses of Parliament. The Church took to itself all legal adjustments which depended on an answer to the question whether the sacrament of marriage had been duly performed; and so all litigations raising the question whether any persons were man and wife, or whether any person was born in wedlock, so as to take the privileges of legitimacy, fell to the ecclesiastical courts. Hence the Lords Auditors, or the Lords of Council, sometimes found that a question raised is not within their jurisdiction, but belongs to the proper ecclesiastical court. They found, too, occasionally, that a person who has entered appearance as a litigant is under sentence of "cursing" or excommunication, and cannot be heard until that ecclesiastical doom is removed. With ecclesiastical tribunals and persons,

---

[1] In one instance, in the record of the auditors, the clerk is found setting down a decision as by "the lords of counsale," but, recollecting himself, he scores his pen through the words and writes "auditors."—Act. Parl., 10.

the Lords, although acting as a supreme court, seem generally loath to be authoritative. In a case before them, for instance, a priest is in possession of writs which will help to a right decision; but the Auditors, instead of taking steps to enforce production of them, apply to the bishop, exhorting and praying him to compel the priest to produce them.[1]

On the proceedings of the Lords Auditors, little appeal business is perceptible. Perhaps they were shy of exercising the power of reversing the judgments of the king's justiciars. Enough appears, however, to show that, holding delegated power from the Estates as the supreme court of Parliament, they counted themselves a court of review on appeals from the king's courts. On any occasion when this power is exercised, the minute of the finding of the Auditors is expressed with unwonted distinctness and ceremonial.[2]

We find this high court of Parliament, in one instance at least, taking upon itself to give such remedy in an international question as we may well believe the inferior courts would not venture to apply. The

[1] Acta, &c., 94.
[2] " The Lords Auditors chosen be the three Estates in this present Parliament for the decision of the dooms, decreets and delivers that the doom given in the Justice Aire of Cupar, in the tolbooth of the same, before John Haldane of Gleneagles, ane of our sovereign lord's General Justice on north half the water of Forth, be the mouth of [ ] Dempster, the 25 day of Februar, the year of God 1477, for the burgh fundin be Alexander Spence, advocate and forespeaker for John Dischinton of Ardross, upon thre breve of mortancestry, purchast be Andrew Bisset, upon the lands of Kinbrachmont, and agane a recontre made be William Richardson, advocate and forespeaker for the said Andrew, was evil given and well again said by the said William, for divers and mony reasons produced and shown before the lords."—Acta, &c., 66. The words " evil given and well again said " are equivalent to finding the court below in error, and admitting the appeal. This mere reversal is followed by findings for putting the judgment of the court of appeal in force.

case is remarkable, from the practical testimony afforded by it to the closeness of the exchange of citizenship between France and Scotland even before the marriage of Queen Mary. A certain William Richardson, who is called a burgess of Dieppe, while his name shows him to be of Scottish origin, had got a decision in his favour against William Lennox of Kail, for the sum of six score pounds, fourteen shillings, and fourpence of Parisian money. The decision was by a French court of law; it was pronounced by "James Disome, licentiate in the law and Lieutenant-General at the Table of Marbre in the Palace of Paris, under a noble lord, Louis, Lord Grauil, Councillor to the King of France, and Great Admiral of France." This foreign decision was held to be authenticated "by a process, sentence, and certain letters executorial direct by the foresaid James Disome, thereupon shown and produced before the lords." Thereupon they directed that the lands and goods of William Lennox should be distrained for the debt decerned against him by the celebrated court of the Marble Table in Paris.[1]

The French connection comes up in another shape, when it was found that the two tribunals—the Lords Auditors and the Lords of the Council—did not work well; and it was judged fitting to recast the administration of justice, and organise a supreme court of law.

Hence in 1532 that Court of Session was created which, modified from time to time, still exists as the great fountain of justice in Scotland. It was formed on the model of the Parliament of Paris; and this French constitution, infused into it at the beginning, gave peculiarities to its constitution all along. The

[1] Acta, &c., 181.

French Parliaments partook of the double nature, of courts of law, and deliberative bodies with powers of a legislative character. The French crown cultivated, under due subordination, the legislative tendencies of the Parliaments, as superseding the functions of the States General, and at last rendering it unnecessary to assemble that troublesome body. In like manner the Court of Session professed general remedial powers, which pressed close on the office of the legislator. So lately as the early part of the eighteenth century, they raised a storm in Edinburgh by fixing the conditions on which it was just and right that the city brewers should brew their ale. Throughout, the propensity of this court has been to give its remedy on a general view of the whole question before it; and only by degrees, and with hard adjustment, has the method, long brought to precision in England, of absolutely separating the law from the fact, been brought into Scottish practice.

This court took two peculiarities by its constitutional descent. It was deemed illogical to appeal from the Court of Session to Parliament, since the Court of Session was but a remodelling of that committee of Estates which was itself the high court of appeal, as exercising the full powers of Parliament. We shall find this specialty opening up troublesome questions in the reign of Charles II. The other peculiarity was, that the practice of the court made no provision for trial by jury. It has been maintained that this, too, was keeping clear of an illogicality, since the court represented Parliament, the grand jury of the nation.

As to the substance of the law administered by the tribunals of Scotland, we have seen that, before the

War of Independence, there was a tendency in this, as in other institutions of the country, to follow the example set by England. After that war, each country went its own way. England, which alone among Christian nations repudiated the Civil law, busily piled up that extraordinary mass of precedents known as the Common law. Much as the civil law was professedly detested in England, the country had to draw upon it for relief from the strange vagaries and utter injustices committed by the chaotic common law when let loose with absolute power. Against it protection was sought in the Equity jurisdiction, presided over by that high officer the Lord Chancellor, and the means of extending such protection to the subject were found in the civil law. Scotland received the civil law as all-sufficient. Hence, looking across the Tweed, the English common or equity lawyer could see a phenomenon not easily understood by him—a country under one harmonious system of jurisprudence; and he could sometimes only express the nature of a thing so monstrous, by saying that the tribunals there were courts both of law and equity.

The English horror of the civil law came of the autocracy at its head, and the ample use made of it in Continental despotisms. It is a flexible system, however, easily adaptable to the desires of a free people. Take from one end of it the divine right prerogative of the emperor, and from the other end the institution of slavery, we have a system made to meet all possible exigencies, on the broad principle that all are equal in the eye of the law. There is no precedent for privilege of peerage, for forest law, or for game law, to be found there; hence it suited Scotland, where the spirit of the community did not readily adapt itself to the prerogatives of class, which the Normans had established in England. There are but scant vestiges of this spirit in the old customs of Scotland. There was no prerogative law of trespass—a law rendering it an offence for a person to be in a particular place whether his being there caused harm to any one or not. Cultivated lands and crops, whoever owned them, were protected by the exaction of damages or recompense from any one doing injury to them. We have seen how certain French visitors were alike amazed and indignant when they found such claims asserted by very peasants. On the other hand, the bare moor was open to all men.

Of the English forest laws—the prolific parent of a troublesome offspring, the game laws of later times—we have seen that they were but feebly and dubiously imitated in Scotland. The country was full of wild animals; the people were active and armed, and fond of field sports when they had no more serious work for their weapons. It could not be, therefore, but that there should be legislation about game. The tenor of this legislation, however, was to render game abundant. and available for sporting purposes, by prohibiting the slaying of animals at the period when slaughter is fatal to their increase, and for the suppression of those methods of killing them which are inimical to sport by facilitating the means of converting the animals into butcher-meat.[1] There were restraints.

[1] Thus there were penalties against taking the eggs or nests of wild fowl: "Wyld fulis—sic as pairtriks, plovers, black-cocks, grey-hens, mure-cocks—sould not be taken frae the beginning of Lentern till August."—Act, 1427. "Na man should slay does, roes, deer, in time of storm or snaw, nor their kids until they be ane year auld."—Act, 1474. Among the precautions for economising the game for the purpose of

at the same time, to prevent mischief-doing in the pursuit of the chase.[1] There are provisions for protecting to the owners the animals within enclosed parks or chases, and some other restraints; but there is no trace of any of those subtle distinctions by which one man might have the possession and cultivation of the ground, while another enjoyed the prerogative right of following the game reared upon it. We must come down to a period later than we have yet reached ere we shall find the Scottish legislature, in imitation of the practice of England, enacting that the ownership of land is a necessary qualification for the privilege of slaying wild animals. The oldest author who professes to give a general survey of the law of Scotland bluntly lays it down, that "it is leasum and permitted to all men to chase hares and all other wild beasts, being without forests, warrens, parks, or wards."[2]

No doubt the feudal aristocracy of Scotland had great power; and where there is power, there will be more or less of oppression and injustice. The events

sport, the use of firearms was prohibited. We must remember that this referred to a heavy machine for deliberate use, a weapon very different from our modern fowling-piece. "The art of 'shooting flying' is one of very recent acquisition, dependent on the improvements in the mechanism of the modern fowling-piece; and the legislation of earlier times, while it encouraged the well-established and authorised use of hounds and hawks, uniformly directed the severest penalties against the employment of such 'indirect' means of destroying game as 'hackbut, gun, net, and fowler's dog.'"—Irvine on the Game Laws, Introduction, xxix. Here will be found the best account of the early legislation of Scotland on the matter of wild animals.

[1] "That na man tak upon hand to ride or gang in their neighbours' cornis, in hawking and hunting, frae the first of Pasch until the time the samen be shorn, and that na man ride or gang upon wheet na time of the year."—Act of 1555.

[2] Balfour's Practiks, 542.

which have been narrated must be left to give their own impression of the relations to each other of the different orders of society. It has been seen that acts were passed for fixity of tenure to the peasant, and for other checks on the abuse of feudal power. But a large specialty may here be noticed, which, as it is negative, does not naturally come up in the narrative. It was in the spirit of the constitution to confer such powers as were deemed fit for public use; but not to confer the empty privileges and exemptions, which are invidious to those excepted from them, and have it in their nature to set class against class. Among the multitudinous exemptions from the obligations binding on common men, which made up the privilege of peerage in England, there seems to be no trace in Scotland. In later times these nearly all merged into the one substantial privilege of exemption from imprisonment for debt.[1]

In the administration of criminal justice there was no separate tribunal of their own for the trial of peers, as there was in England. Important cases of treason were generally tried by the Estates, whether the accused were lords or commoners. The Estates were ever jealous of leaving political offences to be dealt with by the king's courts. But for other offences, however high, a lord had to "thole an assize," or stand by the verdict of a jury, like any other subject. The jury

[1] At the Union the English privileges were extended to all Scots peers, whether they were returned to Parliament or not. The exasperated party opposed to the Union garnered up every testimony to selfishness and corruption which they could cast against its supporters; and among these, it was said that exemption from imprisonment for debt was a cunning device to buy the votes of the impoverished peers of Scotland.

was in some measure modified to equality in rank with the accused. If he were a "landed man," or proprietor of land, the jury must have been chosen from the same class; and if he were a freeholder, a certain proportion of the jury must have held the same rank.

But the best testimony to the character of the national institutions is to be found in the tenacity of the people in holding to their "auld laws and lovable customs." In the hostile face they ever presented to all attempts towards annexation by England, it is not so much the sentiment of a national sovereignty that is at work, as the dread of innovation on the national customs. We have seen how this is specially noted by the English statesmen who reported on the national feeling to Henry VIII., and especially by the acute and observant Sadler. The influence of the feeling was acknowledged in the later attempts at annexation, which were accompanied by engagements to preserve the old laws and customs of the country—engagements which could not be taken with reliance from kings who were ever striving to cancel the charters conceded to their subjects of England.

As yet we have come across no contest of class against class. It would be difficult to trace the history of any other part of Europe, through the same centuries, without finding this sort of testimony to the dissatisfaction of the people with the institutions among which they lived. In Scotland there was no Jacquerie —no Wat Tyler or Jack Straw. Whether or not the Scots were, as some have held, subjected to a hard feudalism, their condition seems to have been congenial to them. High and low, they fought together, and were of one mind; and it was only when the natural leaders were supposed to have betrayed the country to the common enemy that there was variance between classes, and the peasant would no longer follow where his feudal chief would lead him.

In almost all the periods of the history of Scotland, whatever documents deal with the social condition of the country reveal a machinery for education always abundant, when compared with any traces of art or the other elements of civilisation. Perhaps book-learning is the first of the intellectual pursuits which an inquisitive and ambitious people take to, the others following in their turn. We have naturally no statistics of education which would be sufficient to afford an idea of the number of schools in the country, and the matters taught in each, even so far down as the Reformation. But in documents much older than the War of Independence, the school and the schoolmaster are familiar objects of reference. They chiefly occur in the chartularies of the religious houses; and there is little doubt that the earliest schools were endowed and supported out of the superfluous wealth of these houses, whether with the object of supplying a body of scholars from which the Church might take its recruits, or in a general enlightened view of the blessing of knowledge to mankind.[1] In later times, schools are found attached to the burgh corporations. They got the name of grammar-schools, and we see from the way they are spoken of that Latin was taught in them.

In 1496 an Act was passed requiring, "through all

---

[1] The casual notices of schools in the early parts of the ecclesiastical chartularies have been often cited. They will be found summed up in Innes's 'Sketches of Early Scotch History,' 134 *et seq.*

the realm, that all barons and freeholders that are of substance put their eldest sons and heirs to the schools, fra they be aught or nine years of age; and till remain at the grammar-schools until they be competently founded and have perfect Latin; and thereafter to remain three years at the schools of art and jure, so that they may have knowledge and understanding of the laws."[1] The baron or freeholder who should fail in obedience to this injunction was to forfeit £20 to the crown. The forfeiture is to follow upon "knowledge gotten" of the failure—a protective condition, since it must have been hard to prove that the youth, if sent to school, had not got "perfect Latin." But, like many other Scots Acts, this one was in a great measure an exhortation from authority rather than a law to be rigidly enforced.

We hear, at the commencement of the sixteenth century, of men acquiring distinction as mere schoolmasters—a sure sign of the respect in which the teacher's mission was held. Among these were Andrew Simson of Perth, and John Vans of Aberdeen, who was so ambitious as to write a grammar of the Latin tongue. Ninian Winzet or Winyet, a distinguished scholar, was master of the grammar-school of Linlithgow. As a member of the old religion, he was superseded at the Reformation. He went abroad to hold the high office of Superior of the Scots Convent of St James, at Ratisbon.[2] It does not appear to have been thought that the command over this eminent religious house was a startling contrast to the position of teacher of the grammar-school of Linlithgow. Ad-

---

[1] Act. Parl., ii. 238.   [2] See chapters iv. and xii.

vancement it certainly was, but not to a dizzy elevation.[1]

But however powerful the school education of his time may have been, the Scotsman ambitious of acquiring the learning that went beyond the knowledge of languages must have sought it abroad, until the establishment of universities in Scotland. Three universities had been founded in Scotland more than half a century before the Reformation—St Andrews in 1410, Glasgow in 1450, and Aberdeen in 1495. It may with truth be said that, in the history of human things, there is to be found no grander conception than that of the Church of the fifteenth century, when it resolved, in the shape of the universities, to cast the light of knowledge abroad over all the Christian world. The skill and energy brought to its completion were worthy of the greatness of the design. It was a thing altogether apart from the public-school system, which doles out

---

[1] Winzet lamented the necessity that parted him from his old friends and accustomed pursuits. When addressing the "gentil reader," he says, "When I, for denying only to subscrive thair phantasy and faction of faith, was expelled and shot out of that my kindly toun, and fra my tender friends there, whas perpetual kindness I hoped that I had conquest, by the spending about ten years of my maist flourishing age, naught without manifest utility of their commonwealth." His estimate of the office of the teacher seems worth noting, as the utterance of a Scots burgh schoolmaster of the time before the Reformation: "I judgeit the teaching of the youthhood in virtue and science, next after the authority with the ministers of justice, under it and after the angelical office of godly pastors, to obtain the third principal place most commodious and necessar to the Kirk of God. Yea, sa necessar thought I it, that the due charge and office of the prince and prelate without it, is to them, after my judgement, wondrous painful and almost insupportable, and yet little commodious to the commonwealth, to unfeignet obedience and true godlyness, when the people is rude and ignorant; and contrary, by the help of it to the youthhood, the office of all potestates is light to them, and pleasant to the subject."
—Winzet's Tracts ; see Irving, 'Lives of Scottish Writers,' i. 100.

the rudiments of knowledge to the totally ignorant, giving them a little of it with calculated parsimony, as paupers are fed and clothed. The universities called on all the ardent spirits of the age to come and drink their fill at the great fountains of knowledge. Everything about the universities was on a scale of liberality, splendour, and good taste sufficient to adjust them to the habits of the aristocracy. Yet the poorest and humblest among the people—the children of craftsmen and serfs—were tempted to resort to them and partake of their munificence, on the condition of earnestly embracing the scholar's life and devoting themselves to the acquiring of learning.

The university was to be the same in rank, and if possible in wealth and grandeur, whether it arose in the populous capital of some powerful state, or was planted in some distant region among a scanty people, poor and rude. It was to be the same at Upsala and Aberdeen as at Paris and Bologna; the same at Greifswalde, on the flats of Pomerania, then but recently rescued from heathendom by the crusades of the Teutonic knights. Thus were there spread over the world organisations for tending and rearing learning wherever the germs of it were to be found in youth with an aptitude and a will for study. It was the fulfilment of the Church's mission to raise up an intellectual power fit to cope with brute force, feudalism, burgher wealth, and the elements of the material governing influences. Surely, too, it must have been seen by those enlightened churchmen who designed it, that it would prove an organisation to protect the world from the influence of superstition and priestcraft.

In Scotland some curious relics of the ancient universities are preserved; but from England they were so effectually cast forth, that Cambridge and Oxford are in many things antagonistic to the spirit of the institution. In these the original uniformity, with its broad liberal basis, has been eaten out, as it were, by the growth of internal corporations, rich, invidious, and engrossing, under the names of colleges, halls, inns, and entries. These are, doubtless, illustrious institutions; but it is with another glory than that which gave lustre to the university of the fifteenth century. The tendency of their working is not to level material distinctions, and make knowledge all in all. They have got into the hands of the wealthy, who have made them the institutions in which they seek high tuition and all stimulants to scholarship for their sons. Vestiges exist of the old arrangements for securing those scholars who had not worldly means against the pressure of the sordid wants of life. But instead of tending to a general equality of position, as in the old literary republics, they only degrade the stipendiary student by contrast with the luxurious wealth surrounding him. Perhaps it has been from their poverty that the small universities of Scotland have been better custodiers of the traditions of the "universitas" or "studium generale" of the fifteenth century.

In this the Scots universities are perhaps rather to be counted as interesting relics of a grand old policy, than as institutions responding to the spirit and the demands of the present day. However much we might desire it, we could not have a university in the old sense. The essentials of it were that it belonged not to a province or nation, but to the Christian world. The universities were a great conglomerate of co-operations, giving and taking among each other. The man who held a certain rank in one, held the same in all. The catholicity of the rank was not affected by national partitions, or even national conflicts. To make this reciprocity perfect, a head was necessary, and that was found in the Court of Rome. The Pope's bull was the conclusive writ establishing the university, and that franked it as a member of the university system stretching over the Christian world. In whatever efforts there may have been to preserve the spirit of this communication by voluntary concession, England has had no part. Her university honours are her own ; and she neither acknowledges those of other kindred institutions, nor cares to take anything from them. The catholic spirit of the old universities was shown in the division of the students into groups, according to the nations or districts of the Christian world whence they had flocked to the seat of learning. These groups were called the Nations. Among vast assemblages, such as those congregating to the University of Paris. it is easy to understand that this division was of great moment. Each country, or group of countries, associated under one Nation, on the supposition that they had common local interests, had a corporate standing of its own, and was represented in general proceedings by its Procurator. In Glasgow and Aberdeen " the nations " still flourish and act, though their functions may perhaps be counted little better than a mimicry of those originally vested in the institution. There is a nobler remnant of the old spirit at the competition-table for bursaries at Aberdeen, where any man from any part of the world may step forward and sit down among the others; and if he be a better Latin scholar than his neighbours, may, by the rank which his exercise takes in the competition, carry off a pecuniary prize so solid, that it shall provide for all his needs while he sojourns at the university, obtaining there such a training in the higher walks of learning as it is capable of supplying to him.

These things have a place here because, as subsisting relics, they show us how thoroughly the Scottish universities were part of the Catholic Continental system. If the Scots universities had any specialties, they were those of France, whence they came. King's College in Aberdeen was an exact model of the University of Paris. Its founder, Bishop Elphinstone, had been a professor at Paris and at Orleans. Its first principal, Hector Boece, the friend of Erasmus, printed two editions of his celebrated History at Paris. A worthy effort seems to have been made to do credit to such companionship, both in the eminence of the men brought to the spot, and the amenities by which they were surrounded. As the enmity towards the monastic orders did not extend to the universities, the greater part of the original building still remains, retaining more of the seclusion appropriate to the cloister and the ancient retreat of learned leisure, than perhaps anything else in Scotland. It is perhaps from its remoteness that the thoroughly Parisian elements have there, in name at least, had a more tenacious life than with its neighbours. There is still the Chancellor. Of old he was the bishop of the diocese, according to the practice of the Continental universities—a practice from which Paris happened to be an exception. There is the Rector, chosen by the Procurators of "the nations," representing the republican spirit of the institution. There are Regents, who are the governing body as of old, though they are now also the teachers. There are Deans, or doyens, a Principal, and a Sacristan. It is perhaps, however, in the humblest grade that we shall find the most expressive vestige of Parisian customs. The fresh student during his first session receives the name of Bejeant, from the Bejaune—a class for whose protection from the snares by which they were surrounded many ancient regulations of the University of Paris make anxious provision. The Scots universities had privileges of exemption from the jurisdiction of legal tribunals, like their more populous and wealthy contemporaries. As it affected the universities in great Continental cities, to which students flocked by thousands, these exemptions represented a great policy, whether it was a wise one or not. The place dedicated to learning, and those abiding in it, were a separate independent state, with all the necessary machinery of government. The privilege did not end here, where its boundaries were distinct, but followed the denizens of the place when they went beyond its walls, creating inextricable entanglements with other authorities. The great Continental universities enjoyed the countenance both of the civil and the spiritual powers, and carried their privileges with a high hand. In Scotland such instances of a government within a government did not fit easily into the national institutions; and the universities, losing in their infancy, as it were, the protection of the Church, could not fight a strong battle for them. They did, however, occasionally fight for having them in their utmost purity, as they might be enjoyed in Paris or Vienna. Such contests, especially brought down as they were into the eighteenth century, are, when mixed up with the contemporary current of events, only incidental troubles overcome and forgotten. But when we connect them with the history of the great confederation of literary republics to which the humble universities of Scotland nominally belonged, they are curious relics of a great policy, intended to influence the whole Christian world.

Whatever influences for good or evil these privileges may have had, it cannot be doubted that each of these universities was a centre of civilising or enlightening influences. In later times, plans for planting the apparatus of a high education in poor and remote districts have mortified their projectors by imperfect results or utter failure. For a long time, however, the Scots universities were a great success. They came just in time to serve the Reformation party, among whom there had arisen an ardent zeal for scholarship. Their opponents desired to be armed in like manner for the controversy. Hence it was that, during the latter half of the sixteenth century and the early portion of the seventeenth, the foreign universities swarmed with learned Scotsmen. They might be both teachers and learners, for the absolute distinction now established between the two grades did not then exist. The old-established staff of professors in the Scots universities are called regents. The regents, as we have seen, were the governors or administrators of the several establishments, and were not necessarily or exclusively the teachers belonging to it. By later practice, however, the regents monopolised the teaching, and regent and professor became generally synonymous. Of old, however, every graduate had the privilege of teaching.

Thus the Scot, having acquired such learning as his native university supplied, would pass over to foreign parts, and do his work—teaching what he could communicate, or learning what he desired to know, according to the condition of his means and motives. This gave to the Scots, cut off as they were from the natural brotherhood of their close neighbours of the same family, privileges of citizenship and community over Europe, the breadth and fulness of which it is difficult now to realise.

CHAPTER XL.

Condition of the Nation from the War of Independence to the Reformation.

(Continued.)

SCOTTISH SCHOLARS—THEIR EARLY FAME ABROAD—COMMENCEMENT OF NATIONAL LITERATURE—THOMAS OF ERCILDOUN—RISE AND PECULIAR CONDITIONS OF A PATRIOTIC LITERATURE—BARBOUR, BLIND HARRY, WYNTOUN, FORDUN, BOWER, BOECE, MAJOR, BUCHANAN, LESLIE—'THE COMPLAYNT OF SCOTLAND'—INFLUENCE OF THE PATRIOTIC LITERATURE—DUNBAR, MONTGOMERY, AND THE OTHER POETS—LANGUAGE OF SCOTTISH LITERATURE—VESTIGES OF CELTIC LITERATURE—PRINTING—THE ARTS—SIGNIFICANCE OF THE ECCLESIASTICAL AND BARONIAL REMAINS—SHOW THE POVERTY FOLLOWING THE WAR, AND THE INFLUENCE OF FRANCE—MATERIAL CONDITION OF THE COUNTRY—EXPORTS AND IMPORTS—MINING—GOLD, SILVER, LEAD, AND COAL—A SPANISH AMBASSADOR'S ACCOUNT OF SCOTLAND IN THE FIFTEENTH CENTURY.

IT was among the many misfortunes brought to Scotland by her ceaseless struggle for national existence, that an excessive proportion of her intellectual affluence was given to foreign lands. This sacrifice was, no doubt, obvious to the founders of the universities, who thought there might be a fairer balance of trade in the matter of scholarship if their own country could command quiet retreats for learned leisure, amid comfort, the luxuries of the age, libraries, and good society. The earliest native of Scotland to gain a lasting fame in letters was John Duns, commonly called Scot or Scotus. At the time when Robert Bruce was fighting at the head of the national party, John the Scot was teaching divinity and metaphysics in Paris and Cologne, and making to himself so brilliant a reputation that it might be a fair question for discussion whether or not he was the most illustrious intellectual leader of his day. In the religious world, he was the leader of the Franciscans; in the philosophical world, he was so much the author of Realism that the school who opposed the Nominalists got from him the name of Scotists.

Scotland at that time had work all too serious at home to participate in the intellectual treasures which her illustrious son was bestowing on the world. To trace in detail his history, and that of his countrymen who afterwards signalised themselves in the great republic of letters, would be away from the present purpose. Having taken note of him as foremost in the rank of a great body of men who made their country famous abroad, let us turn to such Scottish literature as had a home influence. Of this, even, there can be no room here for a full critical examination. It must suffice that the conspicuous specialties, and chiefly those which had a peculiar national character or exercised a strong influence on national feeling, be noticed.

Whether the metrical tale of Sir Tristrem—belonging to the romance school which dealt with King Arthur and his knights—was written by a Scotsman, is a question that has been discussed in a great critical contest. The author to whom Scott and others, who maintain its

Scottish origin, trace it, is Thomas of Ercildoun, or Thomas the Rhymer. His name was popular in Scotland, and is still remembered. He had the fame not only of an epic poet or bard, but of a prophet, occupying in his own country somewhat of the position held by Merlin in England, and afterwards by Nostradamus in France. All great national events—all national calamities, especially such as the English invasions—were reputed to have been prophesied by him in rhymes repeated by the people. When compared with the corresponding events, it was ever the specialty of the prophecies of "True Thomas" that they had been uttered in vain to a careless and credulous people, who culpably neglected the warning thrown out by the patriotic seer; yet it is hardly consistent with the logic of prophecy that it should preclude its own fulfilment. His fame was founded in other shapes. The wildest and strangest of the fairy ballads of Scotland are devoted to True Thomas, and his dealings in fairyland with the Queen of Elfin and other persons in authority there. It is, indeed, around his name that the great bulk of the fairy lore of Scotland is found to cluster.

Thomas of Ercildoun was a real man; his name was Learmonth, and his property of Ercildoun has been traced in charters. He died a very old man, about the time when Edward I. was shaping his projects against Scotland, leaving by repute, as a legacy to his countrymen, a prophetic warning of the destiny in preparation for them. His name became known abroad as that of a rhymer or poet.[1]

[1] In the Epitome Bibliothecæ Conradi Gesneri, published in 1555, we have—"Thomas Leirmont vel Ersiletonus, natione Scotus, edidit

At the opening of the romance of Sir Tristrem there is mention of Ercildoun and Thomas. Some boy, or mischievous trifler, has, however, mutilated the passage, by cutting out of it an illuminated letter on its reverse, little conscious, no doubt, of the exciting difficulty which the mutilation was to launch into the literary world, in the decision of the question, whether Thomas was referred to as the author of the romance, or in some other capacity.[1] It may be said, however, of Sir Tristrem, and of the romance of Launcelot of the Lake, also attributed to a native of Scotland, that they cannot be counted national literature, in the more interesting shape in which we shall find it growing in later times. There is nothing of a national tone and there are no local allusions in Sir Tristrem, to give help to the argument that it was written by a Scotsman. King Arthur and his chivalry were the materials of a romance literature common to all Europe. To Thomas Learmonth it would have made no perceptible difference in language and tone of feeling, had he lived on the south instead of the north side of the Tweed. It would be known to him only, if he was the prophet he was afterwards held to be, that a time would come when the people inhabiting his Ercildoun and the neighbouring glens would hate, with the deepest feelings of national hatred, their neighbours on the other side of the river.

In the next stage of Scottish literature we find it

rhythmica quædam, et ob id Rhythmicus apud Anglos cognominatus est. Vixit anno 1286." This, with many other valuable notices, is not to be found in the Bibliotheca itself, only in the Epitome.

[1] The substance of the discussion will be best read in Scott's edition of the romance, and in Price's edition of Warton's History of English Poetry.

animated by that hatred. On this account it is a literature coming especially under the notice of the historian, who, when he deals with it, has to regret that its coming was so long delayed. There is, indeed, a great gap in the home sources of Scottish history. It was about the year 660 that Adamnan wrote his Life of St Columba. Adamnan was not a native of Scotland, but he lived in Iona, where he was abbot; and what he gives us of Scots history, or national peculiarities, comes from one who was living in Scotland. We have nothing else written about the annals of the country, by one dwelling in it, until we come to John of Fordun, who wrote about the year 1350—six hundred years later. There is the Chronicle of Mailros, supposed to have been kept by the monks of that great Cistercian abbey. But during the period it covers, which is before the War of Independence, these churchmen were to be considered as Englishmen rather than Scotsmen, owing their spiritual allegiance to the successors of St Cuthbert. The history of Scotland does not preponderate in the chronicle; it receives little more notice there than from the ordinary chronicles of the English monks.

Our excessive poverty in this kind of literature is shown in the greed with which we seize on every crumb that reaches us from the affluent collection of English chronicles. We have first the help to be found in the writings of Bede, exceedingly precious, although they profess only to bear on ecclesiastical matters. They bear their value in their own internal evidence, and it is certified by the precision with which his narrative fits into that of Adamnan. The narrative of both is carried on in the chronicle attributed to

Simeon of Durham; and whether written by himself, or by another monk named Turgot, it is the work of one who lived and saw what was going on in the year 1100. It is from Ailred of Rievaulx and Richard of Hexham, as contemporaries, that we have accounts of Scots affairs at the time of the Battle of the Standard. For what of chronicle information we receive about the wars of Wallace and Bruce's time, we must still take the English chroniclers—the Scalacronica, the Chronicle of Lanercost, Hemingford, Trivet, and Langtoft. The succession of chronicles kept by the monks of St Albans, and especially those of Walsingham and Rishanger, contribute, out of their abundance, notifications about the affairs of Scotland of the utmost value to the gleaner of intelligence. It is, for instance, Rishanger who has preserved to us that signally interesting incident omitted in the English records—that the community of Scotland had put in a pleading against King Edward's claim of superiority, while the nobles and the Church were silent. There are, besides these, Mathew Paris, Roger of Wendover, Florence of Worcester, William of Malmsbury, Henry of Huntingdon, and Mathew of Westminster. One might go on enumerating the English chroniclers to whom Scots history is indebted, but the process would only be a long list of names.[1]

[1] The treasury of English chronicle lore is so vast, that hitherto those best acquainted with it have shrunk from the gigantic task of estimating and analysing its resources, so as to let the outer world have a notion of what they are. A gallant effort in this direction was made by Bishop Nicholson in his three Historical Libraries. We owe much to the labours of Hearne, and not less for the chronicles edited by himself, than for his resuscitation of the memoranda of readings among the chronicles left behind him by that voracious devourer of parchment lore, Leland. Everything that has been done in this shape, however, will be totally

What it is of moment to remember is that, during the several centuries when Scotland had no recorder of passing events, England had always one or more, contemporary with the times of which he was the annalist. It is a necessary result of this that, during a period when she had her life-struggle with her great enemy, Scotland must take the account of her own conduct almost entirely from the side of that enemy. When Scotsmen began to write their own annals, they did so in a tone of vehement patriotism, inspired by the hot struggle not yet over. Barbour's Bruce was written about the year 1350, and Blind Harry's Wallace a full century later. We have seen something of the character of both works, in going over their historical ground. It may be questioned if either author reaches the standard of poetry according to the æsthetic notions of the present day; nor, indeed, did their task, as rhyming chroniclers, demand that they should. But the national feeling, burning within them, forces itself out occasionally in composition which has the dignity and power of the heroic. These passages may be counted as examples of the old Roman idea expressed by Juvenal in his first Satire, that strong passion comes forth in poetry.

In the period between these two, we have another rhymer—Andrew Wyntoun, the Prior of the Mona-

eclipsed by the great work of Mr Duffus Hardy, the 'Descriptive Catalogue of Materials relating to the History of Great Britain and Ireland to the End of the Reign of Henry VII.' Two volumes of this work have been issued, coming down to the year 1200. The service thus already conferred on British history can only be estimated by those who have gone to the book for practical assistance. The learning and sagacity concentrated in this service are on a scale reminding one rather of the Benedictines of St Maur, than of the common run of contributions to English historical literature.

stery of St Serf, on an island in Loch Leven. His was an ambitious project—a metrical history of the world from the creation to his own time. He has given so large a place to his own country in the general dispensation of human affairs that his work is virtually a chronicle of Scotland, burdened with a quantity of surplus matter, easily removed from the part really valuable. Wyntoun is less poetic even than the others; and, from the view which he took of his task, he would probably have been as little grateful for compliments to his poetic power as any historian of later times is to those who call him flowery and imaginative. To many of the metrical chroniclers, indeed, the use of rhyme rather served for restraining verbal luxuriance than for encouraging poetic licence. The couplet became the measure within which a distinct assertion or proposition had to be set forth.

Wyntoun hands us over to the most characteristic class of early Scots authors—those who wrote the complete history of their native land. The "Scotichronicon," so often referred to in these pages, was written, down to the middle of the eleventh century, by John of Fordun; and was thence continued, by Walter Bower or Bowmaker, Abbot of Inchcolm, down to the middle of the fifteenth century. Although it is usual to speak of the work as Fordun's Chronicle, yet the continuation, as coming from one who told of events, all of them nearer to, and some of them contemporary with, his own day, is the more valuable part of the work. In Fordun and Wyntoun we have the earliest detailed narrative of that fabulous history which has had so great an influence on Scottish literature, and even on political events. It owed its most egregious development to Hector Boece, who added to the history of Scotland many wonders, some of which have been already noticed. Through his History—two editions of which were printed in Paris—the wondrous tale of the annals of Scotland got a hold on the European mind. It is noticeable that Hector Boece's narrative, wild as it would now be counted, was skilfully adjusted to the conditions of belief in his own time. In whatever savours of the supernatural, he deals with far more caution and reserve than Geoffrey of Monmouth, the chronicler of the Anglo-British heroics, or Geoffrey Keating, the historian of Ireland. It is easy, indeed, on a comparison, to imagine a time when these would be dealt with as wild romances, while Boece's work might be accepted as sober history. As credulity faded before advancing knowledge, however, there were others to adapt the tale of Scotland's ancient and glorious history to the taste of the age. Even while Boece lived, the sceptical could find relief from his exaggeration in the sobered narrative of John Major, a doctor of the Sorbonne, with a European reputation as a commentator on The Sentences. But it was the splendid History of Buchanan, welcomed by the learned world as the restoration of classic Latinity, that gave the history of Scotland its strong position as part of the annals of mankind. If there were orthodox Romanists to question the tale of the brilliant heretic, there was his contemporary, the devout Bishop Leslie, telling in homelier Latin the same tale, and realising it by the actual portraits of Father Fergus and his descendants, worthily executed for the editions of his History published in the holy father's own capital of Rome. This community of testimony is characteristic of Scottish sentiment and conduct. There was hot controversy between Scotsmen then, and long afterwards; but each party, however fierce in abuse of the other, stood up for the ancient dignity of the native land common to both.

The fabulous history of Scotland, as we are now bound to call it, was brought into existence with a great national object. It was to vie with the equally fabulous history of England, and to establish a case for ancient independence, which might neutralise the story told by King Edward to the Papal Court about Brutus of Troy and his three sons.[1] The tenor of the case for Scotland was as follows: We are first introduced to an unfortunate division in the royal family of Greece at the period of Moses. It ended in Nicolas, King of Greece, sending his son Gathelus out of the country. The young prince went to Egypt, where he became attached to and married Scota, the daughter of that Pharaoh who was drowned in the Red Sea. The young couple took to wandering, and getting out of the Mediterranean, they founded a state called Portus Gatheli, and now known as Portugal. At length they arrived in Scotland, and settled there. Long afterwards, Ptolemy, King of Egypt, sent ambassadors to Scotland, who were surprised to find how well the country, ruled by the descendants of the Egyptian princes, adhered to the ways of the dwellers on the banks of the Nile. "They persaivet," says Bellenden, in his translation of Boece, "the same writs, the same manner of writing, the same tongue, and the same habits and ceremonies, as was usit among the Egyptians." Some time elapsed, however, before the country resolved itself into a firm

[1] See above, vol. ii. p. 318.

monarchy. It was about three hundred years before
Christ that a descendant of Gathelus and Scota, named
Fergus, reigned supreme. Descending from him, the
"Fergus, father of a hundred kings," there was an
unbroken royal line. Malcolm Canmore, the first in
whom we can now, from authentic sources, identify
the attributes of a king of Scotland, stands in this
dynasty as the eighty-sixth king.

So skilfully was this story told that, in the modified
version of Buchanan, it lived after the fabulous elements were deducted from the history of England and
of many other countries. Scotland received homage as
the most ancient of European monarchies. After the
union of the crowns, it was usual to distinguish Scotland from her neighbour as "the Ancient Kingdom."
The fabulous history had great political influence. A
belief in the antiquity of the royal line had a constitutional effect in favour of the monarchy, which was
valuable to those who ruled so restless and self-willed
a people as the Scots. After the Revolution, however,
it had a disturbing influence in favour of the Jacobite
cause. The loss of the house of Stewart was believed
to be the loss of the most august dynasty in the world—
a dynasty that raised Scotland in the scale of nations.
In the thirteenth century, such a house as that of
Guelph, with its legends of Roman ancestry, could only
think of the Stewart of Scotland as the possible descendant of a Norway pirate, holding humble office under
another, who, although he was called a king, had no
nobler origin. The connection with the Celtic house
of Riadha, which opened to it the succession to the
throne, would hardly have given any legitimate lustre
to the house of Stewart. The founding on such a

connection might have carried little more than a plebeian family of later times would gain by establishing a descent from an American cazique, or some questionable Oriental pasha.

When the Hanover dynasty came over to reign in Britain, its best friends would not have measured its ancestral claims with those of the descendants of Fergus. It was not ancestral lustre, but respectability and political utility, that commended the new dynasty. Curious incidents of the picturesque in literature might be found in the rage with which the earliest doubts about the antiquity of the race of Fergus were received. The doubting went on for ages before it established disbelief, if it has even yet done so. The first malignant whisperings came from the English antiquaries Lloyd and Stillingfleet. The doubters were assailed with hearty goodwill by Sir George Mackenzie, in his Defence of the Royal Line of Scotland. Sir George was then lord advocate. He seems to have thought that it became him, as the public prosecutor of offenders, to punish, in what fashion he might, those who threatened to abbreviate the line of his majesty's ancestry; and he hinted that, had the perpetrators lived within the country in which he exercised his powers, he might have felt it his duty to bring them to justice as political offenders against the crown.

The peculiar character and influence of this special literature commend it to the consideration of the historian; but it is not intended, on this occasion, to give more than a brief allusion to other departments of Scottish literature, which, in the eyes of the critic, might be equally or more important. With Major and

Buchanan there arose a school of Scottish authors in prose and verse who, addressing themselves to the learned world at large, wrote in Latin. These were but beginning at the period we have reached, and the bulk of their services belong to a later age. As a characteristic morsel of the patriotic literature of the country, we must include 'The Complaynt of Scotland,' printed in 1548, and proving itself to have been chiefly written while Henry VIII. was pressing on the country with cruel wars and treacherous offers of peace. Who was the author of this piece is matter of dispute.[1] The work is a prose pastoral, with a strong tinge of the practically political. Its writer is by courtesy a shepherd. He thus belongs to the class best fitted to take a survey of human life at large, or any portion of it. They are not subjected to "the corrupt infection and evil air that is generit in ane city, where most confluence of people resorts;" but "we live on the fragrant fields, where we are nourished with the most delicious temperate air, and there is neither hatred, avarice, nor discord among us."[2]

For his meditative and reflective purposes he takes up his position with much picturesqueness :—

"I passed to the green wholesome fields, situate maist commodiously fra distempered air and corrupt infection, to receive the sweet fragrant smell of tender grasses, and of wholesome balmy flowers most odoriferant. Beside the foot of ane little mountain there ran ane fresh river as clear as beryl, whar I beheld the pretty

---

[1] 'The Complaynt of Scotland' was reprinted by Leyden, with a copious introduction, in which the question of the authorship is examined, along with much other matter suggested to that accomplished scholar by the matter of the book.

[2] Ibid., 70.

fish wantonly stertland with their red vermyl finns, and their skails like the bright silver. On the other side of that river there was ane green bank full of rammel green trees, whar there was mony small birds hoppand fra busk to twist, singan melodious reports of natural music in accords of measure of diapason prolations, tripla and diatesseron, that heavenly harmony appeared to be artificial music."[1]

The devious meditations which start so pleasantly, find a gloomy present in the country tortured by the harassing assaults of King Henry, and contemplate a gloomy future, only brightened up by exhortations to the author's countrymen to take heart and fight out the battle of national independence to the last. The book is so saturated in classicalities, that any glimpses we have of the condition of the country have to be seen through a Greek or Roman medium, by which they are sadly distorted; and at the points where curious information might be expected, a grotesque mixture of modern purpose and ancient illustration comes in its stead.[2]

---

[1] 'The Complaynt of Scotland,' 57.

[2] So we have a parable of a cordinar or shoemaker from the internal contests in Rome, after the slaying of Julius Cæsar:—

"He by gret subtlety nourised twa young corbies in twa cages, in twa sundry hooses, and he learned them baith to speke. He learned ane of them to say, 'God save thy grace, noble victorious Augustus Cæsar!' and he learned the tother to say, 'God save thy grace, noble victorious Emperor Anthonius!' Then this subtle cordinar set ane of his corbies that gave loving til Augustus forth at his window in the plain rue when he beheld any gentilman of Augustus allya pass or repass before his hous; and siclike he set forth his tother corby at his window when he beheld any of the allya of Anthonius pass or repass before his house. The whilk thing he did to that effect that he might win the favour of Augustus, and not to tyne the favour of Anthonius. Of this sort he was like to the sword with the twa edges. Then when Augustus Cæsar vanquished Anhonius, and was peaceable emperor, this subtle cordinar presented the

There were several writers in verse who, aspiring beyond the mechanical rhyming of the annalists, aimed at true poetry. Such were King James I., James V., or whoever wrote the poems attributed to him, Henryson, Dunbar, Montgomery, Bishop Douglas, and many others.[1]

Those who, after overcoming the difficulties of the spelling, are able to enter into the spirit of their poems, are generally surprised, when remembering the tenor of the times in which they were written, by the tenderness and beauty of the sentiments, and the polished harmony of the versification. Their tone generally belongs to

corby til Augustus, whilk gave him loving in her artificial speech, of the whilk Cæsar was very glad, wherefore he gave to the cordinar fifteen hundred pieces of gold. But soon thereafter it was reported to Augustus Cæsar that the said subtle cordinar had ane corby that gave as great loving to Anthonius. Then Augustus caused the said corby and the cordinar to be brought to his presence; and when he persavit the cordinar was ane astute subtle fellow, and dissimulate, he gart hang him on ane potent before the Capitol, and his twa corbies beside him."—P. 285, 286. The moral of the story is the folly of dubious councils, and the especial folly of temporising with the King of England, from whom nothing is to be gained or hoped. If he comes in war, let him be resisted; if he comes with proffers of kindness, let them be suspected and flung back upon the treacherous giver. War to the utmost, all men turning "special valiant defenders" of their native country, "is the true policy of Scotsmen." "For as Thucydides says in the thirteenth chapter of his first benk, quoth he, As it is convenient to honest and prudent men to live in peace when their neighbours does them no outrage nor violence; siclike it is honest and convenient to virtuous men to change their peace, and rest in cruel war fra time that they have receivit outrage and violence from their neighbours. For the changing of ane dissimulat peace into a cruel war shall be occasion for ane firm and faithful peace."—P. 290, 291.

[1] For a critical account of the productions of these early poets, see 'The History of Scottish Poetry,' by Dr David Irving, a posthumous work, edited from his manuscripts by his friend Dr Carlisle. Dunbar and Henryson should be read in the accurate versions edited by David Laing, and with the aid of his valuable explanatory matter. Hopes are entertained that we may soon have the works of Sir David Lindsay dealt with after the same fashion, by the same accomplished hand.

what in modern æsthetical phraseology is called sensuous. There are descriptions extremely minute of real objects or real actions, and with these are connected, by the poet's skill, associations and sentiments touched with some passionate thought generally of a pensive kind. These early Scots poets draw largely on nature. They are full of descriptions of natural objects—fresh waters, woods, flowers, and birds. In this dealing with the world of nature there is a notable peculiarity. The present tone of the literature of natural objects would lead us to expect that in Scotland a poet of nature would seek a topic suited to his genius in the mountain scenery of which the country has so many grand examples. We would expect something of the tone of which the poems of Ossian, as rendered by Macpherson, are so full. But the inner eye for these things had not been opened in the early Scots poets. They might have written what they draw from nature and rural life in the flattest parts of England, or in Holland. It is safe to say that, in all this school of poetry, there is not a single reference to mountain gorge or cataract as an object of poetic thought. There is one poem, indeed, that, in the character of a flagrant exception, proves the rule that these poets were incapable of feeling sublimity or beauty in mountain scenery. In the Lament of Duncan Laideus there are pensive reminiscences of some tracts of Highland scenery much beloved at this day by tourists. Now Duncan Laideus was a robber and a cut-throat — a leader of Highland cateran. He is supposed to utter his pensive recollections within sight of the halter. The spots his recollection fondly dwells on are the scenes of his robberies and murders, and the author of the piece thought it good irony to make the man of horrible character talk with admiration and affection of those horrible places.[1]

There were some satirists in this group of poets— among these Sir David Lindsay stood unrivalled. This is the class of poetry that most imperatively of all demands that, to relish its character, we should be conversant with the nature of the times—with the persons and the things on which it alights. Old Davy Lindsay was transcendently popular. We see the marks of his influence on the history of the times, and can understand how it was so, when we read his potent attacks on the abuses of the day. He was a consummate artist. His riotous wit seems to drive him before it; but when his sarcasm is sharpened for a hit it never misses its aim, but strikes the victim right in the face. We have seen in the history of the Reformation some traces of his handiwork.

The literary merits of Knox's works would claim a place here, were they not also referred to in connection with their political influence. It may be mentioned that in more than one quarter Knox was charged with innovation on the old language of his country, which he corrupted by modern innovations. When put in a friendly shape, the import of the charge is that he improved the language of his country, as he reformed its religion; and it is a singular coincidence, that Luther has the fame of reforming the language of Germany, and Calvin of reforming the language of France.

The language of this literature was fundamentally a pure Teutonic of the Anglo-Saxon family. It took

[1] See the Lament in 'The Black Book of Taymouth,' 149.

nothing, as we have seen, from the Celtic dialect spoken by the inhabitants of a great portion of the country—the language of those who gave it the name of Scotland. The relations of Scotland with France were too superficial to affect the structure of the language, or even its vocabulary farther than in the supply of a few words, which avowed themselves to be foreign in the method of their use. The old Scots has less of classic admixture than the old English. This is one of the things that can only be stated as a general opinion taken from general reading. Where such things are matter of degree, there is seldom a means of coming to precise comparison; and here we have it, as a disturbing element, that in both countries some authors affected words of Greek or Roman origin more readily than others. That the Scots should have less of this element than the English, is in conformity with historical conditions. The Teutonic nations of the Continent admit no mixture of the classical—if they have words of Greek or Roman origin, these are distinctly marked off as foreign. There is no doubt that the mixture confers an unexampled richness and subtlety on the English language, by giving the means of expressing abstract or spiritual terms without having recourse to the words used for the practical purposes of everyday life; and affording a double nomenclature, which may be called the real and the ideal, as in the words "cleanness" and "purity;" in "age" or "oldness," as a different quality from "antiquity," and the like.

There cannot be a doubt that England took this, with so many other things distinctive of the English people, from the Normans, who brought with them the language of the most eminent of the Latin races. We have the Anglo-Saxon Chronicle written in the purest of Teutonic while Norman-French was the language of the Court, and there emerges the English of later times enriched with words of classic origin stripped of their French garb. This, like the other novelties coming of Norman usage, spread but faintly into Scotland, and so the language there remained nearer to the character of the old Teutonic stock.[1]

It would be difficult to realise the difference in pronunciation between the languages of the two countries three hundred years ago, and were it conceived it could not be expressed. The living persons are very few who remember the separate language of Lowland Scotland as spoken by people of education and condition. It lingered with a few living secluded lives in remote districts, yet holding a local position which put them above the necessity of compliance with innovating fashions; and those who have heard these lingering vestiges of a national tongue must ever retain an impression of its purity, force, and beauty. It was not the English language of the cultivated classes of the present day; yet though distinct, it was not so far apart from it as the language of the un-

---

[1] An interesting inquiry might be directed to the words belonging to the Scots but not to the English language, which are still used in any of the Continental Teutonic nations; and to make complete results, the next question in each case would be, whether the word common to both was Anglo-Saxon, though it has ceased to be English. Every Scotsman travelling abroad feels that the pronunciation of the languages which have not admitted any classical mixture is more akin to his own than to the English. Three consecutive numerals in Scots will be almost sufficient to show this: *sax, seyven, aucht.* "Half aucht" means half-past seven—an idiom which Englishmen who have been in Germany will at once identify both in pronunciation and idiom with one of the national oddities.

educated in Scotland, and for that matter in England too.¹

To this negative account it is difficult to add anything save further negatives. The spelling of old Scots, tried by the modern powers of letters, is not to be taken as a test of its pronunciation. All readers of old books are familiar with the eclecticism of their spelling—how, even after the art of printing made a pressure on uniformity, the same word might appear on the same page in two, sometimes three, different spellings. Spelling varied more easily than pronunciation; and, apart from any such generality, it can be easily shown that the sounds expressed by letters used in both nations in the fifteenth and sixteenth centuries were quite different from the sounds expressed by the same letters in modern times.²

---

[1] It is fortunate that a man with capacity and patience for the task should have set himself to store up a record of the peculiar language of the Scots people ere yet it had entirely ceased to be spoken by the educated. The Etymological Dictionary of the Scottish Language, by Dr Robert Jamieson, is of great value to the present generation, and promises a value in the future to an extent not to be easily pre-estimated.

[2] Of the language as used in literature, state papers, and some other kinds of documents, several specimens will be found in the preceding pages—specimens, perhaps, all the more suited to afford a fair test of the character of the language, that they have not been selected with that object, but each for some separate purpose appertaining to itself. This opportunity may be taken for explaining the manner in which the author has rendered passages so cited, in the matter of spelling. Words which are especially Scots, whether because they were never used in England, or have become obsolete there, are scrupulously retained. Of words still in use, however, the spelling in which they are found is not always employed. Those who must have *literatim* spelling do not trust to histories, but go to the earliest rendering in manuscript or print. For providing the reader with a notion of the words used, the original spelling would be very fallacious. Besides many instances in which it is likely that letters have changed their powers while spoken words have not, we know many instances in which the change in the power of the letter is certain. There are the well-known instances of *j* for *i*, and

It was not until the year 1507 that the art of printing came in aid of the national literature of Scotland. It was brought in by Walter Chepman, under

v for *u* and *w*. The letter *o* had sometimes the sound of the diphthong *œ* with a leaning to the *e*, as where the pronoun *she* is written *sho*. *Quh* was used to express the sound of *wh*. *Z* was identical with our present *y*, and *you* was spelt *zou* or *zu*. The Scots peasantry, in dealing with names, tell this to the present day. Thus where certain family names are spelt and pronounced by Englishmen thus, Mackenzie and Menzies, they are pronounced by the peasantry as *Mackenyie* and *Menyies*. So of places—Cockenzie, Edzel Castle, and Culzean Castle, which are respectively called *Cockenyie*, *Edyel*, and *Culyean*. The dealing with the letter *y* itself is a specialty of a troublesome kind. It represents one of the last remaining of all the Gothic contractions, which made a theta in the alphabet, as representing the sound of *th*. This letter was very like the *y*, differing only in having the left limb elongated upwards, and a horizontal line from it to the other limb, making a triangle. When this remained as the last of the contractions, the printers of the sixteenth century began to use the *y* instead of it, whence came the well-known *ye* for *the*, and *yat* for *that*. As a specimen of the way in which the author thinks the spelling of these old writings may be changed with every chance of making it a better representative of the sound, the following passage is given as it is *literatim* printed by the scrupulous editor of the State Papers of Henry VIII. It is a passage of no great moment, taken from a letter by the widow of James IV., that Queen Margaret who was an English princess, yet spent the greater portion of her days in Scotland:—

"I haif resaiflit zour lettir be Mons. Gozolis wyth ane letter of ye lordis; ye quhilk hes schawin me ye ordinance yat ze and yai haif maid, and how yai have prait and ordand me yat I sall nocht abide wyth ye kyng my sone, bott tocum quhilles and se hym. My lord, I thynk it rycht strange yat yis is zour will, seing ye gud and trew part yat I haif kepit to ye king my sone, and to zou, and to yis realme, and ye displesure yat I haf had of ye kyng my broyer, my frendis, for zour part."

The author thinks that the words used by the writer will be better rendered to the present generation thus:—

"I have receivet your letter by Monsieur Gonzales with ane letter of the lords; the whilk has shown me the ordinance that ye and they have made, and how they have praid and ordaind me that I sall nought abide with the king my son, but to come whiles and see him. My lord, I think it right strange that this is your will, seeing the good and true part that I have keeped to the king my son, and to you, and to this realm, and the displeasure that I have had of the king my brother, my friends, for your part."—State Papers (Henry VIII.), iv. 59.

the favour of James IV., who, curious in shipping and other mechanical triumphs, seems to have felt much interest in the printing-press. Chepman, with an assistant who is supposed to have provided capital for their joint undertaking, got a grant of exclusive privilege, or letters-patent, as the document might have been called in England. It gave authority for printing the ritual books of the Church; and through Chepman's press there is fortunately preserved to the present day the national service-book, elsewhere mentioned as the Breviary of Aberdeen.[1]

This book of church service, remarkable as a fine specimen of early printing, was, like the foundation of King's College in Aberdeen, due to the munificence of Bishop Elphinstone. When it was issued, copies of the 'Usum Sarum' were excluded from Scotland as contraband goods. Besides the national prayer-book, the Acts of Parliament and other works of public utility were referred to in the grant of privileges to the first printer as books likely to come from his press and to justify the grant of privileges. These were deferred until a later period. The earliest productions of the press in Scotland, so far as vestiges remain, were knightly legends, and the productions of Dunbar and other contemporary poems.[2]

[1] See chapter viii.
[2] A volume of these, of which the only copy known is preserved in the Advocates' Library, was reprinted in facsimile by David Laing, with an instructive introduction. The reprint is an extreme rarity, as the impression was nearly all burned by a fire in the establishment where it was printed. The editor gives, in his introduction, the grant of exclusive privileges by the Privy Council, in 1507, to Chepman and his partner Millar. It is set forth that they, "at his majesty's request, for his pleasure, the honour and profit of his realm and lieges, had taken upon them to furnish and bring hame ane print, with all stuff

The later history of religion and education in the Highlands would not lead us to suppose that the press had early fruit in Gaelic literature; yet of the liturgy commonly called John Knox's, a translation was printed for the use of the Celtic inhabitants of the Isles not long after it had been published in the vernacular.[1] This leads to the recollection that the language now and for long called Scotch is not the only language spoken in Scotland — that indeed there is another, which, whether or not it be older in common use, is certainly older in literature.

Any glance taken over the literature of Scotland at this period will naturally comprise that of the Lowlands only, omitting the Highlands as naturally as the critic of the Elizabethan period of English literature passes by the Welsh bards and anything they have to say. That the sovereign state of Scotland took its name from that of the Irish Celts who colonised the country, and that these were the first to teach the art of writing and to spread learning and civilisation through the country, had been buried under the eventful history of their Teutonic neighbours, who had gradually pressed them out of the districts available for agriculture into the rocky region of the west. That the despised Celt might treasure the remnant

belonging thereto, and expert men to use the same, for imprinting within the realm of the books of the laws, Acts of Parliament, chronicles, massbooks, manuals, matin-books, and partures, after the use of the realm, with additions and legends of Scottish saints now gathered to be eked thereto, and all other books that shall be seen necessary; and to sell the same for competent prices, by his majesty's advice and discretion, their labours and expenses being considered."— Laing's Introduction to reprint of 'The Knightly Tale of Golagras and Gawane.'

[1] Skene, Introduction to the Book of the Dean of Lismore, xxxviii.

of the old heroic poetry sung in the days when his ancestors were civilised and those of the Lowlander were barbarian, was unlikely to occur to the scholars who studied in the French universities, or to the other leaders of opinion in Scotland, at the period we have reached.

It is now known, however, that the traditions of the Irish mythical history, which supplied the skeleton of Macpherson's poems, existed at least down to the Reformation. James Macgregor, Dean of Lismore, the ecclesiastical metropolis of Argyle, who lived nearly down to the Reformation, left a written volume containing transcripts of poems preserved orally or otherwise among the Highlanders. They contained much vague reference to Highland affairs near their own time, and to obscure matters of monkish tradition which may have had a Highland local influence in their day. What gives them their chief interest, however, is that they possess, at least in the names of the heroes who come forth in them, a conformity with those traditions which Irish scholars believed to be history, and out of which James Macpherson made his noble poems. It would be hard to conceive that in the language they were translated from, or in any language into which they could be put, the legends preserved by the Dean of Lismore could take shape as poetry. The tenacity, however, with which the original Irish legends, and especially the notion of a great conquering and regenerating king called Fin or Fian, have been thus preserved, is an interesting feature in ethnology, if not in literature; and it is satisfactory to consider that 'The Dean of Lismore's Book' has been given to the present age with everything that Highland zeal and Celtic scholarship could do for it.[1]

All that can be said of the condition of early art in Scotland comes within narrow compass, but tells an impressive history. A country possessing the means and the skill to raise edifices of stone, or even of brick, is likely in them to leave the clearest testimony to its condition, unless it has advanced so many stages farther in civilisation as to leave a treasury of literature and art. Scotland, before she had many other means of telling her condition to later ages, had buildings ecclesiastical and baronial. These afford, perhaps, but a narrow source of information; but it is, so far as it goes, distinct and complete. We have seen that, down to the opening of the war, many noble churches had been built. They followed or accompanied the procession of the same class of buildings in England. First we have the round-arched Norman—the transition stage between classic, and Gothic or pointed architecture. Next comes the earliest type of pointed architecture, which proves its origin by the name it has been longest known by—the Early English. In the estimation of many this is the noblest style of Gothic architecture—the true type of the school, beside which all others are to be held either as the imperfect development or the degeneracy. Its leading character was the aspiration after loftiness, by a tendency to height rather than breadth in all its features, the spirit of the pointed arch ruling the whole. It was frugal in decoration, trusting more to the general influ-

---

[1] 'The Dean of Lismore's Book, a selection of ancient Gaelic poetry,' edited by the Rev. Thomas M'Lauchlan, with an introduction by William F. Skene.

ence of size and structure. The buildings of this style were lighted by separated, long, narrow windows, terminating in the characteristic pointed arch. When the Gothic shifted out of this solemn simplicity into the next style, called the second-pointed, the most remarkable type of the change was the grouping of these long, solemn, simple windows together, so as to bring them into a structural connection; and next, by narrowing and decorating the separations between the openings, to resolve the line of solemn, separated, pointed openings into the large Gothic window of a later age, in which groups of lights were intersected by narrow stonework, according to the varied fantastic shapes which every one is acquainted with in a mullioned Gothic window.

It is useful to note the facts of this transition, because they interpret the historical testimony which the ecclesiastical remains of Scotland furnish to us. We have seen that there yet exist noble specimens of the Norman. There are vestiges of early English on a yet greater scale; but after this stage in the transitions of Gothic building, the Scottish specimens become distinctly impoverished. It was but a short time before the War of Independence that the early English type shifted to the "second-pointed" in its own country, England; it may have been a generation later in travelling to Scotland. We may count that it took no root there before the war, and that the struggle for national life found the Scots expending their wealth on buildings raised in that noble style of architecture which they had borrowed from their good neighbours on the other side of the Tweed.

Judging from existing remains, the greatest Gothic

buildings Scotland ever had were the three cathedrals of St Andrews, Glasgow, and Elgin. In each of these the architectural forms which Scotland copied from England are so predominant as to fix the type of the building—instances of the styles of other periods are incidental adjuncts. What we know of the history of the buildings agrees with the story told by their fragments. The consecration of the completed Cathedral of St Andrews followed close on the battle of Bannockburn, and was in some measure an act of commemorative homage to St Andrew, the patron saint of Scotland, for that goodwill to the cause of his devotees without which they might not have been victorious. The cathedral had been upwards of a hundred years in building, and was probably almost completed before the war began.

The remains of Elgin give us very beautiful specimens of the early English style. The later work on this building is, in comparison with these old massive fragments, scanty and meaningless. We know, however, that the cathedral had to be rebuilt, as it was said, after its destruction by the Wolf of Badenoch; and perhaps its condition in the earliest representations we have of it, about a century and a half ago, give it much as he left it—the later work having decayed through time, while the more massive masonry of the early English survived alike his burning and the wasting influences to which the fabric was subjected from the Reformation downwards.

Glasgow Cathedral is the only eminent Gothic building in Scotland still in good preservation. The whole tone of the building and the fundamental parts of its structure are early English, what there is of the succeeding stage being secondary detail. We hear of the completion of the building during the War of Independence. Wishart was at that time Bishop of Glasgow. We have seen his name in curious shapes connected with the attempt to subdue Scotland; and his title of the "Warlike Bishop" is in harmony with the charge against him, that having been licensed by King Edward to cut timber for the completion of the wood-work of the cathedral, this timber he employed in the construction of instruments of war for the siege of the Peel of Kirkintilloch, then held by the English.

The second English stage of Gothic architecture, that of second-pointed, had spread to Scotland before the war, but it was not long enough coeval with the fortunate period of the country to produce any great edifice. We owe to it only a change in the later works of the great remnants, and a few secondary buildings. There is visible, to any one who looks at the remains of Scots ecclesiastical architecture, a distinct gap. The war did not at once stop church-building. The finishing touches were given to the great buildings planned and nearly completed, and small buildings arose here and there. But there was a collapse, which lasted so long that, when the country was again able to raise costly churches, the national taste and ways had wandered far away from companionship with England. Foreign types came to predominate; and while the ecclesiastical architecture of Scotland down to the war was identical with that of England, the school which succeeded it was as different from the contemporary method of church-building in England as any other foreign style might be.

The only ecclesiastical building in Scotland that in

magnificence can be compared to those either entirely or nearly completed when the war broke out, is the far-famed church of Melrose Abbey. It was a very ancient convent, and buildings of some sort had belonged to it as long ago at least as the earliest specimens of Scots church-architecture extant. The Cistercian monastery there was a favourite of the great King Robert Bruce, who largely endowed it. When he thus added to its wealth there were, doubtless, the ordinary monastic buildings and a church there, though probably at some little distance from the present ruin. It was, however, some hundred and fifty years after his day ere, from the rents of his endowments and their other wealth, the fraternity were able to build their beautiful church. Perhaps Scotland was then becoming rich enough to multiply such examples of architecture; but the Reformation was not in favour of the development of Gothic architecture, and wealth had no farther opportunity of displaying itself in that shape.

Before Scotland had so far recovered from her depression as to be able to raise distinguished buildings, the style of her church-architecture had long ceased to come from England, and had, indeed, gone into a direction which separated the two from each other by fundamental differences. The best means of briefly estimating the character and extent of the divergence will be by comparing the ecclesiastical architecture of England and Scotland at the time of the Reformation. The style then prevalent in England was called the Tudor, but it has had other names, such as the "perpendicular" and the "depressed." Among eminent specimens of this style are Henry VII.'s Chapel and Christ Hospital Chapel in London, the Chapel at Windsor, and Christ Church Hall and Brazen Nose College in Oxford; but in fact it abounds throughout England in specimens great and small. The contemporary style in Scotland was an adaptation of the French flamboyant, a school utterly at variance with the specialties of the Tudor. In the larger features of the latter, straight lines, horizontal and perpendicular, predominate. The mouldings and other decorations, including especially the mullions of the windows, have a tendency to geometrical division by angles and straight lines. On the other hand, the French flamboyant, sometimes called the florid, luxuriates in curves, and has a tendency to throw out from a centre, or an upright line, a symmetrical design coming out in curves, which return as loops to their starting-point after having thrown out lateral curvilinear tracery, the process going on to any extent. To take a very common form of this process—the centre of the design is parallel to the spring of the arch of a pointed Gothic window, and of course midway between the two sides. If all round this point there are grouped curved or loop-shaped departments of the window, they will be narrow towards the centre and will broaden outwards; hence comes the flame shape of the tracery of the windows which has given to the style the name of flamboyant. Fair specimens of this style may be seen in the Cathedrals of Dunkeld and Brechin, the Church of Linlithgow, and the Chapel of King's College in Aberdeen.

It will perhaps afford a more distinct notion of divergence from English practice to speak of what is to be found there in abundance, and is not to be found in Scotland. The arch of the Tudor period is peculiar to

England. It is neither circular like the Roman and Norman arch, nor pointed like the Gothic of the first and second periods. It is from the peculiarity of the arch that the style has been called the depressed Gothic; and to those unaccustomed to it, an arch of this type is apt to justify the term by suggesting that it had been originally pointed, but that the superincumbent weight had pressed on it on either side, and given a horizontal curve to the ribs of a pointed arch. This form has another name—the four-centred arch, because the variation in the curve requires that on either side it should be drawn from a double centre. This arch is abundant all over England, in buildings both baronial and ecclesiastical: there is probably no English county in which it is not the conspicuous and characteristic feature of several buildings. In Scotland it may be said that it is unknown; if there be a single instance of it, that instance must be an exception of mark.[1]

These facts suggest two inferences. The one that, for many generations after the War of Independence, Scotland had not wealth enough to raise ecclesiastical buildings on the scale of those completed, or nearly completed, when the war broke out. The other is that, when the country was again rich enough to spend

[1] Of course an old exception is supposed. In the attempts at the restoration of Gothic architecture in Scotland, this and all the other features of the Tudor type are common. There can be no objection to this; the style has its merits, and if any modern architect can produce a building vying with Henry VII.'s Chapel, it should be thankfully accepted, without consideration for the ethnical history of the style. It is provoking, however, that restorations of buildings of thoroughly Scottish type have often been made in this style. St Giles's, in Edinburgh, is a flagrant instance. There are windows of the four-centred arch in King's College Chapel, in Aberdeen, which the Author might admit to be the exception he anticipates above, had he not himself seen them let into the wall.

money in this shape, it was no longer England that she sought as her teacher in architecture, but France.

The same conclusions are shown by the remains of baronial or castellated architecture, and perhaps even more emphatically. We have seen that there is in Scotland no known remnant of the Norman school—the method of castle-building, from the Conquest down, let us say, to the reign of Henry III. The oldest existing castles in Scotland belong to the succeeding period, known in England as that of the Edwards. As these are the oldest castles in Scotland, so also they are the most magnificent. Not even Tantallon, Glammis, or Craigmillar, the greatest efforts of any later age, can vie with them. A general mystery hangs over them. We do not seem to have means of knowing, as to any one of them, what particular lord of the soil it was who had it built. The remains of some of them stand on the possessions of the Norman houses which were so eventfully connected with Scotland—those, for instance, of Comyn and Bruce. But it would be difficult positively to contradict any one who should maintain that they were all built by the English invaders. The structural history of this noble class of buildings can be traced step by step from the simple square tower of the Conqueror's reign. It has been the natural growth of European fortification to expand into flanking works. At the period of the War of Independence, castles had so far developed in that direction that they consisted of great walls or screens flanked by strong round towers. In England the process of expansion went on down to the Vauban fortress, spreading over an expanse of country. In Scotland the expansion suddenly stopped; nay, more, castle-building went back to the simple square tower, which was a novel feature in England two hundred years earlier. The two were so much alike that strangers taking a cursory tour in Scotland have returned with the impression that the country contains a great many Norman keeps. A close inspection, however, shows distinctions which to the adept are conclusive. The details of the Norman castles are in the style of work still called Norman— the transition between the Roman and the Gothic. The Scots square towers show the work of the fourteenth or fifteenth century, and in their general masonry are inferior to the oldest English castles.

Among the square towers so large as to be mistaken at a distance for Norman keeps may be counted Clackmannan, Borthwick near Edinburgh, Melgund in Forfarshire, Niddry in Linlithgowshire, Huntingtower near Perth, and many others. The same class of work, however, was repeated in smaller shapes. The country was in one sense amply fortified. The buildings were meagre, significant of the limited means of impoverished builders, but they were very numerous. Many of them, indeed, though for accommodation and the means of domestic comfort they would not have in England been admitted to the rank of yeoman's granges, were still strong fortresses. The peel or bastle-house, which spread a considerable exterior before the eye, would contain three, perhaps only two, small chambers—mere cells let into a solid mass of masonry. These humble fortresses were naturally numerous on the border. Along the banks of the streams they may there be seen at short intervals, more or less in ruins. They are the only remnants of old buildings designed for human habitation in that district. In the border towns, such as Hawick, Roxburgh, and Kelso, the absence of old houses is observable, and at once accounted for by the recollection of the many burnings by the English invaders.

The necessity of some flanking work for these square towers seems to have been soon felt, and the impoverished owner supplied it in an economical shape creditable to his ingenuity. Instead of attempting to run up from the ground flanking round towers like those of the Gothic castles, he perched turrets or machicolations on the corners of the top of the tower. Generally there was one on each corner; but sometimes the laird had to be content with two, which, if placed at opposite angles, would serve to flank the whole four sides of the square block.

Before the time we have reached, the country had been recovering from its prostration, and acquiring the means for enlarged efforts in this and in other directions. It did not, however, follow the example of England; but, as in church-architecture, took its models from friendly France. The spiral character of the French chateau-architecture is well known. It had begun to appear in Scotland, but its full development there was in the beginning of the seventeenth century. Even already, however, it touched the grim square tower with relieving features. The spiral roof of the French flanking tower was set on the corner machicolation, and by the clustering of ornamental chimneys, and other devices taken from the same source, a certain rich variety was given to the top at least of the old peel tower. Had the houses of the gentry been subject to the influence not of the French chateau but of the English hall and mansion style, known as the Tudor, the internal condition of Scotland would not have admitted of such a method of building. It was one incident to a country where there was a strong central government keeping internal peace. The English squire could turn his castle into a mansion two hundred years before the Scots laird could imitate his example.

Some of the royal residences partook in the profusely decorative character of the Renaissance; remnants of it may still be seen in Stirling, Linlithgow, and Falkland. Among feudal castles, the only one that now preserves the ambitious design and extensive decoration belonging to the period which followed the pointed Gothic, is Crichton Castle, the stronghold of that Chancellor Crichton who had a struggle for supremacy with the Douglases in the reign of James II. In its "stony cord," with "twisted roses laced," its "courtyard's graceful portico," and the "fair hewn" facets rising row on row above the cornice, it stands in signal contrast to its grim square neighbour Borthwick. Among the few other instances of ambitious decoration on the buildings belonging to subjects in that early period, the best specimens are to be found in a spot where one would hardly expect to find such things—the village of Maybole in Ayrshire. This, however, was the ancient capital of the bailliary of Carrick, the domain of the Bruces; and within it the Lord Cassilis, the hereditary bailie, and the other magnates of the district, had their hotels or town residences, and formed a little court by themselves.

We know nothing of the personal history, or even the identity, of the architects who planned the palaces, the ecclesiastical buildings, or the feudal castles of the day—we cannot even tell whether they were foreigners or natives.[1] We can only suppose, from other conditions, that Scotland had not within herself sufficient art to compass the finer work in the palaces and churches, and that it was done by foreigners. The mason must go to the spot where the work of his hand is to remain; and whatever was to be wrought in stone by foreigners must have brought them to Scotland.

We have no testimony to the practice of the portable arts, as they may be called—painting and sculpture—in Scotland, within the early period now in view, unless we may count some illuminations on manuscripts made in the cloisters as specimens of art. The carved woodwork of the churches, and the beautiful oaken sculpture in the Palace of Stirling, known as "the Stirling heads," were doubtless foreign work. Perhaps the finest piece of carved work, both for beauty of Gothic design and practical finish, existing in the British Empire, is that of the screens, stalls, and canopies in King's College Chapel in Aberdeen; but it is a testimony to the comparative richness of the Church and her zeal for education, rather than to the progress of national art. While thus artificially destitute and dependent on others for these physical fruits of intellectuality, Scotland was in other departments of intellectual work giving far more than she got. The contrast is a curious exemplification of the conditions necessary to the prosperity of what are called the fine arts. The stuff that made those great scholars and rhetoricians who rendered Scotland illustrious abroad, could have also given inspiration to the painter, the sculptor, and

---

[1] See the observations connected with the violent death of Cochrane the mason in King James III.'s reign.

the architect; but these could only grow in a soil prepared for them by peace and prosperity.

About the material progress of the nation during the three hundred and fifty years since the War of Independence, there is little to be said. Much of stirring life as we have during that long period, there occur no instances of impulse given to trade, manufactures, or the other producers of wealth. We have seen that at the outbreak of the war the elements of wealth and comfort were noticeably large. The impression left on more than one of those who have mused over such testimony as can be had from the records of this long period is, that though Scotland had somewhat recovered from deep depression, the country was not so rich at the time of the Reformation as the long war found it. France gave facilities of trade to her ancient ally, by exemption from customs duties, and otherwise; but the opportunities so offered seem to have met but a languid co-operation. In foreign places where the Scots had a commercial treaty, it became the practice to appoint a "conservator of privileges," whose function resembled that of the consul of the present day; the office, in one instance at least, remained as a sinecure after its uses had come to an end, and even been forgotten; and John Home, the author of Douglas, was provided for as "the conservator of Scots privileges at Campvere."

There is extant the record of transactions or ledger of Andrew Haliburton, conservator of the Scots privileges at Middleburg. It runs over ten years—from 1493 to 1503.[1] He seems to have been himself—as

---

[1] This is likely to be the earliest of the collection of "chronicles and memorials" relating to Scotland to be issued under the auspices of the Lord Clerk Register.

many consuls now are—an agent or dealer in mercantile transactions. The aspect of his book does not assure us of an active intelligent commerce, conducted with the newest arrangements for facilitating business. Book-keeping had advanced so far in practice among the Genoese and Netherlands merchants, that during the period of Haliburton's transactions it had been systematised in a literary treatise. But he has none of it. Further than that there is a separate statement of transactions with each of his employers or correspondents, there is no analysis, with corresponding figures, to enable the state of his business to be posted up. Each account is a history, the money equivalent being stated in Roman figures, and of course supplying no means for arithmetical adjustment. Were one to judge by comparing his accounts with those of the lord chamberlain so far back as 1263, it might be inferred that in the interval there had been no improvement in account-keeping. The transactions are narratives. From these he might have told any correspondent which of the two was the other's debtor, and for how much; but he could not have wrought out his own pecuniary position, by making up anything approaching to the nature and services of a balance-sheet.[1] The goods he receives from Scotland,

---

[1] Of book-keeping as an exact art, which gives no more expression to the success or failure of the transactions recorded in it than so many algebraic formulas, the conservator had so little conception that his entries of pecuniary payments and receipts bear marks of the joys or griefs associated with them. Having to record a hopeless balance against a correspondent, which a modern book-keeper would perhaps "write off" into the limbo of bad debts, he puts a note, "God keep all good men from such callants!" and of another hopeless customer he notes, "He mansworne me with evill malyssious laugag; and to be quyt of hym in tym to cum, I gaf hym a hayll quittans, and whyll I lyff never to deal with him."—P. 269.

and sells abroad, are all raw produce—salmon, herrings, hides, furs, and wool. It would be difficult to find in his record any article of Scots handiwork, farther than that the wools may have been sorted, since they are of various quality. The fish must have been cured for keeping, and the hides probably tanned. He sends back wine, with spices and other articles, now called colonial produce, evidence that Scotland bought these things from the Continental merchants instead of importing them from the place of production. On this side of his transactions are textile fabrics and other manufactures. It is observable that a large proportion of the goods he sends to Scotland are for churchmen, in the shape of books of devotion, sacerdotal robes, reliquaries, images, and the like. Thus we see that the large revenue drawn by churchmen from the land made the supply of their professional and personal wants fill up a great proportion of the traffic of the country—a certain sign of the narrowness of its trade.

The mineral riches of Scotland were so far sought that we can trace a small export trade in metals. We have seen that gold belongs to the geological formation of Scotland. Down to the period we have reached, it seems to have been from time to time found disintegrated from the rock. Bishop Leslie describes the streams of the Lanarkshire heights carrying so much of it in the gravel brought down by the floods, as if each were a very Pactolus; but he makes a significant admission in telling us that the sifting of this gravel for gold is the occupation of the poor.[1]

---

[1] De Origine, &c., 11. The 'Scotiæ Descriptio,' in which such matters are mentioned, has no counterpart in the vernacular history by Leslie, often referred to above.

Among the Acts passed in the busy Parliament held by James I. when he returned from England, gold and silver mines were made the property of the crown, "as is usual in other realms." The form of the Act is peculiar, as being an offering of this prerogative to the crown by the lords of Parliament. At the same time a duty was laid on all gold and silver exported from the realm.[1] At the time when Henry VIII. was casting greedy eyes on Scotland, the richness of the gold-fields of the country seems to have been an object of consideration, as affecting the value of the proposed plunder. Wharton sends a specimen of "gold coined in Scotland, the time of Duke Albany being there," from nuggets found on Crawford Moor, and says, "If it shall so stand with the king's majesty's pleasure, I shall cause the ground to be seen without suspicion thereof, and the manner and order of the work, as the same hath continued and at this present standeth, and shall make certificate thereof accordingly." But Wharton seems to have taken too sensible a view of the affair to stimulate much hope of riches from such a source. Sir Adam Otterburn told him how James IV. "made great work upon the moor, and all that he did find was gold in pieces loose in the earth, and never could find any vein thereof; and, as he said, the charges of workmen surmounted the value of the thing gotten."[2]

Lead was extracted, at a very early period, in the district of the present Wanlockhead mines. The method of separating any portions of silver that might be in the matrix of lead must have been early in use,

[1] Act. Parl., ii. 5.
[2] State Papers (Henry VIII.), v. 575.

as the royalty established in favour of James I. applies to those mines where "three halfpennies of silver may be found out of the pound of lead." Whenever any names come up in connection with mining operations, they generally belong to Englishmen, Germans, or Dutchmen.[1] About the time we have reached, a contract was entered on for giving a foreigner the working of the lead mines, on the condition of his sending a certain amount of silver to the royal cunyie-house, coin-house or mint.[2]

That there was iron in Scotland was known at an early age; but there are but faint, if any, traces of its having been wrought, and there is nothing until long after the period we have reached to show that the country was conscious of the enormous source of wealth it contained in this shape.

Coal was used, but probably only found where it cropped out on the surface of the soil. We are told of its use, and of other customs, by an eminent observer, known to literature as Æneas Sylvius Piccolomini, and to history as Pope Pius II., who visited Scotland in the year 1435, to transact business about some obscure affair of ecclesiastical patronage. The notes left by such visitors are naturally considered very precious; but we may find, as on this occasion, that there is not much of distinct truth to be gained from their appreciation of the broad social conditions of a country. In

[1] See several details about early mining, picked out of charters and other documents, in Chalmers's Caledonia, iii. 733.

[2] "Herefore we bind and oblige us faithfully to the queen's majesty, and her said treasurer in her name, to deliver to her grace's cunyie-hous, betwix this and the first day of August next to cum, forty-five unce of utter fine silver for every thousand stanewecht of the said twenty thousand stanes of led-ore."—The Discoverie and Historie of the Gold Mynes of Scotland, by Stephen Atkinson, Appendix, 88.

his judgment regarding feminine modesty and decorum in Scotland, he utterly contradicts, at least in essentials, another observer, Don Pedro de Ayala, who a few years afterwards had fuller opportunity of noticing the social conditions of the country.

Piccolomini tells—what we can easily believe very noticeable to an Italian belonging to a distinguished and wealthy family—that the country was very poor; that many houses in it were built without lime, and roofed with turf; and that the towns were not fortified. He says something much more distinct to the interests of the present day, when he reports, to his own special audience, a practice of the Scots, which he gives with the exactness of a man who knows that he is telling truth to the incredulous. He finds, among the other poverties and barbarisms of these Scots, that they dig out of the earth a mineral of sulphurous quality, and use it as fuel. He tells, with the misgiving of a man who scarcely expects to be believed, how he first noticed the value set on this black mineral. He observed that the half-naked beggars at the church doors received portions of it as alms, and went away thankful. It is, on the whole, treated compassionately, rather than otherwise, that a people should be reduced to the use of so sordid a fuel. He notes that the country is treeless. Perhaps it was so in the district of the south, which alone he saw. He would have both reason and opportunity for observing the bareness of the ten long miles of country over which he walked twice barefooted on the frozen ground on a pilgrimage, though that district is now thickly wooded.[1] The Highlands, on the other hand, were covered with native forests,

[1] De Europa, Sylvii Opera, 443. See above, iii. 35.

which have been destroyed in later times. John Major, who was acquainted with other countries, mentions the dense forests of the Highlands, or Caledonian Alps, enhancing their inaccessible nature. Hence came a significant element in the distinction between the two races inhabiting the land—the Saxon Lowlander delving the ground, and striving to extract nourishment from the sterile soil on which his lot was cast; the mountaineer hiding in the deep forests which clothed his mountains, and issuing from fastnesses nearly inaccessible, to plunder from time to time his industrious neighbour.

Although it has been noted, as a general impression created by the tenor of the Author's reading, that Scotland was not so rich at the Reformation as at the beginning of the War of Independence, it is proper to note that there was one period of evidently rapid prosperity in her annals. This was during the reign of James IV., when the Wars of the Roses kept the national enemy busy at home. We have seen how, in that reign, Scotland obtained a considerable diplomatic position among the European powers, and how an ambassador from the proud monarchs of Spain was observing, with close interest, the turn of Scottish politics. We have seen his picturesque description of the King of Scots transmitted to his own court. He reported at the same time on the institutions of the country—its agriculture, its trade, and in some measure on its social conditions and customs. He writes as one who had found on his mission a powerful and prosperous community, with which it were better to be in alliance than at war. On the sources of revenue he says, " The import duties are insignificant, but the exports yield a considerable sum of money, because there are three principal articles of export—that is to say, wool, hides, and fish. The customs are worth about 25,000 ducats a-year. They have much increased, and will continue to increase." This revenue on exports would some fifty years ago have been denounced by the prevalent school on the economy of trade as a gross folly, leading to certain national ruin; but the later school of political economy has left import and export duties pretty nearly on a balance against each other.

The ambassador reported to his court on many matters coming under his notice in Scotland. From his Spanish training, even had he cultivated the faculty of observing political institutions at the Court of the Emperor or at Paris, he was not likely to form a clear notion of the political and social condition of such a country as Scotland. In the dearth, however, of notices of the country from without, his should not be thrown away. They want the coherence which might be given to the facts coming under his notice, if we had them now as he got them. In some things, too, he has been mistaken; and his estimate of the force of mounted men available for war in Scotland is so preposterous that we must suppose it to have come of a slip of the pen.

Without seeing a way to anything more precise or instructive by way of commentary upon the following passages, they are given as they stand in the report on the Court of James IV. and the people of Scotland, in the year 1498, sent by the protho-notary, Don Pedro de Ayala, to Ferdinand and Isabella:—

" They spend all their time in wars, and when there is no war they fight with one another. It must, however, be observed that since the present king succeeded to the throne, they do not dare to quarrel so much with one another as formerly, especially since he came of age. They have learnt by experience that he executes the law without respect to rich or poor. I am told that Scotland has improved so much during his reign that it is worth three times more now than formerly, on account of foreigners having come to the country, and taught them how to live. They have more meat, in great and small animals, than they want, and plenty of wool and hides.

"Spaniards who live in Flanders tell me that the commerce of Scotland is much more considerable now than formerly, and that it is continually increasing.

"It is impossible to describe the immense quantity of fish. The old proverb says already ' piscinata Scotia.' Great quantities of salmon, herring, and a kind of dried fish, which they call stock fish (stoque fix), are exported. The quantity is so great that it suffices for Italy, France, Flanders, and England. They have so many wild fruits which they eat, that they do not know what to do with them. There are immense flocks of sheep, especially in the savage portions of Scotland. Hides are employed for many purposes. There are all kinds of garden fruits to be found which a cold country can produce. They are very good. Oranges, figs, and other fruits of the same kind, are not to be found there. The corn is very good, but they do not produce as much as they might, because they do not cultivate the land. Their method is the following: they plough the land only once when it has grass on it, which is as high as a man, then they sow the corn, and cover it by means of a harrow, which makes the land even again. Nothing more is done till they cut the corn. I have seen the straw stand so high after harvest, that it reached to my girdle. Some kind of corn is sown about the Feast of St John, and is cut in August.

"The people are handsome. They like foreigners so much that they dispute with one another as to who shall have and treat a foreigner in his house. They are vain and ostentatious by nature. They spend all they have to keep up appearances. They are as well dressed as it is possible to be in such a country as that in which they live. They are courageous, strong, quick, and agile. They are envious to excess.

"The kings live little in cities and towns. They pass their time generally in castles and abbeys, where they find lodgings for all their officers. They do not remain long in one place. The reason thereof is twofold. In the first place, they move often about, in order to visit their kingdom, to administer justice, and to establish police where it is wanted. The second reason is, that they have rents in kind in every province, and they wish to consume them. While travelling, neither the king nor any of his officers have any expenses, nor do they carry provisions with them. They go from house to house, to lords, bishops, and abbots, where they receive all that is necessary. The greatest favour the king can do to his subjects is to go to their houses.

"The women are courteous in the extreme. I mention this because they are really honest, though very bold. They are absolute mistresses of their houses, and even of their husbands, in all things concerning the administration of their property, income as well as expenditure. They are very graceful and handsome women. They dress much better than here (England), and especially as regards the head-dress, which is, I think, the handsomest in the world.

"The towns and villages are populous. The houses are good, all built of hewn stone, and provided with excellent doors, glass windows, and a great number of chimneys. All the furniture that is used in Italy, Spain, and France, is to be found in their dwellings. It has not been bought in modern times only, but inherited from preceding ages.

"The queens possess, besides their baronies and castles, four country-seats, situated in the best portions of the kingdom, each of which is worth about fifteen thousand ducats. The king fitted them up anew only three years ago. There is not more than one fortified town in Scotland, because the kings do not allow their subjects to fortify them. The town is a very considerable borough, and well armed. The whole soil of Scotland belongs to the king, the landholders being his vassals, or his tenants for life, or for a term of years. They are obliged to serve him forty days, at their own expense, every time he calls them out. They are very good soldiers. The king can assemble, within thirty days, 120,000 horse. The soldiers from the islands are not counted in this number. The islands are half a league, one, two, three, or four leagues distant from the mainland. The inhabitants speak the language and have the habits of the Irish. But there is a good deal of French education in Scotland, and many speak the French language. For all the young gentlemen who have no property go to France, and are well received there, and therefore the French are liked. Two or three times I have seen, not the whole army, but one-third of it assembled, and counted more than 12,000 great and small tents. There is much emulation among them as to who shall be best equipped, and they are very ostentatious, and pride themselves very much in this respect. They have old and heavy artillery of iron. Besides this, they possess modern French guns of metal, which are very good. King Louis gave them to the father of the present king in payment of what was due to him as co-heir of his sister, the Queen of Scotland." [1]

[1] Bergenroth, Simancas Papers, 168-75.

CHAPTER XLI.

Queen Mary.

DEATH OF THE KING OF FRANCE—VISITORS TO THE YOUNG QUEEN—HER BROTHER, AFTERWARDS EARL OF MURRAY—EMBASSY FROM HUNTLY AND THE ROMISH PARTY—PERTINACIOUS DEALING OF QUEEN ELIZABETH'S AMBASSADORS IN FRANCE—QUEEN MARY'S RETURN—HER COMPANIONS—HER RECEPTION—HER PAST AND FUTURE POSITION COMPARED—A PAGEANT—THE RELIGIOUS DIFFICULTY—THE QUESTION OF TOLERATING IDOLATRY—CALVIN CONSULTED—METHODS OF REVILING THE OLD CREED AND CEREMONIES—INTERVIEWS WITH JOHN KNOX—THE FIRST BOOK OF DISCIPLINE—FAILURE OF THE CLERGY TO GET IT CONFIRMED BY PARLIAMENT—REASONS FOR THE LAY MEMBERS OF THE CONGREGATION DISLIKING IT—CONTAINS PROVISIONS FOR APPROPRIATING THE TEMPORALITIES OF THE CHURCH—WOULD THUS TAKE THEM FROM THE LAY LORDS WHO HAD SECURED THEM—INSTANCES OF THE METHOD OF GETTING AT THEM—ROASTING A COMMENDATOR—KNOX'S WRATH—THE COMPROMISE—MURRAY'S MARRIAGE AND ELEVATION—A CLEARING AMONG THE BORDER THIEVES.

QUEEN MARY's husband, Francis II., died on the 15th of December 1560. The effect of such an event is immediately obvious. It was a relief to the great new party predominant in Scotland. It left but little strength in the hold by which Scotland seemed bound over to the ambitious schemes of the Guises. If to a large portion of the Scots people their queen was also to be their enemy, she had lost her power to injure.

Her early return was now desired, and preparations were made accordingly.

In the mean time, one in her position would naturally have to receive important visitors. Among these were two countrymen of her own, who, representing the two opposite parties in the great contest, reached her simultaneously at Vitry in Champagne. The one was her brother, the Lord James. What counsel he gave her becomes obvious from his position as leader of the lay members of the Congregation. The other, who came after him, was John Leslie, afterwards the Bishop of Ross, and her stanch friend and supporter in her adversities. We have his errand from himself. He represented the party of the old Church, especially the Lords Huntly, Athole, Crawford, Marishal, Sutherland, and Caithness. He says he offered the devoted duty of his party, and that it was thankfully received. He further tells the significant fact that he recommended her to land at Aberdeen, where twenty thousand troops would be at her disposal; and that he was accompanied by one high in command in Huntly's armed force, who was to arrange her convoy to Aberdeen, if she consented to land there. This was no less than the offer of the power of the north to strike at once a great blow against the Congregation and for the old religion. However it came to pass, the landing at Aberdeen was not effected; but the proposal will be seen to have an intimate connection with events immediately following the queen's return to Scotland.[1]

---

[1] History, vernacular version, 294. It is in the Latin version that the affair is more distinctly marked as a project of the Romish party, and that the army to be collected at Aberdeen is mentioned. The leader of the convoy was to be "Jacobus Cullenus, ipsius Huntlæi cognatus, vir militiæ terrestris ac navalis scientia plurimum valens, qui illam

She afterwards received sedulous attentions from Bedford and Throckmorton, the English ambassadors at Paris. They were very anxious that she should confirm the treaty of Edinburgh, with its important clause acknowledging Elizabeth as the rightful Queen of England. It might be said that their pertinacity in this matter extended to rudeness, and even cruelty, were not the vital issues at stake an excuse for earnest endeavour. If these veteran statesmen expected to mould the beautiful young widow in her solitude and sorrows to their purpose, they were mistaken; and they got experience to teach them that their mistress had a dangerous neighbour, so far as plausibility and seductive influence might go. On the very weakness of her condition as a new-made widow among strangers, she founded an insuperable barrier against all their efforts. How could they ask her to transact business —important business, too—without her proper advisers about her? Queen Elizabeth had, in a manner deemed presuming, recommended her in all things to follow the advice of the native nobility of her realm. This little offence served her in good purpose. Had not the mistress of her tormentors—the Queen of England, her gracious sister—most kindly advised her in this matter? and would they have her disregard the counsel so graciously given her by their mistress? Oh, and indeed in regard to her they had broken a promise. She and her gracious sister were to exchange portraits. She had sent her own, but she had not got her sister's.

tutam ac incolumem Aberdoniam duceret."—P. 532. These particulars are repeated in Gordon's History of the Family of Gordon (i. 198), whether on Leslie's or other authority. See also Gordon's Genealogical History of the Earldom of Sutherland, 139.

She begged that there might be no delay in the reciprocity; nay, she could not rest until she beheld the dear resemblance.

Before they had done with her they had a sample of another of her accomplishments, and found with what royal grace she could pass a sarcastic rebuke on an unworthy act. She had asked a safe-conduct from Queen Elizabeth, that she might pass through England. It was refused; and indeed it was believed that an attempt would be made to intercept her. She spoke of all this with a kind of easy scorn. Elizabeth's father had tried to kidnap her when she came to France as an infant. He failed; and perhaps Providence would be equally kind to her again, and bring her safe through the traps set by his daughter. And if Queen Elizabeth were successful—well, then, she would be at the mercy, no doubt, of the person who had so acted, and what would be the end? For herself, easy enough—she had but to submit to her fate; but for the other? The end of all was that the ambassadors got no confirmation of the treaty, and scarcely any satisfaction concerning it. Queen Mary embarked to return to Scotland on the 14th of August 1561.

She and her escort sailed from Calais in two of the galleys then almost peculiar to France, as vessels which went before the wind when they could, and were rowed by galley-slaves on benches at other times. Two ordinary sailing vessels attended, the whole making a fleet of four. She was well escorted. There were with her, besides many minor nobles of France, her two uncles, the Duke of Aumale and the Marquis of Elbœuf; her two adorers, Marshal d'Amville, and Chastellar, whose adoration afterwards cost him so dear. There was

Strozzi—apparently the son of the general who besieged St Andrews—and La Noue, afterwards known in the Huguenot wars as Bras de Fer.[1] By far the most interesting, however, of her attendants to us at the present day was Brantome, who sailed in the same galley with her.[2] Her conduct during the voyage has been treasured and told in various shapes; but as the original source of all of them is a few precious sentences by that vivid writer in his little book 'Des Dames Illustres,' it may be well to adhere to what is so said. A light wind sprang up; the crew of galley-slaves were released from their labours, and the sails set. As the lumbering vessels moved slowly away, the queen sat beside the helm, as the place where she would be nearest to the land she was leaving. She gazed on it with her fine eyes, and wept bitterly throughout the remaining five hours of daylight, repeating over and over the simple words, "Adieu, France!" When the sight of land faded into the darkness, she uttered passionate words about the jealous night drawing its curtain before her, and, with tears falling faster and faster, exclaimed that the sight of France was now lost to her—she would never see it more. She then became conversable, and spoke of herself with her eyes bent on the land, dropping a sentiment about her

---

[1] M. de Castelneau, l. iii. ch. i.

[2] It might be inferred, from what Leslie says, that she was then accompanied by her evil genius, Bothwell: "Not long efter, the Earls Bothwell and Eglintoun, the Bishop of Orkney, and sindry other noblemen and clerks, arrivet in France, wha returnet in Scotland with the queen's majesty again."—P. 295. In the Latin version, Bothwell's going to France is mentioned; but in the train coming to Scotland with the queen, only the French are mentioned, as in Brantome. The author of a contemporary diary says: "Upon the 21 day of Februar, my Lord Bothwell landed in Scotland out of France."—Diurnal of Occurrents, 64.

reversing the attitude of Dido, who, when Æneas departed, ever gazed on the sea. She slept on the deck, desiring the pilot to waken her immediately, should the land become again visible at dawn. The wind fell, and the slaves were set to their slow labours again, so that next morning the coast was still to be seen; and sitting up, she looked on it till it vanished, crying—" Adieu la France, cela est fait. Adieu la France, je pense ne vous voir jamais plus!" The fleet, having taken about a week on the voyage, arrived in the harbour of Leith one morning at six o'clock—the exact day is disputed. The arrival of their queen was announced to the nearest inhabitants by the discharge of the guns mounted on the galleys. Whatever arrangements were in preparation for the event had not been completed, and the contrast between Scotland and France was rather exaggerated than modified. She and her following had to wait some time at Leith ere horses—there were no carriages—could be procured for them. Brantome, whose narrative still accompanies us, says the queen burst into tears at the sorry contrast with the gorgeous processions of France. He says nothing more, however, against the equipage, save that it consisted of the horses of the country, with conformable harness; but this he seems to have thought enough.

Some zealous citizens sought to enliven her first night at Holyrood by a serenade, in which it is said that fiddles with three strings bore a conspicuous and discordant part. Whatever effect the discord may have had on the queen herself, it seems to have grated direfully on the nerves of Brantome, who describes the attempt as some five or six hundred " marauds" performing on *mechans violons* and *petits rebecs;* continuing, by way of aggravation apparently, that the music, abominably performed by them, partook of the nature of psalmody. The serenade is described by an observer of a different order in Knox's History, where we are told that "a company of most honest men, with instruments of music and with musicians, gave their salutations at her chamber window," and that the queen said the melody "liked her well," and she wished the same to be continued some nights after.

The spoilt beauty expected to find in the land of her destiny a dreary contrast with that of her adoption, and she found her expectations fully realised. France, though now more closely and economically cultivated, scarcely bears to outward appearance a richer raiment of civilised fruitfulness than it did then. Wherever royalty was likely to resort, there were palaces and chateaux, walled towns, fine churches, and great stretches of pleasure-ground. Scotland was yet ignorant of the high cultivation which has warmed its cold landscape and softened its dreary winds. There was a greater contrast even in the people than in the country. England was behind France in a certain kind of civilisation; the Court and the aristocracy were more homespun and yeoman-like. Scotland was a much greater distance behind England, and lacked the solid respectability which was then ripening into a civilisation more firm and true than that of France. The common people of Scotland were perhaps as well off as those of France, but they were not subdued to the same submissive order, being self-willed, boisterous, and, down to the very humblest grade, even proud. In France, the Court, through its power and wealth, could effectually isolate itself from the people, clearing away whatever was sordid and disagreeable, wherever it moved. In Scotland, the common people, such as they were, pressed close around the palace door, and haunted royalty wherever it went. The contrast between the two nations, thus considerable in the lowest sphere of society, increased rather than diminished with the ascending grades, and was greatest among the courtiers immediately surrounding the throne. There were many country seigneurs in France who practised rough hospitality and tyranny in their own domains, and were seen but on rare occasions at Court, where they were the objects of ridicule and horror. But those who frequented the Court had mounted as high in the scale of external elegance and fastidiousness as the world has ever reached. Though corroding vices were eating all morality out of it, the Court abounded in as much elegant luxury and external refinement as it has ever known at any later age. There was a high polish in the very vices of the period. If there were gluttony and drunkenness, they exercised themselves in the most skilfully prepared meats and costly wines. French cookery had made wonderful strides as a skilful art, and had produced one master mind. Sensuality indulged itself in exquisite works of art and inspired poetry. The men even were profuse in silks and velvets, indulged in perfumes, and kept diminutive monkeys and silky spaniels as pets. Murder itself was refined, by a preference of subtle poisons, skilfully prepared, over the bloody brawls of earlier times. A portion of these vices and trivialities, covered with a thin polish, had been transferred by the French courtiers to their faithful allies of Scotland; but these tended rather to expose and aggravate than to subdue the natural character of the Scottish aristocracy. Their dress was that of the camp or stable; they were dirty in person, and abrupt and disrespectful in manner, carrying on their disputes, and even fighting out their fierce quarrels, in the presence of royalty, which had by no means accomplished the serene imperial isolation which the sovereigns of France had achieved since the days of Francis I. With the exception of one or two castles which had been built in the French style, the best families were crowded into narrow square towers, in which all available means had been exhausted in strength, leaving nothing for comfort or elegance. The royal residences were little better. The more roomy portions of Linlithgow, Stirling, and Falkland, as we now see them, did not then exist. Holyrood, though then very different from what it now is, was probably an exception to the general sordidness. It was the new palace, and was consequently built up to the taste and luxury of the age. It had been completed but a few years previously by James V. The park included the fine mountain-range of Arthur Seat. The lands of Duddingston, with their loch, had just been added to it; and thus, with rocks, trees, and water, the palace and its park bore some faint analogy to the glories of Fontainebleau.

On one important point a difference between the two Courts was disagreeably and alarmingly conspicuous— the unprotected condition of the sovereign and her Court, from the want of any armed force, whose duty it was to guard the royal person. In France, besides many other armed retainers of the household, there was

the thoroughly disciplined body of the Scots Guard—
mercenary foreigners, in the usual phraseology of later
times, but at the same time a body of honourable true
men, entirely devoted to their employer, and by their
foreign birth disconnected with the native aristocracy,
against whom they were the crown's chief support.

While every head of a considerable family in Scotland, down to the humblest landowner, had some regular
armed following, the crown alone had none. The feudal
tenants of the crown were bound, indeed, to furnish
their quotas to the national armament; but the troops so
assembled were entirely under their feudal leaders, and
were often questionable supporters, if not dangerous
neighbours, to the sovereign. Memorable incidents, some
of which were yet to come, show how unprotected the
royal person might be in Scotland. The early Stewart
kings were men and soldiers who could always manage
to keep a force of some sort at their call; but Mary
severely felt the want of a permanent armed body,
whose duty it was, without interference on her part, to
be always protecting her and her feminine Court—and
her son was scarcely better fitted to dispense with it.
All Mary's efforts, however, to establish a royal guard,
were, like the attempt of her mother, sternly resisted,
calling out a deep national antipathy to anything approaching to the character of a standing army. When
an alarm arose in the palace that the excited Earl of
Arran was going to seize the queen, and sudden efforts
were made for her protection against dangers which
soon turned out to be unreal, she was suspected of
having got up the alarm to prove the necessity of
establishing a household guard.[1]

[1] See Knox, ii. 293.

On the 2d of September, a fortnight after her landing, she had to undergo the ordeal of a popular demonstration by the citizens of Edinburgh. They were to make a "propine" or goodwill-offering to her. It was a present of a cupboard "double overgilt," which had cost 2000 merks. The giving of it was to be the occasion of a pageant, which was to salute her in a progress through the city. It was witnessed by one who chronicled in their order the events of the time, and the show delighted him, so far as to inspire some spirit into a narrative, the general merits of which are to be found in the brevity and precision with which he states in their proper order of sequence the events of that stirring period.[1]

[1] The crisis of the pageant is as follows:—
"And thairefter, when she was rydand doun the Castellhill, thair met hir hienes ane convoy of the young men of the said burgh, to the nomber of fyftie or thairby, thair bodeis and theis coverit with yellow taffateis, thair armes and leggs, fra the kne doun, bair, cullorit with blak, in maner of Moris, upon thair heiddes blak hattis, and on thair faces blak visouris, in thair mouthis rings, garnesit with intellable precious staneis, about thair nekkis, leggis, and armes insynit of chenis of gold; togidder with saxtene of the maist honest men of the toun, cled in velvet gownis and velvet bonettis, berand and gangand about the paill under the whilk hir hienes raid, whilk paill wes of fyne purpour velvet lynit with reid taffateis, freingiet with gold and silk; and after thame wes ane cart with certane bairnes, togidder with ane coffer whairin wes the copburd and propyne whilk suld be propynit to hir hienes. And when hir grace come fordwart to the butter-trone of the said burgh, the nobilitie and convoy foirsaid precedland, at the whilk butter-trone thair was ane port made of tymber in maist honourable maner, cullorit with fyne cullouris, hungin with syndrie armes, upoun the whilk port wes singand certane barneis in the meist hevinlie wyis; under the whilk port thair wes ane cloud opynnand with four levis, in the whilk was put ane bonny barne. And when the quenes hienes was cumand throw the said port, the said cloude opynnit, and the barne discendit doun as it had bene ane angell, and deliverit to hir hienes the keyis of the toun, togidder with ane Bybill and ane Psalme-buik coverit with fyne purpourit velvet; and after the said barne had spoken some small speitches, he deliverit alsua to hir hienes thre

The Protestant clergy, and those of their political partisans who were also their followers in religion, had mixed the sentiment of the English Puritan with the Calvinism of the Huguenots, and disliked exhibitions and pastimes. On this occasion, however, there was something to propitiate them. There was the significant presentation of a Bible to the Popish queen; and the children resembling angels, who presented the propine, "made some speech concerning the putting away of the mess, and thereafter sang ane psalm."[1]

There were pageants or exhibitions of a less innocent character, which yet had in them a tendency that made them not entirely unwelcome to the Congregation. These were the ritualistic revels, called by the French the *fêtes des foux*. They are not to be confounded with the legitimate mysteries, which were attempts, however unseemly, to impress religious notions on the people by the acting of the critical events in Scripture history in such a manner as to seize the attention and attract the admiration of the uninstructed. The others had nothing in them professing to aim at the reverent or devout, but were acts of profane ribaldry, of which the point was the travestying, by some lewd and brutal antithesis, the most solemn ordinances of the Church. They were generally pinned to something or other in sacred history. Conspicuous among them was the Feast of Asses. Its chief

writtingis, the tennour thairof is uncertane. That being done, the barne ascendit in the cloud, and the said clud stekit."—Diurnal of Occurrents, 67.

[1] Ibid. See an account of the same pageant, Knox's History, ii. 287, 288. He says, "The verses of her own praise she heard, and smiled; but when the Bible was presented, and the praise thereof declared, she began to frown."

actor was the ass of Balaam, or one supposed to stand beside the manger, or that on which the Saviour rode. Whichever it might be, a donkey clad in grotesque canonicals was brought into the most sacred parts of the church, and there a brutal mob made sport with the beast to the full satiety of their lust of the profane. Another feast, more formidable if less disgusting, was dedicated to the Innocents, and brought the whole children of the neighbourhood to do their will among the vestments, ornaments, and shrines of the church. These things had been allowed to become an established formula of the decorous Church of Rome. How they arose, is a mystery which has defied solution. It has a literature of its own, and is worthy of far more zealous efforts to reach its causes and early history than any yet made.

If such observances were troublesome when the Church was powerful and revered, it is easy to believe what they would become when it was tottering to its fall. If there were rules by which the licensed ribaldry was restrained and measured out, the populace broke through them. They could thus, in following up old traditional usages of the Church, inflict the most stinging insults on the priesthood; and if the Church had thus provided a means of mortal injury in the house of its friends, its enemies were not naturally called on to interfere for its relief.

But the populace was impartial, and would have the revels condemned by the new Church as well as those that might offend the old. Queen Mary had arrived almost in time to find the city of Edinburgh tossed by a bloody tumult. The tradesmen of the city would have the old pageant of Robin Hood and Little John.

The Congregation would not abide it, and they had an Act of Parliament for its suppression, on their side. A riotous shoemaker was committed to the Tolbooth—the well-known Heart of Midlothian. He was so far implicated that death was to be his doom. We see the influence at work in this rigid act, when we are told that his friends besought John Knox to procure his release; but Knox of course was obdurate, and would "do nothing but have him hangit." His comrades collected. They seized and locked up the magistrates, and tore down the gibbet; next they battered in the door of the prison and released their comrade, while, with a goodfellowship common to such occasions, they permitted all the inmates of the prison to escape. There was no force sufficient to contend with them, and the magistrates were glad to make terms on the foundation of a general amnesty.[1]

To return to the young queen, set down amid all these contending elements, great and small. She had many difficulties to deal with, formidable among which was that she, a thorough member of the Church of Rome, had come among a people of whom the greater portion, including all the ruling men, had become Protestants. There was little toleration in that age, and it was a thing undreamed of in France, whence both parties took their principles. When at any time there was religious quietness there, and Protestants had rights as well as their opponents, it was in reality but a truce between enemies prepared soon to fly at each other's throats—each abstaining only because the other was too nearly his equal in strength to be easily prostrated.

[1] Diurnal of Occurrents, 65.

The contest broke out on the first Sunday after her arrival. It was known, of course, that she would hear private mass in her chapel; and whether on the grounds of Christian toleration, or of the promises made to her, it was useless to argue with men who, in the words of Knox, "began openly to speak, 'Shall that idol be suffered to take place again within this realm? It shall not;'" or with the Master of Lindsay and his followers from Fife, " The idolater priest shall die the death according to God's law." Some violence was done to a priest carrying a candle; and the chapel would have been burst open had not the Lord James defended the door—an act for which he was rebuked by Knox, who says in conclusion, "And so the godly departed with great grief of heart."

A proclamation was issued, denouncing, on the one hand, as penal, any attempt to interfere with the form of religion which the queen found publicly and universally standing at her arrival in the realm; and, on the other hand, requiring that her French followers should not be molested in the private exercise of their religion. Inspired by a bold thought, however, the queen resolved to go to the root of the evil, and endeavour to talk over the formidable head of the Church. In demanding an interview with Knox, there is little doubt that she anticipated a triumph from her never-failing blandishments; and she courted the ordeal of the discussion as one seeks an arena where triumph seems secure. She had seen little in France to prepare her for the rugged nature on which she was to play her wit and allurements. No other person was present in the same room but the Lord James. It has been said that the Reformer treated the queen on the occasion with gross insult. It is probable that he did not observe very closely the complicated etiquettes of the French Court; but neither would the Scottish nobles of the day, Protestant or Romish. Her grave brother would, doubtless, have protected her from absolute insult, had any been offered. Though there are many accounts of this renowned dialogue, the one given by Knox himself in his History is the source of all the others, and to that we must go back as the sole authority for the scene.[1] It is extremely picturesque and lifelike, and has the appearance of doing honest justice to the ready wit of the queen, as it certainly does to the relentless bigotry of the narrator. She first rallied him on his attacks upon feminine rule in the tract which had been his stumbling-block with Queen Elizabeth—the Blast of the Trumpet against the monstrous Regiment of Women. He seems to have felt that, with matters of difference behind it far more serious, he need not have a contest on this with the Popish queen; and it was easily, if not gracefully, got over. He did not deny his objection to feminine rule, but he did not intend specially to attack her title— "that book was written most especially against that wicked Jezebel of England," Mary Tudor. For his part in the particular instance before him, "if the realm finds no inconvenience from the regiment of a woman," that which his countrymen approve he shall not gainsay, but shall be as well content to live under her grace "as Paul was to live under Nero." He afterwards, however, gave a casual but significant inference to this strong comparison, by arguments which referred to Paul living quietly at Rome because he

[1] History, ii. 277 *et seq.*

was powerless and could not resist, while the Paul of Edinburgh was powerful, and had another line of duty before him. The queen turned the argument on resistance to princes. Her opponent asked, what would have been the fate of mankind had all adopted the religion of their princes—had Abraham worshipped with Pharaoh, and the apostles submitted to the religion of the Roman Emperors? "and so, madam, ye may perceive that subjects are not bound to the religion of their princes, albeit they are commanded to give them obedience." With a ready dialectic power of which the Reformer, hurried on by his zeal, seems to have been unconscious, the queen marked off the difference between passive resistance, in which each subject individually worships according to his own conscience without regarding the religion of the ruler, and that desire to coerce the ruler to his own views, of which she accused Knox. But the very words of this portion of the dialogue are necessary to express its import. The queen remarked that none of those he had referred to raised their sword against their princes.

" 'Yet, madam,' quoth he, 'ye cannot deny but that they resisted; for they that obey not the commandments that are given, in some sort resist.'

" 'But yet,' said she, 'they resisted not by the sword.'

" 'God,' said he, 'madam, had not given unto them the power and the means.'

" 'Think ye,' quoth she, 'that subjects having power may resist their princes?'

" 'If their princes exceed their bounds,' quoth he, 'and do against that wherefor they should be obeyed, it is no doubt but what they may be resisted even by power. For there is neither greater honour nor greater obedience to be given to kings or princes than God has commanded to be given unto father and mother. But so it is, madam, that the father may be stricken by a frenzy in the which he would slay his own children. Now, madam, if the children arise, join themselves together, apprehend the father, take the sword or other weapons from him, and finally bind his hands and keep him in prison till that his frenzy be overpast, think ye, madam, that the children do any wrong? Or think ye, madam, that God will be offended with them that have stayed their father to commit wickedness? It is even so,' said he, 'madam, with princes that would murder the children of God that are subject unto them. Their blind zeal is nothing but a very mad frenzy; and therefore to take the sword from them, to bind their hands, and to cast themselves in prison till that he be brought to a more sober mind, is no disobedience against princes, but just obedience, because that it agreeth with the will of God.'"

The narrator here tells us that "at these words the queen stood, as it were, amazed more than the quarter of an hour." Nor can this be wondered at, if she saw the full import of the exposition, as showing that her profession of Romanism was like the frenzy of the parent—a thing which entitled the children to seize and bind, in self-protection against the bloody consequences. She spoke of her conscience, but was told that conscience required knowledge, and it was to be feared that of the right knowledge she had none. But she had heard and read—so had the Jews who crucified Christ; they heard the law and the prophets, she the Pope and the cardinals. "'Ye interpret the Scriptures,' said she, 'in one manner, and they interpret in ane other—whom shall I believe, and who shall judge?'" The answer is ready. "'Ye shall believe,' said he, 'God that plainly speaketh in His Word;'" or, as a duller mind than hers would plainly see, she must obey Knox and the Congregation. Throughout the whole dialogue he does not yield the faintest shred of liberty of conscience, or leave it for one moment doubtful that the queen has any other course before her save submission.

And yet the interview seems in some measure to have warped the stern rigidity of his original purpose. He joined with those who were for giving her a trial, a backsliding of which he seems afterwards to have bitterly repented. It was plainly put, he says, that "she will be content to hear the preaching; and so, no doubt, but she may be won—and thus of all it was concluded to suffer her for a time." "So careful was I," he continues, "of that common tranquillity, and so loath was I to have offended those of whom I had conceived a good opinion, that in secret conference with earnest and zealous men I travailed rather to mitigate, yea, to sloken that fervency that God had kindled in others, than to animate or encourage them to put their hands to the Lord's work, whereintil I unfeignedly acknowledge myself to have done most wickedly."

This view of the state of the Reformer's mind at that juncture is singularly confirmed by a remarkable letter written by him to Calvin, which has been lately found. It is dated from Edinburgh on the 24th of October 1561. It is the more curious as a private pouring out of its writer's griefs, that Knox had offered his services to obtain the opinion of Calvin and the fathers of the Geneva Church on the course which the Protestants should pursue in Scotland, and was stayed by Lethington, who offered to take that function on himself—he was trimming at the time between the Court and the Congregation, and Knox charged him with making the offer as an expedient to gain time.[1] Whatever Lethington may have done, the researches of the French antiquaries have shown, by producing the very document, that Knox was not to be deterred from his purpose in consulting Calvin.[2] It is the letter of a man sad at heart, and sincerely penitent for not having, in the hour of trial, been strong enough to do the stern duty which his faith demanded of him, and now willing to atone. He tells the mournful news that the idolatrous mass had again been set up in purified Scotland. There were those of gravity and authority who had thought that they could not in conscience stand by and permit this thing to be done. It had been pleaded that the clergy of Geneva, and himself, Calvin, had expressed an opinion that they were not entitled to prohibit the queen from openly professing her own religion. He desires to know if this is true; he courteously acknowledges how troublesome he has been for advice, but there is no other bosom on which he can repose his cares. He had never before seen how formidable and difficult it was to contend with hypocrisy, disguised under the name of piety. Never, in the midst of his hardest struggle with open enemies, had he despaired of victory; but so wounded was he by this perfidious defection from

---

[1] Knox, ii. 292.
[2] See the letter, which is in Latin, with a facsimile, Teulet, ii. 12.

Christ—which its perpetrators chose to term indulgence—that strength was failing him for the labour before him.

It is probable that this letter never reached its destination. The answer it would have received can be easily anticipated. Even the faint remaining scruples entertained by Knox himself would have been at once dispersed by the conclusive logic of him who knew no doubts, and permitted no paltering between truth and error. We have here the beginning of a series of events in which it will be seen that, when it came to actual deeds, the Scottish nation shrank from enforcing the rules of faith and action which they received from the sanguinary Huguenots.[1]

Knox, before he wrote this letter, had in reality seen grounds for penitence in the alarming reaction towards Romanism. The Congregation had gradually lost a good deal of that absolute power which seemed to leave it as a question of discretion with them whether they would tolerate their sovereign's religion or not. The magistrates of Edinburgh had been in the practice, on their election, of issuing a proclamation against certain classes of criminals and profligates, calling them by names which, however appropriate, it is not now

---

[1] Dr M'Crie, criticising the observation of an anonymous French writer who compares Popery with Calvinism, says of the reception of Queen Mary: "I maintain that, in the state of men's spirits at that time, if a Huguenot queen had come to take possession of a Roman Catholic kingdom with the slender retinue with which Mary went to Scotland, the first thing they would have done would have been to arrest her; and if she had persevered in her religion, they would have procured her degradation by the Pope, thrown her into the Inquisition, and burnt her as a heretic. There is not an honest man who can deny this."—P. 177. Perhaps not, if the affair had taken place in France or Spain. But there is no reason to suppose that any Roman Catholic prince who fell under the power of the French Huguenots would have experienced a better fate.

deemed decorous needlessly to repeat. On this occasion they added to the list the "massmongers" and the "obstinate Papists, that corrupted the people;" "which, blown in the queen's ears," says Knox, "there began pride and maliciousness to show the self." Proceedings were taken against the magistrates, and the town council were constrained to appoint others in their stead, who issued a proclamation of a different tenor, "and so got the devil freedom again where that before he durst not have been seen in the daylight upon the common streets. Lord, deliver us from that bondage!" Such is the pious ejaculation with which the Reformer relieves his mind ere passing from this deplorable event.[1]

At a public banquet given by the city of Edinburgh to the queen and her Court, including her French followers, a mystery was performed, in which was enacted the destruction of Korah, Dathan, and Abiram, for burning strange fire on the altar. There was nothing palpable in this which might not tell against the one priesthood as well as the other, although it might be easy to know which was meant. But when the actors went on to parody the mass, and burn in effigy a priest in his canonicals, the Popish Earl of Huntly was permitted audaciously to suppress the performance. But there were other and more serious indications of the tendency of events, insomuch that "the devil, guiding his reins, ran forward in his course, and the queen took upon her greater boldness than she and Baal's bleating priests durst have attempted before."[2] A sort of crisis was brought on by the solemn celebration of Hallow mass. A meeting of the Congregation,

---

[1] Knox, ii. 289, 290, with Laing's notes.   [2] Ibid., 291.

lords and clergy, was held in the house of Macgill, the lord clerk register, where it was gravely discussed " whether that subjects might put to their hand to suppress the idolatry of their prince." The laymen present, with the Lord James and Lethington at their head, were for the most part favourable to the proposition " that the queen should have her religion free in her own chapel, to do, she and her household, what they list." The ministers seem to have unanimously voted against this proposition, maintaining that ere long " her liberty should be their thraldom." But the lay votes carried the proposition, so far as that meeting was concerned.

Another dispute among the Protestants, in which the clergy, nearly alone, held one side, carried the war into their own ground. They had adopted, besides the Confession of Faith, a Book of Discipline, being an outline of an organisation for the new Church. It is known as 'The First Book of Discipline.' They desired that it should have the sanction of the Crown and Parliament, and be made the law of the land.

The Protestant nobles and lairds were ready to accept all denunciations of Antichrist and Popish idolatry, nor did they hesitate at accepting the Calvinistic doctrines of the new faith just as Knox and his assistant ministers set them forth; they had, hence, at once adopted the Confession of Faith in Parliament. But the Book of Discipline affected practice as well as faith, and enforced certain stringent restraints to which it would have been inconvenient for some who were the readiest to subscribe propositions of theological metaphysics to submit. Several, it is true, had found it expedient to sign the document; but Lethington, with a sneer, asked how many even of these would be subject to the conditions of that book ; and he emphasised the taunt by saying, " Many subscribed these *in fide paren- tum*, as the bairns are baptised," meaning that the sub- scription was but the mere temporary conformity for obtaining an object, which men submit to when they ask for a ceremonial such as a baptism. Knox, whose ire was roused, reminded him that the book " was read in public audience ; and by the space of divers days the heads thereof was reasoned, as all that here sit know well enough, and ye yourself cannot deny." Another of the laymen expressed the general impatience among them, by telling him at once " to stand content—that book will not be obtained." " Let God," said Knox, finding farther discussion useless, " require the lack which this poor commonwealth shall have of the things therein contained, from the hands of such as stop the same." [1]

Elsewhere, in a general view of the dispute, he leaves this emphatic testimony to the conduct and motives of his lay comrades in the work of reformation, when dealing with the Book of Discipline : " Some approved it, and willed the same had been set forth by a law. Others, perceiving their carnal liberty and worldly com- modity somewhat to be impaired, thereby grudged, in- somuch that the name of the Book of Discipline became odious unto them. Everything that impugned to their corrupt affections was called in their mockage ' de- vout imaginations.' The cause we have declared—some were licentious; some had greedily gripped to the possessions of the Kirk ; and others thought that they would not lack their part of Christ's coat, yea, and

[1] Knox, ii. 298.

that before that ever He was hanged, as by the preachers they were oft rebuked. The chief great man that had professed Christ Jesus, and refused to subscribe the Book of Discipline, was the Lord Erskine; and no wonder, for besides that he has a very Jezebel to his wife, if the poor, the schools, and the ministry of the Kirk had their awn, his reckin would lose two parts and more of that which he unjustly now possesses. Assuredly some of us have wondered how men that professes godliness, should of so long continuance hear the threatenings of God against thieves and against their houses, and knowing themselves guilty in such things as were openly rebuked, and that they never had remorse of conscience, neither yet intended to restore anything of that which long they had stolen and reft. There was none within the realm more unmerciful to the poor ministers than were they which had greatest rents of the churches."[1]

The inspiring cause of this wrath was a matter, partly involved in the question of the Book of Discipline, which also came in a separate shape. It was an affair of the keenest temporal interest to both sections of the Congregation—the lay and the spiritual; an interest not common, but antagonistic. It was the weighty question of the temporalities on which the Reformed Church was to be supported. The Protestant clergy had no fixed source of income, though the Book of Discipline dealt with them as persons entitled to and obtaining a comfortable provision. There is, indeed, a savour of practical sense and worldly wisdom in this portion of the original standards of the Presbyterian Church, which says much for the discernment and

[1] Knox, ii. 128, 129.

ability of its founders in matters of secular importance. After setting forth the appointments and supplies proper to a minister's house, in which are included "forty bolls meal and twenty-six bolls malt, to find his home-bread and drink," there is provision for the education and up-setting of his sons, and for his daughters being "virtuously brought up and honestly doted when they came to maturity of years." These requirements, the framers of the document protest, are not so much for their own sakes as for the increase of virtue and learning, and the profit of the posterity to come; for "it is not to be supposed that any man will dedicate himself and children so to God, and to serve His Kirk, that they look for no warldly commodity. But this cankered nature whilk we bear is provoked to follow virtue when it seeth honour and profit annexed to the same; as contrarily, then, is virtue of many despised when virtuous and godly men live without honour. And sorry would we be that poverty should discourage men from study, and from following the way of virtue, by whilk they might edify the Kirk and flock of Christ Jesus."[1]

The Assembly passed some acts or orders professing to exercise authority over the tithes and other endowments of the Church, and charitably resolved "that all such as have been in the ministry of the Pope's Kirk, good and well-conditioned persons, that they shall live upon the alms of the Kirk with the number of the poor." As yet, however, they had not touched the temporalities. These yet remained with those Popish beneficiaries whose ecclesiastical functions were

[1] Buke of Discipline. The Fifth Head, concerning the provision for the ministers, and for the distribution of the rents and possessions justly appertaining to the Kirk.

abolished by law; but, in a great measure, the property was theirs only nominally. Many of the ecclesiastical corporations, hopeless apparently of ultimate victory in the struggle, disposed of the property committed to them in long leases, mortgages, or absolute conveyances, under conditions which would not easily bear inspection in reference to the fairness of the transactions and the disinterestedness of the parties to them. The lords and lairds who obtained legal claims over ecclesiastical property by such arrangements were likely to hold their own with a much firmer gripe than the tottering ecclesiastical foundations, and that was the reason why it was deemed politic to make arrangements with them. For a few years both before and after the eventful epoch of 1560, there was a continued process of absorbing ecclesiastical within temporal domains, or a continuous "birsing yont," as it has been expressively called, by the lay landholders.

The transference was not effected without some pressure on the hopes and fears of the ecclesiastics who had the power to make the desired arrangements, and even some violence to their persons. Of how this might come to pass, the method pursued by Gilbert, Earl of Cassilis, called in his own neighbourhood the "King of Carrick," may be taken as an expressive example. We are told by the family historian that this Gilbert "was ane particular man, and ane very greedy man, and cared not how he gat land, so that he could come by the same." He had his eye on a few of the estates of the Abbey of Glenluce, and had dealings with the abbot about them. That abbot, however, died before the writs were signed, "and then he dealt with ane monk of the same abbaey, wha could counterfeit the abbot's hand-writ and all the haill convent's, and gart him counterfeit their subscriptions." When this was done, fearing that the monk might make unpleasant revelations, he got a certain carl to "stick" or stab him, and then he got one to accuse the carl of theft, "and hang him in Crosragall, and so the lands of Glenluce were conquest."[1]

The next step was the "conqueshing" of the estates of the Abbey of Crossraguel, of which the extensive ruins may yet be seen. The domestic buildings of the fraternity have not here been so completely destroyed as in other places, probably because the "King of Carrick" preserved them for his own use. It was his desire that certain writs should be executed in his favour— to wit, "a five-year tack and a nineteen-year tack, and a charter of feu of all the lands of Crossraguel." The commendator of the abbey was unwilling to sign the writs, and shy of approach. He was waylaid, however, and brought face to face with the "king," who introduced him to a chamber where there was a roaring fire, prepared, as the host said savagely facetious, for roasting meat. The commendator saw his fate at a glance, but held out until he was stripped or "skinned," as the narrator says, basted with grease, and scorched until his hand barely retained power to sign the deeds. The Privy Council so far took notice of this affair as to require Cassilis to find security, to the extent of £2000, not to molest the person or the property of the commendator.[2] Men who had done such things to

[1] History of the Kennedies, Bannatyne's Journal, 55. In Scotland, the landed property which any one has acquired by purchase is still expressly called "conquest," to distinguish it from that which he may have inherited.
[2] Douglas's Peerage, i. 332.

acquire lands were not likely to part with them without knowing why.

The Protestant clergy, sagacious as they were about many things, seem to have made the mistake of supposing that the active energy with which their lay brethren helped them to pull down Popery was actually the fruit of religious zeal, and to have expected that they took from the one Church merely to give to the other. The landholders, on their part, thought such an expectation so utterly preposterous, that they did not condescend to reason with it; but, without any hypocritical attempt to varnish their base selfishness, called the expectations of the ministers "a fond imagination."

There were, thus, three classes of claimants on the property of the Church—the old clergy, the laymen who had obtained rights from them, and the ministers of the Reformation. The Privy Council resolved to deal with this matter by a process which had the merit of simplicity. They were to appropriate to the crown the fourth, and, if necessary, the third of the ecclesiastical benefices for new uses; it was found necessary to take the third, and the transaction is known in law and history as "the assumption of thirds of benefices." It was carried out by a series of Acts of Council, very secular in their tenor, and seeming as if they avoided the nomenclature of the Catholic hierarchy on the one hand, and of Presbyterian perfection and supremacy on the other.[1] The purposes to which these thirds were to be applied are thus set forth: "Sae muckle thereof to be employed to the queen's majesty, for entertaining and setting forward of the common affairs

---

[1] The most accurately printed copies of these Acts of the Council are in Mr Laing's edition of Knox.

of the country; and sae muckle thereof unto the ministers, and sustentation of the ministry, as may reasonably sustain the same, at the sight and discretion of the queen's majesty foresaid; and the excrescence and surplus to be assigned unto the old possessors." One department of ecclesiastical property was to be specially dealt with. The revenues drawn within towns by monastic establishments, whether in the shape of rents of property or in the more invidious form of local taxes or privileges, were specially designed for the entertaining of "schools and colleges," and other like uses; and it was at the same time recommended that, as "nothing is more commodious" for such uses than the friaries and other edifices which had belonged to the monastic bodies, such of them as had not been demolished should be kept up for these uses.

When there was delay in giving in the valuations of the Estates, stewards were sent down by the Council to estimate the "rentals." As these officers would be apt to affix a higher value to the estates than those in possession, the alternative had the effect of stimulating the preparation of the returns in the proper quarter. As a sort of sanction against the under-estimating of the rentals, the tenants on the ecclesiastical estates were authorised to hold the rents returned as the maximum which they were bound to pay; for instance, if a farm were returned by the holder or owner as of so much "rental" or annual value, the tenant farming it was acquitted if he paid that amount of rent.

For all the precautions taken, however, it seems clear that the returns were imperfect and to a great extent false. Of the three parties interested, the ecclesiastics, unless Archbishop Hamilton be an ex-

ception, do not seem to have complained. Such a
remnant of their possessions was a boon which in
recent years had been beyond their expectation; and
if something was taken from them, what remained
was secured, so far as anything could be in that age,
by an adjustment which professed to be final. The
two-thirds of the fund unappropriated were supposed
to remain in the hands of the ecclesiastics of the old
Church, on the principle of each retaining a vested
life-interest in the greater part of his old income. As
these died out, the benefices seem to have fallen to
the Crown for miscellaneous disposal. But there is
no doubt that a very large portion of these revenues
had already, in the manner referred to, got into
lay hands. It might have been expected that these
lay holders, who had come recently into possession,
and held in many instances by questionable tenures,
should have readily acquiesced in an arrangement
which secured to many of them a lion's share in the
two-thirds. But in the general case they seem to
have thought the chance of keeping what they could
with the strong hand a preferable alternative, and
there was on all hands much growling at the dis-
gorgement they were called on to make.

It was to the ministers, however, who were to be
sustained out of the thirds, that the arrangement was
least pleasing, since they had settled in their own
minds that the sudden overturn of the Romish Church
was virtually a transference of its wealth to their own
body. They protested vehemently from their pulpits,
Knox giving them the key-note, and saying, "Well, if
the end of this ordour, pretended to be taken for the
sustentation of the ministers, be happy, my judgment

faileth me; for I am assured the Spirit of God is not the author of it; for first I see twa parts freely given to the devil, and the third maun be divided betwixt God and the devil. Weel, bear witness to me that this day I say it. Ere it be long the devil shall have three parts of the third, and judge ye then what God's portion shall be." A commission collected the money, and adjusted the claims on it. To pay the ministers' stipends was the special function of the Laird of Pittarrow, "an earnest professor of Christ," whose conduct in the business was, however, such as to call forth the suggestive analogy, "Who would have thought that when Joseph ruled Egypt, that his brethren should have travailed for victuals and have returned with empty sacks unto their families?"[1]

The allowance made to the ministers varied from one hundred to three hundred merks a-year. The amount gave rise to a curious comparison, which shows how extremely poor many of the Scottish aristocracy then were, and how considerable were the merely worldly aspirations of the Protestant clergy. It was said that there were many lords who had not so much to spend. Whereon it is remarked in Knox's History, where the justness of the comparison seems to be admitted, "Men did reason that the vocation of ministers craved of them books, quietness, study, and travail, to edify the Kirk of Jesus Christ; and therefore that the stipends of ministers, who had none other industry but to live upon that which was appointed, ought not to be modified according to the livings of common men, who might and did daily augment their rents by some common industry."[2] So enormously rich

[1] Knox, ii. 310.   [2] Ibid., 312.

had the Romish hierarchy become, that a mere fragment of their wealth—much less than a third—was sufficient to endow a ministry on terms bearing comparison with the incomes of the aristocracy.

There were several political causes urging the queen's Government to moderation; and in the person of her brother, the Lord James, who took the helm as if it naturally belonged to him, she had a pilot willing to take this course, and able to keep it with a strong hand. Elizabeth sent her ambassador Throckmorton ostensibly to see to the fulfilment of the treaty of Edinburgh, but at the same time to keep his eye on many other things. The question of Mary's right to succeed Elizabeth in the English throne was opened, and though it was not conceded, neither was it denied. The negotiations on this point went so far that, when a meeting of the two queens in the north of England was proposed, Elizabeth consented to it, though whether she ever intended to be present at it no one can tell—it was never held. The Guises, with a considerable French following, still remained in Scotland; and they thought it wise, while this great question of the English succession stood in doubt, to help rather than interrupt the moderate councils of the Lord James. This able man was gradually strengthening his hands. In 1562 he married the daughter of the powerful Earl Marishal. The wedding was followed by a grand banquet, destined by its magnificence to provoke the cynical reproaches of Knox, who was ever doomed to find the world regaining possession of those whom he fondly believed that he had snatched from its influences. On this occasion Mary performed one of those graceful and effective courtesies for which she possessed a gift. She drank to the health of Queen Elizabeth in a heavy golden cup, which she presented to Randolph the ambassador.[1] The Lord James was at the same time created Earl of Mar—a title presently merged in the earldom of Murray, by which he is better known to the world.

He was immediately afterwards engaged in one of the many expeditions against the thieving borderers. Of this expedition, which must have been full of interest, we have nothing but the results—fifty-three of the most noted outlaws apprehended, of whom eighteen were drowned "for lack of trees and halters," and six were hanged in Edinburgh.[2] There is no trace of these punishments to be found in the criminal records. By a sort of tacit understanding, border thieves, like Highlanders, were not deemed within the pale of the law; and the slaughter of them was a matter of interest solely as to its amount, as marking, like the head of game brought down in a day's sport, a successful or an unsuccessful raid. There are, however, several prosecutions for "abiding from the raid of Jedburgh," as it was called—that is to say, for not complying with the royal proclamation to join the expedition—a defalcation which, in the instance of any border chief, was naturally deemed suspicious. From these trials it appears that the raid lasted for twenty days, beginning on the 13th of November 1562.[3]

[1] P. F. Tytler, vi. 258.   [2] Ibid., 259.
[3] The excuse pleaded for absence was generally extreme ill-health. Ramsay of Dalhousie, for instance, protested that he was "vexed with sic distress in his person that he might not ony ways travel, nother on horse nor foot, to na space, by reason his haill left side was so occupied and troubled with evil and malign humours, sic as he can nought declare nor specify—that his haill arms, fingers, and leg on that side, wherethrough that he might not move the same."—Pitcairn, i. 422.

CHAPTER XLII.

Queen Mary.

(Continued.)

DANGERS IN THE NORTH—POSITION OF HUNTLY AS LEADER OF THE ROMANIST PARTY—MURRAY'S DESIGNS—A ROYAL PROGRESS—HUNTLY'S FEARS FROM IT—HE ARMS—BATTLE OF CORRICHIE—RUIN OF THE HOUSE OF HUNTLY—QUEEN MARY'S POLICY IN ASSISTING IN THE RUIN OF HER FRIENDS—POSITION OF MARY'S GOVERNMENT—ASPECT OF FIRMNESS AND MODERATION—HER HOME-LIFE AND AMUSEMENTS—HER POPULARITY—FURTHER DIALOGUES WITH KNOX—QUESTION AS TO WHAT LANGUAGE THEY WERE HELD IN?—PROSECUTIONS OF ROMANIST PRIESTS—ARCHBISHOP HAMILTON—THE QUEEN'S DEVOTEDNESS TO HER CHURCH—HER FOREIGN COMMUNICATIONS—ASSASSINATION OF HER UNCLE—PARLIAMENT—TENDENCY TO A REACTION AGAINST THE PROTESTANT PARTY—FURTHER ALTERCATIONS BETWEEN THE QUEEN AND KNOX—RIOTOUS ATTACK ON OFFICIATING PRIESTS—THE RIOTERS BROUGHT TO TASK—FEELING AMONG THE PROTESTANT CLERGY.

WE next follow Murray to a contest in the opposite end of the country, the cause and character of which can only be seen by going back a little way into the past. We have found that the policy of the Crown in dealing with the old half-independent districts, inhabited chiefly by people of Celtic race, was to root out the power of their original local chiefs, and to encourage the predominance over them of some neighbouring family of rank and power. Thus, in the west, the house of Argyle governed; in the north, that of Huntly. Even in such hands, however, the spirit of the old troublesome Maarmorate had a tendency to develop an independent principality. The family of Huntly possessed estates on the east coast, estates cultivated by the most industrious among the Lowland tenantry. From these they drew a goodly revenue. This enabled them to keep high court, and strengthen their rule over the vast Highland territory to the north and west; for over all the district now beyond the Caledonian Canal and the lakes it unites, the "Cock of the North" was supreme in one shape or other. He kept princely state in his Castle of Strathbogie; and events afterwards revealed that its sumptuous furnishings shamed those of the royal palace. He had the flourishing town of Aberdeen, with its university and cathedral, by way of capital. Here he seems to have had a small fleet, with which he kept up foreign communications, as little under restriction from the Court of Holyrood as those of the King of Norway or Denmark might be. The Earl of Huntly of that day was an accomplished man and a politician. He frequented the Court of France, where he received the decoration of St Michael, and would be honoured much as the sovereign of any secondary German or French state. What he might be doing in strengthening himself by alliances, or surrounding himself by troops, was not easily to be discovered by those outside of his own dominions. The Government in Edinburgh could but guess at them, as our rulers in India might at the doings of some native prince who professes to hold by British protection in a distant in-

accessible territory. He had been playing some deep
game with the Lords of the Congregation. It seemed
to them at one time that they had him, having bought
him with a price—a large share in the ecclesiastical
estates so profusely distributed. But there is little
doubt that he determined to stand forth as leader in a
great contest for the old faith, and had made arrangements accordingly, treating with the Guises, and organ-
ising the people under his own banner. Murray, when
his followers jostled those of Huntly's ambassador in
the village of Vitry, must have come to the knowledge
that Huntly had deep projects. Whether or not he
knew exactly that an army of twenty thousand men
had been offered to the queen, he knew enough to tell
him that he must crush Huntly ere the power he yet
held as head of the Congregation slipped from his grasp.
Murray had further and personal motives for trying
his strength with Huntly. The estates belonging to
his own new earldom were in Huntly's hands, whether
under any regular title or by mere occupancy, and
would not be got for him who owned them under a
crown charter, except by force.

It was determined that the queen and Murray should
make a royal progress northwards, and visit Huntly.
Ostensibly the Court was to do him honour; but he
had his own reasons for suspecting that something of
another kind was in view. Matters at Strathbogie
Castle were not in a condition to be inspected by eyes
like Murray's. Incidentally we know that the vestments and treasures of the Cathedral of Aberdeen—
the monuments of idolatry, as they would be called
—were deposited in Huntly's stronghold, that they
might be restored to the Church in its day of tri-

umph.[1] These things might be hidden out of sight, to be sure; but it would be impossible to obliterate all testimony that here were the headquarters of the enemy.

An incident that seemed in itself of little moment connects itself with this affair. A quarrel which Huntly's son, Sir John Gordon, had with Ogilvy of Findlater broke into a bloody conflict on the streets of Edinburgh. Gordon was seized, and put in prison; but the Scottish prisons were ever notorious for their unretentiveness of prisoners of his rank. This Sir John, who was not the heir of Huntly, but only his fourth son, was among the countless lovers with whom Queen Mary's name is mixed up. The historian of the earldom of Sutherland says he was "a comely young gentleman, very personable, and of good expectation, whom she loved entirely."[2]

Soon after this affair, the queen with her brother took their royal progress northwards. They started in August 1562. To have gone without a sufficient force, would have been a folly of which Murray was not likely to be guilty; and Huntly felt by no means satisfied with the form in which his sovereign approached him. Wisely keeping at a distance himself, he sent his wife, as a sort of ambassador and spy, to meet the queen at Aberdeen, and try to discover whether she came in peace or war. She was courteously invited to the earl's fortress-palace at Strathbogie. She declined, however, to countenance the house of Huntly while one of its members was a fugitive from justice, and demanded that Sir John Gordon should "enter himself

[1] See Inventories of Queen Mary's Jewels, pref. xxv. p. 53.
[2] Gordon's History of the Earldom of Sutherland, 140.

in ward" again—that is, go back to prison. It appears that he went so far southward with the intention of doing so, but changed his mind. The royal party ran some risk. Murray, had he fallen into the hands of the Gordons, would not have been spared; and they would have had little hesitation in keeping the queen herself in pledge for their lives and fortunes. It appears that when sojourning in the stronghold of the Leslies of Balquhain, of which a battered tower still remains, about twenty miles from Aberdeen, the queen and Murray both made a narrow escape from seizure. They passed on to Inverness, where, desiring admission to the castle, it was closed against them. A siege was begun. In this conflict with royalty, some of the clans which had submitted hitherto to the iron rule of Huntly found that they had an opportunity of deserting with the merit of loyalty. The Clan Chattan remembered how their chief had, a few years before, been beheaded before the gate of Strathbogie Castle; and, with the Frasers and Monros, they abandoned the banner of Huntly. The castle was taken, and the governor hanged. When the queen and Murray retired to Aberdeen, Huntly, who seemed to think that his best chance of avoiding ruin was in war rather than submission, followed them, designing some bold stroke. There was a fight — sometimes called a battle—on the declivity of Corrichie, a long flat hill from fifteen to eighteen miles west of Aberdeen. Huntly's force, which had dwindled down, was easily defeated. The earl was found dead on the field—smothered, as it was said, in his armour. His body was brought to Edinburgh, that doom of forfeiture might be pronounced on it; and there i extant the record of certain payments to an adept for treating it with vinegar, aqua vitæ, powders, odours, and other necessaries, to prevent it from putrifying.[1] Sir John Gordon was convicted of treason, and beheaded at Aberdeen, where the queen attended his public execution.

The power of the house of Huntly was thus broken, and the event, though in the ordinary phraseology of history it was but the suppression of a rebellion and the punishment of its leaders, was an important national revolution. The breaking and dispersal of so great a fabric of power by a single day's events afforded to the Reformed clergy a great occasion for addressing their hearers on the vanity and uncertainty of human greatness, and the punishment which in due time visits those who lift themselves up against eternal power. One of them—no doubt it was Knox himself—in pointing, for the benefit of Mary's courtiers, the moral of the event, affords a curious personal sketch of the public deportment of the great earl: " Unto you do I say, that that same God who from the beginning has punished the contempt of His word, and has poured forth His vengeance upon such proud mockers, shall not spare you, yea, He shall not spare you before the eyes of this same wicked generation, for the pleasure whereof ye despise all wholesome admonitions. Have ye not seen ane greater than any of you sit picking his nails, and pull down his bonnet over his eyes, when idolatry, witchcraft, murder, oppression, and such vices were rebuked? Was not his common talk, ' When the knaves have railed their fill, then they will hold their peace' ? Have ye not heard it affirmed

[1] Laing's Knox, ii. 359 note.

in his own face, that God should revenge that his blasphemy even in the eyes of such as were witness to his iniquity? There was the Earl Huntly accused by you as the maintainer of idolatry, and only hinderer of all good order. Him has God punished even according to the threatenings that his and your ears heard, and by your hands hath God executed His judgments. But what amendment in any case can be espied in you? Idolatry was never in greater zest—virtue and virtuous men were never in more contempt—vice was never more bold, and less feared punishment. And yet who guides the queen and Court? Who but the Protestants? O horrible slanderers of God and of His holy evangel! better it were unto you plainly to renounce Jesus Christ, than thus to expose His blessed evangel to mockage."[1]

That the queen should have dealt so hardly with the champion of that faith to which she was ever devoted, and of which we shall find that she was working for the restoration, has been felt as one of the mysteries of history. She not only did what had to be done, but seemed to do it with heart and will. It was in riding to the field of Corrichie that she was reputed to have said that she wished to be a man, to ride forth in jack and knapscull. But for the solution of such a mystery, familiarity with the tenor of Scottish, or even of English history, does not prepare us. In these we find many deeds of passion, and cruelty, and rapine—some pieces of perfidy too, such as the kidnapping projects of Henry VIII., or his daughter's barefaced mendacity. But all was something utterly different from the profound dissimulation of that political school of which Catherine of Medici was

[1] Knox, ii. 362.

the chief instructor, and her daughter-in-law an apt scholar. Covered over as the underworkings of wickedness were by a fair outside of art, literature, courtesy, gentleness, and loving-kindness, it was likened by the oft-used parallel of a fair country, with its meadows, gardens, and peaceful homes, covering volcanic fires that might any day break through it. To feel the spirit in which this young queen could assist in the ruin of her friend, we must realise the halls of the Louvre, with their splendid tapestries and statues, their perfumes and pet poodles, filled with an assemblage of gallant courtiers and gay ladies, full of wit and pleasantry and courtly kindness, while Henry of Navarre, the gayest of all, his pleasant face beaming with jollity and careless good-humour, has yet all his faculties at their utmost tension to detect the first premonitions of murder; or we must enter the chamber of the wounded Coligny, and find that vain headstrong youth who had tried to murder him, and was preparing to try again, pouring meek condolence into the ear of the wounded man, and seducing him to the belief that his king held him in love and honour.

The queen was in the hands of the Protestant party, and it was her policy to abide by them, and appear to do so with a willing heart; it was her duty, and she endured it, trusting that the day of retribution would come. If we believe one of her faithful friends, this policy was sketched out for her before she left France, by those statesmen who knew by experience what Scotland was: " Monsieur de Martigues, Monsieur d'Oysel, Monsieur la Brois, the Bishop of Amiens, Monsieur Roubay, and sich other Frenchmen as were lately carried out of Scotland within the English ships, resorted unto the queen, and declared unto her the haill progress and success of their pretences. And as well they as the rest of her friends advised her to return in Scotland, and encouraged her with the hope to succeed unto the crown of England, rather than to abide the queen-mother's disdain in France ; and for her best, willed her to serve the time, and till commode herself discreetly and gently with her own subjects, and to be most familiar with my Lord James, Prior of St Andrews, her natural brother, and with the Earl of Argyle, wha had married Lady Jane Stewart, her natural sister, and to use the Secretary Lethington and the Laird of Grange most tenderly in all her affairs, and in effect to repose most upon them of the Reformed religion."[1]

It would be difficult to find in history a closer resemblance than the early government of Mary bore to a strong and deep-rooted moderate policy, holding in check the factious extremes of either side. The country had become Protestant, and the members of the Government were Protestants; yet they desired to protect the queen herself in the exercise of her religion, and broke with the extreme clerical party, which owned Knox as its head. But the elements of the political condition of the country, even without reference to subsequent events, are sufficient to show that the short peace was but an armed truce, in which each party was prepared to fly at its opponent's throat. It was the reproach of both, though pleaded by each in extenuation of its deeds, that the one could not permit the other to live without danger to its own existence.

Protestantism, nominally supreme, asserted its dignity in judicial proceedings against some adherents of the

[1] Sir James Melville's Memoirs, 88.

old religion. On the 17th of March 1562, Sir James Arthur, a priest, was prosecuted for solemnising baptisms and marriages "in the old abominable Papist manner." He came to the queen's will—that is to say, submitted to her mercy, and probably went unpunished.[1]

In spite of the lowering of the political atmosphere, and some actual storms, the first two years of Mary's reign were passed by her in a gaiety and geniality sadly in contrast with the gloomy remainder of her days. She possessed a strong elasticity of spirit, and, after the first shock was over, set herself to draw as much enjoyment as could be extracted from the humbler resources now at her disposal. It was no longer as in France, where a court party, roving on some sudden impulse to the distant bank of a stream, or the centre of a wood, found there all the luxuries of the palace laid at their feet by an expert and costly commissariat. Yet she was not to be imprisoned in a palace, and forfeit all the enjoyments of a free foot. The English ambassador Randolph, in his minute reports, details some little scenes of innocent gaiety, which it would be refreshing to meet with among the partly arid and partly appalling events he has to record, if the reader could feel any assurance that they were the outward symbol of an innocent and guileless heart. She went, for instance, with a few attendants to the house of a burgess in St Andrews. There Randolph followed her, and waited for three days in devouring impatience for an audience. When he could hold out no longer, and pressed through the light fence

[1] Pitcairn, i. 420*. It is curious that the record of his trial bears, that an extract of it was sent to the regent in 1569, as if he might then make some use of it.

which royal raillery had set between them, she said, "I see now well that you are weary of this company and treatment. I wish for you to be merry, and to see how like a burgess's wife I live with my little troop; and you will interrupt the pastimes with your great and grave matters. I pray you, sir, if you be weary here, return home to Edinburgh, and keep your gravity and great ambassade until the queen come thither; for, I assure you, you shall not see her here— nor I know not myself where she is become."[1]

Knox admitted that "in presence of her Council she kept herself very grave," but that the scene was changed when business and ceremony were over; and "how soon soever the French fillocks, fiddlers, and others of that band gat the house alone, then might be seen skipping not very comely for honest women." In weighing the full merit of these old denunciations of the innocent amusement of dancing, it must be remembered that in that age the dance had often a meaning beyond the mere graceful cadenced exercise. The forms of the dance were often symbolical of interesting situations; and of how far these were delicate or decorous, we may judge by the books, such as those of Brantome and Margaret of Navarre, which were the favourite literature of the dancers. Knox lifts his testimony against the dance "called the purpose," which the queen trod with Chatelar, and it is easy to believe it to have been sufficiently indecorous. In fact, the Puritans from that day having taken a loathing towards dancing such as they saw it, shut their eyes to it for the coming ages; and thus, to the amazement and ridicule of later times, blindly continued their old railing against it long after

[1] Raumer, Contributions, 26.

it had been purified of its indecorums. The wrath of Knox on this particular was raised to its climax by a suspicion that the queen made her dancing an active expression of her heterodoxy and malignancy; "and among others, he was assured that the queen had danced excessively till after midnight, because that she had received letters that persecution was begun in France, and that her uncles were beginning to stir their tail, and to trouble the whole realm of France." On this text he preached a stirring sermon, which brought about one of his renowned interviews with the queen. After having given her his mind with his usual freedom and emphasis about her uncles, he concluded by explaining to her that he was a public functionary doing his public duty, from which he was not to be drawn to waste his valuable time in dialogues with individual persons, unless in cases of urgency. "If your grace," he said, "please to frequent the public sermons, then doubt I not but ye shall fully understand both what I like and mislike, as well in your majesty as all others." He had no objection to her solemnly setting apart an occasion for his publicly expounding in her presence "the form and substance of doctrine which is proposed in public to the subjects of this realm"—a suggestion towards which the queen kept silence, probably not without a shudder. "But to wait," he continued, "upon your chalmer door or elsewhere, and then to have no farther liberty but to whisper my mind in your grace's ear, or to tell to you what others think and speak of you —neither will my conscience nor the vocation to which God hath called me suffer it." He was pleased to depart from this interview with "a reasonable merry countenance;" and when he heard it remarked of bystanders that he was not afraid, he made the genial remark often quoted, "Why should the pleasing face of a gentlewoman affray me? I have looked on the faces of many angry men, and yet have not been affrayed above measure."

A question will naturally arise, Were these dialogues held in the language in which Knox reports them? Singularly enough, among the many personal details about Queen Mary, none informs us distinctly of the extent to which she could understand or use the language of her people. It is not likely that she could speak it fluently on her arrival in Scotland, but we hear nothing of progress made in acquiring it; and in the various dialogues in which her sayings are reported —even in these sharp trials of wit and language with Knox—no instance occurs to us in which she appears, or is said to have been, at a loss for a proper expression. When Knox reports the sayings of her mother, they are generally in an imperfect or broken Scots vernacular, as the instances cited in previous chapters have shown. It is clear that her daughter was, while in Scotland, extremely chary of writing in any other language but the French. Running the eye over Labanoff's collection, it will be noticed that a letter taken from an autograph is invariably French. It must be inferred from this that the letters in the vernacular are not only in the handwriting, but in a great measure the composition of a secretary. Sometimes to such a letter there is a postscript, autograph and in French. The only specimen preserved in her autograph in the vernacular seems to be a postscript of a letter to the Earl of Argyle, of 31st March 1566, in these terms : " Wat ever bis sayed, bi sur off my gud mynd, and that ye sal persayve, command my to our bruder."[1] It must be inferred from this that her habitual language was French; and if we are to take from her the merit of disputing with Knox in the language which he learned when a boy in East Lothian, we must concede to him the accomplishment of speaking French so well that he did not fear an encounter in that language with a very clever woman, mistress of every art for enhancing her native qualities which the highest courtly training in the world could bestow. But, indeed, Knox had his own training to the task, for he had lived and preached in France.

The prosecution of a considerable body of recusants in 1563 was preceded by some discussions of a highly suggestive kind. Of course, in a country so little under control, the old religion was privately observed wherever the predominant feudal power of the district gave it any countenance. In the north, though the power of Huntly was broken, there cannot be a doubt that the bulk of the people, in as far as they were Christians, were Romanists; but they were too remote from the eye of justice to be prosecuted, or even watched. In the western districts south of the Clyde the territorial influence was so far divided that in some places the Romanists were enabled to resume their worship and observances, but not without risk from the vengeance of their Protestant neighbours. These were sternly urged by the clergy to put in force those laws against Popery which the Government were neglecting. The brethren "determined to put to their own hands," and "that they should neither complain to queen nor Council, but should execute the punishment that God has appointed to idolaters in His

[1] Labanoff, i. 340.

law, by such means as they might, wherever they should be apprehended."¹ The work was begun, and some seizures had been made, when the queen, who was at Lochleven, desired to have a conference with Knox. He went, and the dialogue is given with the usual emphasis in his History. The question why the royal prerogative was usurped by subjects was at once met by conclusive reasons and apt cases in point. "The sword of justice, madam, is God's, and is given to princes and rulers for one end, which if they transgress, sparing the wicked and oppressing innocents, they that, in the fear of God, execute judgments when God has commanded, offend not God. Although kings do it not, neither yet sin they that bridle kings to strike innocent men in their rage. The examples are evident; for Samuel feared not to slay Agag, the fat and delicate King of Amalek, whom King Saul had saved; neither spared Elijah Jezebel's false prophets and Baal's priests, albeit that King Ahab was present; Phinehas was no magistrate, and yet feared he not to strike Cozbi and Zimri,"—supplying, in the plainest words, the statement of their guilty conduct, which the terms of Scripture leave to be inferred.² The queen, of course, was not prepared to admit the soundness of the principles so explained and exemplified; and "she, being somewhat offended, passed to her supper." Knox, sullen and resentful, determined to return next morning to Edinburgh; but before the early May sunrise, messengers from the queen desired him to stay. They had an interview, in which, judging from the only account of it—that of her antagonist—the queen showed consummate tact. She was "at the hawk-

¹ Knox, ii. 371.   ¹ See Numbers, chap. xxv.

ing," so she chose her own battle-field, suited to
her light weapons and restless strategy. The traces
of last night's anger were totally obliterated — all
was sunshine, gaiety, and good-humour. The talk
skipped lightly from topic to topic at the queen's
guidance, until she could get it settled down on
some topic on which her formidable companion could
be kept interested. There was the offering of a ring
to her by Lord Ruthven—he was one of her Council;
but she could not love him, for she knew him to use
enchantment. This failed to excite much interest.
She next referred to Knox's own movements. He
was going to Dumfries to act in the appointment of
a superintendent of the Church there? "Yes, those
quarters have great need, and some of the gentlemen
so require." She then brings up the claims of the
favoured candidate, Alexander Gordon, titular Archbishop of Athens, a son of the Master of Huntly, who
held high preferment in the hierarchy, and having
turned Protestant, desired to serve the new Church,
and keep the emoluments he had from the old. She
warned Knox against him, saying, "Do as ye will, but
that man is a dangerous man;" and, oddly enough,
Knox shows in his narrative that he afterwards found
this to have been a sound warning. Still the queen,
passing lightly from topic to topic, had found nothing
to interest and enchain her formidable gossip; but she
hit on it at last, by soliciting his services in restoring
the heads of a great family to the observance of
domestic duties and moralities. The Earl of Argyle
had been married in 1554 to the Lady Jane Stewart.
The queen, telling Knox that she must have his help
in one of the gravest matters that had touched her

since she came to the kingdom, threw herself with amiable simplicity on his friendly and confidential assistance, explaining that this sister of hers had not been so circumspect in all things as should be desired; "and yet," said she, "my lord her husband, whom I love, entreats her not in many things so honestly and so godly as yourself would require." The function of mediator, or rather of dispenser of discipline in such a matter, was one thoroughly to Knox's own heart. His colloquy with the queen became cordial and earnest; and he fell immediately to his congenial task, by writing to the earl a letter, setting forth the domestic duties which he had hitherto neglected, and was now called on to perform, with as much peremptory distinctness as it is possible to suppose any like injunction to have been given privily from the confessional. The letter is printed in his History. In the mean time, Knox having become interested in the task before him, the queen seized the favourable moment to get through, briefly and without cross-questioning, with the disagreeable business of their original meeting—the prosecution of the officiating Romanist ecclesiastics. "'And now,' said she, 'as touching our reasoning yesternight, I promise to do as ye required. I shall cause summon all offenders, and ye shall know that I shall minister justice.' 'I am assured then,' said he, 'that ye shall please God, and enjoy rest and tranquillity within your realm, which to your majesty is more profitable than all the Pope's power can be,' and thus they departed." So is the conclusion of the interview set forth in Knox's History. His account of it reads like a true account of the part of the dialogue which it contains, and at the same time does not look as if it suppressed any important part. What afterwards passed through his mind about the whole affair, when he put it in writing, seems to be noted in the following words, with which, referring to the sayings of the day before, he begins the narrative of the second day's conference : " Whether it was the night's sleep, or a deep dissimulation locked in her breast, that made her to forget her former anger, wise men may doubt—but thereof she never moved word."[1]

It must be held as the consequence of her promise that, on the 19th of May 1563, no fewer than forty-eight persons, some of them eminent Romish ecclesiastics, were indicted for celebrating mass and endeavouring to restore Popery in Paisley and Ayrshire. They were charged with collecting tumultuous assemblies—in one instance, of two hundred people. The law which they were accused of transgressing was that dubious proclamation by the queen, requiring that no one should innovate on the state of religion as she found it publicly and universally standing on her arrival in Scotland ; and the accused were said to have transgressed this injunction by "ministering and abusing, irreverently and indecently, the sacraments of haly Kirk—namely, the sacraments of the body and blood of our Lord Jesus—otherwise and after ane other order than the public and general order of this realm was, the time of the queen's majesty's arrival foresaid." Auricular confession was another form of transgression taken at Paisley in the "kirk, toun, kirkyard, chambers, barns, middens, and killogies thereof."[2] The charge of officiating in "middens" or dunghills, and in killogies or kills, which gives a ludicrous tinge to the proceedings,

[1] Knox, ii. 373.   [2] Pitcairn, i. 428*, 429.

shows, in harmony with the tenor of the correspondence of the period, that these recusants courted secrecy. Several of the accused were sentenced to be "put in ward" within the royal fortresses during the queen's pleasure. There was one man, by his station and history, prominent among these offenders—so prominent, indeed, that the prosecution may in some measure be considered a trial of his strength. This was John Hamilton, Archbishop of St Andrews, the illegitimate brother of the head of the house of Hamilton. He had become hateful to the Protestants by the martyrdom of Walter Mill. At the same time there were reasons why neither the Romish party nor the queen's personal friends should then be strongly inclined to back him. Restless, fierce, and ambitious, if he had shown devotion to his Church, he had shown still more devotion to his own interest, and was believed to be working for a compromise between the two extreme parties, in which there would be enough of Protestantism to satisfy the lay Reformers, and enough of Popery to preserve for him his high dignities and emoluments; so that his deficiency in zeal may even have contributed to his sufferings. At the same time he was the leading spirit of the dubious policy of the Hamiltons, and had fought the battle of Arran the regent against the queen's mother. In Knox's History it is told with great glee how the bishop, hesitating to appear as a criminal in the Earl of Argyle's court, was at last "compelled to enter within the bar;" and how "a merry man, who now sleeps in the sod, Robert Norwell, instead of the bishop's cross, bare before him a steel hammer."[1]

But the most instructive consideration in connection

[1] Knox, ii. 380.

with these prosecutions is that, while they were carried on in the queen's name, she was resolutely bent on the restoration of the old religion. It is unnecessary, in confirmation of this, to found solely on that steady unshrinking adherence to her own faith, which must ever stand forth as the noblest, if not the sole redeeming feature of her character. Fragments of correspondence show that, while nominally prosecuting Papists at home, she held close communication with the great leaders of the Romish party abroad, and even with the Pope himself. In January 1563 she wrote to Pope Pius IV., expressing her devotion to the Church, and her readiness to sacrifice for it her life. She mourns over the new opinions and damnable errors which she found prevalent on her return to her kingdom, and regrets that this will defeat a design she would otherwise fain have carried out—to send certain prelates to represent Scotland in the Council of Trent. She writes at the same time to her uncle the cardinal, going over the same topics more fully and earnestly, announcing her desire to restore the Catholic faith in her dominions, though at the peril of her life, and declaring that she will rather die than change her faith, and give encouragement to heresy. The bearer of these dangerous communications was that Cardinal Granville who was conspicuous even among the relentless Spaniards for his zeal in the forcible suppression of heresy.[1]

[1] Labanoff, i. 175 *et seq.* The letters are translated copies, but there is no reason to doubt their genuineness. Since this was written the ground has been gone over by Joseph Robertson (Statuta Ecclesiæ Scoticanæ, Pref. clxiii.) Whoever desires to enter critically into the question how far the tenor of the correspondence here attributed to Queen Mary is supported by evidence, will find there all the information he can desire. But in truth Queen Mary's entire devotion to her Church is so steadily distinct through her whole history as to leave neither excuse nor temptation for resting it on narrow testimony.

We must henceforth, indeed, view Knox and the queen as engaged in a contest, each for the extermination of the other. He also had his correspondents on the Continent, and seems to have known the steady consistency with which she preserved her communications with France, Spain, and the Court of Rome. For all the skill with which she had represented herself as a simple unprejudiced person seeking knowledge and open to conviction, his sagacity early revealed to him that she was an assured unwavering champion of the old faith. So early as October 1561, he said, writing to Cecil, " The queen neither is, neither shall be, of our opinion; and in very deed her whole proceedings do declare that the cardinal's lessons are so deeply printed in her heart that the substance and the quality are like to perish together. I would be glad to be deceived, but I fear I shall not."[1]

But the state of the Continent at that time required that the queen should keep her policy profoundly hidden in her bosom. She had just witnessed, before she left Paris, the reaction against the Guises, and the formidable combination of the Huguenot princes. Catherine of Medici, not having that assured faith which belonged to her daughter-in-law, held herself in grim reserve, watching the contest, and determined not to commit herself until she saw which side should develop the elements of decided superiority. She made herself courteous to the Huguenot preachers, and held colloquies with them like those of Queen Mary and Knox. Then followed the celebrated edict of January 1562, and the establishment of the Huguenots in many of the strongest towns in France, where idolatry was

[1] Quoted, M'Crie, 183.

forthwith suppressed as in Scotland, the religious recluses driven out of their monasteries, and the churches defaced of their sculpture and decorations. It was, no doubt, with secret joy and pride that Mary watched how, step by step, her illustrious uncle consolidated the fragments of the Catholic party, and, after gaining the victory of Dreux, was wrenching from the Huguenots their chief stronghold—Orleans; but all hopes thus excited were doomed to sudden and bitter disappointment, by the news that he had been assassinated by a Huguenot fanatic. He fell on the 18th of August 1563. That was undoubtedly no time for his niece to try the strength of the Catholic cause in Scotland. But in fact it continued from that epoch rapidly to advance in France, with the Guises still at its head. And as it achieved predominance, so we shall find, at humble distance, its champion in Scotland warily stirring herself from the prostrate condition she had found it necessary to accept on her first coming, and arming herself for a conflict which, to all human appearance, was likely seriously to endanger, if not to overwhelm, the cause of the Reformation in Scotland, if not in England too. The concurrence was noticed by Knox in his own peculiar fashion, in the passage already cited, in which he represented the queen as inaugurating the rise of persecution in France by excessive indulgence in the offensive exercise of dancing.

Among the elements of power which she brought into this contest, what she possessed in her own person and personal qualities must not be overlooked. Scarce ever a sovereign entered upon rule with so many attributes of popularity. The blood of an ancient and beloved line of monarchs ran in her veins. She was the descendant of the heroic Bruce, the liberator of the land. With this illustrious blood she united that of the heroic line of Lorraine, with whose deeds Europe was ringing. She herself, by her marvellous beauty, her accomplishments, and her wit, had even widened the renown of her country, known as it was so well over Christendom. She dazzled the commonalty with new court glories to which sombre Scotland was unaccustomed; and her regal pageants were no mere chaotic displays of profuse barbaric splendour, but were brought under the rule of a thoroughly refined taste. The splendours of her Court were not invidious to the people, since they came not from the national exchequer, but were decorated by the jewellery and supplied from the dowry of a queen-dowager of France. The old warlike and chivalrous feeling of the people found more to stir it in this delicate woman than in many a hero. She had often shown her beautiful face under the helmet, mounted on her charger at the head of her troops. In more peaceful days, the peasantry of the borders and the Highlands were familiar with the airy form sweeping past on a milk-white steed, at the stag-hunt or the hawking, followed by all the chivalry of her Court. Such scenes were not confined to the exclusive precincts of parks or royal forests; they were not secluded from a suspected population by a jealous retinue of guards. They were seen by her people at large; and there were few corners of the land so remote but some were there who could tell of having seen them. Hence the queen naturally, from year to year, acquired a strength in her own popularity, which must have weighed formidably against her opponents, and might have served her in good stead had not those things taken place before which no popularity could stand.

There was in the mean time such reaction as chafed the impetuous spirit of Knox, and drew forth the following expressive notice in his History: " While that the Papists were so confounded that none within the realm durst more avow the hearing or saying of mass than the thieves of Liddesdale durst avow their stealth in presence of an upright judge, there were Protestants found there ashamed, not at tables and other places, to ask, ' Why may not the queen have her own mass and the form of her religion? What can that hurt us or our religion?' And from these two—why? and what?— at length sprang out this affirmative, ' The queen's mass and her priests will we maintain; this hand and this rapier shall fight in their defence,' &c." [1]

If Knox and his friends had found reason for genuine satisfaction in the prosecution of Hamilton and the western Papists, it did not last many days. A Parliament was called, from which they expected much and got nothing. It met on the 4th of June 1563. Now was the occasion for ratifying with the royal presence the Reformation, which had been passed in a mere convention, and for devoting to its proper spiritual purposes the Church property which had been seized by the Church's lay friends; but both these objects were effectively evaded. The Acts passed by the convention of 1560 remained unconfirmed, and care seemed to be taken to avoid any reference to the proceedings on that great occasion, as if they involved questions tacitly set aside by both parties for subsequent adjustment. The

[1] Knox, ii. 206.

Estates commenced business by passing an "Act of Oblivion," to protect from prosecution all concerned in the troubles immediately preceding the queen's arrival. The period of time covered by its protecting clauses was from 6th March 1558 to 1st September 1561. The chief object of this Act was to secure from dispute the transactions about Church lands during that period — transactions which the Protestant clergy looked on as a robbery of their Church, but which many of their lay supporters had reasons for keeping quiet, even when adherents of the old Church were the chief gainers by them. For any other purpose than this, the Parliament need not have assembled, since all its other business consisted of petty regulations about cruives and yairs, the export of bullion, the manufacture of salt—unless it may be considered an exception to the general triviality of the proceedings that a statute was passed discharging all persons, of whatsomever estate, degree, or condition, to use any manner of witchcraft, sorcery, or necromancy, under the pain of death, "as well to be execute against the user, abuser, as the seeker of the response or consultation." This is the first announcement on the statute-book of a persecution for which Scotland became rather notorious. It was much desired by Knox, to whom the progress of witchcraft and the kindred arts had been giving alarm; but it was not sufficient to propitiate him in the absence of the more solid results which a Parliament should have brought forth. The proceedings of this Parliament filled up the cup of Knox's gathering wrath against the Protestant lords, on their lukewarmness in the great cause, and over-anxiety about their worldly interests. He signified his displeasure on the occasion by solemnly breaking with Murray. It is very significantly suggested in Knox's History that Murray wanted the estates and honours which he had obtained through the ruin of the Gordons effectively secured; and that these things and other convenient arrangements for supporters being accomplished, he left the rest to the course of events, not choosing to take the strong hand with the queen farther than the assembled Estates might call for it. The feud is thus told in Knox's History: "The matter fell so hot betwixt the Earl of Murray and some others of the Court and John Knox, that familiarly after that time they spake not together more than a year and a half; for the said John, by his letter, gave a discharge to the said earl of all further intromission or care with his affairs."[1]

A few days afterwards, Knox preached a renowned discourse. It was addressed to the Protestant lords, most of whom were present, and was sharpened with all his sternest eloquence, as a last appeal of duty to their obdurate hearts. He described, with picturesque pathos, how he and they had worked together in the evil days of temptation and danger. "In your most extreme dangers I have been with you. St Johnston, Cupar Moor, and the Craigs of Edinburgh are yet recent in my heart; yea, that dark and dolorous night, wherein all ye, my lords, with shame and fear left, this time is yet in my mind, and God forbid that ever I should forget."[2] And where had they cast the great truth for which all this temptation and danger and scandal had been braved, now that the perfecting of it was in their own hands? "Shall this be the

[1] Knox, ii. 382.   [2] Ibid., 384.

thankfulness that ye shall render unto your God, to betray His cause, when ye have it in your own hands to establish it as ye please? The queen, say ye, will not agree with us. Ask ye of her that which by God's Word ye may justly require, and if she will not agree with you in God, ye are not bound to agree with her in the devil." Before concluding, he sounded an admonitory blast of the trumpet on a matter then under busy discussion, although it had not yet pointed to an individual conclusion—the queen's marriage. "And now, my lords, to put end to all I hear of the queen's marriage. Dukes, brethren to emperors and kings, strive all for the best game; but this, my lords, will I say, Note the day, and bear witness after, whensoever the nobility of Scotland, professing the Lord Jesus, consents that an infidel—and all Papists are infidels— shall be head to your sovereign, ye do so far as in ye lieth to banish Christ Jesus from this realm; ye bring God's vengeance upon the country, a plague upon yourself, and perchance ye shall do small comfort to your sovereign."[1]

When Mary heard of this she resolved to have another controversy with her assailant, trusting, as on previous occasions, to her own unaided wit. She had no one present but the pacific Erskine of Dun. It brought her little satisfaction. When asked why he went out of his way as a clergyman to meddle with the affairs of her marriage, Knox explained that it was his duty to admonish, and, where practicable, premonish his congregation of their sins; and if he saw them prepared to stand by inactive, and permit her to take to herself an idolatrous husband, he was constrained to

[1] Knox, ii. 385, 386.

admonish them on their sinfulness and responsibility. According to his own account, he was on this occasion encountered by passionate bursts of weeping. His History states that "the said John stood still, without any alteration of countenance for a long season," until it occurred to him to put in a word of comfort, founded on his domestic experience. Weeping was far from pleasant to him, and he could scarce stand that of his own boys when under paternal flagellation. But on the present occasion, that he should be assailed by tears, was more unreasonable, the queen having no just cause for offence, since he had but spoken the truth, as his vocation craved of him. He was thrust for a time into an anteroom among the queen's ladies, a body for whom he had often expressed intense disgust, railing at their "stinkin' pride," and the "targetting of their tails and the rest of their vanity," all calculated to "provoke God's vengeance not only against those foolish women, but against the whole realm." The grim preacher was probably no more welcome to them than they to him; but he resolved to improve the occasion, and to this accident we owe a sentence of quaint and solemn moralising, which may fairly match with Hamlet's over Yorick's skull: "O fair ladies, how pleasant were this life of yours, if it should ever abide, and then in the end that we might pass to heaven with all this gay gear! But fie upon that knave Death, that will come whether we will or not! And when he has laid on us his arrest, the foul worms will be busy with this flesh were it never so fair and so tender; and the silly soul, I fear, shall be so feeble that it can neither carry with it gold, garnishing, targetting, pearl, nor precious stones."[1]

[1] Knox, ii. 389.

This, according to his History, was spoken by him "merrily," though it is not said to have been received in the like spirit. After a short abiding, he was desired to depart, and the Court ladies and he were relieved of each other's presence.

The conflict between the contending powers was soon afterwards brought to closer issue by an occurrence which did not leave the penal law entirely in the hands of the Protestants, but emboldened the Catholics also to seek its protection. In the summer of 1563 the queen made a progress in the western shires, hunting and hawking as far northward as Argyle. She not only took her idolatry with her, and set it up in sundry places, according to Knox's sure information, but the followers left behind attended mass in the Chapel of Holyrood. One Sunday evening they appear to have been joined by an unusual number of the citizens, " which understanding, divers of the brethren, being sore offended, consulted how to redress that enormity; and so were appointed certain of the most zealous and most upright in religion to wait upon the abbey, that they might note such persons as resorted to the mass."[1] Had the performance merely been deemed a public scandal, this deputation would have been liable to the reproach of increasing the publicity and the scandal. But the act was looked upon as a crime which it is the citizen's duty to detect and denounce. Several persons were thus indicted, according to the established form, for making innovations and alterations on religion contrary to the queen's proclamation, but it does not appear that they were punished.[2] They appear all to have been citizens of Edinburgh, and not the French

[1] Knox, ii. 393. [2] Pitcairn, i. 435*.

followers, whom Knox terms *dontibours*, a term of equivocal origin. The noting and identification of the massmongers, however, being exciting work for the zealous and upright men who undertook it, there appears to have been violence. In Knox's History it is said, " Perceiving a great number to enter into the chapel, some of the brethren burst also in; whereat the priest and the French dames being affrayed, made the shout to be sent to the town."[1] Whatever may have been the extent of the violence committed, two of the party — Andrew Armstrong and George Boyd, burgesses — were indicted for " carrying pistols within the burgh, convention of the lieges at the palace, and invasion of the queen's servants."[2] This gave high offence to the Protestant clergy; and Knox, who said he had been intrusted with authority to convene the champions of the cause in case of danger or emergency, considered that the hour had come for which this precaution was taken, and issued a circular warning to the faithful, calling on them to assemble in Edinburgh on the 24th of October, the day fixed for the trial of Armstrong and Boyd. Such pains seem to have been taken to preserve secrecy in this summons, although very widely circulated, that Knox is loud in his denunciations of the treachery by which it was made known to the queen's advisers. These considered that at last they had Knox at their mercy, with a charge of treason hanging over him for convocation of the lieges. Some efforts of Murray and the Master of Maxwell to get him to accept of leniency, founded on a partial admission of error, were received with haughty scorn, and he was cited to appear before the queen in

[1] Knox, ii. 393.   [2] Pitcairn, i. 434*.

Council. The assemblage does not appear to have been limited to the Privy Council, nor was it a meeting in full of the Estates, but something like a committee of the Government officers and chief members of Parliament. The queen attended, and took a leading part in the business. Her approach is described in her opponent's History as that of a haughty and prematurely-exulting foe. " Her pomp lacked one principal point — to wit, womanly gravity; for when she saw John Knox standing at the other end of the table bareheaded, she first smiled, and after gave ane gawf lauchter; whereat, when her *placeboes* gave their *plaudite*, affirming with like countenance 'This is ane good beginning,' she said, ' But wit ye whereat I laugh? Yon man gart me greet, and grat never tear himself. I will see if I can gar him greet.' "[1] There was a long discussion, Knox stern and unbending as usual. The sum of his defence—or rather justification, for he scorned to demean himself as one pleading to a charge —was that convocation of the lieges for evil purposes was doubtless a crime; but his was for a good purpose, a holy purpose—he was " doing the duty of God's messenger" in writing this letter. The assemblage declined to inculpate him. Their motives on the occasion are not very clear, for there seems to have been a strong feeling, even among the zealous lay Reformers, that it would be dangerous to let such an act pass. It is open to the reader to believe, with the exulting accused, that " there was not ane that plainly durst condemn the poor man that was accused, this same God ruling their tongue that formerly ruled the tongue of Balaam when gladly he would have cursed God's

[1] Knox, ii. 404.

people."[1] It may also have had its influence on the assemblage that, "the bruit rising in the town that John Knox was sent for by the queen, the brethren of the Kirk followed in such number that the inner close was full, and all the stairs, even to the chamber door where the queen and Council sat."[2] On being told that he might depart homewards, he turned to the queen and prayed that God would purge her heart from Popery and preserve her from the counsel of flatterers.[3]

A General Assembly was held immediately afterwards, and there Knox sought, and of course immediately received, a full justification of his conduct. So the affair ended. There are no traces of ultimate proceedings against the rioters. The lay friends of the Reformation got no thanks for any leniency shown on this occasion; on the contrary, from that time the wrath of the preachers became ever louder against them as participators in the idolatry of her they served. They anticipated the Divine vengeance on the land for these sins, and soon found it executed. "God from heaven, and upon the face of the earth, gave declaration that He was offended at the iniquity that was committed even within this realm; for upon the 20th day of January there fell wet in great abundance, which in the falling freezed so vehemently that the earth was but ane sheet of ice. The fowls both great and small freezed, and might not flee; many died, and some were taken and laid beside the fire that their feathers might resolve. And in that same month the sea stood still, as was clearly observed, and neither ebbed nor flowed the space of twenty-four hours. In the month of February, the 15th and 18th days thereof, was seen in the firmament battles arrayed,

[1] Knox, ii. 411.   [2] Ibid., 403.   [3] Ibid., 411.

spears, and other weapons, and as it had been the joining of two armies."[1]

The gloom which had been gathering over the prospects of the zealous Reformers now deepened apace. The clergy besought the mitigation of God's wrath for the sins of the land in their prayers, which, as they freely exposed the great cause of all the evils, became thus a powerful weapon of assault. Knox adopted a form of prayer for the occasion, which he freely repeated when questioned for the last time about his conduct. It was in these terms:—

"O Lord, if Thy pleasure be, purge the heart of the queen's majesty from the venom of idolatry, and deliver her from the bondage and thraldom of Satan, in the whilk she has been brought up and yet remains, for the lack of true doctrine; and let her see, by the illumination of the Holy Spirit, that there is no mean to please Thee but by Jesus Christ Thy only Son, and that Jesus Christ cannot be found but in Thy Holy Word, nor yet received but as it prescribes, which is to renounce our own wits and preconceived opinion, and worship Thee as Thou demandest; that in so doing she may avoid that eternal damnation which abides all obstinate and impenitent unto the end; and that this poor realm may also escape that plague and vengeance which inevitably follows idolatry maintained against Thy manifest Word and the open light thereof."[2]

This prayer came under question in the following shape. A General Assembly was held in the summer of 1564, at which the lay lords expected their clerical friends to take violent measures. At the first sitting, these lay lords, called The Courtiers, were not present,

[1] Knox, ii. 417.   [2] Ibid., 428.

and it was proposed that measures should be taken with them to compel them to do their duty as humble members of the national Church. The courtiers were accordingly summoned to attend, and they appeared next day; but instead of mixing with the assembled clergy and their brother-elders at once, it appears that they passed into an inner council-room to hold a preliminary conference. Thence they sent a message requesting the superintendents "and some of the learned ministers" to confer with them. The Assembly answered that they could not spare their principal members, and that it better became the courtiers to take their part in the general deliberations than to draw away those whose services were the most valuable to the Assembly. After an angry discussion, it was at last agreed that a preliminary conference might be held between the lay and clerical leaders, on the understanding that they should conclude nothing, but that all should be redebated in open assembly. Among the courtiers there were Hamilton, Argyle, Murray, Morton, Glencairn, Marishal, Rothes, the Laird of Pittarrow, and chief of all, as him on whom the labour of the controversy fell, Secretary Lethington. On the clerical side were Erskine of Dun, Spottiswood, Winram, and Willock, who, according to an arrangement for providing a governing body in the new Church, were Superintendents of districts. They were assisted by Row, Craig, and Hay. Knox, who for some unexplained reason seems to have been reluctant to appear, was forced into the discussion on the infallible plea that his own conduct was to be questioned, and his absence would be cowardice. Once there, the whole conduct of the conflict naturally fell into his hands. He was opposed by the ready-debating talent and subtle wit of the secretary. But the laymen had an assailable point, which rendered victory to the others secure from the beginning. A rumour had been ominously whispered about among the clergy, and had gained such palpable force that some of them had in fear and grief sought to relieve their hearts concerning it in their public prayers. It was to the effect that some of their lay friends had been heard to doubt if the queen's mass really were the idolatry which must be punished with death. It was the great aim of Knox's rhetoric and his taunts to drive his opponents to the avowal of this doubt; but whatever they inwardly thought, none of them had courage for the avowal. Thus the clergy had all the advantage possessed by men with one simple clear conclusion which they delighted in avowing, over those who wished to avoid avowals, and to carry the controversy into subsidiary channels. The clergy were charged with dwelling too strongly on the queen's impenitence. Why should they propagate the impression that she was obdurate in her sins? why not make allowance for penitence coming in due time? But this argument tottered under its own inherent weakness. The supposition of her repentance was a farce—nothing was farther from her thoughts; and all of them knew by that time, if they did not before, that she was as thorough a bigot to her own creed as the most zealous of themselves was to his.

Then supposing her to be sinful and impenitent, yet she was a queen, and could not be punished or controlled in her personal actions; and for subjects to rail at them, whether in pulpits or elsewhere, was disrespect to the Lord's anointed, if not worse. Lethington had the imprudence to throw out a challenge that Scripture precedents could not be found for such arraignments of the conduct of princes. This was a call to Knox to draw on the resources of his great arsenal of Bible-learning. He had so abundant a choice, that with characteristic pride he cared not to cite precedents except from the doings of the greater prophets. There were Elisha and King Jehoram; Jeremiah, who cried aloud to the kings Zedekiah and Jehoiakim; and, happiest instance of all, "Ahab was ane king, and Jezebel was ane queen, and yet what the prophet Elijah said to the one and to the other, I suppose ye be not ignorant."[1] "The idolater shall die the death." "God's laws pronounce death to idolaters without exception of any person." Such was the terrible burden of the preacher's argument to the conclusion; and the courtiers had nothing to answer it with. Craig, who had led a strange wandering life, appealed to a precedent of later times, when Protestantism had for a short time dominion in Bologna, and it was resolved by the eminent doctors there that idolatrous rulers must be deposed by subjects sound in the faith.

The discussion was taking a dangerously practical direction, when Macgill, the clerk-register, diverted it by reminding the meeting of the previous proposal to consult Calvin and the Continental heads of the Protestant faith how far obedience was due to infidel princes. Lethington admitted that he had undertaken that duty, but that when it came to be done he shrank from deliberately inquiring of foreigners whether it was his duty to depose his sovereign. Knox was

[1] Knox, ii. 432.

pressed to write such a letter to Calvin, but declined. It is odd enough that he never alludes to his having already written one.[1] The conference ended without any practical conclusion. No vote was taken in the General Assembly; and the reason why there was none appears to be because the committee of leaders, which, as we have seen, the Assembly were averse to sanction, once finding themselves set apart, and divided into two parties eager for controversy, debated so long that the Assembly got tired, and dispersed. The lay Protestants—the Lords of the Congregation—with Murray at their head, had by this time their own deep anxieties to deal with. They could not, on the one hand, bring the clergy to what they thought reason; on the other, they saw more clearly, day by day, that there was no room for a temperate party; that Knox and Craig were right in holding the queen to be obdurate and impenitent in her idolatry, and that in the great conflict hers was the party the more likely of the two to be successful. The point on which the question of Protestant or Roman Catholic appears at that time to turn was the queen's marriage; and before narrating that event, with its wondrous consequents, it may be proper to glance at some of its precedents.

[1] Knox, ii. 460.

CHAPTER XLIII.

Queen Mary.

(Continued.)

THE QUEEN AND HER ADMIRERS — MYSTERIOUS STORY OF THE PROJECT OF ARRAN AND BOTHWELL — BOTHWELL INDICTED FOR IT—HISTORY OF CHATELAR—HIS ADVENTURES—HIS FATE — POLITICAL IMPORTANCE OF THE QUEEN'S MARRIAGE — THE PROJECTS OF THE HOUSE OF GUISE — QUEEN MARY'S OWN VIEWS—PROJECT FOR UNION WITH THE HEIR OF THE SPANISH MONARCHY—POLITICAL PROSPECTS OF SUCH A UNION—MARY'S FOREIGN CORRESPONDENCE ABOUT IT — HER SCHEMES TRAVERSED BY CATHERINE OF MEDICI—OTHER PROJECTS—QUEEN ELIZABETH — HER ESCAPADES ABOUT LEICESTER — PROPOSED MEETING OF MARY AND ELIZABETH — MARY MEETS HENRY STEWART, LORD DARNLEY—MARY'S SECRET EMISSARIES—DAVID RIZZIO—REACTION IN FAVOUR OF THE ROMANIST PARTY—GLOOM AND DIFFICULTIES OF THE REFORMERS—PROTESTANT RIOT SUPPRESSED—QUESTION OF CONSULTING THE ESTATES ABOUT THE MARRIAGE—MARRIAGE OF MARY AND DARNLEY.

EVER since the death of her husband, the admirers of the young queen had been very troublesome. Besides the members of reigning houses who were offered or spoken of after the usual fashion of projected royal alliances, her steps were infested by audacious and demonstrative adorers, who had no claims to such a destiny. Whether the passive influence of her wonderful wit and beauty rendered this phenomenon inevitable, or it might be in any measure promoted by some little touches of seductive fascination in her manner, is a question which students of her history will in general decide for themselves. The most eminent among these miscellaneous admirers, and the one who came nearest to the rank which might have justified the expectation of her hand, was D'Amville, the second son of the Constable Montmorency, who afterwards succeeded to the offices and honours of his family—the most illustrious among the unregal nobility of France. He was one of those who accompanied the queen to Scotland. He had a wife; but to such homage as he was entitled to tender, that was no hindrance.

Arran, the heir of the house of Hamilton, was numbered among the queen's suitors. The position of that family at the juncture of Mary's return was very peculiar, and so was their conduct. The head of the house was next heir to the crown, and held this position not merely by genealogical tenure, but by the repeated acknowledgments of Parliament, which had made provision for his claims being made good if the succession opened. It was not in human nature that the man so placed should enter, with the indifference of an ordinary subject, into questions about the most suitable alliance for his sovereign, and the desirableness of a direct heir appearing to the house of Stewart. Whether from temper or policy, he evaded the usual demands of homage paid by the nobility. His absence from Court was of course noticed, and was in fact rather the assumption of a diplomatic position than an ordinary discourtesy. Something of menace, too, appeared in his movements, and especially in his jealously fortifying and keeping well garrisoned the fortress of Dumbarton. The annalists of the day mention a sudden alarm arising in Holyrood House one summer night in the year 1561, when the Lord James was absent suppressing the borderers, and the palace was peculiarly unprotected. This incident is isolated —unconnected with any train of events preceding or following it. It is briefly recorded in the quaint manner of Knox's History, in a spirit of latent sarcasm: "The queen upon a night took a fray in her bed, as if horsemen had been in the close, and the palace had been enclosed about. Whether it proceeded of her own womanly fantasy, or if men put her in fear for displeasure of the Earl of Arran, and for other purposes, as for the erecting of the guard, we know not. But the fear was so great that the town was called to the watch." The shape into which the cause of this panic was put, was a design by young Arran to seize the queen and carry her into the district where the house of Hamilton was supreme. If the queen had, as Knox and others thought, no ground for her apprehensions, yet such an enterprise was not at all inconsistent with the spirit of the times, and it is impossible to disconnect it with certain subsequent transactions in which the name of so very practical a person as the Earl of Bothwell is mixed up. The alarm in Holyrood must have occurred in November 1561, the date of Murray's absence on the border; the further incidents now to be noticed belong to the spring of the following year. Knox was intimately concerned in them, and they are narrated with much distinctness in his History. The affair begins by Bothwell desiring a private interview with Knox, which was gladly conceded; and they met in the house of James Barron, a worshipful burgess of Edinburgh. The scene resolved itself into a sort of Protestant confessional. The earl bewailed his sinful life, and entered into particulars of his offences, whereof he heartily repented. But there remained behind a practical object in which he desired the Reformer's intervention—it pressed hard on him that he was at enmity with the Earl of Arran, and he solicited Knox's good offices for their reconciliation. Knox undertook the task with hearty goodwill; in some way or other it is evident that the heart of the austere preacher was gained. He said his grandfather, father, and father-in-law had served under the banner of the Hepburns—this by the way, as connecting them together by the obligation of their "Scottish kindness;" but he had another and a more solemn function as the public messenger of glad tidings, and so he bestowed on the penitent a suitable admonition to prove the sincerity of his penitence by his reformation. Bothwell stuck to the practical point—of a reconciliation with Arran. Knox busied himself in the matter, and after overcoming some practical difficulties, he had the satisfaction to see them meet and embrace, the Earl of Arran saying to his new friend, "If the hearts be upright, few ceremonies may serve and content me." Knox, who seems to have been mightily pleased with his handiwork, left them with the benediction following: "Now, my lords, God hath brought you together by the labours of simple men, in respect of those who would have travailed therein. I know my labours are already taken in an evil part, but because I have the testimony of a good conscience before my God, that whatsoever I have done, I have done it in His fear, for the profit of you both, for the hurt of none, and for the tranquillity of this realm."

The good work seemed to be perfected, when next day Bothwell and "some of his honest friends came to the sermon with the earl foresaid, whereat many rejoiced."

But in a few days the scene was changed. Arran came repeatedly to Knox, and poured into his ears a tale how Bothwell had offered to help him to carry off the queen, and put her in his hands in Dumbarton Castle, proposing at the same time the slaughter of Murray, Lethington, and the others that "misguide her." These revelations seem to have gone on for some time, when Knox at last found that his informant was raving. "He devised of wondrous signs that he saw in the heaven; he alleged that he was bewitched; he would have been in the queen's bed, and affirmed that he was her husband; and finally, he behaved in all things so foolishly that his frenzy could not be hid."[1]

He was subjected to the process by which in Scotland insane persons are deprived of the management of their property.[2] His madness cannot be doubted, whether or not it was rightly atributed to his despairing love for the queen. However it arose, his accusations against Bothwell, to which he resolutely adhered, were not only gravely considered and examined at the time, but were three years afterwards, when Bothwell returned from France, solemnly resuscitated in the form of a criminal indictment or summons of treason. In this document it is specifically set forth that Bothwell proposed a plan for seizing the queen when she was hunting in the fields, or in one of her rural merry-makings, and conveying her with a sufficient force to Dumbarton Castle. There she was to be at the dis-

[1] Knox, ii. 322-29. [2] Mor. Dict. Dec., 6275.

posal of Arran; and it was part of the charge that by this Bothwell seduced him to join in the enterprise. As Bothwell did not appear to answer to the charge, he was outlawed, and the affair was forgotten amid the more stirring historical incidents in which he was to figure.[1] As the conclusion of this episode, it is proper to note that in the end of April 1562, a month after the date attributed to Bothwell's conversation with Arran, the Castle of Dumbarton was yielded up to Captain Anstruther, to be held for the queen.[2] In Knox's History the extraction of this fortress from the hands of the Hamiltons is spoken of as a breach of faith, on the ground that the custody of it had been granted to them "till that lawful succession should be seen of the queen's body."[3] Thus the fortress was understood to stand as a material guarantee for the protection of the house of Hamilton's right of succession to the throne.

It has been already recorded how the unfortunate Sir John Gordon, the son of the rebel Earl of Huntly, conducted himself as a lover of the queen. But the most troublesome and preposterous of all her train of admirers was a Frenchman named Chatelar or Chastelard, who also fell a victim to his follies. Little is known of him, except from the pages of Brantome; but his mere appearance there, accompanied by expressions of eulogy and warm attachment, is sufficient to mark him as a man of distinction. The biographer says he was a native of Dauphiné, and a grand-nephew by his mother of the illustrious Bayard, whom he resembled in person. According to the same authority, he owned in a high degree not only all the warlike and

[1] Pitcairn i. 462*.   [2] Diurnal of Occurrents.   [3] Knox, ii. 330.

polite accomplishments of a high-bred gallant of the day, but possessed original literary genius, and could accompany his lute by his own poetry—" usant dune poesie fort douce et gentile en cavalier." He was a follower of the Constable Montmorency, with whom he joined the body of gentlemen who escorted the queen from France. A *gentil mot* of his on that occasion has been recorded—that when a fog sprang up, and the necessity of lights was spoken of, he said the bright eyes of their mistress were sufficient to light the fleet past all dangers.

He had certainly been admitted on terms of some familiarity with the queen. Brantome says her love of letters led her to admire the young man's poems, of which she was often naturally the theme, and that she answered him in verses which raised within him the wildest aspirations. It is difficult to mark the limits within which at that period a royal personage at any of the French or Italian Courts might legitimately flatter and encourage a person of good birth, endowed with the literary accomplishments of the troubadour. The homage paid to Ronsard, by beauties of princely rank, was more like adoration than patronage. But Knox certainly shows ignorance of the fitting usages of a court at that time, when he says, "The queen would lie on Chatelar's shoulder, and sometimes privily she would steal a kiss of his neck; and all this was honest enough, for it was the gentle entreatment of a stranger. But the familiarity was so great, that on a night he privily did convey himself under the queen's bed."[1] That he committed this folly, whatever his encouragement may have been, is beyond doubt, though

---

[1] Knox, ii. 368.

Randolph states that by his own account his hiding-place was a part of the establishment still less adapted for romance or lovemaking.¹ The occurrence was in Holyrood. For this first offence, though flagrant enough, he was spared and warned. Next day, however, as Mary spent the night at Burntisland, on her way to St Andrews, he burst into her private apartment, either to plead a palliation for his conduct or to plead his suit. It is said in Knox's History that Mary desired him to be forthwith put to death, but that Murray, who was present, maintained it to be due to the fair course of justice, and more conducive to her own good repute, that he should be brought to trial. He was tried at St Andrews, condemned, and executed. The records of the Court of Justiciary for that period having been lost, we are deprived of any light which they might have cast on this strange story. Whoever desires to read how he died, like a true knight-errant, turning to the direction of his bright particular star, though obscured from his view, and unheard addressing her as the most lovely and cruel of her sex, may turn to the lively pages of Brantome. Chatelar's adventures fed many preposterous rumours, and the King of Spain was told that he had been hired in France to do as he did, for the purpose of ruining the queen's matrimonial prospects.²

Chatelar had been sent back to France with the other attendants of the queen soon after her arrival, and had found his way back to the centre of attraction. One of the few wise things done by Mary and her advisers was the speedy restoration to their own country of this foreign train, whose presence in Scot-

¹ Raumer, 22. ² Teulet, iii. 1.

land, however discreetly they might have conducted themselves, would have fostered a special growth of jealousies and animosities, in addition to the already luxuriant crop. What the rest would have incurred we learn in the brief history of one of them who remained behind the others—D'Elbœuf, the queen's uncle. He was charged with having joined some dissipated Scotsmen in a nocturnal riot, in which they forced an entrance to the house of a citizen, seeking access to a damsel living there. It is not stated that they committed violence on her, or even got access to her; and her own conduct was so far from being irreproachable, that the affair arose out of a dispute as to the person to whom she had for the time being sold her blandishments, and the object of the riot was to put one of the claimants in possession. The criminal records of the day convey a very false impression of the social condition of the country, if far heavier offences of the same character were not of daily occurrence. Yet the participation of D'Elbœuf raised this paltry riot to a place in history. In Knox's Book it is said that "the horror of this fact, and the rarity of it, highly commoved all godly hearts."[1] A sort of General Assembly was convened on the occasion, who addressed the queen in a long remonstrance about the impiety, "so heinous and so horrible that, as it was a fact most vile and rare to be heard of within this realm, principally within the bounds of this city, so should we think ourselves guilty of the same if negligently, or yet for worldly fear, we pass it over in silence." They predicted that its going unpunished might cause God's sore displeasure to fall on her and her whole

[1] Knox, ii. 315.

realm.[1] The queen resisted the prosecution of the offenders, but promised measures for better order in time coming.

It must be admitted, however, that, so far as the clergy were concerned, they do not seem to have applied to the Frenchman a more rigid rule of virtue than that which they followed themselves and endeavoured to enforce on the community generally. They were under the impulse of that great reaction against the profligacy of the age—the reaction which, driven out of France, where it had its origin, swept England under the name of Puritanism, and established a permanent influence over opinion in Scotland. Calvin had to take his notions of the absolute rule of saintship away from France, where the Huguenots were in a minority, to the small state of Geneva; and Knox sought to establish in Scotland the same iron rule which his master was able with difficulty to hold over that small and peculiar state. The rigidness of the rule by which he and his brethren of the clergy had resolved to walk is better exemplified by one exceptional case of backsliding than by their professions of godliness. One of the new clergymen—Paul Methven, minister of Jedburgh—was accused of connubial infidelity. Instead of any effort to conceal this reproach to their body, they proclaimed it aloud as an awful and inscrutable judgment, and hunted the accused man until, whether guilty or not, he fled from his pursuers. The excitement aroused in a considerable body of men by the revelation among them of this one black sheep, points to the conclusion that such sins were rare in the community to which Methven belonged. Had there been

[1] Knox, ii. 316. Book of the Universal Kirk, 29th May 1561.

other instances of flagrant offence, these too would have been made known; for it was a peculiarity of the Presbyterian bodies to blazon the infirmities of their own members as judgments and warnings, while those of the opposite religion were dealt with by ecclesiastical superiors, and shrouded in what they deemed decorous privacy.

While thus perplexed by immoralities without and within, the new Church had to look to the more serious question of its own safety, and the preservation of the reformed faith. The question, which party should be supreme in Scotland, seemed to depend so much upon the queen's marriage, that both preserved a sort of armed neutrality until that event should take place, and declare for the one or the other. The anxiety on the point travelled indeed far beyond the bounds of Scotland: for if Mary, with her claims on the crown of England, were married to some great Catholic potentate, no one could calculate what strength such an event might bring to the cause of Rome; while, on the other hand, a Protestant king in Edinburgh would secure Scotland, at all events, to the cause of the Reformation. Her ambitious relations the Guises were fully alive to the important influence which the event must have on their own designs and prospects. It is only in the events of later times that we can appreciate the scope and tendency of the projects of that illustrious race, and see how near they were to the accomplishment of a great revolution. They appeared in all their lustre at a time when the French had few great men, and were becoming discontented with the position they found themselves holding among European powers. What the family of Bonaparte has since achieved, this ambitious house were on the point of achieving in the sixteenth century. If we look into the history of each of the several great men of the house, we shall find them all strengthening their position by a marvellously dexterous use of every available instrument, and uniting to propagate an impression throughout the world that some wonderful destiny was in store for them. They gave themselves out as the true descendants of Charlemagne, through that Lothaire, the founder of Lotharingia or Lorraine, whose race was superseded on the throne of France by the dynasty of Hugh Capet; and though they would have found it hard to prove this descent to fastidious genealogists, the history of their family gave plausibility to their claim. When their niece ascended the throne of France, they received a solid accession of power; and whatever may have been the form of their ambitious dreams for the future, they had the certainty, while she and her husband lived, of ruling supreme in France.

The death of the young king was a severe blow to them. They had just perfected their measures for crushing the house of Bourbon, where, from the physical condition of the remains of the Valois family, they saw the future probable successors to the throne of France. With the change of fortune, they were compelled to give up their hold on Condé, Coligny, and the other illustrious victims through whom the cause of the Huguenots and the Bourbon family were to be crushed; and they found in Catherine of Medici, the mother of the boy who succeeded to the throne, one who had the will, and might very soon have the power, to trample them under her feet.

Far from abandoning their great projects, however,

the history of their country has declared how they came back to the contest with redoubled efforts and new resources. The marriage of their niece was again in their hands, as a means of giving strength to their position. They bethought them that, with her claims on the crown of England, were she married to the heir of the King of Spain, the most powerful monarch of the day, there would arise a more glorious prospect for her and themselves than even that which the death of King Francis had extinguished. Accordingly they laboured hard to bring about her marriage with Don Carlos, the heir of the Spanish crown, then in his sixteenth year. The project was unsuccessful, and of the manner in which it was defeated we at least know this much, that Catherine of Medici was indefatigable in her efforts to baffle it. Among other evidence of her industry, some letters written in cipher to the Bishop of Limoges, the French ambassador in Spain, have lately been deciphered.[1] They are interesting in themselves, as specimens of the subtle and tortuous method by which this incomprehensible woman worked for her ends. One reading these letters cannot of course fathom their ultimate objects, which are laboriously concealed from the bishop himself; but the overpowering intensity of her eagerness to stop the match between her daughter-in-law and Don Carlos breaks through all the avowed objects of the correspondence.

Philip's own intentions lie hidden among the other mysteries of his policy; but it seems clear that he entertained, if he did not push, the match. Catherine's suspicions were directed against him at so early a period that, when Don Juan de Manriquez was sent

[1] Chéruel, Marie Stuart et Catherine de Medicis, &c., 22.

from Spain to France on a message of condolence for the death of Francis II., Catherine said this was a pretence; for his actual mission, in which he exerted himself, was to negotiate with the Guises for the marriage of their niece with Don Carlos. The preponderance which such an event would give to Spain, influenced the policy of France in relation to the resumption of the Council of Trent, as seriously affecting the influence which Spain, aggrandised by such an alliance, would exercise among the Catholic powers.[1]

The immediate object most keenly urged by Catherine is a personal meeting with Philip. She seems to have thought that, if she once had an opportunity of talking with him, all her objects were gained —a curious instance of her thorough reliance on her diplomatic powers, since it would be difficult to point in history to a potentate more obdurately and hopelessly self-willed. Intensely as she desired the interview, it must seem unpremeditated; and she laid down a little chain of events through which it might be brought to pass as if it were fortuitous. In September, as she ascertained, the King of Spain would attend a public spectacle in Aragon. Towards the end of July her son would make his public entry into Paris, after his consecration at Rheims. She might herself go as far as Touraine under the natural pretext of visiting Chenenceau, the beautiful chateau out of which she had driven her hated rival, Diana of Poictiers. Her son the king would be with her, and they might probably go on to Gascony, where the King of Navarre had a project for letting the people see their young

[1] Castelnau, Laboureur Additions aux Mémoires, i. 480, 554.

king; so she would be near Spain, and the meeting, which must appear to the world an affair of chance, might be accomplished. If the meeting had been held, she was to prove to Philip that the proposed marriage would in reality be disastrous to the interests of the Church, the promotion of which was the avowed object for urging it. She knew that Philip held the interest of the Church beyond all things at heart; and could she but obtain this interview, there were innumerable shapes in which they could combine to promote that object, the dearest to her heart as it was to his. The Guises, though the self-constituted champions of the Church, were not truly devoted to it—they were too ambitious and worldly. Even now they were in league with the King of Navarre, whose interests would predominate in France along with theirs. Let the King of Spain sap this worldly coalition, and take to his bosom her own young son the King of France, inspire him with true zeal, and so raise up a hero worthy to serve with him in his great enterprise for the restoration of the rights of the Church. This pleading is a signal instance of the plausibility and subtle duplicity of the woman. She was then contemplating and preparing for an alliance of her own interests with those of the Guises, as likely to be the best security for her supremacy; but she did not desire that her prospective ally should acquire an influence which would give him the mastery. She relied thoroughly on the absorbing character of Philip's religious bigotry, though she had none herself; and yet at the same time she laid before him a small temporal bait, in case he should possess some latent element of worldliness, in her allusions to the King of Navarre, who was then disputing with the King of Spain the possession of certain territories.

She did not obtain her interview, but she gained her ultimate end in breaking the match. She bore, in her objections to it, on the King of Spain's ear through all available channels, not forgetting his confessor. Her most available ally, however, seems to have been her own young daughter, who had been married to Philip after the death of Mary, Queen of England. Catherine had known and keenly felt the humiliation of giving precedence to the haughty beauty as reigning queen, on the death of her husband, and could tell her own daughter what she had to anticipate in a similar position. The mother, indeed, suggested that her daughter, the Queen of Spain, should endeavour to keep this preferment for her own young sister, Marguerite of Valois, the same who became afterwards the wife of Henry IV. It appears that at last Catherine of Medici even influenced the Guises to abandon their project.[1] But it was not abandoned by Mary herself. When she was not under the influence of the violent attachments to which she afterwards yielded, and while she viewed her marriage as a politic arrangement, she scorned anything but a thoroughly great alliance. So when it was proposed to marry her to the Archduke Charles, the second son of the emperor, she contemptuously rejected him for substantial reasons. As a stranger, he would have no following or political influence in Scotland. Estimating him among the powers of Europe, he was nothing but a younger son, without fortune or title, and with no power to assert her birthright—the entire sovereignty

[1] See Authorities in Mignet, chapter iii.

of Britain.[1] It was the more mortifying to her also to find that, when this marriage was proposed, Philip II. drew back in courtesy to his uncle the emperor. When he learned Queen Mary's repulse of the German alliance, he reopened the negotiation, observing that he would have been well pleased to have seen his relation the archduke husband to the Queen of Scotland, if that alliance would have furthered the views he had at heart; but he really believed a marriage with his own son would be more effective in settling religious difficulties in England. In the year 1563, when Don Alvaro de la Quadra was Spanish ambassador in England, there was at the same time a Spanish gentleman connected with his embassy named De Paz, who went to Scotland as representative of Spain, with special instructions about the proposed marriage of Mary with Don Carlos, and, to shroud his journey in secrecy, passed round by Ireland.[2]

The negotiations of De Paz, and their immediate result, are as yet buried in mystery. We know, however, that Mary herself renewed the negotiations for the marriage, if they can be ever said to have died. She wrote earnest letters about it to Granvelle, her uncle the cardinal, and her aunt the Duchess of Arschot. Castelnau, when he went to Holyrood after having delivered to Queen Elizabeth the mocking proposal for her marriage with the young King of France, said, probably with truth, that Queen Mary held easy and confidential communications with him about the several princes named to her, as the Archduke Charles, the Prince of Ferrara, several princes of Germany, and the

[1] See Documents, Labanoff, i. 248, 295.
[2] Chéruel, 35. Papiers d'Etat du Cardinal de Granvelle, vii. 208.

Prince of Condé, an alliance with whom would accomplish the desirable end of bringing the house of Bourbon on closer terms with the house of Guise. The ambassador hinted that a marriage with the Duke of Anjou would enable her to return to France. To this she said, with a touch of graceful sentiment quite her own, that indeed no other kingdom in the world had such a hold upon her as France, where she passed her happy youth, and had the honour to wear the crown; but appropriate to this honour, it would hardly be becoming for her to return thither to fill a lower place, leaving her own country a prey to the factions by which it was rent; and then as to the matter of dignity, she had high expectations from certain suggestions about an alliance with Don Carlos, who would succeed to the great empire of Philip II. It was on this alliance that her mind was bent, for she spoke of it twice emphatically, in the midst of the slighting remarks in which she passed the others in review.[1]

She intrusted her secret foreign messenger Raulet, and one less known, called Chesein, to make for her those more full and confidential communications which she could not always trust on paper.[2] What remains of this correspondence shows that much more existed, and that there were many communications to her friends abroad, which she rather trusted to the spoken explanations of faithful agents than to letters.

The fragmentary traces of her exertions in this cause give some insight into the extent of the system of secret communication with her friends on the Continent which she had established. Alava, the Spanish am-

---

[1] Mémoires, liv. v. c. 11.
[2] See Labanoff generally, down to 1564. Chéruel, 37.

bassador in France, is found writing repeatedly to Philip II. himself, in the year 1564 and in the early part of 1565, with statements how Beaton, the exiled Archbishop of Glasgow, whom he calls Queen Mary's secretary, presses for a definitive determination from Madrid on the question whether the marriage is to be or not. On the 15th of March 1565, he communicates the assurance of Beaton that unless the King of Spain come to the rescue, she will be compelled to throw herself away on a cousin of her own—namely, Henry Darnley; and it is represented that she is deserted by her brother Murray, and driven by Queen Elizabeth to this undesirable union. A despatch of the 4th of June states that there is yet time, for she is not yet married, and ardently desires the protection of the King of Spain. This last appeal was written seven weeks before her marriage.[1]

It is doubtful whether Queen Elizabeth, if she knew even that this project had been entertained, was aware how pertinaciously it was pressed. Knox, whose communications gave him means of accurate intelligence from the Continent, seems to have known something of what was going on, when he made those allusions to the queen's marriage which aroused her high displeasure. There is evidence that the ever vigilant Catherine of Medici had considerable knowledge of the affair, and continued to be busily counterplotting. In letters written in cipher she earnestly pressed it on Bochetel, Bishop of Rennes, the French ambassador at the Emperor of Germany's Court, to defeat the Spanish

---

[1] Extraits des Correspondances de Don Frances de Alava, du Secrétair Aguilon, &c., Ambassadeurs ou Chargés d'Affaires de Philippe II. en France de 1563 à 1587.—Teulet, vol. iii. 1 *et seq.*

match by pressing the proposal for Mary's marriage
with the Archduke Charles.[1] She sent Castelnau to
Britain professedly to arrange a marriage between
Mary and her son the Duke of Anjou, the King of
France's younger brother, and consequently the brother
of Mary's dead husband. It was on the same mission
that Castelnau was intrusted with the equally sincere
proposal of a marriage between the young King of
France and Elizabeth.

This king himself was among the reputed expectants
of the hand of Mary; he is even said to have been
deeply in love with her. Any project for their union,
if it was ever really entertained at any time, had not
vitality enough to call out the king's mother's active
opposition, though her opinion against it is pretty clear.
She says the rumours about it were carried so far as
to contain an assertion that the Pope's dispensation
for a marriage so far within the forbidden degrees had
been applied for, and was expected to arrive; but at
the same time she says that this rumour was circulated
for the purpose of concealing a project for marrying
the young king to a granddaughter of the emperor, and
that the author of the rumour was the King of Spain,
who sought in this manner to stop a marriage which
would too closely unite France and the house of
Hapsburg.[2] It is on the correspondence of the period,
too, that, conscious how strongly the poor youth was
attached to her, Mary threatened to accept him, in
the hope that the threat would bring Philip II. to
terms.[3]

---

[1] Additions aux Mémoires de Castelnau, liv. iii. 552.
[2] Ibid.
[3] Spanish Correspondence quoted, Mignet, i. 134.

Among the other Continental dignitaries not already named who, by their own desire or the schemes of diplomatists, were counted among the suitors for Queen Mary's hand, there were—the young Count of Orleans, of the house of Dunois, the nephew of her mother's first husband; the Duke of Nemours, of the house of Savoy; and the Duke of Ferrara. Greater than any of these was the young King of Denmark. The unhappy Eric, King of Sweden, was another competitor for her hand; and his suit was pressed with considerable earnestness for nearly three years after her arrival in Scotland. His subsequent misfortunes were caused by personal defects, which were not likely to be considered in the estimate of his claim. Politically, such a union would have been the best that could be found for the Protestant party; and Queen Elizabeth, if the affair had not been one about which female caprices and jealousies had got possession of her, would certainly have felt that a union between Scotland and a Protestant state fast rising into the position of a great European power was sound policy for the Protestant interest, and would have furthered the claims of the King of Sweden with her usual energy. Mary herself had, as we have seen, her own designs, to which it was not convenient to attract attention by the peremptory rejection of other proposals, and the negotiation with Sweden was allowed barely to live until it exhausted itself.

All this while there passed between the two queens expressions of cordial sympathy and intimacy, Mary throughout leaning with seductive confidingness on the counsel of her royal sister in the serious affair of her marriage. It is observable, however, that among her many letters to Queen Elizabeth which have been preserved, none are in the genial easy spirit of her French letters written with her own hand to her friends abroad. Whether she could write in English or Scotch at that time is, as we have seen, questionable. The few letters to Elizabeth in French, and the much larger number in Scotch, are drawn by secretaries, and only pass out of the etiquette of state papers to express the feeling of cordial attachment and sympathy which the draughtsman was instructed to throw into his communication. Throughout, in the midst of the most profuse professions of regard and confidence, Mary is firm on the one essential point between them —she will give no distinct assent or ratification to the treaty of Edinburgh; and in the arrangements for their meeting, it was stipulated that "the said Queen of Scots shall not be pressed with anything she shall show herself to mislike, before that she be freely returned into her own realm."[1] This meeting, which was never to be, went so far on the face of the negotiations that the French ambassador De Foix reported to Catherine of Medici how it was to be held at Nottingham on the 8th of September 1562. He wrote in great alarm, anticipating a cordial alliance between the two queens, which would extinguish all remains of the ancient alliance with Scotland, and give England such an increase of power as would probably soon be proved in the recapture of Calais.[2]

But at that time the great civil war had begun in which the Guises led the contest against the Huguenots, as representing not only the interests of Catholicism but the throne itself, since the king was in their

[1] Labanoff, i. 152.   [2] Teulet, ii. 24.

possession. Queen Elizabeth sent over troops to aid the Huguenots. Randolph officially communicated this act to Queen Mary, who received the information in sadness, but in candour and courtesy, saying she believed her uncles were true subjects of their prince, and did but execute their orders; adding, that "she was not so unreasonable as to condemn those who differed from her in opinion, still less was she inclined on their account to abate anything of the friendship she felt for his mistress the Queen of England." The astute reporter of this scene assured Cecil, his master, in the end of December 1563, that Mary heard almost as seldom from France as the King of Muscovy.[1]

In fact, the gifted pupil of the Italianised French Court, under her winning smile and the bland courtesy which seemed also so full of candour, kept impenetrably hidden a subtle dissimulation, which was high art beside the clumsy cunning of Elizabeth and her English advisers, who could not rid themselves of the consciousness that they were doing what was uncongenial to British natures, and were ever apt to overact or otherwise bungle their part. At Holyrood the practised statesman felt secure in his communications with a woman, young, gentle, and inexperienced, whose weaknesses were a careless frivolity and too easy reliance on others. At Westminster the same practised statesman would have an uneasy consciousness that there was duplicity in the communication with him, though he might not be able to trace it home.

In the course of the friendly messages between the two queens, which chiefly now bore on the question of the marriage, Sir James Melville was sent to Elizabeth.

[1] Document quoted, P. F. Tytler, vi. 269.

He was a shrewd observer with a strong sense of the
ludicrous, as well as an accomplished courtier; and his
account of the attentions paid to him, the professions
lavished on him, and the tricks, as they might be
termed, to secure his confidence, is highly amusing.
He was not for a moment deceived, and set down the
whole as dissimulation and jealousy.[1] His mission
occurred at a curious juncture in the affair of the marriage, which gives a zest to his personal sketches of
Darnley, Leicester, and other bystanders, as well as
of Elizabeth herself. We are told how she stealthily
shows him Leicester's picture, comparing the handsome courtierly man it represents with "yonder long
lad" the Lord Darnley, and drives the faithful courtier
nearly frantic by determining to have his candid opinion
on her own personal beauty as compared with that of
his mistress. At his wits' end how to give her some
honest praise, he had his opportunity at last, when it
was managed that by chance he should hear her performing on the virginals, and pleaded that while wandering about "his ear was ravished with her melody,
which drew him into the chamber he could scarcely
tell how."[2]

Just before this visit Elizabeth had declared herself
on the question of the marriage. She had objected to
every claimant brought forward by others. Her position seemed unreasonable; but when she changed it
for a positive recommendation, she only added amazement to the other misgivings and difficulties, by proposing her own favourite, Leicester. What did she mean
by this?—was it to extinguish temptation by fixing a
gulf between her and one whom she loved not wisely,

[1] Memoirs, 129.   [2] Ibid., 125.

but too well? Was it to shut the mouth of scandal, by a sort of protest that she was totally indifferent to him? Was it a mere dash into the diplomatic proceedings about her royal sister's marriage, for the purpose of throwing them into confusion? These are questions which those only who know what kind of sentiments may vibrate through such sinewy hearts as hers can profess to solve. The proposal scattered dismay among Elizabeth's sage advisers, who wist not what to do. Leicester had been giving himself airs among them; and though they might consider him a rash young man, whose intellect was inflated by intoxicating draughts of regal caresses, yet some of the wisest of them covertly sought his good wish, as that of the man who might some day soon be their master. Randolph, in his confidential communings with Cecil, muttered his uneasiness in conjectures about "how unwilling the queen's majesty herself would be to depart from him, and how hardly his mind could be diverted or drawn from that worthy room where it is placed, let any man see, where it cannot be thought that it is so fixed for ever, that the world would judge worse of him than of any living man, if he should not rather yield his life than alter his thoughts."[1] Mary not having fallen in love with Leicester—whom, by the way, she never saw—did not abandon her ambitious projects of a great regal alliance; and after having slighted suitors who, if below her mark, were still royal, received the proposal to marry the upstart favourite of her rival with an angry disdain, which she could not or did not wish to conceal. Murray seemed desirous of the match, at least he spoke

[1] Quoted, Tytler, vi. 288.

well of it. Leicester himself seems to have been silent, awaiting his destiny at the hands of Elizabeth.

To this point had come the various negotiations and intrigues for providing Mary with a husband, when the tall person and fresh boyish face of a foolish youth settled the matter by love at first sight. It was at Wemyss Castle, a weather-beaten fortress on a rock rising from the northern coast of the Firth of Forth, that Mary first saw her cousin, Henry Stewart, Lord Darnley, about the middle of February 1565. He had just come from England to join his father, and finding the queen absent from Edinburgh on one of her many progresses, he took the privilege of a relation to push on and visit her. They had no sooner met than the many keen eyes who watched the young widow and the handsome youth saw what was to be.

The meeting was by no means a matter of accident on the part of others, though Mary does not appear to have furthered or expected it. The young man's birth placed him naturally within the view of those who busied themselves about the disposal of her hand. He was of a family which had branched off from the old Stewart stock before it became royal, and several early intermarriages connected his ancestry with the reigning line of the family. His connection with the throne of Scotland followed that of the house of Hamilton. He was more closely allied to the English throne, since his mother, Margaret Douglas, was a daughter of Henry VIII.'s sister Margaret, the widow of James IV., by her marriage with Angus. According to the rules of strict lineal descent, Mary was at that time heir to the crown of England, as the child of Margaret's son, and he was next after her in succession as the descendant of Margaret's daughter. He was the nearest prince of the blood in Queen Elizabeth's Court, and Sir James Melville saw him take that place in one of the ceremonials of Leicester's promotion. There was much parade, and some difficulty, about his father, Lennox, obtaining leave to visit Scotland about his personal affairs, as if both Elizabeth and the other parties concerned felt that there was something more in view than the mere object avowed. It was with the becoming and very natural profession of joining his father that the young Darnley visited the queen, and at once found himself on the summit of fortune's wheel. Elizabeth professed herself extremely indignant that two of her subjects should have taken the opportunity of their leave of absence to transact business so important.

To Murray and the Protestant lords the crisis was now approaching, and they felt it. Darnley belonged to the Church of Rome, and thus the question which religious party should have the influence of the queen's husband on its side was coming to a determination. Matters might have been much worse; and few people either in England or Scotland then knew the imminent risk, that the most powerful monarch of the day, who was at the same time the most ardent champion of the Popedom, might have a legitimate right to dictate to Scotland. The Protestant lords felt, however, that in the prospect of the marriage the queen was showing the flag of her true party.

Murray resolved at this juncture to try his strength in a form which suggests strange associations with subsequent events—he tried it not against Darnley himself, but against Bothwell, who had just returned from France, where he had sought refuge from the criminal

charge already spoken of. That charge Murray now
urged against him — it was the same strange plot
against the queen in which he had the mad Arran
as his confidant and denouncer.

The indictment against Bothwell for high treason
came up for trial on the 2d of May 1564, before the
Earl Argyle as Lord Justice-General, one of Murray's
supporters. It is one of the most remarkable instances
on record of a judicial proceeding being turned into a
trial of party strength, yielding only in this characteristic to another and more memorable trial to which
Bothwell was called. Finding his enemy too strong
for him, he disappeared and was outlawed. Randolph
reported the triumphant support given to Murray in
these terms: "The company that came to this town in
favour of my Lord of Murray are esteemed five or six
thousand, and for my part I assure your honour I never
saw a greater assembly." It was put on the record of
the trial at Bothwell's instance that he "dare not compear for fear of his life at this time and place, by
reason of the great convention of his enemies and
unfriends."[1] Thus, though his power was tottering,
Murray found and showed that he still ruled in Scotland. The terms in which Randolph continues his letter are curious and significant, as the first traces noted
by a contemporary on the spot of the queen's partiality
for Bothwell — yet what the agent meant to convey
was probably rather the evidence of her antipathy to
Murray. "The queen," he says, "has shown herself
now of late to mislike of Murray that he so earnestly
pursued him"—namely, Bothwell; "and further, the
queen would not that the justice-clerk should proceed,

[1] Pitcairn, i. 464*.

which hath bred here so mighty mislike, and given occasion to such kind of talk against her grace for bearing with such men in her own cause, that that which is already spoken passeth all measure. So many discontented, so large talk, so plain and open speech, I never heard in any nation; and, in my simple judgment, see not but it must burst out to some great mischief."[1] These sentences, which, estimated by the light of subsequent events, seem inspired by the spirit of prophecy, are but Randolph hinting, with the proper technical mysteriousness, that Murray is going down, and a new ruling influence arising in Scotland.

It is at this juncture that another remarkable actor in the tragic events to come appears on the stage— David Rizzio, the Italian. As he is never spoken of among his contemporaries except either in contempt or hatred, it is difficult to know his social position and his personal qualities. He certainly had not that distinction of birth which would enable him to refer to his family as one publicly known for its eminence. But people seldom asked about the family of any of the Italians, so numerously scattered among the European courts: they were gentlemen at least by training and education, and able by their subtle talents to hold their own place among the local feudal aristocracy. Buchanan, to whom we owe nearly all that is known of his early history, says he was a native of Turin, and came to Scotland in the train of Morette, or Moretti, the Piedmontese ambassador, who arrived in the year 1561, and that he entered the queen's service as a musician, being a skilful singer and performer.[2] Some writers on the history of Scottish music have

---

[1] Raumer, 46.   [2] Buchanan, xvii. 44. See Teulet, ii. 50, 76.

suggested, but on no better foundation than his reputed skill, that he may have been the author of the old melodies so much loved by natives and admired by strangers. That he was old, deformed, and strikingly ugly, has been generally accepted by historians, but is not said of him by either Knox or Buchanan, both of whom had opportunities of seeing him, and were not inclined to forget anything likely to render him odious. The common notion of his personal appearance seems to have been derived from the account of Adam Blackwood, who is very unlikely to have ever seen him; but it is a matter of no real moment in the events with which the poor man was connected.

It is more important to correct another common supposition, that Mary advanced him to high offices of state. Such an act might seem naturally a continuation of the practice established under Mary of Lorraine as regent; but the two things are, when examined, very different. Rizzio was at best a man who had to find his own livelihood, employed at what his services were worth to his employer; the foreigners promoted by the regent were Frenchmen of high rank sent to Scotland to carry out the French projects of domination. There can be no doubt, however, that the Italian was very valuable to the queen, and very powerful. Knox seems accurately to describe his official position in saying, "The queen usit him for secretary in things that appertainit to her secret affairs in France or elsewhere."[1]

A skilful person, versed in foreign languages, on whom she could rely, was extremely valuable to her at this time. Some other persons flit casually across her

[1] Knox, ii. 422.

own correspondence, and the other letters of the period, in the same capacity. One, named Chesein, carries despatches to her Guise relations and other correspondents, and is also intrusted with verbal communications.[1] A man called Yaxley—an Englishman apparently, who had been secretary to the Council in the reign of Edward VI.—was sent on a special mission to the Netherlands, where, through the Duchess of Arschot, he communicated with the Duchess of Parma, the regent, who thought his communications so important that she passed him on to deliver them at the Court of Spain. This man seems to have been a babbler, who boasted of his diplomatic services and his influences, and there is no trace of his having been again employed. His revelations were reported to Elizabeth, who founded on them in her complaints of the risk she incurred from the machinations of Mary.[2] Another of her emissaries was David Chambers, a follower of Bothwell, a scholar and an author, who had studied and served abroad, knew the politics and the customs of most European states, and had no scruples.

The French ambassador mentions an Italian, Francisque, her *maître d'hôtel*, as one of her confidential advisers; but the one who, next to Rizzio, seems to have been deepest in her counsels, was named Raulet. He was in the Low Countries transacting business with the Spanish authorities at this juncture, while Beaton represented her in France. Rizzio then was virtually her secretary for the foreign affairs, in relation to which these were her emissaries or ambassadors.[3] There was

---

[1] Labanoff, i. 200, 209. See above, p. 253.
[2] Teulet, ii. 53, 84.
[3] Ibid., 76. Labanoff, i. 200, 202.

serious business in hand for them all, since the crisis was approaching which found Mary a member of the Catholic League. It is part of the mystery, however, of the poor Italian's history, that, though he was thus deeply occupied in politics, scarcely any traces of his movements have survived. He is not referred to so frequently as Raulet and Chesein in the correspondence before his death. There is scarcely a known document under his hand, and it has been difficult to identify his signature.

It was rumoured at the time that the Italian did his best to forward the marriage with Darnley. Such a course was natural; it would unite duty with self-interest. Darnley belonged to "The Church," and so the claims of religion were satisfied. He was not a man likely to govern without help, and supersede the queen's adviser; while under any great foreign potentate Rizzio might have been nobody. It was well, too, if other objects did not preponderate, to keep favour by giving the advice most agreeable to his patroness.

On the 15th of May 1565, a special council or assembly of great feudal lords and officers of state was held at Stirling. It was not a Parliament, nor was it a mere Privy Council. There is no authentic list of those present, nor are there the means of ascertaining the criterion on which they were selected. It is stated, however, that among those present were Hamilton, Duke of Chatelherault, always called "The Duke," with the Lords of Athole, Ruthven, Morton, Glencairn, Lindsay, Rothes, Glammis, Semple, Boyd, and several others high in feudal influence. Murray was present; but singularly enough, considering the business to be transacted, the name of Lennox does not occur on the lists.[1] To this assemblage Mary announced her intended marriage with Darnley. A curious incident happened outside the castle where the meeting was held. Throckmorton, coming post from England to argue and protest against the proceedings which were to take place that day, arrived at the gate of Stirling Castle while the lords were assembled. Though he had sent his cousin Middlemore before him to demand an audience, he found the gate shut, and a deaf ear given to all his demands and prayers for admission. He was obliged to seek his own lodging in the town, whence he was afterwards called by the queen to an audience.[2] After his audience was over, Darnley was created Lord of Ardmanach and Earl of Ross, as steps to the rank he was presently to be lifted to. This earldom, bringing down the traditions of the old Maarmorate, was, as we have seen, reserved as a title to the royal family, after the manner in which the French monarchy reserved for the princes of the blood the titles of the royal fiefs which were from time to time annexed to the crown.

Difficulties were now thickening round Murray and the Protestant party. The Lennox family recovered their great feudal power in the west. In the north the Gordons, being left for some time unmolested, were gathering up the fragments of their old authority. Other men of influence, who were secret Romanists or but doubtful Protestants—a body larger among the aristocracy than the Reformation party—now found that they could act according to their inclinations or interests without danger. There was but one reliance for the Reformation party—that England would come

---

[1] Keith (8vo edition), ii. 280. [2] Ibid.

to the rescue. The opportunity for carrying out the policy begun by Henry VIII., and establishing an English supremacy supported by Protestantism in Scotland, had never been so good as now, when two parties, hating each other, and each in fear of extirpation by the other, were trembling in the balance. The opportunity was so good that the Protestant party in Scotland seemed not to doubt that it would be seized. Elizabeth's advisers thought so too, and felt provoked as the time for action slipped past. Randolph, in his impatience, pressed it on Cecil that if troops were not to be sent, money alone, and but little of that, might accomplish great things. "A little now spent in the beginning affordeth double fruit. What were it for the queen's majesty, if she list not to do it by force, with the expense of three or four thousand pounds, to do with this country what she would?"[1]

Elizabeth, however, was sullenly immovable. She had protested in various forms against the marriage, and even by some stretch of the law had got the only member of Darnley's family left in England—his mother, Lady Lennox—committed to the Tower. She had even obtained resolutions by the English Council condemnatory of the marriage, as a matter affecting an English subject of the blood royal and the succession of the crown of England. But there were reasons why the Queen of England's opposition should be limited to mere words. The marriage was, on the whole, not unsatisfactory. It was to the two queens what an act of folly or imprudence is in ordinary life—rivals and competitors must for decency's sake protest against it, but are not sincerely vexed at heart to hear

[1] Quoted, Tytler, vi. 344.

of a fall which will substitute pity for rivalry. If, when the Armada was in the Channel, Elizabeth knew and remembered how near, to all human appearance, her rival was to the throne of Spain, she must have more fully estimated the peril escaped by England and Protestantism in the advancement of her worthless cousin.

The profession of amity, however, between the two queens was kept up, and, on Mary's side at least, with great skill to the last. She commissioned Lethington, who was in England, to press for Elizabeth's approval of the marriage. That rather self-willed and tortuous statesman, however, had his own views, and resolved to pursue them. He was on his way back to Scotland, probably alarmed at the course of matters there, when he met Beaton, Mary's messenger, at Newark, and finding his worst fears confirmed by the instructions sent to him, instead of returning to London, joined Throckmorton, the ambassador sent from England to remonstrate with Mary; and, like the other chiefs of the Protestant party, consulted with him how to thwart the marriage. She sent afterwards John Hay, commendator of Balmerinoch, called also her "principal master of requests," with instructions dated 14th June 1565, in which she professed an anxiety to conciliate Elizabeth, and obtain her approval of the now arranged marriage.[1]

It was necessary, however, that professions of amity between the sovereigns should cease; and Randolph, who had the disagreeable part of the discussion on his hands, was the first to feel the change. Writing to Leicester on the 5th of February 1564, he says in

[1] Keith, ii. 293; Labanoff, i. 271; Teulet, ii. 56.

his simplicity, " It may please your lordship to understand that this queen is now content to give good ear unto the queen's majesty's suit in your behalf." Blandly satisfied about his reception in Scotland, he continues: " Greater entertainment or greater honour could not be done to the greatest ambassador that the queen's majesty could have sent unto this queen than was done to me at St Andrews. For four days together I dined and supped daily at her grace's table. I sat next unto herself, saving worthy Beton, our mistress. I had longer talk and conference with her than any other during the time; enough, I assure your lordship, if I were able to report all, can make all the ill-willers to both these queens' felicities to burst asunder for envy."[1] Afterwards, on the 2d of July, when he had been, partly with persuasion and partly with threat, urging Darnley to go back like an obedient subject to England, and thereupon craved audience of the queen, " I was received," he says, " in stranger sort than ever I was before, as a man new and first come into her presence, whom she had never seen."[2] So far as the Court was concerned, the English connection might now be considered at an end. The Court of France was not in a position to exercise its old influence in Scotland; but when the civil conflicts were over and the Guises supreme, the French alliance might be expected to revive with renewed vigour.

It is stated in Knox's History and elsewhere that the queen strove hard to persuade Murray to assent to the marriage. His determined refusal was the keynote to the views of those who still adhered to the

---

[1] Wright's Queen Elizabeth, i. 188.
[2] Letter to Cecil, Keith, ii. 298.

Protestant party. It was intended to hold a Parliament at Perth, and there solemnly desire the assent of the Estates of Scotland to the union; but the position taken up by Murray and his friends suggested that it would be the safer policy to evade a Parliament, as its concurrence could not be calculated on, and discussions of which no one could foresee the result might arise from bringing together parties fiercely opposed.

A General Assembly meeting in Edinburgh at the time when it was intended that the Parliament should have met at Perth, afforded in the mean time a sort of rallying-point for the more zealous of the Protestant party. This meeting had been preceded by a local event of an exciting nature. It had become the practice to expect a scuffle with the followers of the old religion during their Easter celebrations. It is related in Knox's History how some of the brethren, " diligent to search such things," having with them one of the bailies of Edinburgh, " took one Sir John Carvet, riding hard, as he had now ended the saying of the mass, and conveyed him, together with the master of the house and one or two more of the assistants, to the Tolbooth, and immediately revested him, with all his garments upon him, and so carried him to the market-cross, where they set him on high, binding the chalice to his hand, and himself fast tied to the said cross, where he tarried the space of one hour, during which time the boys served him with his Easter eggs. The next day following, the said Carvet, with his assistants, were accused and convinced by an assize, according to the Act of Parliament; and albeit for the same offence he deserved death, yet for all punishment he was set upon the market-cross for the space of three or four hours, the hangman standing by and keeping him, the boys and others busy with egg-casting."[1]

Then arose a tumult in which the poor priest might have fared still worse, but the provost coming with the town guard carried him back to the Tolbooth. The magistrates received a royal letter, calling on them to prosecute the rioters, and altogether in a more peremptory tone than any of the previous communications from the queen in matters where her own religion was concerned. The priest was released, and the matter went no further.

This was felt, however, as a heavy grievance by the Protestant clergy, and helped with many other things to strengthen the zeal with which they met in General Assembly, in the Nether Tolbooth, on the 25th of June 1565. They resolved, in the first place, "that the papistical and blasphemous mass, with all papistry and idolatry of Paip's jurisdiction, be universally suppressed and abolished throughout the haill realm, not only in the subjects, but in the queen's majesty's own person, with punishment against all persons that shall be deprehended to transgress and offend the same; and that the sincere Word of God and His true religion now presently received might be established, approven, and ratified throughout the whole realm, as well in the queen's majesty's own person as in the subjects, without any impediment."[2]

It was further proposed that there should be a certain amount of compulsory attendance at worship by Act of Parliament. The Assembly took the opportunity to urge that the large ecclesiastical revenues otherwise disposed of, under the arrangement made in

[1] Knox, ii. 476.   [2] Book of the Universal Kirk.

1563, should be transferred to the Protestant Church. Five members of the Assembly were appointed to present these "articles" to the queen; and it is observable that they were all, though worshipful gentlemen, persons of little note in the history of the period, as if the presentation were a mere form, and not an agreeable one. The five commissioners were—Walter Lundie of Lundie, in Fifeshire; William Cunningham of Cunninghamhead, in Ayrshire; William Durham of Grange, in Forfarshire; George Hume of Spot, in Berwickshire; and James Barron, burgess of Edinburgh.[1]

These commissioners went to the queen at Perth, and waited on her, "desiring and requiring her highness most humbly to advise therewith, and to give them an answer." Having retired to their quarters, expecting next morning to be summoned to receive the answer, they found that the queen had slipped out of their hands and gone to Dunkeld. Thither they followed her. They obtained audience, and were told by the queen that she required the advice of her Council in the matter, but that she proposed in a week to be in Edinburgh, and then they would get answer.

The answer, in as far as it has been preserved, exemplifies a peculiar distinction in practice between the two great creeds—that Roman Catholics, when not predominant, profess principles of toleration; while among Calvinistic Protestants, the time when they have least power is that in which they profess their most intolerant doctrines. She assured her loving subjects that as she had not in times past, so would she not hereafter, "press the conscience of any, but

[1] Knox, ii. 486, Laing's note.

that they may worship God in such sort as they are persuaded in their conscience to be best." She meekly desired the same toleration for her own conscience. But even in this placid document there were suggestive allusions to the quarter to which the queen was then looking for strength and support, and it was not one from which the principles of toleration were likely to radiate. Among the reasons why she must adhere to her religion was that by apostasy "she should lose the friendship of the King of France—the married ally of this realm—and of other great princes her friends and confederates, who could take the same in evil part, and of whom she may look for their great support in all her difficulties." The abandonment of the ecclesiastical revenues, so far as they were in the possession of the crown, was civilly declined.[1]

It appears to have crossed the thoughts of the more zealous members of the Assembly in the mean time to organise an armed resistance; for we are told that they assembled on St Leonard's Craig, a small rocky eminence between Edinburgh and Arthur's Seat, "where they concluded they would defend themselves, and for the same purpose elected eight persons of the most able, two of every quarter, to see that the brethren should be ready armed."[2] Four burgesses were cited to answer for this affair; but the prosecution, of which this was the preliminary step, seems to have been abandoned.[3] This incident was supposed to be connected with the designs of Murray, who was then in his mother's Castle of Lochleven, ill or pretending to be so. The queen was living at Perth, where the Parliament was to be held. She had promised to

[1] Knox, ii. 488, 489.   [2] Ibid., 487.   [3] Ibid., 490, Laing's note.

attend the christening of the Lord Livingstone's heir at Callander House near Falkirk, and was prepared to ride thither in company with Darnley. They started together, with a strong escort, at an early hour, and reached Callander by ten o'clock; and the reason assigned for the feat was that thus they avoided an ambush, to be laid by Murray and his confederates, to attack and seize them at a point where the road passed through a rugged defile of the Ochils. The elements of the conspiracy have been very distinctly set forth. Murray himself held Lochleven Castle, on the line of their journey; the Earl of Argyle was to descend with a force from his fortress of Castle Campbell, on the brow of the Ochils; and the Duke of Chatelherault had made his preparations at Kinneil, near to the ferry where the betrothed lovers would cross the Forth. It would not be difficult to believe in such a conspiracy, if tolerably well vouched; but there is scarcely a vestige of evidence in its support.[1] Murray, on his part, maintained that his life was in danger, and kept himself among his own immediate supporters. He was summoned to Court, and offered a safe-conduct for himself and eighty attendants; but he declined to appear—he was making arrangements for armed resistance. To prepare for a crisis, a royal summons was issued on the 22d of July, for a "raid" or general gathering of the crown vassals and their attendants.

The marriage of the queen and Darnley, who had just been created Duke of Albany, was celebrated on the 29th of July 1565. It was preceded by a Papal

[1] See all that can be said for it in Chalmers, i. 140; Tytler, vi. 349; Miss Strickland, iv. 148.

dispensation, on account of affinity in blood, and the ceremony was performed according to the office of the Romish Church. The queen, following the etiquette of a widow of France, wore her solemn state mourning dress, or dule robe, until the festival after the ceremony, when, as a wedded wife, she cast it off, and put on gayer attire. At the festival the ceremonials were imitated from the French Court, which was foremost in the practice of exacting menial services to the person of royalty from subjects of the highest rank. Lord Athole served as sewer, Morton as carver, and Crawford as cupbearer.[1]

[1] Randolph's Letter, in Wright, i. 202, and elsewhere.

CHAPTER XLIV.

Queen Mary.

(*Continued.*)

A STRONG GOVERNMENT—DARNLEY GETS THE TITLE OF KING—PARLIAMENTARY DISPLEASURE WITH THE ASSUMPTION—ARMING OF MURRAY AND HIS SUPPORTERS—THEIR DISPERSAL—PRESENT THEMSELVES TO ELIZABETH—HOW TREATED BY HER—DANGER OF ELIZABETH AND THE PROTESTANT CAUSE—PROJECTS OF THE ROMANIST POWERS — CONFERENCE AT BAYONNE — PHILIP, CATHERINE OF MEDICI, AND ALVA — DARNLEY'S CHARACTER DEVELOPS ITSELF — ODIOUS AMONG THE COURTIERS — HIS WIFE'S APPRECIATION OF HIM — PROGRESS OF RIZZIO'S INFLUENCE—PROJECT FOR PUTTING HIM OUT OF THE WAY—THE BAND FOR HIS SLAUGHTER—ARRANGEMENTS FOR EFFECTING IT—THE SUPPER-PARTY — RIZZIO DRAGGED OUT AND SLAIN — INQUIRY WHEN THE QUEEN KNEW OF HIS DEATH?—HER CONDUCT BEFORE AND AFTER THAT KNOWLEDGE—LURES BACK HER HUSBAND—RETURN OF MURRAY AND HIS FOLLOWERS FROM ENGLAND — MURRAY MAKES PEACE—SECRET ARRANGEMENT OF THE QUEEN AND HER HUSBAND—THEIR ESCAPE TO DUNBAR.

THE world has been so accustomed to treat this marriage as a rash love-match, that what political significance it had is overlooked. This was far less momentous than the questions which a union with Spain or France might have raised, but it was not without importance. Darnley's mother did not forget that she, like Elizabeth, was a granddaughter of Henry VII., with this difference, according to the notion of herself and her religious party, that she was not, like the woman on the throne, tainted with illegitimacy.[1]

The new sovereigns began their reign with measures of successful vigour, which seemed to promise a strong and orderly government under the old religion and the old regal authority. A portion of the Protestant barons, including Murray, Glencairn, Rothes, and Kirkcaldy of Grange, resolved to combine against the new order of things. They stated that the laws against idolatry were not enforced, and that the mass and other abominations were tolerated. They stated, further, that the true religion was oppressed; and though this was not according to strict fact, unless the countenance given to Popery were to be set down as oppression, yet it is plain that Protestantism was in imminent danger; for the queen and her supporters were as fully determined to suppress Heresy whenever they were able, as Knox and his party were to suppress Idolatry. But there were other grounds for opposition of a constitutional character. The queen had not ventured to face a Parliament, and ask their sanction to her late doings. She had not only taken to herself a husband without consulting the great Council of the nation—an indecorous and ungracious thing—but she had proclaimed her husband as King of the Scots. It was maintained that this was illegal, since the monarch reigned by the assent of the Estates of the realm, and could not transfer any portion of the sovereign power to another without the intervention of these Estates. The power asserted by the Estates in such constitutional matters was very wide,

[1] For an animated account of the little opposition court presided over by Lady Lennox, in Yorkshire, see Froude, vii. 387, 389.

and there was at least no precedent to support a denial of the claim in question. The portion of the declaration issued by the discontented barons at Dumfries which refers to this matter is extremely valuable, as one of the few lights, other than what the acts of the Estates themselves give us, on the constitutional power claimed for the Parliament of Scotland. They say—

"Of the same sinister counsel doth proceed that her majesty, without the advice of her Estates, yea, without the advice of the nobility either demanded or given, hath made and proclaimed a king over us, giving unto him, so far as in her highness lieth, power over our lands, lives, and heritages, and whatsoever is dearest unto us on the earth. In the which doing the ancient laws and liberties of this realm are utterly broken, violated, and transgressed, and the liberty of the crown and state royal of Scotland manifestly overthrown, that he was made king over us that neither hath the title thereof by any lineal descent of blood and nature, neither by consent of the Estates."[1] It was afterwards put by Cecil to the French ambassador Le Croc, as a justification of the conduct of Elizabeth, that the assumption of the title of king without the assent of the Estates was contrary to law; and the Frenchman was reminded that even so illustrious a personage as the queen's first husband, Francis, had not taken the title of King of Scotland until it had been accorded by consent of the Estates.[2]

Meanwhile Randolph and Mr Tamworth, who had been sent to join him as a sort of colleague and adviser, with special instructions as to the views of the English Court on the affair of the marriage, found it expedient

[1] Calderwood, Appendix, ii. 573.   [2] Teulet, ii. 73.

A STRONG GOVERNMENT, 1565. 281

to adopt the view of the declaration, and to deny Darnley's right to act as King Henry. Tamworth suffered in the body for a rigid adherence to this principle. Refusing to accept of a safe-conduct in the name of "King Henry," he was detained on his way back to England by the border freebooters, who secured him in Hume Castle, an act which he said had been suggested to them from Holyrood.

Those bound to give suit and military service were repeatedly required to attend the "raid" or array. The absence of important persons from these levies pointed them out as disaffected, and at the same time afforded means of punishing them by feudal forfeitures for default. It was thought fit at the same time specially to cite Murray and a few of the great discontented leaders by public proclamation, with the usual threat of prosecution for treason in case of disobedience. On the 1st of August, Murray was charged to appear under threat of denunciation "to the horn," or by public blast of trumpet; and on the 6th he was denounced accordingly, for, not being a man who would voluntarily place himself in the power of his enemies, he did not appear.

He, with the other discontented barons, assembled at Paisley. Those who had joined the royal raid at the same time marched to Glasgow, so that the two forces were close together. The discontented lords, who with their followers made altogether about a thousand horsemen, passed by Glasgow within sight of the royal pair, and took up their position at Hamilton. The duke was their avowed leader; but he had purposes of his own, differing from theirs, to serve, and they did not work well into each other's hands. They left him, and rode on to Edinburgh. There a provost had been chosen from their own party; but, in obedience to a royal letter, the appointment was cancelled, and a nominee of the Court appointed, who, when the cavalcade approached, directed the alarm-bells to be rung, and endeavoured to prevent the strangers from getting within the gates. They succeeded in entering the town, but were fired at from the castle. They issued missive writings, calling on the Protestants to rally round them; but they utterly failed in their endeavour, and gained no recruits. The royal army, about five thousand strong, had in the mean time marched to Hamilton, and was on its way to Edinburgh. Unable to meet it, the malcontents retreated to Dumfries, whence they issued the remonstrance already referred to.

The king and queen now took prompt measures, for indeed the shortness of the service which could be exacted from the feudal levy required that what was done should be done quickly. They were joined at that juncture by Bothwell, an adherent invaluable when daring and promptitude were needed. This was the beginning of the effective services which placed him, although a subject, in the position of one to whom his monarch owed heavy obligations. He came then from France, bringing with him an agent of many of his doings—David Chambers, a scholar and an author, whose naturally dark and subtle spirit was thoroughly trained in the unscrupulous policy of the Court of France. There arrived nearly at the same time from France the Lord Seton, a zealous member of the old faith, and an able and daring man. He was the head of a house which had been powerful, until the triumph of the Reformation had overwhelmed it; but now, when the day of reaction had come, he returned to re-establish its influence. At the same time George Lord Gordon, the representative of the ruined house of Huntly, who was in law a denounced fugitive, was first relieved from this penal condition, and then step by step restored to the honours and, as far as that was practicable, to the vast possessions which had enabled his father to wage war with the crown. This occurred in August. Some months afterwards, as we shall see, Huntly's sister was married to Bothwell; it was a political alliance for strengthening the cause of the queen and her husband.

They seem in the mean time to have pressed pretty hard on the country in exacting the feudal levy. It could not be detained for a period sufficient for a campaign, and an attempt seems to have been made to remedy this by repeated citation. On the 23d of July, before the marriage, the whole feudal army had been cited to appear at Edinburgh, with fifteen days' provision. On the 6th of August there was another citation of a raid to attend the king and queen on a progress through Fife. On the 22d of August all were again called to Edinburgh, with fifteen days' provision; and on the 17th of September the fencible men of the southern counties were cited to appear at Stirling on the 1st of October. Absence from these raids incurred feudal forfeitures. These had to be levied by the courts of law; and it would depend on the question whether the sovereign or some party among his subjects had the upper hand, how far the penalties would be levied. On the present occasion the crown was triumphant, and the recusants had to fear the worst. Their danger enabled the sovereign to extract aids from them in the shape of compromises, in which the legal proceedings were bought off. Making a progress northward through Fifeshire, money was thus raised from several of the gentry and royal burghs, including a considerable sum extracted from the town of Dundee. Edinburgh was peculiarly disaffected. Certain of the citizens being required to appear at Holyrood, a composition was demanded, which they refused to pay, trusting probably that they would be able to evade or defy its enforcement by the courts of law. A transaction curiously suggestive of the feudal usages of the day followed. Money was much needed by the Court, and if threats would not force enough from the citizens of Edinburgh, any other available means must be taken. In the end a bargain was concluded, and they advanced a thousand pounds, receiving in pledge of repayment the superiority or feudal lordship of the neighbouring town of Leith. The Government repented of the bargain, and tried to cancel it; but the corporation of Edinburgh had already taken feudal sasine, and their hold was absolute, through the unyielding forms of the feudal law. It was the privilege of the burgesses of royal burghs to be the direct vassals of the crown; but by this transaction one corporation was made feudally subordinate to another—an arrangement which naturally occasioned many irritating disputes in later times.

Mary loudly demanded aid from France, and had it been obtained the peril of Elizabeth's crown and the Protestant cause would have been greatly increased. But it was not for Catherine of Medici, if she could decently help it, to let the fast ally of Philip of Spain and her own old rival in France become Queen of England. Castelnau de Mauvissière was sent to

Scotland to keep matters quiet, and a better messenger for such a purpose could not be found. Grave, conscientious, friendly, and peaceful, he was beyond his age, and was peculiarly free of the impulsive, warlike, and ostentatious propensities which have characterised his countrymen in all ages. His lengthy, and to all appearance faithful, record of his endeavours, only recently become known, throws a powerful light on the inner workings of the political mechanism. He brought with him certain letters from the young King of France to the discontented lords, urging them to quietness and to compromise. This, it will be observed, was in accordance with that patronising practice of the French Court, which was apt to overlook the diplomatic rule that sovereigns are only to communicate with sovereigns. In a four hours' interview which Castelnau had with Mary, she tried on him all the various resources of her passionate and subtle nature. She became tempestuously angry, she cried, she besought him with seductive remindings of his old kindly attachment to the house of Guise—surely he would not do to her, a crowned queen, the dishonour of holding communication in name of another sovereign with her rebel subjects. Rather let it go forth that his mission is to arrange for the powerful armament that is to be sent by her brother of France to crush them. She spoke, seemingly, with the vehement impetuosity of one who had cast her fortunes on a die and was to abide the issue. The Frenchman spoke earnestly of the miseries of civil war, of which he had seen only too much at home; it might be so, but she was a sovereign, and was not to let her kingdom become a republic—she would die sooner; and so, whether helped from France or not, she would go at the head of her faithful subjects and put down the rebels. Castelnau, following his instructions, and totally unsuspicious of what was to occur in his own country, told her that the discontented lords only sought what was conceded to the Huguenots of France—permission to follow in peace their own religious observance, what we in this day call toleration; but she indignantly answered that they were her rebellious subjects, that they were conspiring against her own and her husband's life.

Castelnau ventured respectfully to hint that this was an exaggeration put into her head by their calumnious enemies; for courts, he said, were haunted by backbiters, who attacked the absent and defenceless; and as to the faults of her subjects, it were better that she should overlook these than drive them to the extremity of civil war. Those councillors who were loudest for war were not always the most valiant when it came to action; and many were the princes who had begun a civil contest in the haughty resolution of humbling ambitious subjects, and had come to see the day when they would have been glad to buy peace with the concessions at first arrogantly denied. The sage and moderate statesman pleaded in vain; the haughty queen had now taken the course she had long kept in the impenetrable recesses of her own bosom. It is significant that, in the same Memoir in which he describes the beginning of her headlong career, he mentions Bothwell as her right-hand man, and likely to be made lieutenant-general of the kingdom — so began this man's disastrous influence.[1]

[1] Discours sur la Voyage de Sieur de Castelnau en Escosse; Teulet, ii. 101.

On the 8th of October the royal army, with the queen and her husband at its head, left Edinburgh and marched by Stirling and Crawford towards Dumfries. On their approach the discontented barons retreated into England, abiding at Carlisle, and dismissing their small band of followers. To all appearance the Reformation had now been virtually subdued, and the old Church was again predominant in Scotland. At Queen Elizabeth's Court this was naturally deemed a serious calamity. It has been seen that she was recommended to strike a blow before the fatal marriage was accomplished. If she ever entertained such a design, she hesitated in execution till it became too late. Circumstances had now greatly changed. To have conferred on Murray and his party an overwhelming power, while they were yet nominally at peace with their sovereign, would have seemed nothing else than strengthening the established Government. The queen would have found it necessary, with all proper grace, to submit to the influence of the Lords of the Congregation, as she had done in the campaign against Huntly and the punishment of the western Romanists. But now these lords were in arms against their sovereign, and to support them would be countenancing a principle for which Elizabeth had a despot's thorough detestation. When the lords, therefore, applied to her for an army of three thousand men and a fleet, they received no answer. At the same time, if it could be done with propriety and safety, it was extremely desirable that Murray and his party should be saved from utter extinction. The English representatives, Randolph and Tamworth, gave them encouragement, and raised expectations not to be realised. There has long been known a characteristic letter from Elizabeth to the Earl of Bedford, Warden of the Marches, which develops with clearness and precision the policy of the English Court on this nice question. If Murray is in such want of money that a thousand pounds will be of service to help him to defend himself, it may be conveyed to him as from Bedford himself. As to armed assistance, she had "no intention, for many respects, to maintain any other prince's subjects to take arms against their sovereign;" but in this instance there were to be diplomatic representations made, not only by herself, but by the French ambassador, that Murray and his friends might have a fair trial and a just and merciful consideration—that they were not then in a position to levy actual war, but were in reality offering to submit themselves as good subjects, and were only defending themselves from extermination. The matter being viewed in this light, Bedford might secretly gather a small force by way of strengthening the garrison of Carlisle, as a Scottish army was about to approach the border. If he found he could make this force effectual for the protection of the lords, he might then, at the critical moment, move on Dumfries.[1]

As a key to the significance of these events, and especially of Elizabeth's share in them, it is necessary to remember that the cause of the old religion had received at that juncture a great impulse in Europe, which had not yet been met by a reaction. There was good ground to apprehend that France and Spain were to abandon their rivalry, and, with the guidance and temporal aid of the Supreme Pontiff, to enter on an alliance to crush heresy wherever they could find it.

[1] Robertson, Appendix, xiv.

Scotland, the Italian states, and the Catholic states of Germany, were converging to the same centre of action. The French Huguenots felt the peril which afterwards drove them into civil war, but were not yet prepared to act. In the north of England a large body of Romanists were restless and expectant. The Scottish queen, by declining to accept of the treaty of Edinburgh, adhered to her claim on the English throne; and the Catholic powers, leagued as they were together, would seize it for her if they could. A letter of private information by the French ambassador De Foix to Catherine of Medici, dated 29th September 1565, in its calm and guarded estimate of Queen Elizabeth's position, gives a lively notion of the dangers of the juncture. He is of opinion that Queen Elizabeth cannot give any assistance to the rebel lords; she has enough to do to protect herself. Though he has heard that Queen Mary made the idle boast that she would march at the head of her army until it reached London, he gives it as his own mature opinion that she will not venture to cross the border. But then the council which Elizabeth had summoned, separated, not without a suspicion that some favoured the claim of Queen Mary. The Lords of Northumberland, Westmoreland, and Cumberland were summoned to Court, that they might be delivered from the temptation of joining Queen Mary's army if it crossed the border. To these symptoms—which to the Frenchman were matters not of alarm, but of study—was added the news that the great O'Neil—whom he calls "Le Grand Honvel"—had taken two of the principal royal fortresses in Ireland in the service of Queen Mary as Queen of Ireland, and that to arrange about this affair, she sent over to him two Highland ambassadors—gentlemen " du pais des sauvages d'Ecosses"—who could speak his language.[1]

The juncture was one of imminent peril to the liberties and the Protestantism of England. Elizabeth dared not quarrel with any of the powers which looked on England with silent menace, and she found it absolutely necessary to propitiate them, each in its turn. She was not in a position to attack the Queen of Scots. She was especially anxious to retain the amity of France, and professed even to encourage a proposal for becoming the wife of the young king. Both the Spanish and French ambassadors at her Court dropped ominous hints of suspicion that she was secretly aiding the Protestant lords of Scotland in rebellion against their sovereign. So pressed, Elizabeth did not hesitate to cast them off, and succeeded in doing so with flagrant publicity. Murray and the Commendator of Kilwinning went to London to plead the common cause. They were received, no doubt by prearrangement, in the presence of the French and Spanish ambassadors, where, to their amazement, they encountered a hearty scolding for their audacity, rebels and traitors as they were to their legitimate sovereign, in appearing before her, a sovereign too. She demanded of them a declaration that she had never given them any countenance in their traitorous resistance. Murray knew very well that if he attempted to thwart her, he was ruined for ever. He deemed it the wiser policy—and the result showed him to be right—to play into Elizabeth's game, and clear her of suspicion. The reward of the sacrifice had to be patiently waited for.

In tracing the direct effect on Scotland of the impulse

[1] Teulet, ii. 85.

given to Romanism abroad at that time, it is convenient to look at events occurring in the remote French town of Bayonne, on the Spanish frontier. Catherine of Medici had repeatedly expressed an eager desire to have a personal interview with her son-in-law, King Philip of Spain, and planned a method of accomplishing such a meeting without attracting suspicion to it as a solemn conference, by suggesting that Philip should hold a progress through the north-eastern provinces of his dominions, while she and her son held a like progress in the south of France. Each might then step a short way aside, and meet, as it were, by a fortunate casualty. Such a progress Catherine and her son made in the beginning of the year 1565, passing deliberately from town to town with great pomp and splendour, and slowly approaching the Spanish frontier. Catherine's daughter, the Queen of Spain, went dutifully to Bayonne to meet her mother. Philip himself did not join them, but he sent one well fitted to represent him—his destroying general, Alva. From his recently-discovered letters we have his own account of the secret conclaves to which the two dark spirits retired from the ostensible gaieties of the royal meeting. They soon found that, though each was unscrupulous, their aims were not in unison. Philip had one single object before him—the Church, of which he had become the sworn champion. For the Church, but for the Church alone, and for nothing else in this world, he was prepared to plunder and torture and forswear himself—to do anything required. It was not external conformity that, like politic and worldly princes, he looked to, but sincere faith and true belief. He therefore, instead of waiting till it made itself visible, tried to find heresy wherever it lurked, that he might extirpate it by fire, axe, and cord; believing that whatever cruelties brought the victim to orthodoxy, and consequently to salvation, were, in a higher estimate than that of the world, acts of beneficence, and that if the cruelty failed to convert, it accomplished the next best thing, by destroying the earthly tabernacle of heresy.

In this spirit Alva addressed the Italian, demanding of her why heresy was not extirpated in France. When he was told of the strength of the Huguenot party, he considered its existence all the greater a scandal. Not only could he see no reason why greatness and power should save any one from the destruction that was his due, but he flung it as a reproach on the Government of France that there were princes of the blood and heads of the first houses favourable to the heretics, and the very chancellor himself was a Huguenot. It was put as an immediate practical measure of a modified kind, that France should expel the Huguenot clergy and exact conformity, or should, as an alternative, try to strike terror by cutting off some five or six of the principal heads. The Italian tried her diplomatic art by suggesting some royal marriages advantageous to both countries, and hinting that, if these were brought to a satisfactory conclusion, France might join Spain in the good work of extirpation; but these suggestions were haughtily checked as evidence that France had not her heart in the cause, since, instead of going straight to the good work, she made it a matter of policy, and indeed sought a bribe. The subtle Montluc, who was present, agreed in opinion that it would have been better had the right course been taken in time, and before the political power acquired by the Huguenots had rendered its adoption precarious; but he pledged himself that the queen was thoroughly sincere, and would rather be cut in two than become Huguenot. Alva, however, was dissatisfied and disappointed, though the Frenchmen whom he met, especially the Cardinal of Guise, gave him thorough sympathy.[1]

The object of Philip II. in this famous conference was known at the time—probably through the active emissaries of the Huguenots. It was not known that his proffers met a cold return, and naturally the subsequent massacre of St Bartholomew was set down as the consummation of a plot then prepared. Famianus Strada, the great Romanist historian, the only person who professed to know something about the conference from an authentic source—a letter about it from Philip II. to the Duchess of Parma, his sister—rather confirmed this notion by saying dryly, that whether the massacre was planned on this occasion he has no means of asserting or denying, but he rather thinks it was.[2]

The impression at the time was that a special religious league had been contracted between the two powers. The foolish young King of France was supposed to reveal the secret by the looks and words which he cast at the Protestant leaders. His savage nature seems to have been roused by the persuasion of the Spaniards, which his wily mother heard impassively. It went forth that he deeply pondered on a metaphor of

[1] Papiers d'Etat du Cardinal de Granvelle, ix. 312-324. See also Wiesener, 'Marie Stuart et le Comte de Bothwell,' p. 86, and his reference to the letter of the Bishop of Mondovi in Labanoff, vii. 107.
[2] De Bello Belgico, lib. iv.

Alva's, that one salmon was worth a multitude of frogs, as illustrating the view that the more effective and economic method of suppressing heresy was to cut off the heads of the party by some sudden stroke, rather than to fight out the question in controversies and battles. The Huguenot leaders, thoroughly frightened for their heads, and knowing that the tempting moment for a stroke or *coup* was when they were assembled in council or near each other, separated as far apart as they could, each occupying and fortifying one of his own strongholds.

These Huguenots communicated their peril to the Protestants of Scotland, who in their turn believed that Mary had joined the league. A French envoy, who brought the insignia of the order of the Saint Esprit to be conferred on Darnley, was believed to have brought the league for Mary's signature, and to have obtained it.[1] Randolph wrote to Cecil in February 1566 : "There was a band lately devised, in which the late Pope, the Emperor, the King of Spain, the Duke of Savoy, with other princes of Italy and the queen-mother, were suspected to be of the same confederacy to maintain Papistry throughout Christendom. This band was sent out of France by Thornton, and is subscribed by this queen."[2] If such a bond existed, the French Government was no party to it. But whether in the form of a bond or not, beyond doubt Mary was the close ally of the King of Spain in all his formidable views and projects for crushing the new religion.

Indeed the state paper which reveals the true history of the conference at Bayonne is followed by a letter from Alva, undated, but seemingly also written from

---

[1] Tytler, vii. 15.   [2] Wright's Queen Elizabeth, i. 219.

Bayonne, in which he explains to his master the manner of his carrying out the policy he was authorised to use towards Scotland. At the solicitation, he says, of the Cardinal of Guise, he gave audience to an envoy from the Queen of Scots. That envoy told him there would certainly be a revolution in England, and he desired to know what course his mistress ought to adopt. That, he was told, would depend on the strength of parties. Mary must in the mean time conduct herself not merely with reserve, but dissimulation towards Elizabeth. If she conducted herself to the satisfaction of the King of Spain, he would bring to her such aid, at the time when it was least expected, that she would certainly accomplish her object. Here was laid the scheme of the Armada, which was designed to place Mary on the English throne, and restore with her the old religion. By the signal tardiness of its projector it was cast forward into a later historical period, when all the conditions on which it depended for success had passed away. It is remarkable that Alva pressed on the envoy the necessity of keeping this intimation a dead secret even from the Guises; for, once in their possession, Catherine of Medici might get at it. The envoy, whose name is not mentioned, enchanted with the brilliant prospect, sent his brother to Scotland to tell the happy news.[1]

But at this time events fast following upon each other cleared away alike the hopes and the fears that Scotland was to prove the means of subduing the British Isles to the dominion of the old Church. The period during which the marriage of Mary and Darnley had the aspect of a happy union was short. If there

[1] Papiers d'Etat du Cardinal de Granvelle, ix. 329.

had not been worse qualities in either of them, there was an utter incompatibility. The wife had great genius and sagacity; the husband was a fool, and a vicious and presumptuous fool. There is scarcely to be found in his character the vestige of a good quality. The resources of his power and rank seem to have been considered by him only as elements of animal enjoyment, and of a vainglorious assumption of superiority. He indulged in every vicious appetite to the extent of his physical capacity; he surrounded himself with all manner of costly luxuries, over-ate himself, and drank hard. He did his wife that wrong which to a woman who retains the smallest remnant of attachment is the sorest of all. His amours were notorious and disgusting, and they had not the courtly polish which would entitle them to the compromising designation of intrigues; for he broke the seventh commandment with the most dissolute and degraded, because they were on that account the most accessible, of their sex. Such is a general summary of the character and habits which appear in those numerous accusations by his contemporaries, from which no one seems to have thought of vindicating his memory.[1] Without any ambition to govern, he was haughty and supercilious to a pitch that drove the proud Scots nobility rabid; and in his irritable or drunken fits he could not restrain his hand from the blow, inflicting on fierce and vindictive men the insult never to be forgiven.

Apart from her own injuries as a wife, the queen had too much natural good taste, and was too thorough

---

[1] The philippic of Buchanan, which must be dealt with afterwards, may be thought an exception; but there the faint praise is put in for artistic effect.

an adept in the court polish of Italy and France, to tolerate vice in such a form as this. Not many weeks of their married life seem to have passed before coldness appeared, and it soon deepened through estrangement into enmity. Their domestic bickerings became offensively notorious. Darnley ostensibly fixed his quarrel on her in the shape of a complaint that she had promised him the crown-matrimonial, and had afterwards refused to take any steps for accomplishing this promise. In his foolish passion he offered violence to the high officer of the law who brought him the disappointing intelligence that he was unsuccessful. How this expression "crown-matrimonial" came into use, and what it meant, have already been referred to as difficulties arising out of the schemes of the Guises. A French politician is the best interpreter of the term; and we find Mauvissière saying that, in the case of Mary's death, it would have passed the crown to her husband entirely, and then to his heirs. If this arrangement were absolute, then a daughter by Mary might have been superseded by a son born to a subsequent wife; but whether it went thus far or not, it was one of the matters in which the Hamilton family had the chief interest, and probably through their influence it was that the claim was defeated.

On the 24th February 1566 there was a marriage-ceremony, which would not have belonged to history but for after-events. Bothwell was then married to the Lady Jane Gordon, a daughter of the Earl of Huntly. This was made a Court affair, and there was a royal banqueting for five days. The queen took an interest in the lady, and specially bequeathed to her some jewels. She belonged to the old Church; and it is said in Knox's History that "the queen desired that the marriage might be made in the Royal Chapel at the mass, which the Earl of Bothwell would in nowise grant." The interest she took in this marriage has been pitted against the many presumptions that her heart then belonged to Bothwell. But experience in poor human nature teaches us that people terrified by the pressure of temptation do sometimes set up barriers against it which they afterwards make frantic efforts to get over. In the natural course of things a crisis was now at hand; for the Parliament was to meet on 4th March 1566, and the question was whether Murray and his exiled companions would appear there and fight their own battle, or would stay away and be to a certainty outlawed, and stripped of every dignity and every acre of their possessions.

The spies of Queen Elizabeth were in sore perplexity, watching the shadows of coming events; and their correspondence has the tone of men labouring under a weighty consciousness that terrible explosions were coming, yet without any certain indication when or in what form they may be expected. This correspondence is very interesting and suggestive, if we take its general tone; but, written without that distinct knowledge of the mighty projects of the inscrutable King of Spain, which were at the back of all that was doing in Scotland, the letters do not throw a steady and distinct light on the causes of what followed, and indeed contain so many rumours and predictions—some of which were fulfilled, while others were not—that the advocate of almost any historical theory about subsequent events is apt to find among them something temptingly calculated to support his views. We hear that Darnley is in danger of his life: so is Rizzio; so is the queen herself; so is Murray, who is said to be, unfortunately for his own safety, in possession of a secret involving his sister's fair fame. On one significant affair we can depend on these newswriters, because it was not a guess or prognostication, but a matter of fact passing before their eyes; and also because, although subsequent events confer a momentous import on it, yet it was looked on as but an ordinary matter at the time. Bothwell, whether for public or private reasons, was rising high in the queen's favour, and beginning to wield an influence in rivalry of the king's. "This also," says Randolph, "shall not be unknown to you, what quarrels there are already risen between her and her husband: she to have her will one way, and he another; he to have his father lieutenant-general, and she the Earl of Bothwell; he to have this man preferred, and she another."[1]

But another actor in the great tragedy was to precede him. The Italian was daily becoming more offensive; and, utterly unconscious of his position, he flaunted before the eyes that looked murder on him, giving himself many arrogant airs, decorating his person extravagantly, and dealing offence in the very state and rank betokened by his costume. He seems to have felt no fear, and even to have disdained some friendly warnings. He was sure of the favour of the queen, and he was not accustomed to governments in which those who are well with the supreme power need be afraid of what subjects can do. His thorough and almost exclusive knowledge of the great secrets between his mistress and the King of Spain very prob-

[1] Raumer, 69. See this referred to by Mauvissière, in Teulet, ii. 99.

ably added to his arrogance; and a dim consciousness that he was working at Popish intrigues made him all the more dangerous and odious to the Protestant party. The miscellaneous circle of enemies who aggregated round the poor man secured the aid of Darnley by the most powerful of motives—he became, or he was made, jealous of the Italian, and coarsely expressed his suspicion that he and the queen were too intimate. Mary, no doubt, held him in her usual chains; for she seems to have been incapable of holding converse with any one of the male sex without setting her apparatus of fascination at work. Farther than this she is not likely to have gone; but the ugly stories that long prevailed are aptly attested by the saying attributed to Henry IV., that King James's title to be called the Modern Solomon was, doubtless, that he was the son of David who performed upon the harp.

It was settled that the man should be put to death, and that before the great parliamentary contest about the exiled lords came on. A band or bond was entered into, according to the old practice in Scotland, in which those concerned owned their responsibility for the deed, and their resolution to stand by each other. It was absolutely necessary to have a hold like this on so slippery a person as Darnley, whom no one trusted. Or as Ruthven puts it, "they, considering he was a young prince, and having a lusty princess to lie in his arms afterwards, who might persuade him to deny all that was done for his cause, and to allege that others persuaded him to the same, thought it necessary to have security thereupon." It is worthy of remark that the bond contemplates more than one victim, the whole being described as " certain privy persons, wicked and ungodly, not regarding her majesty's honour, ours, nor the nobility thereof, nor the commonweal of the same, but seeking their own commodity and privy gains, especially a stranger Italian called Davie," whom they mutually engage to punish according to their demerits; "and, in case of any difficulty, to cut them off immediately, and to take and slay them wherever it happeneth." If any of the banders should get in trouble for doing so, Darnley stipulates to fortify and maintain them to the utmost of his power, "and shall be friends to their friends, and enemies to their enemies." The document, drawn by a skilful lawyer, ends with a specific clause that, "because it may chance to be done in presence of the queen's majesty, or within her Palace of Holyrood House, we, by the word of a prince, shall accept and take the same on us now as then, and then as now; and shall warrant and keep harmless the foresaid earls, lords, barons, freeholders, gentlemen, merchants, and craftsmen to our utter power. In witness whereof, we have subscribed this with our own hand at Edinburgh the 1st of March 1565-66."[1]

Darnley's side of the bond has been preserved, but not the other, so that we do not know with certainty who all were concerned in the plot. On the 6th, Bedford and Randolph thus intimated to Cecil that it was presently to come off: "Somewhat, we are sure, you have heard of divers disorders and jeers between this queen and her husband, partly for that she hath refused him the crown-matrimonial, partly for that he hath assured knowledge of such usage of herself as altogether is intolerable to be borne, which, if it were not overwell known, we would both be very loath to think that it

[1] Ruthven's Relation.

could be true. To take away this occasion of slander, he is himself determined to be at the apprehension and execution of him whom he is able manifestly to charge with the crime, and to have done him the most dishonour that can be to any man, much more being as he is. We need not more plainly to describe the person—you have heard of the man we mean of."[1]

There was at the same time another bond, involving ostensibly much larger political adjustments, in which Darnley was on one side. Those on the other side were in the same interest with the banders against Rizzio, but there is no evidence that they were exactly the same persons; and, indeed, it might be supposed that they were persons of too much dignity and seriousness of character to entertain a proposal for the murder of a minion. If we may believe Ruthven's account of the origin of this band, when Darnley besought him to get Rizzio disposed of, he protested that he would have nothing to do with the matter unless Darnley would bind himself to "bring home" Murray and the others, "who were banished only for the Word of God," as Ruthven put it. Darnley, to carry his point, agreed to the terms. "After long reasoning and divers days' travelling, the king was contented that they should come home into the realm of Scotland, so that the said Lord Ruthven would make him sure that they would be his, and set forward all his affairs. The said lord gave answer to the king, and bade him make his own security, and that he should cause it to be subscribed by the aforesaid earls, lords, and barons." The title of the formal document they subscribed is instructive. It is called, "Certain Articles to be ful-

[1] Tytler, vii. 25.

filled by James, Earl of Murray; Archibald, Earl of Argyle; Alexander, Earl of Glencairn; Andrew, Earl of Rothes; Robert, Lord Boyd; Andrew, Lord Ochiltree; and their complices—to the Noble and Mighty Prince Henry, King of Scotland." The subscribers bound themselves to "take a loyal and true part with the said noble prince in all his actions, causes, and quarrels, against whomsoever, to the utmost of their powers; and shall be friends to his friends and enemies to his enemies, and neither spare their lives, lands, goods, nor possessions." They specially undertake to do their best in Parliament to secure for him the crown-matrimonial, and promise their interest to secure for him the friendship of Queen Elizabeth and the relief of his mother and brother from detention by her. Darnley, on the other hand, engages to do his best to protect the exiled lords from punishment, and to restore to them their estates and dignities. Nothing is trusted to generalities, but the course he is to adopt is set forth with specific distinctness by some able conveyancer—probably Balfour, who afterwards drew another band in which Darnley was concerned, but to which he was no party. He was not to suffer any forfeitures to pass against them, nor to let them be accused in Parliament, and, if need be, was even to prevent the holding of a Parliament; and if he succeeded in obtaining the crown-matrimonial, he was then to use his prerogative in their favour. The safety of the Protestant religion—the really important part of the arrangement—is provided for, with a curious circumlocuitous shyness, as "the religion which was established by the queen's majesty our sovereign shortly after her arrival in this realm, whereupon acts and proclamation were made, and now again granted by the said noble prince to the said earls, lords, and their complices."[1]

Thus had the Protestant cause received a new and unexpected ally. Mary says afterwards, in a letter to her councillor, Bishop Leslie, that the arrangement was kept a dead secret from her, and that she was unconsciously arranging for her Parliament, "the spiritual estate being placed therein in the ancient manner, tending to have done some good anent restoring the auld religion, and to have proceeded against our rebels according to their demerits."[2] All was now ready for the blow. The Parliament assembled, the exiled lords were on their way back, and the time and method of disposing of the Italian were adjusted.[3]

On the 9th of March, Morton, the chancellor, commanded the force who were to act—about a hundred and fifty men. Having the king with him, he got

[1] Ruthven's Relation.
[2] Labanoff, i. 342.
[3] The account of its execution I propose to take from three sources: first, the queen's own statement, sent to her faithful adviser, Bishop Leslie; second, a state paper drawn up by the Earl of Bedford and Randolph for the information of the Privy Council of England. It is the fruit of inquiries made of the actors themselves after they had taken refuge in England, and from other sources, the whole being sifted and examined with the practical acuteness with which the authors of the paper were so amply endowed. The third is a narrative professing to have been written by Lord Ruthven, the chief actor in the affair. All the three correspond with a precision uncommon in the accounts of exciting events; but the third is the most minute in its detail, and the most practical and lifelike throughout. Queen Mary to Bishop Leslie; Labanoff, i. 341. The Earl of Bedford and Randolph to the Council of England; Wright's Queen Elizabeth, i. 226. 'A Relation of the Death of David Rizzio, chief favourite to Mary, Queen of Scotland, who was killed in the apartment of the said Queen on 9th of March 1565-66; written by the Lord Ruthven, one of the principal persons concerned in that action.' Printed in 1699, and reprinted in Scotia Rediviva, 1826. It is also in the Appendix to Keith, book ii. No. xi., and in Triphook's Miscellanea Antiqua, 1814.

possession, silently and without contest, of the great
gate and the various outlets of the Palace of Holyrood,
so as to make prisoner all within it. A considerable
part of his force seems to have been stationed in
the royal audience-chamber down-stairs. From this
Darnley brought some of them into his own chamber,
whence he ascended, by a secret stair, to the queen's
apartments, showing Ruthven, who was to follow, the
way. It was seven o'clock. Darnley had supped early,
to prepare for work. The queen, who had two chambers entering to each other, was in the inner, called
the cabinet, twelve feet square. She was seated at a
small table on a couch, or "low reposing-bed," as
Bedford and Randolph call it, with the Lady Argyle
and Rizzio, who sat, as it was noted, with his cap on;
and this sight was perhaps the more offensive that a
few Scotsmen of good rank—her brother the Commendator of Holyrood House, Arthur Erskine, the
Laird of Creech, and others attached to the household
—seem to have been in attendance as domestics, while
"Signor Davie" sat with his cap on. He was clothed
in "a nightgown of damask, furred, with a satin
doublet and hose of russet velvet." The little party
seem to have been unconscious of anything unusual,
until after Darnley, who put his arm round his wife's
waist and chatted with her kindly, was followed by
the grim Ruthven, who had risen haggard from a sick-
bed, and required to be helped up-stairs, though he
was clad and armed more suitably for a foray than a
queen's cabinet. He told his business forthwith. "It
would please your majesty to let yonder man Davie
come furth of your presence, for he hath been over long
there." Then there was a sharp dialogue, in which, as

in all the dialogues even reported by an opposite party, the queen appears to have held her own. She wanted to know why her servant should be demanded. She was at last told, in terms sufficiently suggestive, if not quite explicit.

"It will please your majesty, he hath offended your majesty's honour, which I dare not be so bold as speak of. As to the king your husband's honour, he hath hindered him of the crown-matrimonial, which your grace promised him, besides many other things which are not necessary to be expressed. And as to the nobility, he hath caused your majesty to banish a great part, and the most chief thereof, and forefault them at this present Parliament, that he might be made a lord;" and so he passed to particulars. He then tells how, when he had finished, the queen rose up. She stood before the recess of a window. The Italian drew his hanger mechanically, as it appears, with no spirit to defend himself; for he seems to have read his doom in the face of the intruder, and he crouched behind his mistress, clutching at the folds of her gown. Ruthven was alone all this time, and nothing had occurred to tell the inmates of the cabinet that there were others at hand. As Ruthven was palpably rude, the attendants laid hands on him; but he shook them off fiercely, drawing his hanger and saying, "Lay not hands on me, for I will not be handled!" and as he spoke others rushed in, filling the small apartment, and upsetting the supper-table with the candles on it. The Lady Argyle snatched up one of the candles, and preserved the group from darkness. There was some rough scuffling ere the wretch could be torn from his clutch of the queen's gown; and she declared that a hanger was thrust at David over her shoulder, and a hackbut or pistol held as if aimed at herself. In the end, Ruthven took the queen and placed her in her husband's arms, telling her not to be afraid—they would sooner spend their own hearts' blood than she should suffer harm, and they were doing but the bidding of her own husband. So they passed her, and dragged the trembling wretch out of the recess of the window. It had been their intention to take him to Darnley's chamber, there to hold a sort of court of judgment on him, and afterwards hang him; but in the press and confusion he was hurled into the queen's "utter chamber" or anteroom, and the crowd of enemies about him "were so vehemently moved against the said Davie that they could not abide any longer." All that could get near enough stabbed him, until "they slew him at the queen's far door in the utter chamber." The body was hurled down-stairs to the porter's lodge, where the porter's assistant, stripping off the fine clothes as it lay on a chest, said, "This hath been his destiny; for upon this chest was his first bed when he entered into the place, and now here he lieth again, a very ingrate and misknown knave."

Those great officers who had apartments within the precincts of the palace, including Bothwell, Huntly, and Athole, were naturally surprised and angry at the presence of the large addition unexpectedly made to the armed inmates of the palace; and there was likely to be a contest between their followers and the followers of the conspirators. Darnley intervened and kept peace, owning the strangers as his own men; and there was much rapid talk, with explanations and some professions of reconciliation, in the crowd of men—several of them at feud with each other—who had been so singularly brought together. Very few on either side seem to have yet known of the slaughter. A body of the townspeople, armed, and headed by the provost, hearing that there was turbulence and drawing of swords in the palace, hurried thither; but, assured by Darnley that the queen and he were uninjured, and all was right, they went their way, also ignorant of the tragedy of the night. While these things were going on, Ruthven and Darnley were back in the queen's cabinet, talking to her; and she also was ignorant of her favourite's fate. Ruthven, indeed, assured her that he was safe, and for the time in her husband's apartment, where he supposed the body to be safe in his own sense of the word. The queen uneasily observed the absence of her husband's hanger. It was left sticking ostentatiously in the Italian's body, as a testimony whose deed the slaughter was; but she professed to be satisfied that nothing more had taken place but what she had seen, and then began a wordy war between the husband and wife.

He charged her with the change in her ways towards him "since yon fellow Davie fell in credit and familiarity" with her. Especially she used of old to seek him in his chamber; and now, even if he came to hers, there was little entertainment for him there, save so far as Davie might be the third with them; and then they set to cards, and played on till one or two of the clock after midnight—late hours certainly for that age. To this she made answer with her usual felicity, that "it was not gentlewomen's duty to come to their husband's chamber, but rather the husband to come to the wife's chamber, if he had anything to do with her." He rejoined, like a petulant boy, "How came ye to my chamber at the beginning, and ever till within these few months that Davie fell in familiarity with you? Or am I failed in any part of my body? Or what disdain have you at me? Or what offence have I made you, that you should not use me at all times alike, seeing that I am willing to do all things that becometh a good husband to do to his wife?" These words recalled the outrage that had just taken place, and were followed by a little outburst from her, very remarkable when contrasted with the tone we shall find her taking when she knew that her favourite had been actually put to death. " Her majesty answered and said, That all the shame that was done to her, that, my lord, ye have the weight [blame] thereof; for the which I shall never be your wife, nor lie with you, nor shall never like well till I gar you have as sore a heart as I have presently."

Here Ruthven interposed with good-humour, recommending the queen to take a sensible view of things, be reconciled with her husband, and with him follow the advice of good friends. Exhausted apparently by this effort, a little scene follows, which must be told in his own words. "The said lord being so feebled with his sickness, and wearied with his travel, that he desired her majesty's pleasure to sit down upon a coffer, and called for a drink for God's sake; so a Frenchman brought him a cup of wine." His interruption of the matrimonial colloquy, and his insolent familiarity, turned the storm upon himself; and he says that, "after he had drunken, the queen's majesty began to rail against the said lord." She alluded to her position, having been six months pregnant, and said that if she died, or her child, in consequence of what had been done, she was not without friends capable of revenging her. There was the King of Spain, the Emperor, the King of France, and her uncles, not to speak of his holiness the Pope. Ruthven answered, with grave sarcasm, " that these noble princes were over-great personages to meddle with such a poor man as he was, being her majesty's own subject." Then there was a partly political discussion, in which Ruthven maintained that the queen had abandoned her constitutional advisers, and sought counsel of the Italian and other strangers, who taught her to set her own arbitrary power above the Estates; that she had especially interfered to name the Lords of the Articles in the ensuing Parliament, for the purpose of securely crushing her brother Murray and the other exiled lords. It is observable that, while this brisk dialogue went on, not a word came from Darnley, though Ruthven appealed to him. At last he observed that the queen was tired, and advised her husband to bid her farewell. She was left with certain attendants who could be trusted, and Ruthven kept charge of Darnley, with whom he had business still to transact. Ere they separated two proclamations were adjusted, to be issued next day by Darnley as king. The one called a muster of the well-affected inhabitants of Edinburgh, who were to keep ward in the streets, " and to suffer none others to be seen out of their houses, except Protestants, under all highest pain and charge that after may follow." The other proclamation discharged or dissolved the Parliament, requiring all the members to leave Edinburgh within three hours, save such as the king might specially require to remain. Having adjusted these matters to his satisfaction, we are told that, "the gates being locked, the king being in his bed, the queen's majesty walking in her chamber, the said Lord Ruthven took air upon the lower gate and the privy passages." One other event, however, happened in the night, not so propitious as those which preceded it. Bothwell and Huntly managed to make their escape; and, from Mary's own account of the matter, it would seem that they had contrived to establish a communication with her, engaging to relieve her from without, or to help her to escape.[1]

The great affair of next day, which was Sunday, was the arrival of the banished lords, who reached Edinburgh about seven o'clock in the evening. Thus were they on the spot to profit by the recent tragedy without having defiled themselves with it. There can be little doubt that they were prepared for it. Among the many scraps of paper which contain merely the rumours of the day, Murray is set down in some as a contriver in the plot. There is no sufficient evidence that he was so, and such a thing is not consistent with his steady, careful, decorous walk in life. That, knowing it was likely to take place without throwing any responsibility on him, he should have gone out of his way to hinder it, was beyond the human nature of his age. The name of Knox, too, is to be found on these lists. It is still less likely, however, that he should have compromised his position as a minister of the Word by either executing or plotting an assassination. Whether, knowing that it was to be done, he would have interrupted it, or would have bidden the perpetrators God-speed, is an idle question, since, with his usual candour, he has left in his History his thorough ap-

[1] Labanoff, i. 348.

proval of the deed. Moralising on the fallen condition of the conspirators afterwards, when they became fugitives, he utters a warning against supposing that they are deserted of God, who may yet raise them up again to His glory and their comfort. "And to let the world understand in plain terms what we mean, that great abuser of this commonwealth, that poltroon and vile knave Davie, was justly punished on the 9th of March, in the year of God one thousand five hundred threescore five [six], for abusing of the commonwealth, and for his other villany, which we list not to express, by the counsel and hands of James Douglas, Earl of Morton, Patrick, Lord Lindsay, and the Lord Ruthven, with others assisters of their company, who all, for their just act, and most worthy of all praise, are now unworthily left of their brethren, and suffer the bitterness of banishment and exile."[1] Much of the accusation and defence wasted on the characters of that age arises from the supposition that, like a well-principled citizen of the present day, any one hearing of an intended crime was expected to go and inform the police. People in the public world had too much anxiety about themselves to think of others, and only the strongest personal motive would prompt one to interfere with any act of violence. An attempt to thwart a crime by which his cause would profit, might have justly exposed a man to the charge of insanity or gross duplicity.

Sunday the 10th was a busy and anxious day at the palace. At what time the queen heard of Rizzio's death is not certain; it must have been pretty near the time when she also heard that the banished lords

[1] Knox, i. 235.

were to arrive.[1] It is certain, however, that she at once altered her tone to Darnley. She resolved on luring him back, along with such of the other enemies sur-

[1] The question when and how the queen knew of Rizzio's death seems to be of great moment, in its bearing on the evidence against her for the murder which followed. It is quite clear that Rizzio was not, as is generally supposed, slain before her face. In Bedford and Randolph's narrative it is said distinctly, " He was not slain in the queen's presence, as was said, but going down the stairs out of the chamber of presence." In her own narrative sent to her faithful councillor, Bishop Leslie, she says, " The said Lord Ruthven perforce invaded him in our presence (he then for refuge took safeguard, having retired him behind our back), and with his complices cast down our table upon himself, put violent hands on him, struck him over our shoulder with whinyards, one part of them standing before our face with bended dags, most cruelly took him furth of our cabinet, and at the entry of our chamber gave him fifty-six strokes with whinyards and swords." This tends to confirm Ruthven's narrative, by showing that Rizzio was taken alive out of the cabinet and killed in the anteroom. It is not a necessary inference that he was wounded, though she says they struck him over her shoulder with whinyards; their object, undoubtedly, was to get him out of the queen's presence in the first place. In the queen's short account of her controversy with Ruthven, when speaking of Rizzio, she says, " whom they had actually put to death." If this stood alone, it might be doubtful whether she mentions that as a fact merely which she might afterwards have known, or states that she was told it at the time by Ruthven. In the narrative of Bedford and Randolph, who were undoubted masters of all the facts, it is stated that, in her conversation with Ruthven and her husband, the queen spoke for Rizzio's safety partly in entreaties, partly in threats, saying, " Well, it shall be dear blood to some of you if his be spilt." In whichever sense it be taken, this explanation is further proof that she did not see him slain (see the letter in Labanoff, i. 344, 345). Spottiswoode (p. 195) gives the following distinct account of her acquaintance with the end: " The queen, bursting forth in many tears after a great tiding she kept with the Lord Ruthven, sent one of her maids to inquire what was become of Davie, who quickly returning, told that he was killed; having asked her how she knew it, the maid answered that she had seen him dead. Then the queen, wiping her eyes with her handkerchief, said, '*No more tears—I will think upon a revenge.*' Neither was she seen after that any more to lament." For this account, accepted in several quarters, I am aware of no better authority than Spottiswoode's mere statement, and the dubious memoirs attributed to Lord Herries. If better vouched, it would be formidable evidence of her intention to work for what afterwards came to pass.

rounding her as she could win over. With her foolish husband she accomplished her purpose with the ease of a great artist; the others seem to have kept themselves beyond the magic circle. It was part of her policy to make him think she believed in his absurd protestations that he had no concern in her favourite's death. The day was spent by Darnley in vibrating between the two parties—coming from the queen to demand concessions for her, getting scolded for his weakness and the peril he was bringing them all into by yielding to her blandishments, and going back fortified against her, to return again as her humble messenger. Early in the day she recovered her women, through whom she communicated with Bothwell, Huntly, and other friends. The alarm was more than once raised that a miscarriage was approaching, and the necessary attendants were summoned; but Ruthven thought he saw under all this a project for her escaping among the miscellaneous throng of women hurrying out and in, and it was regulated, much to the queen's annoyance, that no gentlewoman should pass forth " undismuffled."

It was arranged, as a signal token of reconciliation, that Darnley was to share the queen's couch that night. As men will do, however, when they have got a heavy piece of business satisfactorily through, he took a drowsy fit—probably, too, he was saturated with wine; so he fell dead asleep in his own chamber, and when he awoke too late, scolded those who had failed to break his slumber. Probably the queen did not much regret a new insult which relieved her of a portion of her work of dissimulation. She was next day all smiles and caresses. The meeting with the banished lords cannot be better told than in Ruthven's own words :—

"She took purpose, and came out of the utter chamber, led by the king. The said earls and lords sitting down upon their knees, made their general oration by the Earl of Morton, chancellor, and after their particular orations by themselves. And after that her majesty had heard all, her answer was, that it was not unknown to the lords that she was never bloodthirsty nor greedy upon their lands and goods sithence her coming into Scotland, nor yet would be upon theirs that were present, but would remit the whole number that was banished, or at the last dead, and bury and put all things in oblivion, as if they had never been; and so caused the said lords and barons to arise on their feet. And afterwards her majesty desired them to make their own security in that sort they pleased best, and she should subscribe the same. Thereafter her majesty took the king by the one hand and the Earl of Murray by the other, and walked in her said utter chamber the space of one hour, and then her majesty passed into her inner chamber."[1]

The desire that they should "make their own security" had reference to a new band appropriate to the occasion, which a skilful conveyancer was in fact at that moment preparing, under the vigilant inspection of the returned exiles, or of the king's party, as they were then—but only for a few hours—named. Soon after six o'clock in the evening the king joined them, or at least their committee, consisting of Murray, Morton, Ruthven, and Lindsay, who handed to him their band of security, ready for his signature and the queen's,

[1] Ruthven's Relation.

"which the king took in hand, as soon as he had supped, to be done." He made a request, however, which inflamed their still slumbering suspicions, by desiring them to remove their own people, and leave the queen in the hands of her proper guard. The lords had been telling Darnley all along, in pretty plain terms, that there was duplicity at work and they were only led on to be betrayed; and at this proposal Ruthven, bursting out in anger, told him that what should follow and what blood he shed should come on his head and that of his posterity, not on theirs. The guards seem not to have been removed; but the lords themselves adjourned to Morton's house to sup—a step attended with risk, yet in which there was a certain policy, because it was expedient that the queen, in whatever she signed, should have as much appearance of free will as it was safe to allow. After supper they sent Archibald Douglas to see if the queen had subscribed the band. No, she had not; the king said she had read the articles and found them very good, but she was sick and going to bed, and delayed the subscribing until the morning.

About an hour after midnight the queen and Darnley managed, by connivance, to slip out through the wine-cellar. Outside, Arthur Erskine, captain of her guard, met her by arrangement with six or seven mounted followers. The queen seated on a crupper behind Erskine, they all rode straight to Seton House, where the Lord Seton gave them an escort on to Dunbar. The governor of that strong fortress was amazed, early on Tuesday morning, by the arrival of his king and queen, hungry, and clamorous for fresh eggs to breakfast.

CHAPTER XLV.

Queen Mary.

(*Continued.*)

THE CONFEDERATE LORDS AND THEIR DANGER—PROJECTS OF RETALIATION—THE SLAYERS OF RIZZIO SEEK REFUGE IN ENGLAND—A PARLIAMENT—THE FIT OF CONJUGAL ATTACHMENT PASSES—SYMPTOMS OF MARY'S FEELING TOWARDS HER HUSBAND—HE IS AVOIDED, AND BECOMES ALARMED—RISE AND CHARACTER OF BOTHWELL—HISTORY OF HIS HOUSE AS RENOWNED FOR ROYAL LOVE-AFFAIRS—WOUNDED IN A BORDER SCUFFLE—THE QUEEN'S RIDE FROM JEDBURGH TO HERMITAGE TO VISIT HIM—BIRTH OF THE PRINCE—PECULIAR CIRCUMSTANCES OF HIS BAPTISM—PROJECTS AGAINST DARNLEY MOOTED—DARNLEY'S ILLNESS—THE QUEEN'S NEW PROFESSION OF RECONCILIATION, AND VISIT TO HIM IN GLASGOW—HIS FATHER AND HE AFRAID OF MURDER—HIS OWN EXPRESSIONS ON THE MATTER—DARNLEY BROUGHT TO THE KIRK-OF-FIELD—A BAND FOR PUTTING HIM OUT OF THE WAY—THE PREPARATIONS—THE COMPLETION OF THE MURDER.

THUS the confederate lords arose in the morning to find themselves outwitted and in great danger. They despatched a messenger to Dunbar on the useless errand of procuring that signature to their band which the royal fugitives had neglected to leave. The messenger was detained two days before his message could be delivered, and it was not even honoured with the formality of an answer.

The queen dictated letters pleading her cause and vindicating herself. One letter to Queen Elizabeth has been preserved. It is dated from Dunbar on the 15th of March, and contains this passage: "We thought to have written this letter with our own hand, that ye might have better understood all our meaning, and taken mair familiarly therewith; but of a truth we are so tired and evil at ease, what through riding of twenty miles in five hours of the night, as with the frequent sicknesses and evil disposition by the occasion of our child, that we could not at this time, as we was willing to have done."[1]

Bothwell meanwhile was busy in collecting a force for the queen's protection. He seems to have immediately brought to Dunbar a sufficient number of followers to render an attack on that fortress desperate; and on the 28th of March he accompanied the royal pair back to Edinburgh at the head of two thousand horsemen. The opposition had in the mean time, with few exceptions, either fled to England or retired to a safe distance. The exiled lords who had returned from England made their appearance at the Tolbooth, where the Parliament was held, on the day for which they were cited—the day after the escape. There was of course no Parliament, for it had been dissolved by the proclamation which they had influenced Darnley to issue; but there was some subtle technical fencing, the lords protesting that they had appeared when summoned, and since there was no one to arraign them, all charges against them fell; while on the other hand, Robert Crichton, the queen's advocate, entered a counter-protest on such grounds as he

[1] Labanoff, i. 337.

thought most tenable. The lords thought it wise to retreat to Linlithgow. There was, however, no intention of pressing further on them as a party—the cause of the restoration of the old religion, which was the cause of antagonism to them, had to be abandoned for more urgent contests. The queen gave several of them letters of remission. Melville, as interim secretary, was occupied in preparing these documents at Haddington while the Court was on its way from Dunbar to Edinburgh.[1] They were not, however, directly received into favour, but were desired to retire to their own estates; and they professed to obey this instruction, remaining sharply on the watch for each turn of events.

The recent outrage was the point on which all political events for the present turned. Rizzio's body was removed from the Canongate graveyard, where it had been buried, and was solemnly, and with the proper rites of his Church, laid with the dust of the kings of Scotland within the Chapel of Holyrood. In scornful bravado the queen appointed the dead man's brother, Joseph Rizzio, a youth who had just arrived to seek his fortune, to the office of her foreign secretary. The one object of her life seemed then the avenging of the murder, and the one class of men who felt that there could be no compromise for their lives were those who could be proved to have actually committed the deed. Morton, Ruthven, Lindsay, Douglas the Postulate, Ker of Faudonside, and several others, were cited to answer for the murder, and having fled to England, were outlawed and "put to the horn." A few minor persons forming part of the force which held the palace were convicted and executed.

[1] Melville, 132.

Darnley showed the reckless perfidy of his nature by eagerly helping to denounce and capture his fellow-murderers. In speaking of them to Melville, he used an expressive trope applicable to men left to their doom, "As they have brewed, so let them drink."[1] It was not part of his wife's policy to attempt to bring him to justice with the others; and so, to put a decorous appearance upon his position, he acted the farce of solemnly declaring his innocence of the crime before the Privy Council—at least the queen assured Beaton, her own ambassador, that he had declared to herself and the Council "his innocence of this last conspiracy; how he never counselled, commanded, consented, assisted, nor approved the same."[2] His reconciliation with the queen had, however, now served its turn. She no longer required to separate him from the party of the exiled lords, who had more to trust to from herself than from him. The distaste she had felt before, deepened by the intervening tragedy, broke out in a palpable loathing visible to every one around them. Melville noticed it even on the journey from Dunbar, and he thought the subsequent rapid movements of the queen were for the purpose of avoiding her hated husband. Melville takes credit for having pleaded, until he received a rebuff, for the unhappy young man. Randolph, whose eye caught the sudden change of conduct, attributed it to Mary having been shown the band for the murder of Rizzio, with her husband's signature to it; but a woman of her penetration, and with her opportunities of knowing the facts, did not require such evidence.

Her wretched husband had now effectually divested

[1] Melville, 153.   [2] Labanoff, i. 119.

BIRTH OF A PRINCE, 1566.

himself of every hold he ever had on any party or considerable person in the realm. Grave and calculating statesmen distrusted and despised him from the first. Desperate plotters convicted him of the unpardonable crime of treachery to his banded confederates. The Protestant party hated him, and the scorn of the queen cast him off from the Romish party; and so, as Melville says, "he passed up and down his alane, and few durst bear him company." There was not even the external pretence of consulting him on business; and he had nothing to do but to go about like a tabooed schoolboy, bemoaning his condition to any, whether Scots or foreigners, who would listen to him—a practice which, by exposing the family brawl to the world, only made him the more odious and despicable to his wife.

An event occurred, however, which for a short time suspended the matrimonial discord. Mary had retired to the Castle of Edinburgh, as a safe retreat for the occasion; and on the 19th of June a son was born to her, afterwards known as James VI. of Scotland and I. of England. It was noticed at the time as a memorable fact that Darnley acknowledged the infant as his own; and that this should have been deemed a fact of importance is curiously suggestive of the unsatisfied and suspicious feelings which had become prevalent. Sir James Melville was sent to announce the auspicious news at the Court of England, and he has left an amusing picture of the rigid Elizabeth yielding to an impulse of curious vexation when abruptly startled by the news in the midst of a Court banquet at Greenwich, and lamenting that the Queen of Scots was the mother of a fair son while she herself was but a barren stock. Next day, however, at a public audience, she was kind and courteous, and profuse in her congratulations and the proffers of her sympathy.

The family quarrel was suspended only for a brief period by this event. The position of Darnley was ever becoming more conspicuously isolated and feeble, by the queen's policy of reconciliation with those who had been her political enemies. All but those who had actually laid hands on Rizzio were welcomed back. Thus Murray, Argyle, Glencairn, and even the man she most feared and disliked on public grounds, Lethington, with other minor persons who had been in disgrace, were received into favour, and, nominally at least, co-operated with Bothwell and Huntly.

Darnley in his desolation seems to have become alarmed for his safety. He resolved to go to France " in a sort of desperation," as the French ambassador called it—in short, to escape. His father, Lennox, who suffered with his declining fortunes, and seems to have shared in his alarm, wrote to the queen about this design, and said there was a ship ready to receive him. She, however, resolved that he should not go. Something is muttered in the correspondence of the time about his forming a party with the Romanists against the queen, on account of her favour to the Protestant party and her abandonment of the project of restoring the old religion; but Mary and her policy were far too deeply rooted in the councils of Rome and Spain to give the foolish young man the smallest chance of doing mischief—there was no danger in that direction, and there can have been no genuine fear. The reason for detaining him seems to have been that which Le

Croc refers to—the scandal that must arise from the separation and its manner, aggravated as it would be by the young man's incontinent tongue. He knew too much, foolish as he was, to be safely trusted at a distance.

His wife took this occasion to put herself in the right and him in the wrong, and did so with her usual skill. She said she had discussed the matter with him in private, and could get no satisfactory answer; so she resolved on a matrimonial dialogue in solemn manner, before an assemblage of the nobility—both those who were her confidential friends and the others who were for the time being her political allies.

Le Croc was brought within the charmed circle over which Queen Mary exercised her influence—she had taken great pains apparently to gain him. "I be not able," he says, "sufficiently to express the honour and bounty the queen here shows me; for she often prays me to ask money from her, or any other thing I stand in need of." And he paid her back, by intimating to his Court, "I never saw her majesty so much beloved, esteemed, and honoured, nor so great a harmony amongst all her subjects, as at present is, by her wise conduct." Of the scene of matrimonial diplomacy which he was called on to witness, the ambassador gives the following distinct and animated account:—

"And thereafter the queen prayed the king to declare in presence of the lords and before me the reason of his projected departure, since he would not be pleased to notify the same to her in private betwixt themselves. She likewise took him by the hand, and besought him for God's sake to declare if she had given him any occasion for this resolution; and entreated he might deal plainly, and not spare her. Moreover, all the lords likewise said to him, that if there was any fault on their part, upon his declaring it, they were ready to reform it. And I likewise took the freedom to tell him that his departure must certainly affect either his own or the queen's honour—that if the queen had afforded any ground for it, his declaring the same would affect her majesty; as on the other hand, if he should go away without giving any cause for it, this thing could not at all redound to his praise : therefore, that since I was in this honourable employment, I could not fail, according to my charge, to give my testimony to the truth of what I had both formerly seen and did presently see. After several things of this kind had passed amongst us, the king at last declared that he had no ground at all given him for such a deliberation; and thereupon he went out of the chamber of presence, saying to the queen, 'Adieu, madam; you shall not see my face for a long space :' after which he likewise bade me farewell, and next turning himself to the lords in general, said, 'Gentlemen, adieu.'"[1]

It was about this time becoming evident that there was something in the queen's sentiments towards Bothwell of a warmer character than could be rationally attributed either to a just sense of his public merits or simple gratitude for his services to herself. That she should fix her love on him has always been deemed something approaching the unnatural ; but when the circumstances are considered, the conclusion ceases to become so absolutely startling. Mary was evidently one of those to whom at that time a great affair of the heart was a necessity of life—a necessity increased

[1] Keith (8vo ed.), ii. 451.

in intensity by her utter disappointment in her last attachment, and the loathing she entertained towards its object. Who then were near her to be the first refuge for her fugitive affections? None but her own nobles, for she was not in a position to treat with a foreign prince; and in looking round among the most eminent of these, including Huntly, the brother of a former suitor, Argyle, Athole, and Arran, there were none who, on the ground of rank and position, had claims much higher than Bothwell, unless it might be Arran by reason of his royal blood, and he was already a rejected suitor. In personal qualifications Bothwell was infinitely above them all. He had a genius for command, with a dash of the chivalrous, which made Throckmorton describe him to Queen Elizabeth in 1560, as "a glorious, rash, and hazardous young man."[1] He had lived at the Court of France, and thus had over his harder and more effective qualities the polish and accomplishments which were all that Darnley had beside his handsomeness to recommend him. Bothwell was restrained by no conscientious scruples. They were not, indeed, a necessary of life, or even an ordinary possession of the social circle in which he figured. There, unless a man were notoriously addicted to vices now unnamed—Bothwell was but faintly accused of them by bitter enemies—he might keep his fame clear. For the matter of ordinary profligacy, it lay between himself and his physical constitution; and a man like Bothwell had, whether from judicious control or the strength of his northern constitution, the satisfaction of keeping his head clear and his arm steady long after many of his

[1] Hardwicke's State Papers, i. 149.

companions in like courses had sunk into premature senility. He was at a period of life when the manly attractions do not begin to decline, for he had just passed—if he had passed—his thirtieth year. Tradition says that he was ill-favoured; but I do not remember any contemporary authority for the assertion, except the cursory sketch of him by Brantome, who may have met him, but does not speak as if he had.[1] The question cannot now be decided by the eye, for there does not exist a picture which has even the reputation of being his portrait.[2]

With regard to his rank, it aimed at something higher than his means. He was comparatively poor; but his recent ancestors had been the rivals, and in some measure the successors, of the Douglases, who themselves had been the formidable rivals of

---

[1] "Ce Bothuel étoit le plus laid homme et d'aussi mauvaise grace q'il se peut voir."—Des Dames Illustres, Disc. iii. Buchanan speaks of him as like an ape; but this was when writing at him, and is no more to be taken as accurate than any other scolding objurgation.

[2] The Author happened once to be reading in the Library of the Antiquaries, in Edinburgh, when, shifting his position, a small picture caught his eye and kept it. It represented a human head with a rather aquiline nose and high cheek-bones—a Scotch face, and decidedly of the humblest plebeian type. Something like a dirty shepherd's plaid wrapped round the neck seemed in harmony with this character in the face. There was a pinchedness about the features which, along with the copperish colour of the skin, seemed to speak of extreme old age. One eye seemed injured, the other was closed in what seemed a drunken sleep. Altogether there was something loathsome about the picture, and it was a loathsomeness that somehow fascinated the eye. All this was felt before it was known what the painting represented. It was a portrait of Bothwell's head, painted by Otto Bache, when his embalmed body was disentombed in 1861. The editor of Queen Mary's Inventories gives an account of the circumstances in which the likeness was taken (Preface, xcv.), and he quotes the remark of Mr Horace Marryat, "I defy any impartial Englishman to gaze on this body without at once declaring it to be that of an ugly Scotsman." But who is to say how much of this ugliness may have been contributed by an abode of three centuries in the tomb?

the crown. He was thus in the interesting position of the head of a decayed house striving to restore its ancient lustre. In that age of revolutions and forfeitures, when property and power rapidly changed hands, such a man, to make himself the most powerful subject in the realm, required only royal favour; and this, as we shall presently see, was not denied him.

It is incidentally curious that Bothwell's family had acquired a reputation for affairs with royal ladies, and is in some measure significant, as helping to mitigate that colour of the marvellous in which his audacious projects and their success are generally painted. In the Castle of Dunbar, held by his father's great-grandfather Hepburn of Hales, the widow of James I., the renowned and beautiful Joanna Beaufort, spent her latter days and died. She had lived in a questionable obscurity for some time; and how or why she was under the same roof with Hepburn, whether by her own consent or by force, was matter of unsatisfied conjecture at the time. A son of this Hepburn was reputed among the many lovers of Mary of Gueldres, the widow of James II. Bothwell's father, according to the chronicles, was the rival of Darnley's father, Lennox, as a suitor of Mary of Guise.[1] The expense which the disappointed aspirant had incurred in sunning himself at Court in his wooing contributed, it was said, greatly to the decay of the family.

It has to be added to all this, that Bothwell had proved the devoted champion of the queen, protecting her alike from the calculating ambition of her brother and the base insults of her wretched husband. The turning-point seems to have been the murder of Rizzio,

[1] Pitscottie's Chronicle, 452. See Wood's Douglas, i. 228.

when Darnley showed how much treachery and cruelty could be the companions of his folly and feebleness; and her champion, by his dexterous escape and rapid muster of followers, placed her at once in safety and power. In fact, but for the crimes which paved the way to the conclusion, the union of Bothwell and Mary would have been the natural winding-up of a legitimate romance. Remove the unpleasant conditions that both were married, and that there was a husband and a wife to be got rid of ere the two could be united, substitute honour and virtue for treachery and crime, and here are the complete elements out of which the providence which presides over romance develops the usual happy conclusion.

The fluctuations in the old property of the Church at that time afforded substantial prizes for a powerful favourite. Bothwell got out of this affluent source the two rich Abbacies of Melrose and Haddington.[1] He was invested with the lordship and fortress of Dunbar. He was appointed Lord High Admiral and Warden of the Scottish Borders. This last office made him the most powerful man in the kingdom. Of course it was necessary to confer the wardenship on some local magnate whose territories and leadership gave him inde-

[1] The editor of Queen Mary's Inventories has added a very curious item to valuables with which the queen endowed Bothwell. There is an entry—ten pieces of caps, chasubles, and tunicles taken from Huntly's castle, whither they had been sent from the Cathedral of Aberdeen for their safety. On these the recipient notes: "In March 1567, I delivered three of the fairest, whilk the queen gave to the Lord Bothwell; and mair took to herself a cap, a chasuble, four tunicles, to make a bed for the king—all broken and cut in her own presence."—P. 53. Here the object of the gift is not so remarkable, as that so zealous a devotee of the Church should have turned ecclesiastical robes to secular purposes.

pendent authority there; and when to this was added the royal authority to command all the other border magnates, the powers of the warden were so great that the Government was extremely chary in the bestowal of the office. To break up the power so exercised among rivals, it was usual to appoint three wardens—one for the west, another for the middle marches, a third for the east—and it was an unusual, as well as significant fact, that the whole three were conferred on Bothwell.[1] In England, also, there were three wardens. We can see the sagacity of the two crowns in this arrangement, by looking to the origin of certain minor royalties in Germany called Margraviates, made out of the power coming to the hands of the great officers commissioned to protect the marches.

Of the influence he held at Court, contemporary estimates, however imperfect, are far more valuable than those made with a view to account for subsequent events. So on the 27th of July, Bedford the English ambassador wrote to Cecil, " Bothwell carries all the merit and countenance in Court. He is the most hated man among the noblemen, and therefore may fall out somewhat to his cumber one day, if the queen takes not up the matter the sooner ;" and a few days later, " It is said that the earl's insolence is such as that David was never more abhorred than he is now." Again, on the 12th, " I have heard that there is a device working for the Earl of Bothwell, the particularities of which I might have heard, but because such dealings like me not, I desire to hear no farther thereof. Bothwell has grown of late so hated that he

[1] Laing, and Wood (Peerage, i. 230) say the wardenships never had, on any previous occasion, been united.

cannot long continue. He beareth all the sway, and though Murray be there, and has good words, yet can he do nothing."[1]

A memorable occurrence is connected with the execution of his duties as warden of the marches. There came one of those times of more than average harrying and quarrelling which arose at intervals, and it was determined to hold a solemn justice aire at Jedburgh, which the queen herself was to countenance by her presence. Bothwell went to his own Castle of Hermitage, in the centre of the disturbed district, to collect offenders for trial at the great court. His function was more like that of an invading general than a head-constable. He had a good deal of hard fighting, in the course of which he was dangerously wounded by Elliot of Park. There are disputes about the manner of the event, but this is of less consequence than that it occurred on the 7th October. Next day the justice aire was opened. When the proceedings had gone on for a week, Mary took horse one day and rode to the Hermitage, where Bothwell lay awaiting recovery from his wound; and according to Lord Scrope, who sent the news to Cecil, she remained two hours, "to Bothwell's great pleasure and content," and then galloped back to Jedburgh. She had with her there, as official documents show, Murray, Huntly, Athole, Rothes, and Caithness, with three bishops and the judges and officers of court; but to what extent she was attended on her ride is not very clear. It is certain that she could not have had a force sufficient to make the adventure safe in a country which was not merely lawless in the usual sense of the term,

[1] Raumer, 86-88.

but where the sovereign of Scotland was looked on as the great public enemy. The double journey extended to at least forty miles over a country which would be felt as singularly wild, difficult, and dangerous to a rider of the present day.[1]

About the strength and courage necessary to such a feat there can be no question. About the motives which induced the queen to perform it there have been disputes. The affair looked as if she had been under that irresistible influence over which selfish reason has no control—to know by the sight of the eyes and the hearing of the ears the chances for life or death of some beloved object hovering between the two. On the other hand, it has been supposed that she thought it right to undertake this journey in the way of business, that she might confer with the wounded warden of the marches on details connected with his performance of his official duties. Whatever was her motive, she paid the penalty of her exploit in a strong fever, which ran its course, leaving the issues of life and death uncertain until the tenth day, when she began to revive physically, while those around her still noted symptoms of mental suffering, for which each accounted according to his prepossessions and knowledge.

When able to move, she went by short journeys to Craigmillar, close to Edinburgh. There Le Croc saw her in the beginning of December, and said: "She is in the hands of the physicians, and I do assure you is not at all well; and I do believe the

[1] The Author knows, from having walked over the ground, that Hermitage Castle is a stiff twenty miles' journey from Jedburgh. It is reported, on the authority of tradition, that her horse floundered in a marsh, thence called the Queen's Myre; but if she passed this spot, she must have diverged from the direct track.

principal part of her disease to consist of a deep grief and sorrow—nor does it seem possible to make her forget the same. Still she repeats these words, 'I could wish to be dead.' We know very well that the injury she has received is exceeding great, and her majesty will never forget it. The king her husband came to visit her at Jedburgh the day after Captain Hay went away. He remained there but one single night, and yet in that short time I had a great deal of conversation with him. He returned to see the queen about five or six days ago; and the day before yesterday he sent word to desire me to speak with him half a league from this, which I complied with, and found that things go still worse and worse. I think he intends to go away to-morrow; but in any event, I am much assured, as I have always been, that he won't be present at the baptism."[1]

A document of later date throws very instructive light on the condition of the Court at this time. It is called "The Protestation of the Earls of Huntly and Argyle touching the Murder of the King of Scots."[2] It opens with an enumeration of the group surrounding the queen at Craigmillar, including the protesters themselves, Bothwell, Murray, and Lethington. The two latter, it states, came to Argyle's bedroom before he had risen. Lethington spoke of the hardship of Ruthven, Morton, and the others continuing in banishment for the affair of Rizzio, seeing it was done to stop the Parliament and prevent the forfeiture of Murray and his friends, and said they thought him bound in

---

[1] Keith (8vo ed.), xcvi.
[2] This document has been frequently printed. It is in Keith, Book II. App. xvi.

all fairness to use his influence for their restoration. Lethington then proposed, as the best means of gaining the queen's consent to the restoration, to find means of divorcing her from Darnley. Huntly was then sent for, and the matter propounded to him, with the special inducement that the opportunity might be taken to do something in his own favour by the restoration of forfeited lands. He said he would not stand in the way of the project, and the four then went to lay it before the queen. Lethington, still acting as spokesman, opened up on the "great number of grievous and intolerable offences" which her ungrateful husband had perpetrated against her, "and continuing every day from evil to worse." The divorce was then proposed as her best mode of relief. After they had plied her with persuasions, the reception given by her to the proposal is thus stated by the protesters: "Her grace answerit, that under twa conditions she might understand the same—the ane, that the divorcement were made lawfully; the other, that it war not prejudice to her son—otherwise her hyness would rather endure all torments, and abyde the perils that might chance her in her grace's lifetime. The Earl of Bothwell answered, that he doubted not but the divorcement might be made bot prejudice in anywise of my lord prince, alleging the example of himself, that he ceased not to succeed to his father's heritage without any difficulty, albeit there was divorce betwixt him and his mother."

That she should fear the effect of a divorce on the legitimacy of her child is at first calculated to start strange suspicions as to the facts which such a process, if founded on the respective conduct of the husband

and wife, would disclose; but Buchanan, in his celebrated Detection, lets us see that the ground of divorce pointed at on the occasion was consanguinity. There next follows a passage of a strangely suggestive kind: "Then Lethington, taking the speech, said, 'Madam, fancy[1] ye not we are here of the principal of your grace's nobility and Council that sall find the moyen that your majesty sall be quit of him without prejudice of your son; and albeit that my Lord of Murray here present be little less scrupulous for ane Protestant nor your grace is for ane Papist, I am assurit he will look throw his fingers thereto, and sall behold our doings, saying nothing to the same.' The queen's majesty answered, 'I will that ye do nothing whereto any spot may be laid to my honour or conscience, and therefore I pray you rather let the matter be in the estate as it is, abiding till God of His goodness put remeid thereto; that ye, believing to do me service, may possibly turn to my hurt and displeasure.' 'Madam,' said Lethington, 'let us guide the matter amongst us, and your grace sall see nothing but good, and approved by Parliament.'" There is reason to believe that this conversation is pretty accurately reported. In the first place, Huntly and Argyle were men of such repute for probity as the times permitted; and Murray, not criticising the accuracy of the statement, merely denied that he had entered into any band or engagement for the murder, and in fact justified the expressive gesture described by Lethington, of holding his hand before his face, as if to hide what was in progress from his eyes, yet seeing

---

[1] This word "fancy" is supposed to be a mistake for "soucy"—*se soucier*; but whatever may have been the intended word, it does not much affect the tenor.

it all the while. Let us look at the object of the protestation. Its object was to vindicate the queen from the charge that she had been "of the foreknowledge, counselled, devised, and commanded the murder." The protesters count that Lethington, in the words quoted, did announce the murder; and the manner in which they make this bear on the queen's vindication is that, being assured that the deed would be done by others, there was no occasion why she should dip her own hands in blood—no occasion for her to "counsel, devise, persuade, and command" the deed. True, what was to be done was to be "approved by Parliament," and Parliament did not approve of it in the way in which it came to be done. But whether there was a sincere intention to walk in such a manner as to secure the sanction of the Estates, the one thing clear is that a promise was made to rid the queen of her unendurable husband, and that without a divorce. Huntly and Argyle, it may be noticed, did not pen their protest for an age when it would be considered either very improbable or very horrible that a woman situated as Mary was would be glad of the assurance that she would be relieved of her husband without requiring to do anything that would compromise her own safety.

As all seemed to expect, Darnley was absent from the baptism of the young prince on the 7th of December; and his conduct was the more emphatic, as he was then living in Stirling Castle, where the ceremony was performed. Bothwell did the honours of the occasion, as one to whom such a function came naturally; and it was remarked as rather anomalous that a Protestant should have been selected to adjust and direct a ceremonial conducted under the forms of the Romish

Church. The despised husband went about pouring his grievances into all who would listen to them, and became so troublesome that the French ambassador had to threaten that if Darnley entered his house by one door he would himself leave it by the other. Meanwhile, among the events now hurrying upon each other, those who pressed for the pardon of Rizzio's murderers were successful as to all but George Douglas and Ker of Faudonside, who had committed, or at all events threatened, violence in the royal presence.

Darnley was now seized with a sudden and acute illness, which broke out cutaneously. Poison was at first naturally suspected. The disease was speedily pronounced to be smallpox; but it has been conjectured that it may have been one of those forms of contamination which had then begun to make their silent and mysterious visitation in this country, while the immediate cause by which they were communicated was yet unknown. From what occurred afterwards, it became a current belief that he had been poisoned. He was removed to Glasgow, and tended under the direction of his father, Lennox.

His enemies waited to see if nature would relieve them of the work before them; but as he began to recover, they began to be active. Their hands were strengthened by the assistance of Morton, Ruthven, and the other fugitives who had been pardoned, and whose restoration was no doubt facilitated by the work in prospect for them. That all things might be done duly and in order, a bond for the slaughter of the king was prepared. The drafting of this important document was committed to James Balfour, the greatest lawyer of his day. No copy of it has been preserved, and what we chiefly know about it is from dubious sources.[1] In the confession afterwards uttered by Morton on his downfall, he stated that Bothwell met him at Whittinghame, and in a long communing tried to persuade him to join in a plot for the murder of the king, telling him it was the queen's desire that he should be removed, and "she would have it to be done." Morton says, having just got out of one troublesome affair, he was averse to immediately engaging in another; and put it off at the time by desiring, before he committed himself, to be assured of the queen's wish under the evidence of her own hand. He says that afterwards, when he was in St Andrews visiting the Earl of Angus, Archibald Douglas came to him from Bothwell to press the matter; but he had now the good excuse that he had been promised a writing under the queen's hand, and had not received it. When asked why he did not reveal the plot, he said, significantly, "I durst not reveal it for fear of my life; for at that time to whom should I have revealed it? To the queen? She was the doer thereof. I was minded, indeed, to the king's father [viz., Darnley himself], but that I durst not for my life; for I knew him to be such a bairn, that there was nothing told him but he would reveal it to her again."[2]

Completely in harmony with the part acted by

[1] The Laird of Ormiston, in his confession, professed to cite a part of it from memory, to this effect: "That for sacmickle it was thought expedient and maist profitable for the commonwealth, by the haill nobility and lords under subscryvit, that sic ane young fool and proud tyrant suld not reign or bear rule over them; and that for divers causes, therefore, they all had concluded that he suld be put off by ane way or another—and whosoever suld take the deed in hand, or do it, they suld defend and fortify it as themselves."—Pitcairn, i. 512*.

[2] Confession, in Bannatyne's Memorials; Bannatyne edit., 317.

these performers in the tragedy, a change came over the conduct of the queen. She employed her ductile arts on her diseased, suspicious, terrified husband. She set herself to the task of quieting his fears and luring him back to her arms. She announced that she would visit him on his sick-bed; and she set forth on her journey on the 22d of January 1567. A gentleman of his father's household, named Thomas Crawford, was sent to meet her. Crawford was a confidential adherent of Lennox, intrusted to attend this critical meeting between the husband and wife, and to observe and tell to his lord all that passed. It was a duty of some moment; for Lennox evidently believed that the visit was connected with some deadly purpose, and he was striving to fathom it. Crawford was instructed to report everything he saw and all he heard passing between the two. The question how they conducted themselves and what they said to each other became afterwards momentous, and holds so important a place in the history of a year or two later, that we may pass it over for the present, merely noting that Mary prevailed on her husband to agree that, after he had made some advance towards recovery, he would live at Craigmillar Castle for a time, and take the bath there.

After the queen departed, there came a word or two between her husband and Crawford, remarkable in their way. The sick man asked Crawford what he thought of the project for removing him. Crawford did not like it. Taking her husband to Craigmillar instead of his own place of residence was odd—it seemed as if she were going to take him more like a prisoner than a husband. Then came this from the sick man: "He answered that he thought little less himself, and feared himself meikle — save the confidence he had in her promise only; notwithstanding, he would go with her, and put himself in her hands, though she should cut his throat, and besought God to be judge unto them baith." [1]

A few days afterwards she had her husband removed to Edinburgh, so that he arrived there on the last day of January. The purpose of conveying him to Craigmillar was changed. Yet he was told that he would not be taken to Holyrood, but to a place close to the city wall called the Kirk-of-Field. He knew that there stood the great hotel of the Hamilton family, and expected to be taken to it; but the house destined for him was a smaller building, the residence of the provost of the religious house of St Mary-in-the-Fields, which conveniently belonged to Robert Balfour, the brother of the drafter of the bond. This was one of the monastic establishments wrecked by the English invaders. From this or some other cause the provost's house seems to have been singularly destitute of defences for a building of that age; and Nelson, Darnley's page, tells that a small door, which appears to have given access to the whole building from the courtyard, was taken off by the queen's orders, to cover the vat or tub in which the convalescent took his bath, as if nothing more appropriate could be found for such a purpose. Several incidental details speak clearly of the hasty occupation of a building which, however suitable for other purposes, was not adapted to tranquillity and security. An effort seems to have been made to give comfort and even a touch of regal magnificence to the apartments by hangings and furni-

[1] Record Office, Scotch Correspondence, vol. xiii. No. 14.

ture, conveniently afforded from the affluent supplies obtained by the plunder of Strathbogie in the conflict with Huntly.[1] For all that could be thus superficially done for it, the establishment seems to have been of the most sordid and slovenly character. The key of a door leading out through the city wall could not be found, and the door had to be nailed up from within. Of the other keys it was remarked that they were left in the possession of Balfour's people; and the conspirators appear, for more security, to have forged duplicates of them in case they should have been required to give them up.[2]

[1] "The hall was hung with five pieces of tapestry, part of the plunder of Strathbogie. It had a high chair or chair of state covered with leather, and a dais or cloth of state of black velvet fringed with black silk. The walls of the king's chamber on the upper floor were hung with six pieces of tapestry which, like the hangings of the hall, had been spoiled from the Gordons after Corrichie. The floor had a little Turkey carpet. There were two or three cushions of red velvet, a high chair covered with purple velvet, and a little table with a broad cloth or cover of green velvet, brought from Strathbogie. The bed, which had belonged to the queen's mother, was given to the king in August 1566. It was hung with violet-brown velvet, pasmented with cloth of gold and silver, and embroidered with cyphers and flowers in needlework of gold and silk. It had three coverlets, one being of blue taffeta quilted. ... The wardrobe, which seems to have been on the upper floor, was hung with six pieces of tapestry, figuring a rabbit-hunt. Here there was a cabinet of yellow shot taffeta, fringed with red and yellow silk. In a chamber on the ground floor, directly under the king's chamber, there was a little bed of yellow and green damask, with a furred coverlet, in which the queen slept on the nights of Wednesday and Friday, and intended to sleep on the very night in which the king was murdered."—Queen Mary's Inventories, Pref. xcviii.-c.

From the same accurate pen we have the following estimate of the accommodation of the house: "The provost's place contained a hall, two chambers or bedrooms, a cabinet, a wardrobe, and a cellar, besides a kitchen, apparently under another roof. Of these rooms only three or four seem to have been furnished from Holyrood."—Ibid.

[2] Buchanan, in his Detection, gives a hideously-eloquent description of the sordidness of the place; and as he appealed to a public who knew it as well as he did, he cannot well have gone beyond bounds:—

Sunday, the 9th of February, was at last fixed for the great project, probably because, being the marriage-day of the queen's favoured French domestic Bastiat to one of her women, the ceremonials and festivities of

"Whidder then is he led? Into the maist desolate part of the towne, sumtyme inhabitit while the Papische preistis kingdome lestit, bot for certane yeiris past without ony dwaller, in sic a hous as of itself wald haif fallin downe, yif it had not bene botched up for the tyme to serve the turne of this nichtis sacrifice. Why was this place cheifly chosin? Thay pretend the helsumnes of air. O gude God! going about to murther hir husband, seikis scho for ane helsum air? To what use? Not to preserve his lyfe, bot to reserve his body to torment. Heirto tend hir wyfelie diligent attendance, and hir last cair of hir husbandis lyfe. Schoe feiris leist he suld, be preventing deith, be delyverit from pane, schoe wald fane have him feill himself die. Bot let us se what maner of helsumnes of air it is. Is it amang deid mennis graves to seik the preserving of lyfe? For hard by thair were the ruynes of twa kirkis: on the eist syde, ane monasterie of Dominike freiris; on the west, ane kirk of our Lady, whilk, for the desolatenes of the place, is callit the Kirk in the Feild; on the south syde, the towne wall, and in the same, for commodious passage every way, is ane posterne dure; on the north syde ar ane few beggeris cotages, then reddy to fall, whilk sumtime servit for stewis for certane preistis and monkis, the name of whilk place dois planely disclois the forme and nature thairof, for it is commounly callit the Theif Raw. Thair is never ane uther hous neir bot the Hammiltounis hous, whilk is about ane stanis cast distant, and that also stude voyde. Thether remuisit the Archebischop of Sanctandrois, wha alway befoir was wont to be ludgeit in the maist populous partis of the towne. He also watchit all that nicht that the king was slane.

"Now I beseik yow, sen ye cannot with your eyis, yit at the leist with your myndes behald, ane hous whilum of auld preistis, amang graves, betwene the ruynes of twa tempillis, itself also ruynous, neir to the theifis hant, and itself ane resetter of theifis, not far from the fort and garrisoun of his enemeis, that stude richt over aganis the dure, be whilk yif ony man suld fle out, he culd not eschaip thair traterous ambuschment. The vermay schape of this place, when ye considder in your mynd, when ye heir of the ruynes of kirkis, graves of deid men, lurking corneris of theifis, bordelhousis of harlotis,—dois not, I say, not the hous only, bot also everie part neir about it, seme to proclame mischeif and trecherie? Semis heir ane king to have gane into a hous for ludgeing, or to be thrust into ane den of theifis? Was not that desolate waistnes, that unhantit place, abill of itself to put simpill men in feir, to mak wyser men suspicious, and to give nouchtie men schrewit occasionis?"
—P. 66-69.

the occasion afforded opportunities for doing what was to be done. From the testimony and confessions afterwards taken, imperfect as they are, a clear enough history can be gleaned of the greater part of the doings of the active hands, even if we should exclude from consideration those portions in which they exculpate themselves, along with those which, as directly inculpating the queen, are maintained by her champions to be incredible.

To follow accurately the course of events, it is necessary to keep in view one or two specialties which will enable one to single out from existing Edinburgh the geography of the ground gone over. The town formed itself then on the two great thoroughfares running east and west, the High Street and the Cowgate. The city wall cut through on the line where St Mary's Wynd and Leith Wynd now meet at the foot of the High Street, and there stood the Canongate Port, the space between it and Holyrood being occupied by the suburb of Canongate. Where the wall passed the Cowgate, at the foot of the present St Mary's Wynd, was the Cowgate Port. The wall there kept the same southerly direction to a bastion or turret near the present Infirmary, where it turned at right angles, running west. The next break was the Potterrow Port, before reaching which it passed close on the grounds of the Kirk-of-Field, the nearest existing landmark to which is the present College.

The persons known beyond the arch-conspirator as having had an actual hand in carrying out the plot were, Nicholas Hubert, called French Paris, a creature of Bothwell's, whom he had brought from France and placed in the service of the queen; George Dalgleish and William Powrie, in Bothwell's service and confidence; Hepburn of Bolton, his relation; Patrick Wilson, his tailor or master of the robes; Ormiston, the laird of that ilk, and his uncle, called Hob Ormiston; and Hay, the heir of Talla, a district in the wildest part of the border mountains.

The first event noticed on Sunday was that Murray, after breakfast, bade a formal farewell to the queen as he was departing to join his wife; and Hubert, who took note of this, says he saw that that good man desired to be away while mischief was going on. The queen attended the marriage of her favourites, partook of the marriage-dinner, and then supped with the Countess of Argyle, apparently about four o'clock. Hubert, who stood behind a chair, says she was solicitous about a coverture of marten-skins which she had directed him, through Margaret Crawford, to remove the day before from the Kirk-of-Field. She asked him now if it had been removed, and he satisfied her that it had. Bothwell was among the guests; and when they rose, he went to his mother's apartments, attended by Hubert. They then went and found Ormiston and his uncle Hob, with whom they joined Hay and Hepburn on the street of the Canongate. Bothwell then took Hubert to the Kirk-of-Field, and gave him such directions that, when the others came to transact business there, he should be on duty in the king's chamber.

The rest returned to the abbey or palace, where it has to be observed that Bothwell had permanent apartments. In these a quantity of powder was stored in bags or "pocks." Two large receptacles were provided for the removal of these, one of them apparently a common trunk, the other a mail or travelling-trunk. These were carried by two horses, and it took two journeys to remove the whole. They were taken round by the outside of the wall. Near the Kirk-of-Field there was an old gate in the wall, called the Blackfriars' Gate, not one of the regular occupied ports. Ormiston managed to get on the other side of the wall by the help of some ruins, and opened the gate. They had brought a cask with them to stow the powder in, but it was too large to get admission to the room where the train was to be laid. This room was the queen's bedroom, just under the king's, and her bed had to be shifted to make room for the train. It was brought in by the men in the original sackfuls, and this appears to have been a long, silent process. Bothwell at one time feared that it might be heard in the room above, and with a fierce whisper enjoined more quietness. They were at a loss for light; and, among other incidents, we are told that they bought six halfpenny candles from Geordie Burns's wife in the Cowgate.

Powrie and Wilson took back the empty boxes, and on their way saw "the queen's grace, with torches before her," going along the Blackfriars' Wynd to join the king. This seems to have been about ten o'clock. It was understood that, according to recently-established practice, she was to sleep that night in the chamber under the king's. She went first, however, up to the king's chamber, passing the door of her own, like an affectionate wife, whose first care was her sick husband. There was general conversation in the room, in the midst of which she suddenly recollected that she had promised to attend the masked ball to be held in the palace in honour of Bastiat's marriage, and must be off immediately. She bade her husband a very affectionate farewell for the night, and departed. Had she gone into her own chamber, she would have seen the bed removed and the sacks of powder lying there. But she did not go to it; and it is for every one to conjecture whether it was or was not known beforehand that she would keep out of that apartment. To prevent stray intrusions, Hubert kept the key.

The queen and her attendants, including Bothwell, having gone, Hepburn of Bolton and Hay of Talla only of the conspirators remained. How they occupied themselves is now the chief mystery in the whole affair; and from subsequent circumstantial evidence it has been conjectured that the intended victim, with his page, discovered them, attempted to escape, and got even over a wall into a garden, when they were seized and strangled. They were found without any marks from the explosion, but *with* marks of other violence.

Bothwell went to his apartments in the palace and changed his black velvet hose and doublet of satin, both trussed with silver, for a coarser doublet and dark muffled cloak, such as the Schwartz-ritters wore, and passed forth, accompanied by his immediate followers, Dalgleish, Hubert, Powrie, and Wilson. They were challenged by the sentinels on duty at the palace, but they said they were friends—friends of the Earl of Bothwell, and this powerful name silenced everything. They came to the Canongate Port, and finding it closed—for it was now twelve o'clock—called out to Galloway, the keeper, to open for friends of my Lord Bothwell; and here, again, there was immediate obedience. They took this way apparently that they might pick up Ormiston; but he managed not to be found, though he told in his confession that he was in bed asleep, and the rest went down by the Blackfriars. There Bothwell left his followers behind the wall, and joined Hepburn and Hay, who had already lighted the train. It seems to have been carefully laid, and burned so long that Bothwell, overcome by impatience, was on the point of going to look at it when the great crash came.

He was not a man to do things by halves; and he seems to have provided so large a train that the effect exceeded his expectation. Little was known then of the expansive force of gunpowder, and the extent of its destructiveness when confined within walls; and the building was so completely shattered, as to lead to the supposition that it had been systematically mined. The explosion shook the earth, and all Edinburgh was roused from sleep. The murderers had to escape rapidly, and it is probable that they may thus have been obliged to abandon a small detail necessary for the completion of their work in a satisfactory manner. Certainly they either intended to kill their victim by the explosion, or make it appear that he had been so killed. If he was killed in trying to escape, then of course it would have been desirable that the body should be taken back into the house, that it might, wherever it should be found, bear marks of the explosion, from which it was observed to be exempt. If he tried to escape, and was murdered after the lighting of the lint, it was too late to bring the body back; and, with all the world rushing to the spot, it was hopeless to remedy the matter after the explosion. The party were within the town walls, and seemed desirous to escape through the streets by an outlet distant from the Kirk-of-Field. They attempted what they thought a weak part of the wall at Leith Wynd, but found it too high for them, and had to apply again to the keeper of the Canongate Port, who again yielded to the demand of the Lord Bothwell's friends, and let them pass. Bothwell got as rapidly as possible to his apartments in the palace, took a draught of wine, and tumbled into bed, to be roused, as if from slumber, half an hour afterwards, by a messenger informing him of the tragedy. He called out treason, donned his garments, and went forthwith to the queen, along with Huntly, who joined him. It was then, apparently, between three and four o'clock.

Of the way in which the masked ball came off, we hear but little. It was probably a very gay and joyous affair; for Bastiat, in whose honour it was held, was a merry fellow, and especially expert at getting up mummeries. It was he who, on the occasion of a Court pageant, had disturbed the equanimity of the English embassy, by the provocative manner in which his satyrs wagged their tails in the face of these grave personages. The mask was long over, and all had retired before the explosion roused them. Bothwell and Huntly, when they sought audience of the queen at an untimely hour, had of course the excuse of a general alarm; and ostensibly, it appears that they informed her that there had occurred an accident from gunpowder at the Kirk-of-Field, as to which immediate inquiry was promised. Bothwell, it appears, returned between eight and nine o'clock to inform her that she was a widow, and held audience with her within the curtain of her bed—a matter which the royal customs of the time render of no further moment than as it imported that the communing was close and secret, excluding all other of the queen's advisers.[1]

Meanwhile a crowd gathered round the scene of the explosion, eager and anxious to find what the late dawn of the winter sun would reveal.

[1] Sir James Melville says that "Bothwell, when he came furth, told him that her majesty was sorrowful and quiet." He then told Melville that one of the most extraordinary things had come to pass—that powder had come down from the "luft" or sky, and burnt the house of the king, whose body was found under a tree. He recommended Melville to go and see the body, and observed "how that there was not a hurt nor a mark in all his body;" but Sir James was not successful in his attempts to get access to the place where the body lay.—Memoirs, 174.

CHAPTER XLVI.

Queen Mary.

(*Continued.*)

THE MORNING AFTER THE MURDER—DOINGS AT HOLYROOD—FEELING OF THE PUBLIC—DISPOSAL OF THE MURDERED MAN'S BODY—SUSPICIONS AND ACCUSATIONS POINTING TO BOTHWELL—WHISPERS ABOUT THE QUEEN—CORRESPONDENCE WITH DARNLEY'S FATHER, WHO DEMANDS A TRIAL—HOW IT WAS EVADED—BOTHWELL ADVANCED AND FAVOURED—THE QUEEN GETS WARNINGS—SOJOURN AT SETON—THE SUPPER AT ANNESLY'S—THE BAND FOR BOTHWELL'S MARRIAGE WITH THE QUEEN—THE INTERCEPTION AND CARRYING OFF OF THE QUEEN TO DUNBAR—HER FORMAL ENTRY INTO EDINBURGH—BOTHWELL'S DIFFICULTIES AS A MARRIED MAN—ARRANGEMENTS FOR BEING RID OF HIS WIFE—HOW THE PROTESTANT PARTY AND THEIR CLERGY TAKE MATTERS—THE MARRIAGE OF MARY AND BOTHWELL—THE MARRIED COUPLE—HER APOLOGY FOR HER CONDUCT.

THE smallest doings at Holyrood immediately after the murder, the very inertness itself, almost reaching a sort of political paralysis, deserve close attention from their significance. It is useless to join in the common wonder, founded on the practice regarding crimes in the present day, why immediate investigation was not made as to the procuring and carrying of the powder, the making of the false keys, the movements of the perpetrators, and the like. The question was not so much who *could* speak, as who *would*; and the latter question would have to be decided by the tenor of political events. In fact all the world knew who were the doers of the deed. Among persons conspicuous in the history of the time there was one, and only one, person who seemed to be ignorant of the party guiltiest of all. It was a knowledge along with which some entertained an approval of the deed, while others were prepared to employ it in punishment if they should have the opportunity. The one exception to this general admission was the queen, who could not or would not believe that her beloved follower was the great criminal.

Bothwell immediately did the part of the prompt and considerate friend, who in the hour of calamity relieves the bereaved of the irksome duties of the household. He took on himself, in fact, the functions of Governor of Scotland, and with immediate success; for there was nobody who could cope with one so prompt and audacious, supported as he was by the devout reliance of his royal mistress. As morning dawned, the citizens naturally continued to gather to the Kirk-of-Field. Bothwell sent a strong guard to the spot, and directed the bodies to be removed. During the day the ambassadors of France and Savoy desired an inspection of the king's body, which was refused. This was cited, along with other like instances, to show that the murderer was keeping out of sight the chief real evidence of his crime; but such suspicions are natural to such an event. They are caused by excitement and disappointed curiosity. In this instance there was little concealment or motive for it. No one pretended that the death had been accidental, or breathed a doubt that there had been murder.

Mary at first adopted the decorous gloom proper to her situation, and shut herself out from the world. It was a carriage not only blameless but laudable, yet it aptly served the purpose of him who was becoming the ruler of her actions. On the second day of her widowhood we have the earliest indication of the policy she intended to pursue. It is addressed to her worthy councillor, Beaton, the Bishop of Glasgow, in whose eyes she ever wished to stand well. The letter is so significant that it is given in full:—

"Most reverend father in God, and trusty councillor, we greet ye well. We have received this morning your letters of the 27th January by your servant, Robert Dury, containing in ane part such advertisement as we find by effect over true, albeit the success has not altogether been such as the authors of that mischievous fact had preconceived in their mind, and had put it in execution, if God in His mercy had not preserved us, and reserved us, as we trust, to the end that we may take a rigorous vengeance of that mischievous deed, which or it should remain unpunished, we had rather lose life and all. The matter is horrible and so strange, as we believe the like was never heard of in any country. This night past, being the 9th February, a little after two hours after midnight, the house wherein the king was lodged was in an instant blown in the air, he lying sleeping in his bed, with such a vehemence that of the whole lodging, walls and other, there is nothing remained, no, not a stone above another, but all either carried far away, or dung in dross to the very ground-stone. It mon be done by force of powder, and appears to have been a mine. By whom it has been done, or in what manner, it appears not as yet. We doubt not but, according to the diligence our Council has begun already to use, the certainty of all shall be usit shortly; and the same being discovered, which we wot God will never suffer to lie hid, we hope to punish the same with such rigour as shall serve for example of this cruelty to all ages to come. Always, whoever have taken this wicked enterprise in hand, we assure ourself it was dressit as well for us as for the king; for we lay the most part of all the last week in that same lodging, and was there accompanied with the most part of the lords that are in this town that same night at midnight, and of very chance tarried not all night, by reason of some mask in the abbey; but we believe it was not chance, but God that put it in our head.

"We despatched this bearer upon the sudden, and therefore write to you the more shortly. The rest of your letter we shall answer at more leisure, within four or five days, by your own servant. And so for the present commit you to Almighty God. At Edinburgh the 11th day of February 1566-67."[1]

The original of this letter is now lost, and we have not the means of knowing whether it was written in her own hand. The probability is that it was not.[2] But there is no doubt that it is her own. Whether her own device or that of her master, it was a bold stroke. It was to stamp at once the impression that she was to have been one of the victims, and that her own escape was a great marvel of the tragedy. The attempt was a failure. Circumstances at once showed that the safety of the queen was essential to the designs of the conspirators, and they were too expert to

[1] Labanoff, ii. 3, 4.   [2] See above, p. 211.

be likely to make any serious blunder. There is a secondary point in this letter, in which it agrees with the first impression made by the immediate aspect of the affair. She promptly assumes that the explosion came from a mine. This idea prevailed elsewhere, and the question of her good faith in starting it depends on whether she knew or did not know that the powder was piled in her own sleeping-room.

On Wednesday, two days after the discovery of the bodies, proclamation was made that a reward of two thousand pounds would be paid to any one who would reveal the author of the murder. Among the community, who knew perfectly the chief actor at least, none ventured to earn this money by an open denunciation; but a writing was affixed to the door of the Tolbooth or Parliament House, naming Bothwell, Balfour, Chambers, and "black Mr John Spence" as the guilty persons. Another placard followed, naming, as inferior actors in the tragedy, Signor Francis, Bastiat, John of Bordeaux, and Joseph Rizzio.

The event seems to have caused much more excitement among the citizens than its perpetrators expected. The age and the country were familiar with violent deaths. In France, Spain, and the Empire, the labours of the civilians had surrounded sovereigns with a sort of sanctity which claimed inviolability for their persons. Violence to monarchs was thus by degrees removed into a separate category from other outrages, and partook of sacrilege. This doctrine had, however, but faintly penetrated to Scotland, where the people were practically familiar with stories of the death of kings. A party was arising who argued that rulers should be specially responsible for their misconduct;

but then these were people of sober rigid walk, who abjured crime and violence, and demanded that the responsibility should be enforced with order and decorum. The method, too, of the deed, developing in an astounding manner the unknown, and it might be illimitable powers of the mysterious chemical agent just added to the forces at the command of man, was far more adapted to rouse the populace than any common stabbing or hanging. The feelings of the citizens of Edinburgh rapidly heated up to strong excitement, and Buchanan mentions that voices were heard in the street at dead of night denouncing the murderers.[1] It was a natural result of the general excitement that those who dared not speak openly should give utterance in the dark, and also that midnight denunciations were heard with mysterious awe.

Two days after the proclamation, the body of the murdered man was buried in the Chapel of Holyrood with a secrecy that attracted as much attention as any

[1] As all the picturesque accounts of the state of the public mind at this time are taken from Buchanan, we will get at the clearest statement by taking his own words : " Leist the mater suld seme not to be regardit, out gais ane proclamation with rewardis promysit to him that culd gif information of it. But wha durst accuse the quene ? Or (whilk was in maner mair perillous) wha durst detect Bothwell of sic ane horribill offence, specially when he himself was baith doer, judge, inquyrer, and examiner ? Yit this feir whilk stoppit the mouthis of everie man in particulaire, culd not restrane the haill multitude in general; for baith be buikis set out and be pictures, and be cryis in the darke nicht, it was sa handillit, that the doeris of the mischevous fact micht esilie understand that thay secreitis of thairis wer cum abrode. And when everie man was now out of dout wha did the murther, and wha gaif furtherance unto it, the mair that thay laubourit to keep thair awin names undiscloisit, sa mekle the pepilis grudge restranit, brak out mair oppinlie."—Detection, Anderson, ii. 25, 26. More tersely it is put in his History : "Nam et libellis propositis, et pictura, et nocturnis per tenebras clamoribus effectum est, ut patricidæ facile intelligerent arcana sua nocturna in vulgus prodiisse.—Lib. xviii. 20.

feature of the affair. It is noted that on the day of the funeral Bothwell obtained an accession of fortune in a gift of the reversal of the feudal superiority over the town of Leith, and that Darnley's servant Drummond, who stood under heavy suspicion of treachery, got a pension and an office near the person of the infant prince.[1] Two days afterwards, on the Sunday after the murder, the queen went to Seton Palace, in Haddingtonshire, about twelve miles from Edinburgh.[2] There she had for her Court the ever-present Bothwell, with his supporters Argyle, Huntly, Seton their entertainer, Secretary Lethington, and John Hamilton, the restless Archbishop of St Andrews.[3]

The caterers for information to be sent to England picked up expressive stories of the way in which the group conducted themselves. The queen and Bothwell, it was said, amused themselves in shooting at the butts, and having together won a match against Seton and Huntly, the losers entertained the winners at dinner in Tranent.[4] What means that place possessed for entertaining royalty in the sixteenth century it were hard to say: it is now a smoky, cindery, colliers' village, rife with whisky-shops, and lately achieved notoriety, in the course of the Government sanitary inquiries, by its excessive filth and unhealthiness. The

[1] Laing, i. 49.
[2] The best authority for the exact sequence of the events is the Diurnal of Occurrents.
[3] In the Diurnal of Occurrents, however, it is stated that she "left the Erlis of Huntly and Bothwill in the Palice of Halyrudhous, to keip the prince unto her returning."
[4] Drury to Cecil, cited by Tytler. That there were light doings at Seton is asserted also by Buchanan. In a diary of occurrences marked by Cecil (Forbes, ii. 269), it is said that at Seton she and Bothwell "passed their tyme meryly."

queen's visitors are justified in holding that such a scene was much at variance with the usual decorum of her deportment, and the less partial will admit it to be inconsistent with her powers of dissimulation; but there remains the consideration that she was then the victim of an infatuation which broke through all the defences of her strong nature. However it be, she had presently more important matters to occupy her. The denunciatory placards were repeated, and Joseph Rizzio, Bastiat, and the other humble foreigners whose names appeared on these formidable documents, prudently managed one by one to slip out of the country, knowing that whatever turn matters took they must be in imminent peril.

A new actor now steps upon the scene—one likely to bring practical conclusions out of the general chaos of doubts, mysteries, and suspicions. The father of the murdered man demands justice, and calls on the widow, as the person who has the power, and ought of all others to be the most earnest towards that end, to take vigorous steps for the discovery of the guilty persons. The correspondence between the queen and old Lennox is among the most significant of all the tell-tale documents of that crisis, and is well worthy of careful examination. Unfortunately the beginning, a letter from Lennox and the queen's answer, is lost. The reply of Lennox on the 20th of February is as reverential as, coming from the meanest of the queen's subjects, it could have been. He has received her most comfortable letter, for which he renders her highness most humble thanks, and he trusts never to deserve otherwise than as he has received of her highness's hands. Since she takes in good part his simple advice and counsel, he ventures to continue therein. As he sees that all the travail and labour she has manifested have hitherto come to naught, he makes bold to put his poor and simple advice in a practical shape, " that your highness wald with convenient diligence assemble the hail nobility and Estates of your majesty's realm; and they, by your advice, to take such order for the perfect trial of the matter," as he doubts not through God's grace shall so work on the hearts of her majesty and her faithful subjects as that the bloody and cruel actors of the deed shall be manifestly known. A sprinkling of piety there is towards the conclusion; but the last words have a touching simplicity, in desiring that she will bear with him should he seem troublesome, " being the father to him that is gone."

This appeal received prompt attention. It was written at Houston, in Renfrewshire, on the 21st of February, and the queen's answer left Seton next day. It was written in excellent taste, with such courtesy as a young sovereign might show to a venerable subject parentally related to her. The kindness and goodwill for which Lennox was so grateful were but her duty, and came of that natural affection, of which he might feel as assured himself at that time, and so long as God gave her life, as ever he had been since the beginning of their acquaintance. Then to business. For the assembly of the nobility and the other Estates of Parliament, which he recommended "for a perfect trial of the king our husband's cruel slaughter," she so entirely concurred in that plan, that before receiving his letter she had ordered a Parliament to be proclaimed, " where first of all this matter, being maist dear to us, sall be handlit, and nathing left undone whilk may further the clear trial of the same." This state paper does credit to the diplomatic skill of its author. Lennox was at once taken up as desiring a formal meeting of Parliament. As of course something must be done, no step could be more desirable than that, since it was a matter of parade and delay, which would give a long breathing-time. The Estates, in fact, did not assemble until the 14th of April. What Lennox wanted was a general assembling of the chief subjects of the crown, that counsel might be taken among them, the hands of justice strengthened, and assurance given to those who were afraid to reveal what they knew.

The next letter from the old man slips into the tone of one who is angry at being made a mockery of. After short words of courtesy, he explains the misapprehension of his meaning. With a touch of sarcasm, he expresses his assurance that, although her highness is pleased to await the assembling of Parliament, she will feel the time as long as he does until the matter be tried, and the doers of the deed condignly punished. The matter is not for Parliament, but the criminal administration of justice; and " of sic wecht and importance, whilk ought rather to be with all expedition and diligence sought out and punished, to the example of the hail world." He reminds her that certain persons have been denounced on the Tolbooth door as the murderers, and comes to this practical conclusion : " I shall therefore most humbly beseek your majesty, for the luif of God, the honours of your majesty and your realm, and well and quietness of the same, that it will please your majesty forthwith, not only to apprehend and put in sure keeping the persons named in the said tickets, but also with diligence to assemble your majesty's nobility, and then by open proclamation to admonish and require the writers of the said tickets to compear." If, assured of full protection, they failed to come forth and back their secret denunciations, then these would go for naught.

In the queen's next letter, dated the 1st of March, there is some fencing about the cross purposes concerning the Parliament. She did not mean that the affair was for the Parliament, or that it should lie over until the Estates met; "but rather wad wish to God that it might be suddenly and without delay tried, for ay the sooner the better." Then coming to the point: "And where ye desire that we should cause the names contained in some tickets affixt on the Tolbooth door of Edinburgh to be apprehended and put in sure keeping—there is sa mony of the said tickets, and therewithal sa different and contrarious to [each] other in compting of the names, that we wit not upon what ticket to proceed." Perhaps this was the best subterfuge that could be found, but it was lamentably inferior to the subtle device in the previous letter. If Mary expected it to go for anything but an effort to gain time, this would strengthen the other evidence that the terrible strain on her nervous system was telling on her intellect. She ended by saying that, if he would intimate to her the names of any of the persons denounced whom he thought deserving of being brought to trial, she would direct them to be brought to trial according to law; "and being found culpable, sall see the punishment as rigorously execute as the weight of the crime deserves." On this hint Lennox spoke, and that plainly: "And for the names of the persons foresaid,

I marvel that the same has been keeped frae your majesty's ears, considering the effect [purport] of the said tickets, and the names of the persons is so openly talkt of—that is to say, in the first ticket the Erle Bothwell, Master James Balfour, Mr David Chambers, and black John Spence; and in the second ticket, Seigneur Francis, Bastian, John de Bourdeaux, and Joseph, Davie's brother, whilk persons, I assure your majesty, I for my part greatly suspect. And now your majesty knawing their names, and being the party, as well and mair nor I, although I was the father, I doubt not but your majesty will take order in the matter according to the weight of the cause, which I maist entirely and humbly beseek."

This bears date the 17th of March. On the 24th the queen intimated to him an entire compliance with his demands. Next week the nobles were to convene, and the persons denounced by the earl to be put to trial, and punished if guilty; and then comes an injunction such as would make one in Lennox's position ponder : " We pray you, if your leisure and commodity may suit, address you to be at us here in Edinburgh this week approachand, where ye may see the said trial, and declare thay things which ye knaw may further the same; and there ye sall have experience of our earnest will and effectuous mind to have an end in this matter, and the auctors of so unworthy a deed really punished."[1]

Here there is a formidable change of tone, which was not without its sufficient cause. In the oscillations

---

[1] The set of these letters is completed by using Anderson's Collection and Keith's History with Labanoff, who gives the most reliable rendering of the queen's part of the correspondence.

of immediate events the tables had been turned. The man sought as a criminal was himself the pursuer, and the accusers had to look to themselves.

It was consistent neither with the nature nor the designs of the man against whom so many accusations were levelled to act the part of the hunted hare. On the contrary, he took his stand as the great statesman— the actual governor of the realm, insulted by base and skulking calumniators, who dared not confront him. He swore vengeance against the authors of " the tickets ; " and inquiry was made, or professed to be so, for their exposure and punishment. Picturesque descriptions were furnished to the English Court how, in his rage and defiance, he rode through the town of Edinburgh with fifty of his armed ruffians, and there before the multitude told how he would serve the authors of the tickets if he could find them.[1] As a small incident, showing the contempt with which such accusations were received, a pension was bestowed on the Signor Francis so often referred to, the grant being dated at Seton on the 20th of February.[2] For nearly a month there was inaction in Court while the story of accusation raged outside; and men passed from Bothwell, as the principal criminal, to seize on the name of one still higher. It is remarked that the Privy Council, the natural immediate resort on a political emergency, did not assemble between the 12th of February, when the reward for the detection of the murderers was issued, and the 1st of March, when it met to transact mere routine business.[3] Another equally barren meeting was held on

---

[1] Letters cited in Tytler, vii. 74.
[2] Privy Seal Record, quoted, Laing, i. 50.
[3] Ibid.

the 11th, where it is noticed that Murray was present.[1] He had the day before obtained leave to retire to France, and departed a few days later, not much to the regret, it may be believed, either of his sister or the man in whose hands he left her.

As to him, the career of Court prosperity, in which he had been advancing, now took a rapid run—it could not but compromise the giver as well as the receiver of the rewards; and that he should have pursued his fortune so eagerly at such a juncture, may be attributed either to the recklessness of his ambition and greed, or to the necessity of fortifying himself from the coming attack, as the governor of a threatened garrison seizes the latest opportunity afforded to him to run up fresh defences.

Meanwhile those who were near enough to the Court to see what went on there found themselves driven to a new and astounding conclusion. They saw such distinct evidence of the queen's infatuated love for Bothwell that they believed she would marry him, and that the merely superficial impediment of his having a wife alive would be got over. There is little satisfaction in the accounts which those professing after the event to recall what they expected to happen say about their suppositions. We all like to be considered sagacious and prophetic; and the most candid will give a touch of strength to their anticipations when recording them after the event. We have, however, to the present point a narrative of incidents, small in themselves, but sufficient to show that there was a practical belief, even while they were enjoying holiday life at Seton, that these two would be united in wedlock. These inci-

[1] Laing, i. 55.

dents are given us in the Memoirs of Sir James Melville, where they follow on a remark that the "bruit" began to arise that the queen would marry the Earl of Bothwell, "who had six months before married the Earl of Huntly's sister, and would part with his own wife;" "whereat," he continues, "every good subject that loved the queen's honour and the prince's security had sad hearts, and thought her majesty would be dishonoured, and the prince in danger to be cut off by him who had slain his father." He then tells how the Lord Herries, coming to Court, attended by fifty followers, on a special errand for the purpose, told her in the plainest terms the tenor of the rumours, "requesting her majesty most humbly upon his knees to remember her honour and dignity, and upon the security of the prince, whilk would all be in danger of tinsell in case she married the said earl, with many other great persuasions to eschew such utter wrack and inconvenients as that would bring on." Her majesty, it seems, marvelled at such bruits without purpose, "and said that there was na sic thing in her mind." Herries, having done what he deemed his duty, fled quickly with his followers to his own country, to evade the wrath of Bothwell.[1]

A story like this is always liable to be inaccurate; but in what follows Melville was himself a party, and must be correct, unless we charge him with wilful fabrication. He says he had made up his mind to speak to her majesty in the same terms as Herries. One Thomas Bishop, however, whom he describes as a Scotsman long resident in England, and a warm advo-

[1] There seems to be no reference to this in the 'Memoirs' attributed to Herries.

cate of Mary's title to the English throne, anticipated his intention by writing a letter, which he desired Melville to show to the queen. It took up the same tone as the warning by Herries, " but more freely, because he was absent in another country." Telling how the rumour of the coming event had penetrated to England, he assured her that if it came to pass she would lose her own reputation, the favour of God, and the kingdoms of England, Ireland, and Scotland— " with many other dissuasions and examples of histories, whilks wald be ower lang to rehearse." He says that he showed the letter to the queen, as he was desired; and when she had read it, she called out to Secretary Lethington that she had been shown a strange writing, " willing him also to see it." He asked what it was, and she said, "A device of his own, tending to the wreck of the Earl Bothwell." Melville continues, " He took me by the hand and drew me apart; and when he had read it, he asked what was in my mind, and said, ' So soon as the Earl Bothwell gets word, as I fear he shall, he will not fail to slay you.'" Melville muttered something about its being a sore thing to see that good princess running to utter wreck, and nobody to warn her ; but Lethington, telling him he had done " more honestly than wisely," became more specific in his warning, and recommended Melville to be off before Bothwell should come up from his dinner. He took the advice, and says he was hotly pursued. He says the queen interceded for him once and again. On Bothwell's rejecting her first intercession, she " was miscontent, and told him that he would cause her to be left of all her servants." He then promised to spare Melville —so much influence had the siren still on the savage humour of her lord. Melville says that, when he afterwards saw the queen, he reverted to the matter, backing Bishop's counsel with his own. The last touch is curious, and carries an unsatisfied impression: "She said, matters were not that far agaitwart, but she had na will to enter in the terms."[1]

From other quarters come warnings equally significant. We have seen how the queen wrote to Beaton, her ambassador in France, endeavouring to stamp on the first news of the tragedy the impression that she had herself made a providential escape. He expresses in his answer his thankfulness that she has been preserved to take a rigorous vengeance for the crime committed, and then says, "Rather than it be not actually tane, it appears to me better in this warld that ye had lost life and all." Unless this be an implied rebuke on her pretence, he passes entirely the ideal danger, but presses on her solemnly the dangers that were real and imminent. All Europe rings with the terrible story and the wretchedness of poor Scotland; nay, people make free with her own name, and in short charge her with the deed. These are calumnies, no doubt; but they bring deep sorrow on all her faithful servants, and she must nerve herself to such action as shall for ever confute them. "It is needful," he says, "that ye show now rather than ever before the great magnanimity, constancy, and virtue that God has granted you, by whose grace I hope ye sall overcome this most heavy envy and displeasure of the committing thereof, and preserve the reputation of all godliness ye have conqueshed of long, which can appear no way so clearly than that ye do

[1] Memoirs, 175-77.

such justice as the haill world may declare your innocence, and give testimony for ever of that treason that has committed, but fear of God or man, so cruel and ungodly a murther."[1]

It must ever be kept in view, as the key-note to all that preceded and followed, that never was wretched victim more distinctly and loudly warned of the gulf that was opening at her feet. She had still not finally committed herself at the date of a letter in which Kirkcaldy of Grange, writing to Lord Bedford, expresses his belief that the marriage will occur. He quotes a saying reported of the queen. Whether he gives it accurately or not, it imparts his belief in her infatuated devotion to the lord of her heart. It bore that "she cared not to lose France, England, and her own country for *him*; and shall go with him to the world's end in a white petticoat before she leave him."[2]

The tone of the history of Scotland now takes a peculiar turn. Events on the surface contradict the tenor of the influences below; and the plot hurries on, like that of a romance or a drama, to be reversed when the unseen powers find their opportunity and reveal themselves. The death of Darnley was not an event to be regretted or very zealously avenged; but a new light sprang up in men's minds when they saw the mighty reward at which the chief actor aimed. Then, indeed, it was time for them to act too. In the mean time, however, their enemy was too strong; and the policy adopted was to let the evil destinies that ruled the land have their swing. Lethington, Morton, Lind-

[1] Keith, i. civ.
[2] Quoted by P. F. Tytler, vii. 88.

say, Murray, all the subtlest and boldest spirits of the day, were alike silenced for a time. The political conditions of the situation were unprecedented in Scotland. On some occasions the crown had been strong enough to bear hard on the great local potentates. In others, some potent feudal house had been able to defy the crown for a time. But here was a new combination, showing what might come of a connivance of the crown with such a feudal house. The result for a time was the existence, at least in the south of Scotland, of a despotism which it was hopeless to resist until the time for reaction came.

The first performance on the stage thus cleared for the movements of the great actors was the trial which was to cleanse the hero of the piece from all taint, and especially to put matters finally right at the foreign Courts, where an inconvenient amount of interest was shown about the recent transactions in Edinburgh.

The proceedings taken were exceptional and anomalous. The established practice was, when a criminal prosecution was determined on, for the crown to take the office of accuser, treating any persons who had been the first accusers or informers merely as witnesses. In the documents connected with Bothwell's trial Lord Lennox is brought up as the accuser, and the tenor of the procedure looks like an arbitration in a dispute in which he and Bothwell hold opposite sides. On the 28th of March the Privy Council gave instructions for the trial. There were nine councillors present: Bothwell himself; the Lords Huntly, Argyle, and Caithness; Leslie, Bishop of Ross; Gordon, Bishop of Galloway; Secretary Maitland; Stewart, the Treasurer; and Justice-Clerk Bellenden. The Act of Council appointed the

12th of April ensuing for the trial, and directed that Matthew Earl of Lennox be warned personally, or at his dwelling-place, as well as all others who came forward as accusers. Royal letters were issued for the citation of Lennox; and in these, instead of the crown, according to usual form, setting forth the accusation, in name of the crown counsel it was stated that these gentlemen " are informed that our well-beloved cousin and counsellor, Matthew Earl of Lennox, father of our most dear spouse, has asserted that James Earl of Bothwell, Lord Hailes and Crichton, &c., and some others, were the contrivers of the traitorous, cruel, and detestable murther," &c. As another reason for the proceedings, which kept up their tone as a settlement of a dispute rather than a trial of a murderer, is " the humble request and petition of the said Earl Bothwell made to us, and in our presence, offering to submit himself to a fair trial of what he is charged with." The messengers intrusted with the citation of Lennox made formal returns, importing that they did not get access to him personally, but took the usual means for making their citations public and notorious.[1]

Lennox did not appear. Sir James Melville says he was ordered by the queen to bring none with him but his own household. He had a body of men-at-arms—three thousand, it was said—prepared to follow him. And there is no doubt that the policy which allowed the accused to be undisputed master of the capital, obviated what would probably have been the most bloody of all the street-conflicts that had disturbed Edinburgh.

There exists a letter from Lennox to the queen. As

[1] Anderson's Collections, i. 50.

it bears date on the previous day, it may be questioned whether it was delivered before the trial. It pleads sickness as his reason for not appearing, but shows that he did not think himself safe in Edinburgh. He begs that the trial may be postponed until he can prepare his evidence, and convene his friends for his protection. He demands that, like other persons accused of crimes, those charged on this occasion shall be taken into custody; and throws out a taunt that, instead of being treated as suspected criminals, they are not only at liberty, but great at Court, where they enjoy her majesty's special countenance and protection.[1]

On the day of the trial a messenger arrived with a letter from Queen Elizabeth to Queen Mary, but in the confusion and excitement of the event of the day it is not known whether she received it.

From the same authority which mentions the arrival of this letter it has been inferred that the queen openly showed before the citizens her sympathy with the accused, as an affectionate wife might telegraph her good wishes to a husband going forth to a contest or other critical ordeal.[2] But these specialties are of small moment beside the larger facts, among which the most significant is that Bothwell had four thousand armed men on the streets — an overwhelming force in itself — in addition to his command of the presiding fortress.

The proceedings of the day were pedantically formal. The Earl of Argyle presided as justiciar. Fifteen jurymen were empanneled, according to the practice of Scotland, and the Earl of Caithness was chosen their

---

[1] Anderson's Collections, i. 52.
[2] Documents quoted by Tytler, vii., App. v.

chancellor or foreman. John Spence, the queen's advocate, and Robert Crichton, appeared for the prosecution. Still, however, the distinction was kept up, that it was not a case taken up by the crown, but a contest with Lennox, who was called upon to appear as a party. There came forward a gentleman of his household, Robert Cunningham, who explained that the earl could not appear in safety, and protested against the proceedings, should they end in the acquittal of those notoriously known to have been the murderers of the king. To meet this the earl's letters, demanding a speedy trial, were read and recorded, and the court solemnly decided to proceed with business; "and therefore the said Earl of Bothwell being accused by the said dittay of the crime foresaid, and the same being denied by him, and referred to the deliverance of the said assize, they removed furth of the said court, and altogether convened; and after long reasoning had by them upon the said dittay, and points thereof, they, and ilk ane of them for themselves, voted, delivered, and acquitted the said James Earl of Bothwell of art and part of the said slaughter of the king."

Through the pedantic formality of the proceedings it is visible that the jury did not like what they were set to do. It was a practice of the time to put jurors on trial for false verdicts, or, as it was termed, "wilful error." Lord Caithness and the rest of the jurors had honesty and courage enough to record a protest that they ought not to be liable to such an ordeal for acquitting the person accused before them, because not a particle of evidence was given in—there was nothing whatever put before them but the indictment. They therefore had no alternative but to acquit. The chancellor of the jury was at the same time so punctilious as to insist on having it recorded that this their verdict was not founded on a quibble which the indictment put at the service of the jury, by stating the date of the crime as the 9th of February; "for that in deed the murther was committed the next day, being the x day, in the morning at two hours after midnight, whilk in law was, and ought to be, truly accompted the x day."

A careful study of the proceedings—so much of them as we have—leaves the impression that judges and jury were anxious to put on record what would tell that, if there were a defeat of justice, it was not their fault. They could not be blamed for their acquittal of the accused—they had everything, resting on the maxim that rigidity of form is the safety of the innocent, to justify them. All they had was an accusation put into shape. No evidence was called to justify the accusation, and so the jury acquitted. If the world knew no more than the record of the trial, nothing would seem more fair and appropriate. The affair ended in a bravado, the acquitted man offering, by public cartel, to fight, after the old way of the ordeal of battle, any one who should still charge him with the murder.[1]

The Estates met on the 14th of April; and were one to judge solely from the internal evidence of the formal procedure, never did Parliament assemble under conditions of more quietness and order. Yet it might be fancied that, in the very cautiousness of all its transactions, there were symptoms of apprehension that a storm was coming. It was a Parliament of precautions

[1] The record of the trial in State Trials, i. 902.

and confirmation of acquisitions. It began by exonerating Erskine of the command of Edinburgh Castle, acknowledging that he had held his trust as a good and true soldier, and would never be liable to question for what he had done in the course of his duty. There comes next an Act in favour of religious peace and toleration. It narrates how thoroughly the queen had kept her word, in her promise not to attempt anything contrary to the religion which she found "publicly and universally standing at her arrival;" for which all her subjects who have so enjoyed the rights of conscience in peace shall have occasion to praise God for her good, happy, and gracious government, and crave of Him, from the bottom of their hearts, that He would, of His infinite goodness, prosper and bless her majesty and her posterity with long life, and good and happy government, to rule and reign over them. We have not here the equivocation of supporting the Church by law established as in the Act of 1563. But through its multifarious clauses, promising and reiterating protection to the persons referred to in the exercise of their religion, there is an exceeding care to avoid any specific definition of what that religion is, whether by the use of the nomenclature or the characteristics of Protestantism, or by the points of its difference from the Church of Rome. Such as it was, Bothwell had the credit of having gained this boon to his own ecclesiastical party. It did not propitiate them, however. If, as it would seem, he expected to secure the Reformation party, he was signally defeated. They were becoming the champions of Puritanism as well as Protestantism, and looked askance at murder, though the victim was a Papist and the doer one of themselves. There were several ratifications of private gifts of estates. Lethington looked after himself on this occasion; and David Chambers, one of the Lords of Session, was rewarded with domains " for the good, true, and obedient service done in all time past to her majesty's honour, well, and contentment," and that through imminent peril and danger. He was an able man, a jurist and historian, writing both in French and Latin; but he was a creature of Bothwell's, and so vehemently suspected of participation in the murder, that his name appeared on the midnight placards. Morton and Murray were confirmed in their acquisitions at great length; so was the queen's other illegitimate brother, Robert, the Commendator of Holyrood House. There were several other such ratifications, the most significant of which was the virtual restoration to Huntly of a large portion of the old domains of his house. He was expected to reciprocate in services of a peculiar kind. Bothwell, of course, comes in for his share of the royal bounty. In general terms his right is confirmed to all and sundry " his lordships and barony of Hailes, Crichton, and Liddesdale; and all others his lands, lordships, baronies, castles, towers, fortalices, mills, fishings, woods, parts, pendicles, &c., together with the offices of admiralty of Scotland, and the offices of the sheriffships of Edinburgh principal, and within the constabularies of Haddington and Lauderdale." But there was a more special object in the ratification, narrating her highness's regard and consideration " of the great and manifold good service done and performed, not only to her highness's honour, well, and estimation, but also to the commonwealth of this realm and lieges thereof," by which he " superexpended himself" and burdened his lands. This was, indeed, the fact. Most of his great territories he had from his ancestors; but by his own extravagant living, succeeding that of his father, he became hard pressed for available means, and the estates were heavily burdened. The object of the ratification was to amend this defect; and to enable him to support his rank as Governor of the Castle of Dunbar, certain lands in its neighbourhood, apparently of considerable agricultural value, were vested in him. His wealth and power were now enormous. He had the command of Edinburgh Castle and of the county of Edinburgh, with Haddington and Lauderdale. The two great feudal towers, still remaining, twelve miles from Edinburgh, Crichton and Borthwick, were his. He had the original possession of his family—Hailes—and the friary lands of Haddington. This almost joined his lordship round Dunbar, where he commanded a strong fortress. Another, the Hermitage, guarded his estates in Liddesdale, which were almost joined to the rich possessions of Melrose Abbey in the vale of Tweed; and he was Warden of all the three marches, and Lord High Admiral. One significant feature in the legislation of the session was for the suppression of the anonymous denunciations which had been so troublesome. Any person first seeing or finding such a document was to destroy it, otherwise he would be punished as an accessory to its promulgation. This was no novel effort of ingenuity; it was, in fact, the old Roman law of *famosi libelli*, and the Act was little more than a translation of the provisions which may be found in the 47th book of the Pandects.

Parliament rose on the 19th. On the afternoon of

that day there was a great supper of the influential members in a tavern owned by a man named Annesly. They had the distinction to be surrounded by an armed guard of Bothwell's followers. Suppers were at that time, like state dinners of the present day, a suitable occasion for political movements. This one began at four o'clock, and went, amidst much carousal, pretty deep into the night. Before the revellers separated a document was presented for their acceptance, drawn up with that special skill for such draftsmanship which Balfour had more than once exhibited. It contained, in the first place, an assertion of Bothwell's innocence, and a resolution to hold it against all impugners. There is next an obligation, in the usual tenor of bonds of man-rent, to stand by Bothwell in all his quarrels. Then comes last the great stroke. In case his distinguished services to her majesty, "and his other good qualities and behaviour," should move her to condescend to receive him as her husband, all the undersigned determine to further and promote such a marriage to the utmost of their capacity ; and they recommend it as a proper step to be taken for the public good in the widowed condition of the queen. That there was shown to the assembled magnates a writing expressive of the queen's desire for the match is a disputed question. What is, however, a lamentable fact is, that the document was adopted by a meeting of the first men in the country. This is an affair which not only lacks sufficient explanation, but scarcely affords material for a plausible theory. Simple coercion will hardly account for it. Among the men there assembled the vices were many and grave, but poltroonery was not conspicuous among them. It was noticed that next morning the bulk of them rapidly dispersed to their separate territories, leaving the political epoch to its own development.[1]

Events now followed each other rapidly, and thickened to a conclusion. On the 21st of April the queen went to Stirling to visit her child; and so dangerous a repute did she carry with her, that Mar the governor was frightened into vague fears about his precious charge, and would not permit the mother to bring into his presence any other attendants than two of her women. Bothwell prepared to intercept her on her return, and whether this was done by her own connivance is one of the secondary questions in the great controversy. Whether she were aware of the enterprise, it was so well known to others that, between her departure and return, one of the Edinburgh correspondents of the English Court writes to say that the Earl of Bothwell has gathered a body of men professedly to ride to the border, but the writer believes that presently after he writes they will be employed to intercept the queen and take her to Dunbar; and he sarcastically asks the receiver of the letter to judge whether this be with her will or not.[2] Sir James Melville in his Diary dryly says he was told by Captain Blackadder that the queen was seized by her own consent, but he does not give us the benefit of his own comment on this assertion. Bastiat, the French page, says in his testimony or confession that, on the

---

[1] Anderson's Collection, i. 107-111, iv. 60. There are lists of the parties to this manifesto; but they are given from memory, and not to be depended on. The name of Murray, for instance, occurs in them, though, apart from all question of probability, he was absent from Scotland at the time.

[2] Cited by P. F. Tytler, vii. 88.

evening before the seizure, the queen sent him from Linlithgow with letters to Bothwell, who bade him in answer assure her majesty that he would meet her on the road at the bridge. Bothwell took with him eight hundred spearmen to the western entrance of Edinburgh; he had military resources at his disposal which, for any such enterprise as he had on hand, might be called inexhaustible. The spot where he met the queen is now called Fountainbridge, a sort of mixed suburb to the west of the old town of Edinburgh, having to the south the new suburbs of Greenhill and Merchiston, and to the north the western verge of the new town. The affair passed quietly.[1]

It is provoking when men who have partaken in critical events tell of them, and yet tell so sparingly and dryly as to leave a world of untold matter which every reader longs to know; but such are often the very points on which practical men's words are fewest, because they do not like to commit themselves. Sir James Melville, who has left so many lively sketches of more trifling matters, was one of the queen's escort on the occasion, and he tells us nothing more than that "the Earl Bothwell was in her gait with a great company, and took her majesty by the bridle. His men took the Earl of Huntly, the Secretary Lethington, and me, and carried

[1] Buchanan finds a very subtle plot in the "Ravishment." It was desirable, all things considered, that Bothwell should be furnished with the technical protection of a royal pardon. It was the practice in such documents to set forth the principal crime committed by the malefactor, that the boundaries of the indemnity might be fully defined, and to slump minor offences in a general definition. It was not expedient to name the murder of her husband; but a treasonable attack on her own person was a very heavy crime, and by a little sophistry might be made out to go further than the other, so as to leave it in the group of minor offences.

us captives to Dunbar; all the rest were letten go free." Next day Melville himself was released, so that, if he held his tongue about what was afterwards done within the grim fortress, he disappointed no just expectations. A young and lovely princess taken captive and immured in the fortress of a profligate and unscrupulous baron is one of the most approved elements of old romance, giving room for the imagination to revel in all horrors and tyrannies. On the question whether or not the queen was treated with violence in Dunbar Castle there is no end of speculation, but there is very little means of distinct knowledge. To the shifting unsatisfactory character of all foundations for a conclusion she herself added, by expressions which were intended, and with subtle skill adapted, to raise a doubt about her exemption from personal violence, and to leave that doubt unsolved.

The next step was to rid Bothwell of the burden of his existing wife, and make him free to take another. In the letter in which the English statesmen are told of the intended seizure, they are also told of the intention to separate Bothwell from his wife—so well was it known that this was to be, although the method might not be exactly anticipated. Since it had to be forced through, the method adopted is instructive about the state of the public institutions of Scotland at that time, as well as of the character of the persons concerned. The old power of the Romish hierarchy to judge in matters of marriage and divorce as part of the canon law was abolished by the Acts of 1560, which abolished the Papal supremacy. As there was at first no distinct substitute for the power so exercised, some inconvenience was felt. By a suppliant to the Court of

Session in 1562, it was represented "that, because the consistorial jurisdiction is abolished, the said complainer could get no cursing"—that is to say, no civil process followed on the excommunication which the ecclesiastical court could launch against the person who had wronged him in a matter in which the canon law, as administered by the old hierarchy, would have given him redress.[1] To fill up the gap thus caused in the administration of civil justice, a court of four commissaries was erected by royal authority in 1563, and was recast in 1566. In this court Bothwell's wife sued out a divorce against him on the ground of adultery; and it appears to have been very easy to find, on an analysis of her husband's actions, enough to justify a decision in her favour. Sentence of divorce was accordingly pronounced against him, at the instance of his wife, on the 3d of May.[2]

The exceptional condition, however, in which her destined successor stood made something more necessary for the satisfactory conclusion of the affair. The superseding of the bishops' court by that of the commissaries was occasioned by those reforming Acts to

[1] Riddell's Peerage and Consistorial Law, 427.

[2] The marriage with Lady Jane Gordon was on the 22d of February 1566, so that she was his wife for a year and two months. It is curious to trace, in the pages of the genealogists, the after-life of one who was in a manner drifted in among the stormiest incidents of her day, and then after a short interval floated off into calm waters. She lived to an old age, which left far behind all the political conditions of her first-married life, and passed through successive scenes performed by successive relays of actors. She had her vicissitudes, but the way in which she took them showed a quiet spirit, fitted to make the best of existing conditions. The account given of her in Wood's Peerage, after her first marriage is disposed of in proper form, is, "Secondly, 13 December 1573, to Alexander, eleventh Earl of Sutherland, and had issue; thirdly, to Alexander Ogilvy of Boyne; and died in 1629, ætat. eighty-four. She was a lady of great prudence."

which the queen had never given the royal assent, which she believed consequently to be invalid, and which everybody believed she in her secret heart intended to repudiate when the proper time came. Farther, by the doctrine of her own Church, and the practice of the old consistorial tribunal in Scotland, separation of man and wife for adultery was not that nullifying of the marriage which permitted the divorced person to marry again.[1] It was, therefore, desirable to get the marriage annulled under the old law, and by the old hands, on such grounds as would admit of Bothwell marrying again. There were many difficulties in the way of this, and the steps taken to overcome them make a rather complicated history.

According to the view of the queen, and doubtless of all sincere followers of her Church, the Acts abolishing the power of the Romish hierarchy were a nullity; but it would not do to publish such a view by acting on it, and that on a very critical and conspicuous occasion. By a warrant of the queen, acting under her notions of prerogative, the consistorial authority was formally restored, with the Archbishop of St Andrews as its head. This court was constituted in the month of December 1566, and therefore that act in itself cannot have been done, as historians generally say it was, for the special purpose of carrying out this divorce. It was, in fact, an attempt following up the triumph of the Romish party—a trial how far a quiet step could be safely taken for the restoration of old things. It did not pass in silence,

---

[1] The General Assembly in 1566 desired the resumption of this principle—viz., that the culpable party in such a divorce should not be free to marry.—Book of the Universal Kirk, 54.

for the Reformed Church uttered a loud testimony against it. The General Assembly memorialised the Privy Council, saying that although the commission included some of themselves, "yet can the Kirk noways be content that the Bishop of St Andrews, ane common enemy to Christ, use that jurisdiction, and also in respect of that coloured commission he might again usurp his old usurped authority." They attribute it to their own negligence that Satan had so far prevailed within the realm of late days. "We therefore," they say, "in the fear of our God, and with grief and anguish of heart, complain unto your honours; yea, we must complain unto God, and to all His obedient creatures, that that conjurit enemy of Jesus Christ and cruel murtherer of our dear brethren, most falsely styled Archbishop of St Andrews, is reponed and restored by signature to his former tyranny." They strongly suspect that the end of such things will be "to cure the head of that venomous beast whilk once within this realm, by the potent hand of God, was so banished and broken down that by tyranny it could not hurt the faithful." And then follow some protestations, instructive in communicating to us the constitutional notions prevalent at the time. "The danger may be feared, say ye; but what remedy? It is easy, and at hand, Right Honourable, if ye will not betray the cause of God and leave your brethren, whilk never will be more subject to that usurped tyranny than they will unto the devil himself. Our queen belike is not well informed. She ought not, nor justly may not, break the laws of this realm; and so, consequently, she may not raise up against us, without our consent, that Roman Antichrist again, for in ane lawful and free Parliament as ever was in the realm before was that odious beast deprived of all jurisdiction, office, and authority within this realm."[1]

The new tribunal thus protested against did not supersede the Protestant court, and does not seem to have transacted judicial business.[2] Its history stands by itself entirely clear of the great personal question of the day. In fact, before the severance of Bothwell from his wife could be accomplished, Mary had to come personally forward and issue a special authority for that end.

On the 27th of April the queen issued a special commission to the archbishop and certain other clergy, to give judgment in an action of divorce by the Earl Bothwell against the Lady Jane Gordon, on the canonical ground of relationship within the fourth degree of consanguinity, and the celebration of marriage without the necessary dispensation.[3] So rapidly did this tribunal get through its one piece of

[1] Book of the Universal Kirk.
[2] The "signature", or commission under the sign-manual restoring the consistorial jurisdiction of the archbishop is in the Register of the Privy Seal (vol. xxxv. 99). It is in absolute terms, superseding the authority of the Commissaries and the Court of Session, and providing compensation for the judges of that court, whose salaries partly consisted of commissariat fees. It bears date 23d December 1566. The remonstrance of the Assembly bears date 27th December. It is addressed to the Privy Council, requesting them to "stay" the commission. The record of the Great Seal, which, however, is imperfect, does not contain the completed commission, nor is there any evidence of its having been accepted by the Privy Council. From this, and the circumstances mentioned in the text—viz., the proceedings before the Commissaries and the separate commission to the archbishop to adjudicate in the special case—it may be questioned whether the restoration of the archbishop's jurisdiction passed through all the proper forms, or was, on the other hand, "stayed."
[3] Riddell's Peerage and Consistorial Law, 433.

work that the proceedings, begun on the 5th of May, were finished by judgment of divorce on the 7th. The peerages and genealogies will be searched in vain for the evidence of propinquity. His mother was a Home and hers a Keith. It has been noticed that both houses — the Hepburns and the Gordons — were descended from the Earl of Buchan, the illegitimate brother of James II.; but this circuitous connection would bring Bothwell as near in consanguinity to the queen as to Lady Jane. By the practice of the Church of Rome in Scotland and some other countries, the rule that the prohibition extended to affinity by marriage as well as by blood was extended to concubinage. If, therefore, Bothwell had had illicit intercourse with any relation of the Lady Jane, that would impart to him the same nullifying privilege which he would have held had he himself been as nearly related to her as his paramour was. It seems probable, therefore, that in this, as in the other process, he was favoured by his extensive participation in the prevalent vices of the day.[1]

[1] Buchanan asserts that this was the method in which he got his divorce: "Apud judices Papisticos, ordinum quidem decreto vetitos, tamen ab Archiepiscopo Sancti Andreæ ad hanc caussam cognoscendum datos, accusatur, quod ante matrimonium *cum propinqua uxoris stupri consuetudinem habuisset:* celato interim Pontificis Romani diplomate, quo venia ejus culpæ facta erat."—Detectio, Jebb, i. 248. A portion of the proceedings in both suits is given by Principal Robertson in his Appendix, No. xx. In the process before the Commissaries, a certain Bessie Crawford has a story to tell, which removes all difficulties. As appropriate to the whole occurrence, the French ambassador commented on the peculiar facilities for divorce in Scotland: "Ilz ont une coustume estrange en Angleterre, mais plus prattiquée en Escosse, de pouvoir se répudier l'un l'aultre quant ilz ne se trouvent bien ensamble;" and then he cites instances.—Teulet, ii. 157. But that the French too were familiar with such things, is shown by an apt case in point. When, on Queen Mary's first widowhood, the Duke of Aumale

There still remains a nicety in this complicated business. It was the policy of the Church, in stretching her authority over the social as well as the religious condition of the people, to find a method of counteracting every power she exercised. If she helped those who were eager to break the marriage-tie, she could protect those who desired to make it indissoluble. Hence it was customary for the prudent relations of a bride to obtain a Dispensation from the nullifying influence not merely of actual propinquity, if such there were, but of anything that might be founded on the vicious life led by the other party. We find Buchanan asserting that such a Dispensation had been obtained on the marriage of Bothwell with Lady Jane Gordon, and that it was abstracted or concealed : as the charge stands in the vernacular version, "All this while they kept close the Pope's bull, by whilk the same offence was dispensed with."

In the process for the dissolution of the marriage it is expressly set forth that no dispensation had been obtained, and the statement to the contrary was generally set down as one of Buchanan's calumnies. Later inquiries, however, show that such a dispensation existed, that it was granted by Archbishop Hamilton in virtue of his legatine powers, and that, although he did not bring it up to interrupt the divorce, it was per-

was making love to her, the gossips of the Louvre had it that she would marry him if he were free—" qu'elle declara, qu'elle l'epouscroit, si par la mort de sa femme, Antoinette de la Marck fille du Duc de Bouillon, ou autrement, il rentroit en liberté de se rémarier."—Mem. de Castelnau, i. 528. The gossips were at fault, for, as we have seen, the young widow had other designs ; but it is clear that the Duke's having a wife was considered only a temporary impediment to such a marriage if the two desired it.

mitted, whether through his connivance or not, to get into the possession of the house of Hamilton, who had a strong interest to preserve a document that might some day or other prove that offspring of Queen Mary was illegitimate.[1]

[1] There is still a mystery about this Dispensation. If the ground on which it proceeded is given accurately in Tytler's Inquiry (edit. 1790, p. 401), it sets forth what is contradicted by all the books of genealogy, that an Earl Bothwell was married to Margaret, daughter of George, second Earl of Huntly. A key to all available information on this affair will be found in p. 181 of the Preface to the Statuta Ecclesiæ Scoticanæ, by the late Joseph Robertson.

On this, the last occasion in which I have to seek help from his last work, I cannot avoid the opportunity of dropping a few words about its author. In making use of his admirable account of the Provincial Council of 1549, I described it as the work of a "living" author. When the passage came to be corrected in proof, this description was no longer applicable. His recent death is a blow to all who take interest in historical literature; but it concerns myself in an especial manner. It is not only that he and I followed common pursuits. He was my companion in boyhood, and from that time my steadfast friend on to the end. Many years ago, from the peculiar knowledge he had stored up, I had set before him, as his special duty, the work which I have myself attempted in these volumes. The bent of his mind was, however, rather towards archæology than history; and thus it may be said that he preferred the science to the art. We had a constant interchange of ideas, suggested by what we read from time to time; and to those who knew what was in him, I need not observe how largely the balance of benefit from such a commerce was on my side. In fact, intercourse with a mind like his, so accurate and sagacious, was a sort of education or training in archæological science.

He was profuse, almost to a weakness, in giving away to every claimant the fruits of his skill. Where others would have complained of discoveries appropriated without acknowledgment, he was content to see that the truth was spreading into new quarters. If you had a casual discussion with him on some obscure point, you were sure to receive from him next morning a letter full of minute and curious erudition concerning it. He was ever ready with his help. I know that I could have counted on him to revise the sheets of this book, had I wished him to do so. I hold, however, to the opinion that no one should venture on the publication of a work unless he is prepared to take the undivided responsibility of everything contained in it. He took a keen, friendly interest in the progress of my book to the last; and desired to see what I had printed, after the

The affair of the divorces was adjusted, though not concluded, while the queen was still in Dunbar Castle. On the day when the Protestant divorce was issued, the two entered Edinburgh with a large body of followers, who on the journey threw away their arms, to give the assemblage the appearance of a peaceful pageant. On the 12th occurred one of those curious pieces of pedantic formality which accompany the several steps of this wild story. It was said that the supreme courts of law had doubts whether their proceedings were valid while the queen, in whose name they

end was so near that it was necessary to circumscribe his sources of interest or excitement. Among the last words whispered by him to a dear friend common to both was an injunction to keep me right " about that charter of William Rufus."

Of the kind of work in which his strength lay he had that early presentiment so often the companion of true genius. Rummaging among old letters, I find signal evidence of this. He wrote to me on the 7th of August 1833, saying, "The *Ultima Thule* of my desires would be a situation in the Register House." Then, diverging into other plans and possibilities, he comes back in the end to the same point, "My desires are towards the Register House, and about January I shall make a set upon it, and, if unsuccessful, then consider what is to be done next."

He had to wait just twenty years for the fulfilment of this dream. He was then let into the establishment to hold a small appointment, for which little was given, while little service was expected in return. It was enough, however, that he got access to those grand sources of knowledge on which his heart was set. For many years the great institution he now belonged to had been treated merely as an establishment for the concentration and hoarding of the records of the current business of the day. The proceedings of the courts of law, the transactions as to property, the vital and social statistics of the country, were here registered. These objects were duly seen to; but it had been long forgotten that here also was the great storehouse of the national archives—of all that remained to show the career of Scotland as an independent sovereignty. It was on these that Robertson's designs lay; and if working among them he was unnoticed and unremunerated, it was well also that he was unmolested.

At length external changes brought a kind and discriminating eye to bear upon him and his services. A new head came to the institution, who, seeing that there had been a long dormancy in some of its departments, resolved to bring all into life again. In that inner recess where

acted, was a captive. Whether or not they really experienced such doubts, the opportunity was taken for a solemn proclamation of their groundlessness. It is on record in the proceedings of the Court of Session, which mentions the presence of the prelates, the high officers of state, and the Provost of Edinburgh. The "declaration of the queen's liberty" followed that equivocal tone in which she all along spoke of the affair: "Albeit her highness was commovit for the present time of her taking at the said Earl Bothwell, yet since syne, by his guid behaving towards her high-

Robertson had been toiling in silence and almost in secrecy for twelve years, he found much of the work done ready to his hand, and he resolved that the public benefactor should not go unrewarded.

Robertson's day had now dawned. His name was to have an honourable place in connection with his services, and his income was to be in better harmony with their value. Social position, distinction, wealth, were to be his. It would surely be hard to find a sadder example of that uncertainty in human affairs, ever teaching the lesson that neither skilfulness of arrangement nor excellence of aim can make the projects of man secure. The flame was too nearly burnt out for fresh nutriment to aid it. January was to see him enter on his new fortunes, but he was buried in December. None felt more keenly than the high officer with whom he was to co-operate the greatness of the loss to the world.

It is generally difficult to take a measure of the loss caused by the death of an intellectual worker—sometimes difficult to prove that it is a loss at all. The poet, the novelist, the leader of opinion, may have exhausted his mission. The literature in which he has excelled changes its tone. A new school prevails; and it is idle to ask whether the dead man, had he lived, could have kept his own in the face of it. But here the work to be done was all laid out. The sheaves were piled on the threshing-floor, awaiting the work of the husbandman. This will have to be left undone, or to be done by other hands. It will be a hardy aspiration in any one to expect to match the samples by which such work must be tested. It is my belief that time will raise the public estimate of Robertson's powers, as shown in the works he has left. When no more is expected from the same source, the world will go back on them, and find them isolated from others in that exhaustiveness of examination and perfectness of finish which give them a place by themselves in the triumphs of archæological scholarship.

ness, and haifing sure knowledge of his thankful service done by him in tyme bygone, and for mair thankful service in tyme coming, that her highness stands content with the said earl, and has forgiven and forgives him and all others his complices." She intimated that she was minded to promote him to further honour for his services foresaid.[1] The first instalment of the further honour made its appearance on the same day, when he was created Duke of Orkney and Shetland.

And now the wedding was to come on. Some of the preliminaries had already been adjusted. To those who knew the character of the queen, the tendency of these must have been the most astounding evidence yet furnished of the absoluteness of the mastership that had been established over both her heart and her intellect. No man's life could more thoroughly deride the Puritanic religion professed by him than Bothwell's; yet he, an adventurer eagerly grasping at the advancement in his reach, would take it in no other than the Protestant form, while she, the bigoted devotee of the old Church, who was sacrificing everything else, sacrificed this too, and accepted the new form. The ecclesiastical functions proper to the occasion would have rested with Knox. He, however, was absent, a thing to be regretted by all who would desire to add an additional touch of picturesqueness to the scene. His assistant John Craig, however, represented him pretty faithfully. Craig proclaimed the banns from his pulpit, and when afterwards called in question for doing so by the General Assembly, he gave this account of the transaction. He had refused to make the proclamation,

[1] Acts of Sederunt.

when a messenger came from the queen to desire it.
Being afterwards shown a command under her hand,
he consulted his session or congregational court. Their
discussion seems to have been strong; but the conclusion come to was, that the intention of the sovereign
might be announced, leaving the final responsibility
on those who should carry out such intentions; and
Craig, in giving effect to this view, argued ingeniously
enough that, if the act to be carried out was so outrageous and abominable as it was pronounced to be, it
was doing good service to give the world previous
warning of the intention to perpetrate it; and it was
not his proclaiming, but the silence of others, that permitted the event to come to pass. The session came
at the same time to a resolution that they could neither
assist in nor approve of such a marriage, as it was contrary to a resolution of the General Assembly to unite
again in wedlock a person divorced for misconduct.
He made it, he says, a condition of the proclamation
that he should declare his mind to Bothwell himself in
the presence of the Privy Council. It seems to have
been thought prudent to submit to this; and Bothwell
had to listen to a castigation, for his conjugal misconduct and other irregularities; "the suspicion of collusion betwixt him and his wife; the sudden divorcement and proclaiming within the space of four days;
and last, the suspicion of the king's death, whilk his
marriage wad confirm." The object of this tirade
naturally enough, as its author says, "answerit nathing
to my satisfaction." Craig threatened to carry his views
before a more congenial audience; and he kept his
threat next Sunday, when from the pulpit, as he
says, "I took heaven and earth to witness that I ab-

horred and detested that marriage, because it was odious and scandalous to the world; and seeing the best part of the realm did approve it either by flattery or by their silence, I desired the faithful to pray earnestly that God would turn it to the comfort of this realm that thing whilk they intended against reason and good conscience." On this he was called before the Council for having passed the bounds of his commission, and there, still following his own narrative, "I answered, the bounds of my commission, whilk were the Word of God, good laws, and natural reason, were able to approve whatsoever I spake; yea, that their own conscience could not but bear witness that sic a marriage wad be odious and slanderous to all that should hear of it, if all the circumstances thereof were rightly considered."[1]

On the 14th, the day before the marriage, two documents were executed. One of them was a short assurance by the queen, that the persons who had signed the bond urging Bothwell on her as a husband should never be called in question for doing so. It is doubted whether the bond referred to is that signed at the celebrated supper, or one of later date. The other paper is a contract of marriage. It is cleverly and plausibly drawn, probably by that accomplished draftsman Balfour, and manages with much skill to neutralise the inequality of the match between the widow and "the right noble and potent prince, James, Duke of Orkney, Earl Bothwell, Lord Hailes, Crichton, and Liddesdale, Great Admiral of this realm of Scotland." With equal skill it throws the responsibility of this step on the distinguished persons who recommended it, and represents

[1] See the proceedings in Anderson, ii. 278.

her majesty as yielding, after full consideration, to their urgent prayers, because she considered their choice so thoroughly appropriate. There was no discussion, as on the two previous occasions, about the crown-matrimonial; but she virtually did her best to raise him to a joint occupancy of the throne, by stipulating that the signature of both should be necessary to all state documents passing under the sign-manual.[1]

A fit person for the performance of the ceremony was found in Adam Bothwell, who had been Roman Catholic Bishop of Orkney, and was a convert or an apostate, according to the estimate people took of his sincerity. The ceremony was performed on the 15th of May. Sir James Melville says he went little about Court at that time ; but it seems he could not resist the temptation to be present at so remarkable a wedding, though he entertained considerable fear of Bothwell, which would hardly be modified by his consciousness that he was then negotiating for his enemy's destruction. Bothwell's savage nature, however, seems to have been soothed by prosperity. He had some familiar talk and banter, trying to act the condescending prince to one whose sphere he had now left far below him. There was but little said, and that not very brilliant ; but it is valuable, as the sole instance in which one finds that mysterious demon of our history unbending into anything like geniality: "I found my Lord Duc of Orkney sitting at his supper. He said I had been a great stranger, desiring me to sit down and sup with him. I said that I had already supped. Then he called for a cup of wine and drank to me, that I might pledge

[1] The two documents here referred to have often been printed, and are in Labanoff, ii. 22, 23.

him like a Dutchman. He bade me drink it out to grow fatter; 'for,' said he, 'the zeal of the commonweal has eaten you up and made you sa lean.' I answered that every little member should serve to some use; but that the care of the commonweal appertanet maist til him and the rest of the nobility, who should be as fathers to the same. Then he said, I wist well he would find a pin for every bore." This was in reference to an old allegory about nature having made so many circular holes and so many angular, with a set of pins made to fit each, but mismanagement so confused the whole that the angular pins were forced into the circular holes and the circular into the angular. Bothwell, in administering the high functions likely to devolve on him, was not to make this mistake—a conceited announcement arrogating capacities for statesmanship which his career by no means warrants. The conclusion of the short scene is characteristic: "Then he fell in purpose of gentlewomen, speaking sic filthy language that I left him and passed up to the queen, wha was very glad of my coming."[1] If in this sort of eloquence he could shock one who had seen in that age so much of the world, and that not always the best of it, he must have been a master indeed in the invention and expression of lubricity.

Although one chronicler mentions that the ceremony was performed in the Chapel Royal, the probability lies with the other authorities who name the Council Chamber as the place. Le Croc, the French ambassador, said he was urged to attend, but declined. The attendance was meagre, the ceremonial strictly in the Protestant form. It was noted at the time, as one

[1] Melville, 178.

type of the reckless haste with which the affair was driven through, that it was not delayed to the expiry of the month of May, held by an old traditionary prejudice to be unpropitious to the nuptials it claims as celebrated within its own limits. The prejudice still has a lingering existence. As placarding had become the received method of expressing public opinion, a line from Ovid's Fasti, importing that they turned out to be wicked women who accepted wedlock in that forbidden month, was affixed to the palace door on the night after the wedding.[1]

The beginning of their wedded life resembled that of any innocent young couple affluent in the sources of magnificence and luxury. They were a good deal seen in public, and frequently rode together in much bravery. Stories were told how, when he, still preserving the etiquette of sovereign and subject, would attend her cap in hand, she would playfully snatch it and place it on his head. It may, indeed, be counted one of the most remarkable phenomena of the whole situation, that one of the subtlest and acutest women ever born should, in her fool's paradise, have been totally unconscious of the volcano she was treading on.

Some business had to be done, however; and, among other things, came up the proper diplomatic communication of the event to foreign Courts. A long document of extreme interest contains her instructions to William Chisholm, Bishop of Dunblane, sent as a special envoy to France to convey the intelligence and

---

[1] "Nec viduae taedis eadem, nec virginis apta
    Tempora; quae nupsit non diuturna fuit.
    Hac quoque de causa, si te proverbia tangunt
    Mense malas Maio nubere vulgus ait."
                                    —Fasti, lib. v.

The last was the line selected.

make suitable explanations. This document is curiously wavering and inconsistent. It begins with a eulogistic biography of her husband—what the French would call an *éloge*. His great services and merits are set forth at length; and since it has to be admitted that he was sometimes under the cloud of the royal displeasure, this is attributed to the envyings that ever dog high merit, and are successful for a time in obscuring it. In this portion of the document it is made clear that Bothwell amply deserved his preferment.

Having shown that what she had done was exactly what in justice and duty she should have done, she next tells how the surrounding conditions coerced her, so that, as a political necessity, she could not do otherwise. She found that his eminent services to the state and to her own person had not been achieved without exciting ambitious thoughts. She saw the somewhat audacious tenor of these, and tried to administer a judicious check to them. She failed. There was another element besides ambition which made him rash and headstrong in his acts—a devouring love for her. These combined motives conduced to rash acts, which brought her into his power. Then, when she considered her position, it was not merely that she was at the mercy of a man exulting in the consciousness of unparalleled heroism and statesmanship, and frantically in love with herself, but the whole nation was with him. She referred to the bond signed at the notable supper as a great demonstration of the chiefs of the state, such as a sovereign cannot without danger resist. The current in Bothwell's favour was so strong that not one man in Scotland appeared to stand up for her. Then she bethought her if she was right in her obstinate resistance. She began to yield to the wishes of her people, and at the same time her heart relented to the merits and the deep affection of her lover. Further, wearied out by the turbulence of the country she has to rule over, she feels how great a relief it will be to herself, how great a gain to law and order, that she shall have for her husband a man who has command in his nature, and can be trusted to rule her fierce subjects. These, indeed, would never "digest a foreign husband;" and of her own subjects "there was none, either for the reputation of his house or for the worthiness of himself, as well in wisdom, valiantness, as in all other good qualities, to be preferred or yet compared to him whom we have taken." Again the document takes a twist. There must be something said to palliate the extraordinary haste in this royal marriage. Such alliances were generally affairs on which a sort of congress of friendly royalties deliberated. It was but common decorum that she should have consulted the King of France, the queen-mother, her uncle the cardinal, and some others. Here, again, she throws the blame on the importunity of her lover, and the impatient pressure of the ruling powers of the country. Then, as if the writer felt alarm that what she said in her own vindication must react against the other, she pleads vehemently that all her friends must be the friends of him who is inseparably joined to her. The past is past. If he has been to blame, it was because his devotion overcame his discretion.

In some measure there is a key to the enigmas of this set of instructions, in another given to Sir Robert Melville for his guidance in explaining the affair to Elizabeth. This document is much shorter than the other. It bears solely on the political necessities which brought about the marriage—the necessity that she should have a husband capable to rule her turbulent people, their detestation of foreigners, the eminent services and merits of her husband, and the pressure of the ruling families. Nothing is said about the machinations of Bothwell, so fully set forth in the other letter. If we abstract these portions from the instructions for France, the remainder is in substance identical with the English letter. A comparison of the two leaves the impression that a note of the general policy to be adopted in communicating the marriage to foreign powers had been drawn up with care and deliberation, and that the queen had added her own particular story to the French instructions. This would account for the motley and almost contradictory character of the document. It is unsafe to adopt absolute theories on such internal evidence; but there is no escaping the vivid impression that, however the document was put together, those portions which narrate the personal conduct of Bothwell towards her are directly from herself. They endeavour to make out that she yielded to what could not be resisted; yet there is a consciousness throughout that she was guilty in not resisting. While she makes out to her old friends of France that the man she has married is in every way deserving of her love and of his eminent position—that he was the man of all others best fitted to be her husband—that political conditions made the act a necessity,—how comes it that she gives other and meaner reasons for her conduct, and gives them in an apologetic—a pleading—almost a penitential tone? My own opinion is, that her conscience then accused her of her one act of disaffection to the Church of Rome. On all other occasions—when she pursued Huntly to ruin and death —when she engaged to support the Church by law established—when she tolerated, or even caressed her brother and his heretic followers—she could plead that she bent to circumstances, in order that, when the right time came, she might stand up in fuller strength as the champion of the Church. But here she was struggling, and struggling in vain, to prove that the force of an engrossing passion had swept her for a time away from her allegiance; nor could she well assuage her own conscience or the wrath of her party by a brief declaration that, though forced to unite herself to a heretic, she will hold fast by her religion, and does not intend to leave the same for him or any man upon earth.[1]

The newly-wedded couple were left much to each other's society. Le Croc, the French ambassador, notices the melancholy emptiness of Holyrood, with a touch of the ennui which people of his nation are apt to feel in deserted banquet-halls.[2]

[1] These letters are published by Keith from what he calls "shattered MS." They have been on all hands accepted as genuine, and are reprinted by Labanoff, ii. 31 et seq. Obtaining them from a printed source, that careful editor was not able to follow towards them his laudable practice of explaining whether each document printed by him was taken from a contemporary copy or from the original, and in the latter case whether it was merely signed by Mary or holograph. It cannot be believed that she was sufficiently acquainted with the vernacular to have written the long letter for France straight off in her own hand. But whether or not it be a contemporary translation of a letter written by her in French, I believe that virtually all that criticises her husband's conduct is her own.

[2] Teulet, ii. 155.

CHAPTER XLVII.

Queen Mary.

(*Continued.*)

SYMPTOMS OF A RISING—THE QUEEN AND BOTHWELL TAKE ALARM AND LEAVE HOLYROOD—THE QUEEN IN BORTHWICK—ESCAPES THENCE AND JOINS HER HUSBAND—THEY TAKE REFUGE IN DUNBAR—PROVISIONS FOR THE SAFETY OF THE INFANT PRINCE—THE CONFEDERATE LORDS GET POSSESSION OF EDINBURGH—THE ARMED CONFERENCE AT CARBERRY—THE QUEEN'S SURRENDER, AND REMOVAL TO EDINBURGH—DIFFICULTIES IN DEALING WITH HER THERE—SHE IS TAKEN TO LOCHLEVEN—DISCOVERY OF A CASKET—ITS CONTENTS SAID TO BE POEMS AND LOVE-LETTERS ADDRESSED BY MARY TO BOTHWELL.—HOW THE CONFEDERATES RESOLVED TO DEAL WITH THIS DISCOVERY—EXAMINATION OF THE LETTERS—THEIR NARRATIVE OF THE QUEEN'S VISIT TO DARNLEY AT GLASGOW COMPARED WITH ANOTHER NARRATIVE OF THE SAME BY LENNOX'S SPY—QUEEN MARY ABDICATES—CONCLUSION OF A HISTORICAL EPOCH—ACCOUNT OF BOTHWELL'S ADVENTURES AND FATE.

SOME time passed over before anything occurred to break the surface of the tranquil happiness which the new-married couple appeared to enjoy. The first alarm of danger seems to have occurred in this manner. On the 28th of May the usual proclamation was issued for a "raid," or assemblage of the feudal force, for an attack upon the border marauders. The array was called upon to meet the queen and "her dearest spouse"—the force of the midland counties on the 15th of June, that of the border on six hours' warning.[1] It was said at the time that the intention was to use the army when assembled for other purposes. However this may be, instead of the usual clanging and bustling preliminaries of such a gathering, there was an ominous silence; and whatever was doing among the barons and their retainers, they were not flocking to the border. Those who were absent from Court stayed at home; those who had remained in Edinburgh slipped gradually away. Among them was Lethington, who said his life was in danger. It was as with Macbeth when he said, "The thanes fly from thee." Frightened by this silence, and probably by other hints, on the 6th or 7th of June the queen and her husband suddenly left Holyrood, and shut themselves up in Borthwick Castle, twelve miles from Edinburgh. Edinburgh Castle would have been the natural place of retreat; but that, for reasons to be presently mentioned, was not available. They were scarcely safe in Borthwick when the Lords Morton and Hume suddenly appeared with a hostile following of some six or eight hundred men—these were part of a larger force which had crept from various districts towards Edinburgh, expecting to seize the queen and her husband in Holyrood.

Borthwick, a thick-walled square tower like the old Norman keeps in England, was strong for a private fortalice, but could not stand artillery, as Cromwell afterwards showed by the results of a round or two. It could not accommodate a sufficient garrison to cope with an army such as was gathering round it, and the fugitives in their haste had not brought even such a

[1] See the proclamations in Keith, 395.

garrison as it could hold. There was nothing for it but flight or surrender for Bothwell; as to the queen, the muster professed rather to deliver than to attack her. Bothwell managed to escape. The queen might have joined the party arrayed against the castle; for if she had hitherto acted under either coercion or fear of her husband, both were at an end. With him all was suddenly over—there was not the faintest chance of his finding a party that would hold out for himself alone.

She took a different course, however. At dead of night she got herself let out alone, dressed as a page, and, mounting a pony, rode out upon the wild moorland. About two miles south-west of Borthwick is the tower of Cakemuir or Black Castle. There she met Bothwell with a small party of followers. There could be nothing more natural and seemly, under ordinary conditions, than that the captive wife should flee into the arms of her husband; but the specialties of the event made it significant and unfortunate for the stability of some amiable theories. They rode through the night to Dunbar; and thus, on a third memorable occasion, the queen entered that fortress.

So came the outbreak of a combination which had been rapidly maturing. The royal pair, having made no preparation to meet it, seem not to have been conscious of their danger; but it was palpable to the French ambassador, who, within three days after the marriage, wrote home that Bothwell was a doomed man.[1]

Before the marriage, the leading barons had been arranging with each other to cope with Bothwell.

[1] Teulet, ii. 155.

Gradually their objects went farther, and they spoke of dealing with the queen herself as one whom it was dangerous to leave in possession of the power she held. They opened communications with Elizabeth's ministers. That active spirit, Kirkcaldy of Grange, was the soul of their consultations and projects. He was one of themselves, as a landed man, who could bring some followers into the field; yet was he not restrained to the diplomatic reserve of the heads of the great houses, but could go about making himself busy everywhere as adviser, exhorter, or messenger. When they had felt their way so far as to know what reliance they could place in each other, they sought Elizabeth. She was so far with them that she was prepared to express any amount of reprobation against the chief actors in the late events in Scotland. There is reason to believe that these really vexed the rival, and rather malignant rival as she was, of the great actress in them. The utter ruin of one rival is not always pleasant to the other. It annihilates those elements of comparison which impart a zest to emulation and rivalry. There is nothing either to boast or feel internal satisfaction at in being something better than an utter wreck. Elizabeth had thus sufficient inclination to pour any amount of censure on the offenders; but she was startled when the Scots spoke to her about bringing their queen to justice, and making a new provision for the head of the government in the name of the infant heir. All her sensitiveness to the danger of letting subjects question the doings of their sovereigns was roused at once. To meet the exigency that the young prince was in danger, she offered to take him into her own charge—a proposal likely to excite derisive smiles among the Scots lords, who felt that the essence of their whole strength lay in the existence and the possession of the puling infant.

The question, indeed, of his safety proved an important turning-point in the progress of events. Mar, who had him in charge in Stirling Castle, was uneasy for his safety, judging the castle not sufficiently strong. Sir James Melville hints, but does not flatly say, that the queen herself had pressed Mar to give up the custody of her son, and that he had resisted, refusing to do so without the authority of the Estates of Parliament.[1] The question was, What was to be done in the difficulty of all the places sufficiently strong to retain so precious a charge being in the hands of the enemy?

Melville claims much credit for the diplomatic skill with which he conquered this difficulty. Edinburgh Castle was in charge of one of Bothwell's creatures, Sir James Balfour. His master, however, had lately shown some suspicions that his devotion was not sufficiently implicit. Melville, giving a direction to the uneasiness thus created, informed Balfour that he had it from Whitelaw, the captain of the Castle of Dunbar, that Bothwell was determined to take Edinburgh Castle from its present captain, and appoint the Laird Beauston, a Hepburn, in his place. Melville then enlarged on the great part Balfour would play, if he

[1] "My Lord Mar, wha was a true nobleman, wald not deliver him out of his custody, alleging that he could not without consent of the three Estates. Yet he was sa oft pressed be them that had the autority in their hands, that he was put to ane strait after that he had made divers refuses; that he made his moan to me among others, praying me to help to suif the prince out of their hands wha had slain his father, and had made his vaunt already among his familiars that, if he could get him ains in his hands, he suld warrant him fra revenging of his father's death."—Melville, 179.

should be the means of saving the queen and the prince from the man who was also going to sacrifice himself.[1]

The immediate consequence of this dealing seems to have been that, contrary to the general expectation, when the confederates returned to Edinburgh from Borthwick they were not fired on from the castle, but easily forced the city gates and entered—welcome to the inhabitants, who saw them pour in from the alleys leading to the gates and form on the High Street. James Beaton, the archbishop's brother, having gone to offer his duty to the fugitives at Dunbar, was sent by them with a message to Balfour to hold the castle for the queen and punish the rebels.[2] He found that the confederates had established a watch on the Castle-hill; and having managed to pass it, two of the leaders—the Lairds of Tullibardine and Rossythe—followed him to within twenty paces of the castle gate and brought him back. He managed afterwards to evade their diligence and get access to Balfour; but he found "the captain very cauld in his answering to her majesty's commandments." Presently afterwards Secretary Lethington appeared among the confederates—a token that there was life in their cause, and more to be thrown into it. He went to the castle, and, according to Beaton, "spak with the captain the space of three hours." This seems to have been conclusive, and the great fortress passed from Bothwell to the confederates. These took rapid steps to bring the machinery of government into their own hands, to be worked, of course, in the queen's name, and for the

[1] Melville, 180.
[2] Letter printed in Laing, ii. 106.

purpose of releasing her out of the restraint in which she was held. They invaded the "cunyie-house" or mint, and took possession of the fount and the "cunyie irons," or matrices for stamping coins. They offered a bounty for recruits, and readily obtained them. Finding themselves decidedly popular with the citizens, they made a curious appeal to their susceptibility by hanging up a picture of the finding of Darnley's body, the young prince bending over it with the legend, "Judge and avenge my cause, O Lord!"

One of the earliest steps of the confederates was to issue a manifesto; and as they were strong and in command of the capital, it was pitched in a high tone of authority. It is dated on the 11th June. It is a powerfully-reasoned and eloquent document—very different in tone from the pedantic formality of the bonds and other documents so plentiful on the other side. It refers to the murder in due terms of horror and indignation; and points out that, in a nation where such crimes not only go unpunished but uninvestigated, no one knows what deeds may be committed, and no one, high or low, can feel security for life. They are banded together for the investigation of this crime; for the release of the queen from the bondage in which she is held; "to cause justice be ministrate equally to all the subjects of this commonweal, and to purge this realm of the infamy and slander wherewith as yet it remains bruited among all nations." In this document there is not a breath of suspicion or disloyalty to the queen; the object held most prominently forward of all is to rescue her from her present misfortunes.[1]

[1] Anderson, i. 128.

Next day a proclamation was issued in the name of "the Lords of the Privy Council and the nobility." It charged Bothwell with having murdered the king, and afterwards used other unlawful means to seduce his sovereign into "ane unhonest marriage." It narrates, in its own way and with its own colours, the other events that had occurred, and asserts that he had made preparations "whilk we look can be with na other effect but to commit the like murther upon the son as was upon the father." Officers-at-arms are directed to pass to the market-crosses of Edinburgh, Perth, Dundee, St Andrews, Stirling, and other places, and charge all the lieges to be ready, at three hours' warning, to join their banner, and aid them in delivering the queen from captivity, punishing the murderers, and rescuing the royal infant from his father's fate.[1]

On the night of the 14th the confederates heard that Bothwell was approaching Edinburgh with a force, and they resolved to go forth and meet him. One of their reasons for not abiding his attack in their stronghold appears to have been that they could not have much reliance on the new-born virtue of the captain of the castle, should he be tempted by the presence of his old master at the head of a considerable force. They marched at two o'clock next morning. They were in all eighteen hundred horsemen and four hundred footmen—half of these were craftsmen, accustomed to watch-and-ward duty in the town. They came in sight of their enemy as they approached Musselburgh.

Let us look now to the other side. The fugitives reached the fortress of Dunbar at three o'clock in the

[1] Anderson, i. 131.

morning. The author of the Diary, attributed to the captain of Inchkeith, hearing of their arrival, set off to join them. He found them at Dunbar with hardly any one but a few domestics. He noticed the peculiarity of the queen's dress, especially the brevity of the red petticoat, and that she had prepared a couple of casts of hawks and two single birds for the field. She had other matters, however, to busy her, and was deep in despatches and messages to bring together a force. She set off next day to Haddington, with a guard of two hundred harquebussiers and sixty horsemen. By her own exertions and her husband's, she had six hundred horsemen round her when she reached Haddington. Their recruiting was in the very centre of the estates and jurisdictions with which she had invested him; and the old retainers of his house on the border, where he reigned almost supreme as warden, were within reach. The queen went on to Seton, her old haunt, and when there she could count sixteen hundred followers. At what point in the progress her husband joined her, those who narrate the affair, otherwise so minute, give no information. On the 15th, however, he had a gathering that, in numbers at least, seemed fit to cope with the confederates. These, however, had greatly the advantage in condition for the field. With the exception of a few sturdy burgesses, as the eyewitnesses note, they were mounted gentlemen, trained to fighting, and in excellent condition and discipline. Eighteen hundred of them were mounted; and in the sixteenth century, though artillery was breaking down the enormous superiority of horsemen over footmen, that would have been a formidable element in a considerable army. Le Croc, who noticed the preponderance of horsemen and their fine condition, also noticed, as a specialty he seems not to have seen before, that the Scots horsemen when halting abandoned the saddle, and only mounted for actual fighting. Bothwell's men were hastily collected; there had been no time to handle them, so as to know what they were fit for. He had no good captains; and, as an onlooker remarked, they were chiefly "commons" or peasants. He had with him a few cannon brought from Dunbar, and a portion of these he posted at a ford a little above Musselburgh.

To those anywise acquainted with the ground, it will be best understood how the two armies stood to each other by noting that the Esk, which passes Dalkeith and Musselburgh, was between them when they first saw each other. Bothwell's troops were on the southeast side, keeping the upper ridge of the hills or banks. The confederates crossed the river, and competed for the higher ground. They seem to have fidgeted about, trying as well to occupy high ground as to get rid of the annoyance of the sun being in their face, for it was a clear hot day. The country presents no decided sweep of predominant rising ground, but undulates; and so both forces occupied an elevation, with a burn running in the declivity between, now cut by a branch railway. The position taken up by Bothwell on Carberry Hill, where there remained some of the earthworks left by the English army after the battle of Pinkie, is still called Queen Mary's Mount.

While they were watching each other, Le Croc, the French ambassador, appeared on the scene, his diplomatic mind sorely perplexed by the anomalous sight. Here was royalty on the one side, and rebellious subjects on the other. With these was the bulk of the rank, statesmanship, and military capacity of the country—the men with whom he used to hold counsel as its government heads—here, too, was an army, small, but respectable both for the social condition of the men and their effective training. On the side of royalty he saw crime, folly, a few border lairds for a court, and a force of undrilled peasants. Le Croc, however, wished to be of service. He was a man of kindly nature, and, as representing the crown that had so long exercised a high influence in Scotland, he sought to do what he could to stay a conflict that must be the first of a civil war. In fact he must have felt that whatever he did on the occasion might have a material influence on the interests of his own country, and on his own position and repute as a statesman. The tone of the diplomacy of the day shows that the French Court at once took the alarm about the ancient alliance. It was predicted that the end of the doings at Holyrood would be that Scotland, severed from France, would be attached to England. The instructions to Le Croc and others pressed him to do his utmost to avert this calamity; and, in the sincerity of urgent pleading, the importance of keeping a hold on Scotland was set forth in terms that would have made any true Scot on either side indignant.[1] His way led first to the force of the confederates. With these he held talk, but not so long as to give the impression that he favoured their cause. Finding there no opening for accommodation, he left them, and

---

[1] "Le désir et intention principale de sa majesté est de conserver le royaume d'Escosse à sa devotion."—Memoir to, or communicated to, Le Croc; Teulet (8vo ed.), ii. 324.

returned in three hours to find the aspect of things unchanged. He besought them, for the love of God, and in the name of his master, who wished well both to the queen and to them, to try and find a way to accommodation. They said there was no other but the queen's giving up her husband to them. Speak of it, he said, as they would, their act was war against their queen; and should God favour them so that they gained a battle, they would be more than ever at a loss how to act. They said there were just two ways of averting bloodshed: the one was for the queen to part with the traitor in whose hands she was, the other was for him to step forth prepared for single combat. He would find one ready to fight him, and another, and another, up to ten or a dozen, if he desired it. The ambassador said both alternatives would be offensive to the queen, and he would have to do with neither: had they nothing else to offer? No, nothing; and in strong language they swore that they would get the truth of the king's death laid bare. He seems to have found himself in controversy with them. He intended, apparently, if he saw any hope of good results, to have passed at his ease between the two forces, bringing matters by degrees to a reconciliation. Having found as yet nothing but defiance among the confederates, he proposed to cross over and speak with the queen. This was objected to. He complained loudly of the awkward position in which he was thus placed. Communicating with them alone, he would appear to throw his weight into their side. They had no right to put him in that position; he must retire if he were not to see the queen. No restraint was put on him; but to pass over to the queen's force he required to have a proper convoy. He does not tell who they were who were so discourteous as to refuse him this; but he describes with vividness how Secretary Lethington came forward with graceful courtesy, expressed his respect for the ambassador of so great a king, to whom he and his friends offered their humble duty, desiring earnestly that the old alliance between the two nations might exist uninterrupted. He told the ambassador frankly that he was free to come and go at his will between the two forces, and would be provided, so far as concerned their side, with the means of doing so. They gave him an escort of fifty horse, who had to take him beyond their own proper lines; for he found that there had already crossed the brook, in advance on the queen's party, some two hundred troopers, with nine hundred as a support.

He was brought first in presence of the queen alone; and having paid his duty, he told her what grief the knowledge of her present position would bring to the King of France, and also to the queen—as to whom, however, the sincerity of his remark may be doubted. He told her that he had spoken with the confederate lords and what they had said, begging her to weigh their words and intentions well; for they were still her loving subjects, though the position they had taken might look otherwise. She said that they used her very ill, since she had only complied with their own bond, and taken the husband they had dictated to her. Nevertheless, if they would acknowledge his position and ask his pardon, she was ready to open her arms to them.

At this point the husband came up. He and the ambassador saluted each other; but the proud Frenchmen specially notes that he declined the embrace of friendship. He tells how Bothwell demanded, with an air of assurance, and in a loud voice that his followers might hear, if it was he that was wanted. The ambassador answered aloud that he had spoken to the other force, and they had assured him they were the very humble subjects and servants of the queen; and then, in a whisper for his own particular ear, that they were *his* mortal enemies. Bothwell, again speaking so as to be heard around, asked what he had done to them. He had never wished to offend any one, but desired to please all; they were influenced by mere envy of his greatness; but every man was free to enjoy his own good fortune; and there was not one of them but would gladly be in his place. Then he became very earnest, and besought the ambassador, for the love of God, to relieve the queen from a position which gave him great pain, and also to prevent bloodshed. Le Croc was free to tell the confederates that, though he had the honour to be husband to the queen, he would enter in gage of battle with any of them, provided he were of proper quality; and he would fight, holding his cause to be so just that he felt assured God would be with him. But the queen forbade this, and Le Croc declined to take the message.

Bothwell then remarked that more talk was useless; he saw his enemies coming, some of them having passed the brook. He hinted to the ambassador that, if he desired to imitate him who mediated between the armies of Scipio and Hannibal, he should hold himself impartial, and take part with neither side, but stand aloof during the fighting, and see the best fun that ever was; and if he would imitate this example, he would have the like, for he would see good fighting. Le Croc said it was not where the queen and these two armies were concerned that he would enjoy such a sight; on the contrary, it had never been his lot to behold a scene that could so grieve him. Some more talk of a general character they seem to have had before parting. Bothwell boasting of his own strength, the other admitted that he had a greater number of men—four thousand, while they had some five hundred fewer, and he had three pieces of artillery—but were all to be trusted to hold by his cause? Le Croc had just come from a force gallantly and sagaciously led, where there were several wise heads, and all were resolute; but here was no one to be depended on but the leader, and he questioned if more than a half would stand by him. In fact several slipped over to the other side, and the force was much weakened by many others falling out to refresh themselves in the hot day. Le Croc bade adieu to the queen with extreme regret, leaving her with the tear in her eye. He went back to the confederate lords, and told them the condition on which the queen would be reconciled to them; but they were resolute, and would have no more talk; and each taking his morion in his hand, bade him for God's sake depart, thanking him for his well-meant efforts. He withdrew accordingly, and returned to Edinburgh with a heavy heart.

After he went, the two forces, which had stood immovable from eleven in the forenoon till five in the afternoon, crept near each other; but each still sought an elevation, and when they were very close, it required that the one making the attack should go down into a little valley in the first place. The ambassador noticed the banners. The queen's was the royal lion; that of the confederate lords, their favourite picture of the murdered man and the infant prince.[1]

Presently a small party of the queen's force descended and proffered a parle. They were joined by a like body on the other side, and it was determined between them that the gage of battle should be tried. Tullibardine, understood to have been active in the affair of the accusatory placards, came forward, but Bothwell declined to acknowledge him as of sufficient rank. He wished to measure swords with Morton, but this life the confederates thought too valuable to be so risked. Lindsay was the next. He imitated, so far as was consistent with Protestant usage, the religious ceremony of the old gage of battle, and prayed on his knees conspicuously between the two forces. When the queen's consent was asked, she wavered, appeared to yield to such a sacrifice for the avoidance of bloodshed, but in the end forbade the combat.

The confederates now were determined to advance; and it became clear to Bothwell that his own party, thinned by deserters, and not all disposed to combat, would not stand the charge of the well-disciplined force descending into the hollow. Seeing this, it became part of the policy of the confederates to prevent the

[1] Le Croc describes it: "Une enseigne blanche, où il y avoit ung homme mort auprès d'un arbre, et ung enfant qui est à genoulx, representant le prince de ce royaume, qui tient ung escrit où il y a 'Revenche, O mon Dieu, de ma juste cause!'" The captain of Inchkeith, who seems to have had a heraldic mind, describes it with a characteristic difference: "Une ansigne blanche en quoy estoit tiré ung arbre vert, ayant une branch rompue, ung homme mort au pied, vestu d'une chemise blanche, dans un champ vert, et ung enfant assis audessus de son chef, tenant ung escriteau en sa main, disant, 'O Seigneur, juge et revange ma querelle!'"—Teulet (8vo ed.), ii. 306, 318.

escape of Bothwell; and Kirkcaldy of Grange was detached, with two hundred mounted men, to flank the enemy, and intercept his retreat to Dunbar. The queen observing Kirkcaldy, sent a message desiring to have conference with him; and having got a safe-conduct, he consented. He appears to have bluntly told the queen that all would honour and serve her if she would abandon the murderer of her husband. Melville tells us that, while he so spoke, "the Earl Bodwell had appointed a soldier to shoot him, until the queen gafe a cry, and said that he should not do her that shame wha had promised that he should come and return safely." This incident is not mentioned by the other narrators. It is not quite clear whether it was then, or when called on a second time to confer with the queen, that the confederates grew uneasy about his detention, and continued their advance. A hasty stipulation then passed that Bothwell should, unmolested, depart for Dunbar, and the queen render herself. They parted, as we are told, like fond lovers, with many kisses, and much sorrow on her part.[1] He mounted and galloped off with a slender train. His last words to the queen were an exhortation to continue true to her plighted faith.

At that moment the cup of the wretched woman's bitterness must have been filled to the brim. One by one every refuge had been closed; and over the wide world at home, as well as abroad, there was no quarter to which she could look for countenance. England from the first was not to be thought of. But at the Court of France the door was even more hopelessly

---

[1] "Avecque grande angoise et doulleur de son cousté; et plus souventefois s'entrebessèrent."—Captain of Inchkeith; Teulet, ii. 307.

closed. There was strong suspicion there of her guilt; and the deed was not one of those acts, perpetrated with Italian subtlety and external decorum in the inner recesses of courts, of which people circulate timid whispers, but was a flagrant act—the common talk of her own people. At all events she had become the husband of one guilty beyond all question of the crime held in chief abhorrence at Court; and not only so, but she had brought scandal on the royalty of France—she, the queen-dowager, allying herself with one too well known in Paris—noble, no doubt, as all Scots were, but a needy adventurer, seeking fortune wherever and however he could find her, and notorious for indulgence in vices of a low cast. Then the bulk of what was honourable and respectable among her own subjects had taken arms against her, and the rest would not strike in her defence. But sorest, perhaps, of all the arrows at her heart, was the unkindness of him for whom she had encountered all. This dread skeleton in the house can generally be kept in its secret receptacle in the courts of princes, and even the abodes of moderate respectability; but everything in Holyrood went on too passionately and flagrantly for concealment. Many noticed that she was an oppressed, insulted wife. But little incidents referred to by persons present are more expressive than general accusations. Le Croc said that, immediately after the marriage, she was curious to know whether he had noticed somewhat of her husband's strange usage towards her, and told him not to wonder if her manner were sad, for she was in deep distress. Once, too, in an inner chamber, where she was alone with her husband, she was heard to weep, and to say she wished she had a knife, that she might put an end to her existence. By a rare coincidence this was heard both by Le Croc and Melville — it was reported by the former to the King of France, and recorded by the latter in his Diary.

Such incidents are serviceable to those who hold that the unhappy woman was the mere helpless victim of fraud and force—a sort of realisation of the old stories about giants and enchanters, or of the romances with the tyrant lord who, gifted with powers almost as preternatural, seizes and imprisons the doomed princess. But there is another cause for such phenomena, with which the daily world is unfortunately more familiar —the woman with many gifts, and the one fatal weakness that induces her to throw them at the feet of an unworthy object; the victim of a blind imperious passion, giving herself over, body and soul, to one so thoroughly selfish and brutal, that no attachment or gratitude, no prudential restraint, will even for a brief space suspend the impulses of his sensual and tyrannical nature.

Whatever at that moment passed through her mind, the queen acted her part with her usual grace and princely decorum. According to Melville's Diary, she said, "' Laird of Grange, I render me unto you, upon the conditions ye rehearsed to me in the name of the lords ;' and gave him her hand, whilk he kissed, and led her majesty by the bridle down the brae unto the lords, who came forward and met her." Her selection showed a sagacious instinct, and her courtesy that day is believed to have won for her a champion. We are told that the lords used all dutiful reverence; "but some of the rascals cried out despitefully," until they were put down by indignant remonstrances and chastisement. And so the queen returned to Edinburgh.[1]

The confederates were not destined to find in their captive the meek resignation of a broken spirit. After the first touch of depression was over, a reaction seems to have come, which hurried her on into one of those outbursts of rage which, more than once in the course of her life, got the better of her usual subtlety. She let loose her formidable tongue, and hit right and left with maddening effect. She seems to have been particularly successful in finding a sore in the gruff and surly Lindsay, and to have torn at it remorselessly with her sharp sarcasm, while he, accustomed to weapons of a different kind, could retaliate nothing. What was more serious, however, than all this, she swore she would have all their lives; and spoke, even as she then was, like one luxuriating in the execution of her vengeance.[2]

When the captive reached Edinburgh, the procession got an ugly reception from the common people. The great High Street was filled with a mob deeply excited, who uttered revilings and accusations in abundance.

---

[1] The account of these transactions is, with some little assistance from Melville's Diary, taken from the accounts of three eyewitnesses, all happily uniting in the minuteness and the general conformity of their details. One is the 'Letter of James Beaton, the Archbishop of Glasgow's brother, to his brother Mr Andrew, to be given to the archbishop, containing the Proceedings in Scotland from the 11th to the 17th of June 1767;" printed in Laing, ii. 106. Another is a long letter by Le Croc to the King of France; printed by Teulet (8vo), ii. 312. The third is called 'Récit des Evénements du 7 au 15 Juin 1567, par le Capitain d'Inchkeith;' printed by Teulet, ii. 300. The Captain was a Frenchman; it was agreed at the treaty of Edinburgh that a small French garrison should continue to occupy this island in the Forth.

[2] "Ne parla jamais que de les faire tous pendre et crucifier, et continue tousjours."—Le Croc to Catherine of Medici; Teulet, ii. 310.

It was observed that the loudest and fiercest denunciations came from her own sex, and not the most virtuous portion of it. The scene in the celebrated banner, drawn apparently on a large scale, was spread before her, with sedulous endeavours to catch her eye whatever way she turned. A portion of the natural excitement of the time appears oddly enough to have expended itself on painting. Several representations seem to have been made of the discovery of the body, with more or less of allegorical machinery; and several other pictures made their appearance, which, either through allegory or an attempt to represent facts, gave shape to the feelings of their producers. Caricatures they could not be called, for they had a deadly earnestness about them—and still less were they entitled to be called specimens of historical art; but they were deemed as signs of the times, so important that some of them may now be found among the documents of the period, which were preserved in the State Paper Office.[1]

Another phenomenon of the time may be found in the creation of the Edinburgh mob. The strange exciting history passing before it gave it life; and, finding its strength, it continued, down to within the memory

[1] There is one in which an attempt is made to represent the whole scene of the murder—the shattered house, the Duke of Hamilton's house beside it, the city gate and wall, the remnant of the old Kirk-of-Field, the bodies, and the assembled crowd of citizens. A copy of this will be found in Chalmers's Life of Queen Mary. It is curious to observe how that industrious and earnest author, while deeply immersed in the furtherance of one of his hobbies, the vindication of Queen Mary, seizes the passing opportunity to give a lift to another which bore on the prevalence of the Celtic language and customs in Scotland. He takes the slight liberty of dressing about one-half of the attendant mob in the kilt and other elements of the modern Highland costume. A more correct rendering of the picture will be found in Laing's 'Registrum Domus de Soltre.'

of persons still living, a permanent and formidable institution. The well-trained force of the confederates was perhaps sufficient to control any actual violence. The condition of the town, however, was from the first embarrassing. It appears to have been owing to this that it was thought imprudent to convey the captive down the High Street and Canongate to Holyrood. Hence she was lodged in the house of the provost, which stood on the north side of the cross, where the Council-house and the Exchange buildings now stand.[1] Her conduct there is one of the most astounding features in the whole narrative. Several times during the afternoon she appeared at the window so scantily and carelessly dressed that the sight was inconsistent with proper feminine decorum; and there she moaned and cried and wailed to the mob that gathered thick upon the street. Beaton, with a touch of good feeling and that minute attention to detail which makes his story so valuable, says, "Na man could look upon her but she movit him to pity and compassion. For my ain part, I was satisfied to hear of it, and micht not suffer to see it." That she, who never was known to depart from the etiquette of her rank except to dignify that departure by her grace and wit, should so revolt against her proper nature, was an expressive addition to the astounding events that had excited the Edinburgh populace. It goes, with other incidents, to show that the terrible excitement of her recent life must have in some measure disordered her brain.

[1] Le Croc, when reporting this to his master, makes haste to remove the impression likely to be created at the French Court by this *bourgeoisement* treatment of royalty: "Je sais bien, sire, que ce nom de prévost sera bien odieux en France, mais en ce pays c'est comme la principale maison de la ville."—Teulet, ii. 319.

Lethington was an eyewitness of this scene. He went into the provost's house, and tried to soothe the queen. The street in front was cleared of the mob; but the excitement of the people had got an impulse, and Le Croc found that by evening there was much alarm about the preservation of peace in the city. Le Croc expressed himself satisfied that the confederates were reasonable in their ultimate views—that they only wanted to get her separated from Bothwell, in the belief that they might then safely return to their duty towards her as their sovereign. His chief anxiety, indeed, was lest they should not feel strong enough to cope with their enemy, and might seek assistance from Elizabeth, a contingency that might be fatal to the French alliance. He seemed to hint to them that, rather than this should be, they might expect aid from France; but he implored them, if possible, to get this affair brought to a conclusion.

But under Le Croc's eyes, and even while he was explaining these views to Lethington, the affair took a sudden and disagreeable turn. Believing that the queen led a miserable life with her husband, the confederates thought she would be easily severed from him. Her wild talk the night before, however, had led them to suspect that she was frantic to return to his arms, and she had acted so as to confirm this view. Le Croc was told by Lethington that he had had a conversation with her, in which she reproached him for severing her from the husband with whom she hoped to live and die with all the satisfaction in the world. He answered that he and his comrades were far from feeling that they did her injury by this separation; on the contrary, they believed it to be in every way the best thing for her future honour and tranquillity. He tried what jealousy would do, and said her husband was still in correspondence with his former wife, and had told her that she was his real wife and the queen his mistress. The queen gave an angry denial to this, and he shortly replied that the letters would show it. Lethington said the conference ended by her asking if she and her husband would be permitted to depart together in a ship, to sail where fortune should direct. To this draft on the precedents of the romances the "Chameleon," as Buchanan calls him, made answer, evidently in a vein of dry sarcasm, that, provided the pair did not happen to land in France, he thought it about the best thing they could do. It seems clear, too, that she wrote a letter to her husband, which the messenger she had hired to convey it faithlessly delivered to the confederates. Melville renders its purport as " calling him her dear heart, whom she should never forget nor abandon for absence ; and that she sent him away only for his safety, willing him to be comforted, and to be upon his guard."

In this state of matters—the city in commotion, a frantic queen within it, and an unscrupulous enemy at hand, whom she would do everything to help—the leading men seem to have adopted a hurried resolution that there was no alternative but to get the queen " sequestered " in some place, quiet, remote, and safe. Le Croc, who carefully watched what was doing, and immediately reported it home, was unable to give the same satisfactory account of these hasty movements as of the deliberate proceedings of the confederates. He knew that at nine o'clock in the evening she had been conveyed to Holyrood as if to reside there in her usual state, but that during the night she had been taken to the port of Leith, where a vessel received her with her attendants and a guard. Farther than this he was at fault. In his letter to his king dated 17th June, he presumed that their destination was Stirling; but in his next he said the queen had been taken to Loquelin, or Lochleven.

The 20th of June, three days after these stirring events, is the date of an incident small in itself, and known at the time to few, which proved, however, of mighty moment in the politics of the day, and has since given occasion for a whole library of critical and disputative literature. Bothwell, in his hurry to leave Edinburgh, left behind him, as people on such occasions are apt to do, an article which he highly valued. It had been taken with him into the Castle of Edinburgh, and there left. It is described as a casket about a foot long, decorated with silver over gilt, and bearing the crown of France and the initials of Francis II., from whom it had passed to his widow, and then to her third husband. It contained papers of value, and Bothwell was very anxious to recover them. He sent his servant, George Dalgleish, to bring the casket from Edinburgh to Dunbar. The man was intercepted, however, and the casket found its way to Morton's hands. It is possible that a hint may have been given of the removal by Balfour the governor; but as Dalgleish was then wanted as an accessory of the murder of Darnley, the probability is that he was apprehended on this ground, and the casket found with him. The papers afterwards produced as the contents of this casket, whether, indeed, they were its real contents or mere forgeries, were the ground on which the subsequent actions of Queen Mary's opponents rested; and hence it is that the little incident of the discovery of the casket expands into a great political event.[1] Besides the contract of marriage already referred to, and some other documents, the momentous portion of these papers consisted of eight letters and some poetry called sonnets, all declared to be in the handwriting of Queen Mary, and in that Latin or Italian form of writing which she was about the first to practise in Scotland, and which at once distinguishes her manuscripts from the ordinary Gothic writing of the period.

The literary history of these letters and sonnets is curious. The originals have long been lost. They were among Morton's effects when he was executed; and there has been an impression that they passed into the hands of King James, by whom they were destroyed.[2]

[1] The chivalrous class to whom Mary's innocence is a creed rather than an opinion will not blame me for having constructed my narrative without reference to the contents of the casket. In the supposition that they are genuine, they were a secret between two criminals which did not yet begin to influence others; and it seemed to be the historian's proper duty to deal with what was known to, and consequently influenced, the actors at large on the political stage. From the 20th of June 1567, however, the ruling power in Scotland took its stand upon the import of these letters; and it is, therefore, from that day that they properly become a part of public history.

[2] In a letter to me by the late Joseph Robertson, one of the last he wrote, is the following curious passage :—

"I have often puzzled myself as to the fate of the letters produced from the silver casket. I am not satisfied with the story which Principal Robertson tells in a note to the later editions of his History, and which may now be read at more length in Sir R. Bowes's Correspondence, printed by the Surtees Society. To my mind, there is a more significant passage in a book where no one would think of looking for such a thing, in Round's edition of Bishop Ken's Prose Works, London, 1838. It is in a letter from the nonjuring antiquary, Dr Thomas Smith, written in 1707 :—

The source from which we now know their nature is a Latin translation of them appended to Buchanan's Detection of the Doings of Queen Mary, published in 1572. In the translation of that work, which appeared in the same year, and is attributed to Buchanan himself, there is a rendering of the whole into the Scots vernacular, and of nearly the whole into French. Having them in this shape, we have no means of critically judging of the style of the original; and any evidence that might be found in the minuter turns of expression, sometimes so effective when the general tenor of the writing is ambiguous, is lost. The tone of these papers is, however, so impetuous, and their tenor so emphatic and distinct, as to leave, at least in the essentials, no doubtful meanings which a reference to the original might have cleared. These same qualities render it practicable to give a description of the documents, and a brief rendering of their more emphatic

" ' However the great ministers by whose counsels she [Q. Eliz.] was influenced and governed, thought fit to have registered the commission by which Q. Mary was tryed, and the whole processe of her tryall, amongst the rolls of the Exchequer: of which I shall give your lordship a briefe account from a paper under the hand of Mr Arthur Agard, one of the Deputy Remembrancers of the Exchequer, which I met with in the Cottonian Library, and signed by him in February 1603:—

" ' " The Commission, with a written booke touching the execution of it, was delivered into the receipt office of the Exchequer, Westminster, by the L. Treasurer Burleigh in the year 1595, but was taken thence by the command of K. James, 20 June 1603, and delivered to the L. Treasurer Buckhurst, and was never restored though demanded."

" ' I conclude, I think not unjustly, from this last passage, that it was utterly destroyed, K. James I. taking effectual care that this record should never appear in after times to the infamy of the queen his mother.'—P. 91, 92.

" King James did not reach London till the 7th May 1603, and his possessing himself of the proceedings against Q. Mary on the 20th June 1603, a month before his coronation, is a curious proof of his zeal to destroy everything which told against her."

passages, without the risk of injustice. To feel the significance of these passages, it is only necessary to keep in view the chain of events which begins with the queen's visit to her sick husband in Glasgow.[1]

The first letter is very long. It goes over many minute transactions, to some of which we have now no clue. It is apparent, however, that to a forger they must have been perilous material, as affording numerous points from which his work might be assailed. She apologises, indeed, for writing about everything, however trifling, in order that the receiver of her letter may have the means of estimating the significance of all the occurrences. In this abridgment it is considered unnecessary to glean from the document anything that has not in itself a plain meaning, or a reference to some known and significant event. She begins with a sentiment: having gone from the place where she had left her heart, it will easily be believed how unable she was to enjoy society, insomuch that, until dinner-time, she spoke to no one, nor did any one venture to address her. Four miles from Glasgow she was met by a gentleman of Lennox's household—the same Crawford whose account of these transactions is elsewhere referred to. There was some rather exciting talk. Crawford had to explain how Lennox did not come in person—he was scared by the harsh words the queen had used to Cunningham—probably the same who after-

---

[1] It is scarcely necessary to inform the reader where he will find the documents at length. They have been repeatedly printed, and are given in nearly every one of the voluminous pleadings on both sides of the great controversy. The most carefully edited copy of them is, however, undoubtedly that given by M. Teulet in the volume of 'Lettres de Marie Stuart,' which he published for the purpose of supplying deficiencies in Prince Labanoff's Collection.

wards represented Lennox at Bothwell's trial. The queen remarked that Lennox would not have been afraid to come had he not been conscious of guilt. She then stood on her dignity, and closed the discussion. Others she encountered, with whom her conversation was still more obscure and incidental; but she remarked that none of the Glasgow citizens came to see her, whence she inferred that they were on her husband's side. Of him the first note we have is an inquiry of one of the domestics of the queen, why she lodged not beside him. If she did so, he would rise the quicker from his sick-bed; and he was anxious to know whether her visit was intended as a step towards reconciliation. He particularly desired to know if Bothwell himself were in his wife's train, and also if she had made her "State." He wanted to know if she had taken Paris and Gilbert into her service, and was to send Joseph Rizzio away. She expressed extreme annoyance at his being thus accurately informed of her private motions—he spoke even of the marriage of Bastiat! When they met, she taunted him with some complaints in his letters about the hardships he had to suffer. He, instead of answering to the point, gave words to his astonishment and excessive joy at seeing her—he believed he might die of gladness, but he rallied her on her pensiveness. In a second visit which he begged of her, he said his sickness was caused by her unkindness—he would make no testament, but only leave everything to her. Then comes an outpouring, which she professes to report in full: "You ask me what I mean by the cruelty spoken to in my letters. It comes of you alone, who will not accept of my promises and repentance. I confess I have been in fault, but not in the shape which I ever denied. So also I have failed in my duty to some of your subjects, but this you have forgiven. I am young. You will say you have forgiven me over and over, and still I repeat my offences. May not a man of my age, for lack of counsel, fall twice or thrice, or fail in his promises, yet repent, and be chastened by experience? If I be forgiven, I protest I shall never sin again. I desire nothing whatever but that we may live again at bed and board together as husband and wife; and if you will not consent to this, I shall never rise out of this bed. I pray you tell me your resolution. God knows how I am punished for making my god of you, and for having no other thought but on you. And if I am remiss towards you, you are yourself the cause; for when I have cause of offence, if I might take my complaint to yourself, I would go nowhere else; but when I hear rumours while you are estranged, I am of necessity compelled to keep it to myself, and this irritates me until it makes me beside myself with anger."

She says she answered him on each particular, but her part of the discussion was too long to be set down. Then follows the general purport of a talk about her husband's suspicions as to plots for his assassination, and his plans to escape abroad. The matters are briefly touched, as if the writing were to be read by one minutely acquainted with the particulars. Among these there is a certain "purpose of Heigate"—referring to a person so named, a servant of Bishop Beaton, whom Mary herself had charged with propagating a tale that the king was to take the young prince and have him crowned.[1] The impression made by these explanations,

---
[1] Letter to Beaton; Labanoff, i. 396.

as by several others of a like kind dispersed through the correspondence, is that she has exhausted all the particulars of his fears, suspicions, and general grumblings, as completely as an able counsel draws out of an unwilling witness everything he knows.

She describes with a slight touch of scorn how she brings him on from suspicion to unwelcome demonstrations of tenderness. He wants her to sleep in his lodging, to walk with him, and to take him away with her when she goes. He refers at the same time to the terrors now dispelled. He believes she, his own flesh and blood, would do him no harm; and he boasts that others would find it difficult to assail him. Then comes one of the significant passages. If she did not know that his heart was of wax, while her own was of diamond, incapable of being penetrated from any quarter but the adored one she addresses, she might have almost had pity on the poor creature. But no fear; she will hold out: let him she addresses take heed that he be not seduced by that false race, his wife's family. A little farther down she says they are coupled with two false races. "May the devil sever us from them, and God unite us together for ever!" Between the two allusions to the false races she asks if he is not inclined to laugh to see her lie so well, or at least dissemble with gleams of truth between. Next she is getting tired, and thinks of postponing her task till the morning; but she cannot sleep unless it were, as she would desire, in the arms of her dear love. Here she desires him to tell her what he intends to do in the matter he knows about, that nothing be mismanaged. Then come more tokens of weariness, and remarks on her husband's disease, which perhaps would not sound so offensive in the original French as in the translations. His breath, she says, has nearly slain her; and to realise its offensiveness, she tells Bothwell that it is worse than his own uncle's. She had almost forgotten to say that, in presence of the Lady Reres at supper, Livingston had rallied her on the sorrowful condition in which she had left a certain person at a distance.

The continuation appears to be a resumption next day. She had worked two hours at a bracelet for her beloved, trying to make it lock; he must be careful not to show it, for it has been seen, and will be at once traced to her. She is now going to recommence her detestable purpose. The lord of her heart makes her dissemble, so that she feels like a traitress; if it were not in obedience to him, she would rather die than do it—her heart bleeds at it. She found she had the work to do over again, and her husband was by no means so compliant as she had left him the evening before. He will not come with her unless she agree to live with him at bed and board as before; and his suspicions crop out again, to be smoothed down by her skilful tongue. He will do whatever she desires, and will love herself and all that she loves. Then follow a few penitential words, and the old excuse that she is led by a hand she cannot resist. As a token of the implicitness of her obedience come in some words—very few, but so significant that they must touch with awe whoever comes incidentally across them, whether he believe them to be the woman's own, or forged by others for her condemnation. She prays her lord to consider whether the deed might not be done in some more secret way—by medicine, for there must be medicine with the bath at Craigmillar. Then another passionate wail about her horror of deceit—she would not do it for her own particular revenge, she does the bidding of the spirit that has mastered hers. A good deal there still is in the letter; but it is incoherent repetition about her husband's suspicions and her own spells to lull them, the bracelet she sends as a love-token, her jealousy of his wife's influence, and her assurance that she is ready to sacrifice honour, conscience, rank, and life itself for her chosen lord's love.

There are eight letters in all, but this one alone is longer than all the rest together. It bears a general date, January 1567. The second in order is specially dated 25th January. It is a short querulous letter, complaining of forgetfulness and neglect; her husband is still in a trusting and caressing humour; she playfully remarks that her true lord may think he is making love to her and with success, but his very presence renews her infirmity in her side. One articulate announcement there is—she brings the man with her to Craigmillar on Monday, and there he will remain all Wednesday, while she goes in to Edinburgh to be bled.

The third letter, set down as written from Glasgow in January, but not on a specific day, is rather purposeless. It shows that Bothwell apprehended danger from her profuse writing and her many messages, and she craves forgiveness for disobeying his injunction neither to write nor send; and yet there seems to be no practical object to be served in the letter—it looks like a mere irrepressible outburst of suspicion and jealousy of her rival the existing wife. She wonders whether that rival is to win over her what the second love of Jason won. There is something dramatic in the effect of this allusion to the Medea. The mind worked up to the point on which it tells, conscious that the letters recall some vision of love and jealousy drawing on their victim to hatred and murder, might, even unaided by the hint, have remembered the terrible creation of Euripides.[1] After much amorous and jealous raving, the letter ends with a brief notification that she was afraid to write in the presence of Joseph (Rizzio), Bastiat, and Joachim, and had to wait till they departed.

The next is a short letter in the same tone as the rest, but bearing on some incidental grumbling of her lord, as to something that one of her women had done which frightened or displeased him.

All these letters are attributed to the month of January; the next is, on the same ground—internal evidence—referred to April. It deals with the plot for carrying her off to Dunbar. She is distracted by the uncertainty of the arrangements and the insufficiency of his information for her guidance. Then comes to her in her perplexities his false brother Huntly, who, professing to act as his messenger to fix the time and place where he was to intercept her, breaks in with his croakings : It was a foolish enterprise, and with her honour she could not marry the man who carried her off while yet he was the husband of another; and then her majesty's guard in attendance would never be got to submit to such a humiliation.

[1] In the 'Inventory of the Queen's Books in the Castle of Edinburgh, delivered by the Earl of Morton to King James VI.,' is 'The Historie of Jasone.'—Inventories, cxlvi.

But she has now gone so far that she is resolved to complete the work. No persuasion, not the prospect of death itself, can shake her resolution. Then come jealous and querulous railings. Why call on her to fix the place? He should have adjusted all that, and told her. He has risked all through that false brother whom she does not trust with her letter; but if failure be the end, she will never raise her head again. The bearer will tell him her miserable plight; and what effect his vacillations and indistinct counsels must have on it let him judge. She had expected other things, but she sees the influence of absence and of that other one. He must not send an answer by Huntly; and so God give him good-night.

The next letter is a short piece of subtle casuistry. It looks forward to the way out of the difficulty into which they are plunging. She thinks his services, and the good esteem long entertained for him by his brother lords, may justify his pardon, should he take on himself beyond the duty of a subject—not to restrain her, but to assure himself of such a place near to her, that the persuasions or interference of others may not prevent her from consenting to realise the hopes which he may have founded on his services. To be short, let him make himself secure of the lords and free to marry; and let him represent that, to be able to serve his sovereign faithfully, he was driven to join an importunate act with a humble request. He knows, if he likes, how to set the matter in right trim, and will not neglect many fair words to Lethington. If he like not the deed, let him say so, and not leave the whole burden on her.

Circumstances gave those who had the handling of

the letters the means of precisely dating the next on the 22d of April. It begins about his brother-in-law that was. There are no jealousies or suspicions of treachery in that quarter now; but he has perplexed her with doubts about the affair to come off the day after to-morrow, because there are many, and among them the Earl of Sutherland, who will rather die than see their sovereign lady carried off when under their protection. She is assured that he wishes to be honest, but she sees that he fears a charge of high treason. All this must foster caution and care. They had yesterday three hundred horse, including Lethington's; for the honour of God, let her lord be accompanied with rather more than less; and so she prays God that they may have a happy meeting.

There remains yet one letter, perhaps the most remarkable of all for the passionate vehemence with which it expresses the unconditional surrender of the writer's heart, its utter hopeless captivity, its owner's abject resignation to the will and humour of the victor, mixed with faint but agonised wailings about the incompleteness of the return, the stint of that full flow of entire reciprocity which is now the breath of her life. There is now no jealousy of another. There are no uncertainties or plans or difficulties. It is fervid passion throughout, pressing forth with a vehemence that seems almost to choke the utterer. It is coloured throughout with extreme dejection and sadness, like a consciousness of the shadow of coming calamity.

Of the tell-tale contents of the casket there still remain to be dealt with some verses called " The Sonnets." They are divided into sets of fourteen lines each; but there is no separate unity of purpose in each of these sets, nor do they contain any other specialty of the sonnet proper. That she was acquainted with these specialties is shown by a real sonnet written after long imprisonment and affliction. It condenses into unity those solemn verses scattered through the ninth and tenth chapters of the Epistle to the Hebrews which speak of the old material sacrifices of slain animals as superseded by one atonement, which requires of mankind only the purifying qualities of faith and humility. It is clear that the casket sonnets have been a continuous poem, cut up by the translator or editor into pieces of the canonical length of the sonnet, but without entire success, since the whole was not divisible by fourteen, and the last of the sonnets contains only six lines.

There is, in fact, a unity of purpose throughout the whole. It is a wild wailing of love, jealousy, and despair. She is withheld from the object of her frantic adoration by the double marriage—nay, worse, by his attachment to her rival. And what sacrifice does that rival make to be set beside all that *she* is prepared to lay down? If the other gives love, she has love in return. She is protected by the respectable bond of matrimony. She has been a worldly gainer, for she has been elevated by the favour which the devotion of another has conferred on her husband. And that other—what is *she* not ready to sacrifice? Rank and position; but these are nothing. Her life, her fair fame, her infant child, her immortal soul—all will be thrown at his feet.

There is no Latin translation of the sonnets; and in their Scots and French guise they have little to adorn them but the sheer fervency of their passionateness.[1] Brantome spoke of them as unworthy of her pen; but there is scarcely any chance that he could have seen the contents of the casket, and a retranslation from Scots into French would be poor material for testing the merits of the original. Nor is it quite clear whether he is giving us his own opinion, or merely the result of conversation with others. French critics of the present day do not confirm the popular notion that Queen Mary was gifted with the genius of poetry. They even talk disrespectfully of those lines on the death of her husband which Brantome himself preserved and published as a testimony to her genius.[2] French critics have gone farther of late, and deposed poor Mary from the poetical rank which she held as the reputed author of some pretty lines bidding adieu to her beloved France.[3]

[1] As printed in the Detection they are called "Certane Frenche sonnettis writtin be the Queen of Scottis to Bothwel befoir hir marriage with him, and (as it is said) while hir husband levit, but certainly befoir his divorce from his wyfe, as the words themselfs shaw."—Forbes, ii. 115.

[2] M. Chasles, in his 'Etudes sur W. Shakspeare, Marie Stuart, et L'Arétin'—a curious conjunction—calls these lines "rimes barbares," and says, "L'expression en est dure et la pensée vulgaire."—P. 23.

[3] "Adieu, plaisant pays de France !
O ma patrie,
La plus chérie,
Qui as nourri ma jeune enfance !
Adieu, France ! adieu, nos beaux jours !
La nef qui dejoint nos amours
N'a eu de moi que la moitié
Une parte te reste, elle est tienne,
Je la fie a ton amitié
Pour que de l'autre il te souvienne."

M. Philarete Chasles having started a doubt as to the reputed authorship of these lines, the question was taken up and hunted to its conclusion by Fournier, and the result will be found in that amusing book, 'L'Esprit dans l'Histoire.' He proves that the lines were written in

There is still another piece of poetry—the admitted work of Queen Mary—with which the sonnets may be compared. When her councillor and ambassador, Bishop Leslie, was imprisoned in the Tower for his zeal in the cause, he wrote a book of meditations, which he sent to the queen. She was pleased with the gift, and comforted by its perusal; and under this influence sent in return, in a poetical shape, her own meditations upon his.[1] An effort, supposed to be longer and more ambitious, on 'The Institution of a Prince,' has unfortunately been lost sight of.[2]

There are two theories on which the guilty conclusion to which the casket documents point has been resisted with great perseverance and gallantry: the one is that, as we now see them, they have been tampered with; the other, that they are forgeries from the beginning.

All questions raised on the prior theory are at once settled by the fact that those to whom the letters were

Queen Mary's name by Meusnier de Querlon, and first published by him in 1765 in his 'Anthologie.' It gives a zest to his success to be able to quote from the pompous M. Dargaud, who, speaking of Mary and her genius, says, "Ces vers sont désormais inséparables de son nom." Querlon was accustomed to such tricks; or, as Fournier says, "Prenait volontiers plaisir à ces sortes de mystifications littéraires." He published a little book called 'Les Innocentes Impostures;' but all his were by no means innocent. He was the editor of one of the editions of the infamous book, 'Meursii Elegantiæ Latinæ Sermonis,' in which the foulest pruriences that the language could express were published as the production of a virtuous and distinguished scholar.

[1] 'Meditation fait par la Reyne d'Escoce, Dovairière de France, recueillie d'un Livre des Consolations Divines, composez par l'Evesque de Ross;' Bannatyne Miscellany, i. 343.

[2] "The queen, his majesty's mother, wrote a booke of verses in French, of the Institution of a Prince, all with her ounc hand, wrought the cover of it with her needle, and is now of his majesty esteemed a most precious jewel."—Montague's Preface to the Works of King James. It is stated by the same author that Darnley translated Valerius Maximus.

first shown drew conclusions from them as damnatory as any they can now suggest. Little more than a month after the documents were in possession of the confederates—on the 25th of July—Throckmorton, the English ambassador, got sufficient information to write home that "they mean to charge her with the murder of her husband, whereof, they say, they have as apparent proof against her as may be, as well by the testimony of her own handwriting, which they have recovered, as also by sufficient witnesses."[1] Farther still, Sir Ralph Sadler made what may be called a *précis* of the significant portions of the documents. According to the natural practice on such occasions, he briefly sweeps over the trivial or indistinct passages, and dwells on those which convey significant conclusions, translating them at full length; and these translations echo the corresponding passages in the letters, as we now possess them, with decisive precision.[2]

The theory of an entire forgery seems not to have occurred to any of those friends or foes of the queen who saw the documents. In the Parliament held in December there were several of her partisans present, such as Huntly, Athole, Errol, Herries, and others; but we have no hint anywhere that they stood up for her fame, or had anything to say, when, in the very body of an Act of Parliament, the nature of the documents

---

[1] Keith, 426.
[2] Sadler State Papers, ii. 337. Sadler, with his usual methodicalness, divides his notes of the papers under three heads: 1. "The special words in the Queene of Scotts' lettres, written with her oune hande to Bothwell, declaring the inordynate and filthie love betwixt hir and him." 2. "The specyall words in the said lettres declaring her hatred and detestacion of her husbande." 3. "The specyall words of the saide lettres touching and declaring the conspiracie of her husband's deth."

and the guilty conclusion drawn from them were set forth in the plainest and severest terms.[1] The theory of forgery, indeed, seems to have become prevalent only after any appeal to the original writings, and to the recollection of the persons referred to in them, had ceased to be practicable. And it is impossible not to connect the absence of contemporary impugnment with a notable peculiarity in these documents. They are so affluent in petty details about matters personally known to persons who could have contradicted them if false, that the forger of them could only have scattered around him, in superfluous profusion, allusions that must have been traps for his own detection.

Wherever any of these petty matters comes to the surface elsewhere, it is in a shape to confirm the accuracy of the mention made of them in these letters. For instance take the "purpose of Heigate," referred to in the first letter. In no history, letter, or state paper of the day is that matter referred to except one, and that is a confidential letter by the queen herself to Archbishop Beaton, in which she desires him to warn his servants not to prate on such matters, and refers, just as in the casket letter, to the story having been spoken of by Walker, a servant of Beaton's, and told to Lennox by the Laird of Minto.[2] Again there is a reference in the same letter to a matter, the explanation of which has cast up only the other day. Among other inquir-

[1] "Anent the Retention of our Sovreane Lord's Motheris Person" (Act 1567, c. 19). Here the Parliament, among their reasons for their conduct towards her, say it is to be attributed to "her own default, in sa far as be divers her privie letters written halely by her aun hand, and send be her to James, sometime Earl of Bothwell, chief executer of the said horrible murther, as well before the committing thereof as thereafter." —Act. Parl., iii. 27.

[2] Labanoff, i. 397. See above, p. 427.

ies which teased her, as showing that the sick man knew more about her doings than she liked, was an inquiry whether she "had made her State." This State is now visible in the papers published by M. Teulet; and a very important document it is, being a recasting of the pensions and salaries of officers chargeable on Mary's income as Queen-dowager of France. The sum total, of which it records the distribution, exceeds thirty thousand livres—an enormous sum in that day. The unseen existence of this separate expenditure, and of the official persons to whom it passed, has caused occasional tripping among historians, who are at a loss to account for persons who, like Rizzio and his brother, are spoken of as holding distinguished offices, while no trace of them in their official position can be found in the constitutional records of the country. The document is signed by the queen and her private secretary, Joseph Rizzio; and its date, 13th February 1567, coincides with its being under consideration about the time of the momentous visit to Glasgow.[1]

It will not readily be admitted that any weight should be given to coincidences between the casket letters and the facts narrated in the dying confessions of the inferior persons executed for the murder. There

[1] 'Estat des gaiges des dames, damoiselles, gentilzhommes, et outres officiers domesticques de la Royne d'Escosse, Douairière de France;' Teulet (8vo), ii. 268. This document would be sent to France as a warrant for the respective payments announced by it. By far the greater portion of the recipients are French; and some who perhaps are not so are not easily recognisable as Scots—for instance Ceton for Seton, and Letinthon for Lethington. The highest salary, however, goes to a Scot—Beaton, Bishop of Glasgow, who gets 3060 livres. It may be noted, for what it is worth, that Bothwell's name does not occur in this list of beneficiaries. The editor of Queen Mary's Inventories notices the identification of this document with the "State" mentioned in the casket letter.

was a person less open to suspicion, however, who was an eye and ear witness at some of the scenes described in these letters, and his testimony concerning them was recorded in a very peculiar manner. This was Thomas Crawford, an adherent of the house of Lennox, who was in personal attendance on Darnley, when he was sick in Glasgow and received the memorable visit from his wife. It is stated, in the Journal of the commissioners who sat at York, that this man was brought to give evidence before them. It was found that the evidence he had to give was something much more clear and specific than any mere recollection of past events. He stated that old Lord Lennox, being afraid, as we have seen, to trust himself away from his own fortress and his own people, while he was in a state of great anxiety and suspicion about the object of the unexpected visit, had instructed Crawford carefully to note down all he saw or could learn of what went on. Crawford said he not only set down in writing what he was witness to, but that the king was very communicative to him about the private interviews with the queen, at which no third person was present. According to the record of his testimony, he stated " that he did, immediately at the same time, write the same, word by word, as near as he possibly could carry the same away; and sure he was that the words now reported in his writing concerning the communication betwixt the Queen of Scots and him upon the way near Glasgow, are the very same words, on his conscience, that were spoken; and that others being reported to him by the king are the same in effect and substance as they were delivered by the king to him, though not, percase, in all parts the very words themselves." This document being read to the commissioners, Crawford affirmed it, " upon his corporal oath there taken, to be true."¹

It has often surprised me that, although casually referred to as in existence, this paper should not have been printed among the documents, many of them less expressive, which have been heaped together in the collections regarding Queen Mary. It could not fail to be extremely instructive on the one side or on the other. Guided to its existence in the Record Office at the Rolls by the Calendars recently issued, an opportunity has been found of comparing it with the casket letter.

Of the result I can only say that the two agree together with an overwhelming exactness.² Of course

---

¹ The Journal of the Commissioners, apud Westminster, die Jovis, nono die Decembris 1568; Anderson, iv. 169.
² The following may suffice as a specimen:—

CRAWFORD'S TESTIMONY.	THE CASKET LETTER.
" She asked him of hys sicknesse; he annswered, that she was the cause thereof. And moreover, he saide,' Ye asked me what I ment bye the crueltye specified in mye lettres; yat procedethe of yow onelye, that wille not accepte mye offres and repentance. I confesse that I have failed in som thingis, and yet greater faultes have bin made to yow sundrye times, which ye have forgiven. I am but yonge, and ye will saye ye have forgivne me diverse tymes. Maye not a man of mye age, for lacke of counselle, of which I am verye destitute, falle twise or thrise, and yet repent, and be chastised bye experience ? Gif I have made anye faile that ye but thinke a faile, howe soever it be, I crave your pardone, and proteste that I shall never faile againe. I desire no other thinge but that we maye be together as husband and wife. And if ye will not consent hereto, I desire never to rise forthe of this bed. Therefore, I praye yow, give me an aunswer hereunto. God knoweth howe I am punished for	" ' Ze ask me quhat I mene be the crueltie contenit in my letter; it is of zow alone, that will not accept my offeris and repentance. I confes that I have failit, bot not into that quhilk I ever denyit; and sicklyke hes failit to sindrie of zour subjectis, quhilk ze have forgevin. I am zoung. Ze wil say, that ze have forgevin me oft tymes, and zit yat I returne to my faultis. May not ane man of my age, for lacke of counsell, fall twyse or thryse, or in lacke of his promeis, and at last repent himself, and be chastisit be experience ? Gif I may obtane pardoun, I protest I sall never mak fault agane. And I craif na uther thing, bot yat we may be at bed and buird togidder as husband and wyfe; and gif ze wil not consent heirunto, I sall never ryse out of yis bed. I pray zow, tell me zour resolutioun. God knawis how I am punischit for making my god of zow, and for having na uther

every one is at liberty to maintain that Crawford's statement is entirely false, and that it was got up to support a forgery. In such repudiations, as in the length to which St Denis could carry his head, the first step is everything. It might also be maintained that

making mye god of yow, and for having no other thought but on yow. And if at anie tyme I offend yow, ye are the cause; for that when aine offendethe me, if for my refuge I might open mye minde to yow, I woulde speake to no other; but when anie thinge is spoken to me, and ye and I not beinge as husband and wife ought to be, necessite compellethe me to kepe it in my brest, and bringethe me in suche melancolye as ye see me in.'

"She aunswered, that it semed hym she was sorye for his sicknesse, and she woulde finde remedye therfore so sone as she might.

"She asked him whye he would have passed awaye in the Englishe shippe.

"He aunswered, that he had spoken with the Englishe man, but not of minde to goe awaie with him; and if he had, it had not bin without cause, consideringe howe he was used. For he had neather to susteine him sellfe nor hys servantes, and neded not make farder rehersalle thereof, seinge she knewe it as well as he.

"Then she asked him of the purpose of Hegate. He aunswered, it was tolde him.

"She required howe and bye whome it was tolde him.

"He aunswered, that the L. of Minto tolde him that a lettre was presented to her in Cragmillar, made bye her owne divise and subscribed bye certaine others, who desired her to subscrive the same, which she refused to doe; and he said that he woulde never thinke that she, who was hys owne propper fleshe, woulde do him anie hurte; and if anie other woulde do it, theye should bye it dere, unlesse theye tooke him slepinge, albeit he suspected none. So he desired her effectuouslye to beare him companye. For she ever founde som adoe to draw her sellfe from him to her owne lodginge, and woulde never abyde with him paste two houres at once."

thocht bot on zow; and gif at ony tyme I offend zow, ze ar the cans, becaus quhen ony offendis me, gif for my refuge I micht playne unto zow, I wald speik it unto na uther body; bot quhen I heir ony thing, not being familiar with zow, necessitie constrains me to keip it in my breist, and yat causes me to tyne my wit for verray anger.'

"I answerit ay unto him, bot that wald be ovir lang to wryte at leuth. I askit quhy he wald pas away in ye Inglis schip. He denyis it, and sweiris thairunto; bot he grantis that he spak with the men. Efter this I inquyrit him of the inquisitioun of Hiegait. He denyit the same, quhill I schew him the verray wordis was spokin; at quhilk tyme he said that Mynto had advertisit him that it was said that sum of the Counsell had broeht ane letter to me to be subserivit to put him in presoun, and to slay him gif he maid resistence. And he askit the same at Mynto himself; quha answerit, that he belevit ye same to be trew. The morne I wil speik to him upon this point. As to the rest of Willie Hiegait's, he confessit it; bot it was the morne efter my cumming or he did it."

THE CASKET DOCUMENTS, 1566-67. 443

the memorandum of Crawford being true, afforded the conspirators the materials from which they could work up the details of their little picture of a domestic interior. Before adopting, however, any theory against the genuineness of this document, it would be well for the enthusiast to weigh the possible influence of that darkly suggestive conversation between Darnley and his domestic, in which they exchange their suspicions about the unexpected visit — suspicions in which murder is an element.[1]

Such theories, and the impossibility of confuting them to the conviction of those who choose to maintain them, is one of the incidents of the rather forensic tone in which the great controversy about Queen Mary has been conducted. A leaf has been taken from the Old Bailey, and it has been maintained that she should be counted innocent until she is proved guilty. But in the legal sense this is impossible about long past events. To comply with it, we would require to place Crawford in the witness-box, cross-question him, and search the world for testimony until we fill up all gaps and explain all inconsistencies. These things are the strong securities with which the law surrounds the rights of living men, especially their lives or their liberties. We all know multitudes of things which are not judicially proved, which we could not judicially prove; yet the law requires that before we act on them, to the injury of our neighbour, they shall be so proved. If the life or liberty of a British subject could be made to depend either on proving Queen Mary guilty or proving her innocent, neither could be made out in such a manner as to secure a verdict. At

[1] See above, p. 338.

the present day we have no evidence on which we could hang Felton, who stabbed the Duke of Buckingham in Charles I.'s time, or even the man who shot Spencer Perceval. It would be the same with the death of Cæsar and the execution of Charles I. Such a way of going to work would blot out history, by making its parts extinguish each other, like the equivalents in an equation. If Queen Mary is entitled to the benefit of all doubts, the confederate lords who brought the charges and evidence against her are entitled to the benefit of all doubts to protect their character from the stigma of conspiracy.

The judge may be bound to release the accused, although in his secret heart believing him to be guilty; but in history belief is all, and belief cannot be resisted when it comes, nor can a leaning to the stronger probabilities where there is doubt, let the effect on the fame of some long dead actor in the history of the world be what it will.

But while thus tenacious of the privileges of an accused person, these enthusiasts demand a conclusion from which such a person is excluded by the act of seeking their protection. The verdict of "not guilty" founded on imperfection in the evidence, is no proclamation of innocence. Its tenor is generally more distinctly interpreted by an expressive form in use in Scotland. When the jury do not find reason to proclaim a case of calumniated innocence, but give the accused the benefit of defective evidence, they find a verdict of "not proven." It would perhaps surprise some enthusiasts of the present day to find contemporary vindicators going no farther than the demand

of a verdict of "not proven." Their reason was the
same material one that influences modern trials. They
maintained that there was no sufficient case made out
for depriving her of her queenly rights. The evidence
was not conclusive, and she should have had the
benefit of the doubt. Those who believe in her as a
saint martyred by wicked men, would find disagreeable revelations in reading what is said by the early
class of vindicators.[1]

Though this controversy has produced dazzling
achievements of ingenuity and sagacity, I would be
inclined not so much to press technical points of evidence as to look to the general tone and character of
the whole story. In this view, nothing appears to me
more natural than the casket letters. They fit entirely
into their place in the dark history of events. They
are thoroughly characteristic of one who, inheriting
the common blood of James IV., the Tudors, and

[1] Take, for instance, this passage from 'A Defence of the Honour of
the Right High and Noble Princess Marie, Queen of Scotland and Dowager
of France :' " I would, then, farther demand of them what authority
they had to summon and assemble a Parliament ? And whether this
fact of hers, supposing she were shown guilty, deserveth in her, being a
prince, and considering how heinously the Lord Darnley had offended
her and the crown of Scotland, such extreme punishment to be levied
upon her for one simple murther, especially by them that committed
that shameful murther upon her secretary, that have committed so
many treasons, and daily do commit so many horrible murthers upon
the queen's true loving subjects ? How many, and how cruel and terrible
deaths do such traitors deserve ! We have, moreover, to demand of
them, whereas they pretend a marvellous and a singular zeal to religion
and holy Scripture, and to measure all their doings precisely by Scripture and order thereof, what sufficient warrant they have therein, by
their private authority, to lay violent hands upon their anointed prince ?
I find there that King David was both an adulterer and also a murtherer.
I find that God was highly displeased with him therefor ; yet find I not
that he was therefor by his subjects deposed."—Anderson's Collection, i. 56.

the Guises, was trained at a Court where good faith, justice, and mercy were represented by Catherine of Medici, and the social morals were those of the 'Dames Galantes' of Brantome and the novels of Queen Marguerite.

Suppose it to have been settled in conclave that such a set of letters were to be forged, who was there with the genius to accomplish the feat? Nowhere else, perhaps, has the conflict of the three passions, love, jealousy, and hatred, been so powerfully stamped in utterance. Somewhat impoverished though it may be in the echo of a foreign medium, we have here the reality of that which the masters of fiction have tried in all ages, with more or less success, to imitate. They have striven to strip great events of broad, vulgar, offensive qualities, and to excite sensations which approach to sympathy with human imperfections. And, indeed, these letters stir from their very foundation the sensations which tragic genius endeavours to arouse. We cannot, in reading them, help a touch of sympathy, or it may be compassion, towards the gifted being driven in upon the torrent of relentless passions, even though the end to which she drifts is the breaking of the highest laws, human and divine. A touch of tenderness towards those illustrious persons who show their participation in the frailty of our common nature by imperfections as transcendent as their capacities, is one of the mysterious qualities of the human heart, and here it has room for indulgence. In fact it is the shade that gives impressiveness to the picture. With all her beauty and wit, her political ability and her countless fascinations, Mary, Queen of Scots, would not have occupied nearly the half of her present place in the interest of mankind had the episode of Bothwell not belonged to her story.

The question, Who could have forged such documents? receives in no quarter a distinct answer. In other instances of attempted identification, as of Eikon Basiliké, or the Letters of Junius, attempts have been made to bring the matter home by identifying specialties of style, method of handling, and turns of thought. No one, however, has tried to prove that these documents resemble any one's acknowledged writings.

Buchanan is the person naturally hinted at as the author of the contents of the casket, having been the first to draw public attention to them. But if we suppose him morally capable of such an act, it is pretty clear that it did not come within his intellectual capacity, extensive as that was. The little domesticities in the letters would not suit the majestic march of his pen. In the Detection, to which he appended the documents, he shows that, had he prepared these himself, he would certainly have overdrawn them. In fact, in that philippic the great scholar and poet shows that, although he may have known politics on a large scale, he was not versed in the intricacies of the human heart. Everything is with him utterly and palpably vile and degrading, without any redeeming or mitigating element. The love that, if wicked, yet takes the tone of feminine attachment and pure devotedness, becomes in his hand mere lust, breaking out in brutal and degrading acts. The flagrant proceedings of this guilty couple, and their pander the Lady Reres, a cast-off mistress of Bothwell's, sometimes even admit of ludicrous postures, which the author describes with sarcastic zest. The quarrels of the

king and queen are like those that might pass between
a passionate strolling actress and the good-for-nothing
husband she has to support by her talents. She starves
him and lets him go in rags, while the favourite fares
sumptuously and is endowed with stately dresses and
jewellery. She grudges him the charge of a physi-
cian in his sickness. She carries off his service of plate,
and replaces it with pewter. A quantity of incredible
charges are heaped up; and among others, that she
tempted her husband into acts of low profligacy, that
she might get him divorced, " to make empty bedroom
for Bothwell." She sleeps soundly, with a satisfied
mind, when she hears that her husband is dead—she
gloats over his dead body, unwilling to take her eyes
from so delightful a sight — she insults it with the
sordidness of the funeral appliances — her glee is
irrepressible, and will not be controlled by any
usages of Court etiquette or even common decorum.
She lays plots to open a deadly feud between her
husband and Murray, in the hope that one of them
may fall—little matter which, it will be a hatred the
less to her. And what was he for whom she sacrificed
herself, body and soul? He was not only polluted by
the vilest crimes, but he had none of the external
qualities with which bad men varnish their wickedness. He was hideously ugly, boorish in manner, a
babbler in talk, and a coward in action. Where, then,
was the attraction? In the common degradation of
the two—their cruelty, falsehood, and lust. It is, perhaps, not the least incongruous feature of this picture,
with its blacks and whites, that the victim stands, in
contrast with his slayer, as endowed with constancy,
truthfulness, and general goodness.

But while those who have gone into the intricacies of the story cannot accept the conclusions of the Detection, they cannot read it without acknowledging that it is a great work of rhetorical art. It bears up throughout the grand forms of ancient classical denunciation, rising, with blow after blow, up to the thundering climax. It is for this reason that it is so extravagant. It was among the rhetoricians a *tour de force*, as the French say, to make the denunciation perfect—a total annihilation of a cause or a character; and any ray of light or hope, any redeeming touch, was a defect, almost an infringement of the great principles of rhetoric.

Such a work, put forth in the common language of the learned by its greatest master, had immense influence over Europe. It was paralleled by a scarcely less remarkable translation for the benefit of the people of Scotland. This conveys a very distinct impression of the power of the old Scots tongue, and its capacity to march alongside of the language of Rome, preserving the same grand historic step. It will be found to differ much from Knox's style, though both wrote powerfully, and were adepts in denunciation. To say that Knox has a touch of vulgarity would not be correct; but he is more homely. He affected to write in the English of the day; and though his style is abundantly rich, it wants a certain sinewy terseness which his friend and coadjutor finds in the old Scots tongue.[1]

[1] " Albeit thir thingis were thus done as I have declairit, yit thair ar sum that stick not to say that the quene was not onely hairdly, but alswa cruelly delt with; that efter sa detestabill ane fact, sche was removit from regiment ; and quhen they cannot deny the fact, they complane of the punischment. I do not think thair wil be any man sa schameles to think that sa horribill ane fact aucht to have na punischment at all ; bot if thay complane of the grevousnes of the penaltie, I feir leist to all gude men we may seme not to have done sa gentilly and temperately

With all its exaggerations and extravagancies, the Detection is the work of a man thoroughly sincere. Buchanan believed in the fundamental fact of the guilt, and he brought out his belief in the fashion of his special accomplishments as a classical scholar, with due devotion to the method of the rhetoricians. There are accusations in the Detection not to be believed, and yet the statement of them there is an important revelation. It gives us the popular feeling about Queen Mary. This feeling, of course, arose and had its chief seat among the populace of Edinburgh, before whom the tragedies of her reign had been acted. But it was a period of action and excitement, and whatever moved the centre was taken to the extremities of the

---

as lously and negligently, that have laid sa licht ane pane upon ane offence sa haynous, and sic as was never hard of befoir. For quhat can be done cruelly aganis the author of sa outragious ane deid, quhairin all lawis of God and man ar violatit, despysit, and in maner haillely extinguischit ? Everie severall offence hes his punischment baith be God and man appointit. And as thair be certane degreis of evill deidis, sa ar thair also incressis in the quantiteis of punischmentis. If ane have slane a man, it is ane deid of itself verray haynous. Quhat if he have slane his familiar freind ? Quhat if his father ? Quhat if in ane foull fact he had joynit all thir offencis togidder ? Surely of sic a ane nouther can his lyfe suffice for imposing, nor his body for beiring, nor the judge's policie for inventing, pane aneuch for him. Quhilk of thir faultis is now comprysit in this offence ? I omit the meane commoun materis—the murthering of ane young gentilman, ane innocent, hir countriman, hir kinnisman, hir familiar, and hir cousing-germane. Let us also excuse ye fact, if it be possibill sche unadvisidly, ane young woman, angrie, offendit, and ane of greit innocencie of lyfe till this tyme, has slane ane lewd young man, ane adulterer, ane unkynde husband, and ane cruelle king. If not ony ane, bot all thir respectis togidder, wer in this mater, thay aucht not to availe to schift of all punischment, bot to rais sum pietie of the cace. Bot quhat say ye, that nain of thir thingis can sa mekle as be falsly pretendit ? The fact itself, of itself is odious in ane woman; it is monstrous in ane wyfe, not onely excessively luifit, bot also maist zealously honourit—it is incredibill. And being committit aganis him quhais age craifit pardone, quhais hartly affectioun requyrit

country by the burgesses and lairds who attended the Estates, and the clergy and lay members of the Assembly. It is its foundation on popular feeling that gives the Detection its tone of vehemence and confidence. The declaimer will not be at the trouble of going into the evidence; the thing is notorious, the public voice is filled with it.

The fallaciousness of such a test is notorious. The atmosphere of public rumour that surrounds any marvel is sure to exaggerate and distort it. But the existence of that atmosphere is in itself an important psychological phenomenon; and of such a phenomenon we have a vivid picture in the Detection. It is a truer echo of public opinion than we can find

lufe, quhais neirnes of kyn askit reverence, quhais innocencie micht have deservit favour—upon that young man, I say, in quhome thair is not sa mekle as alledgeit ony just caus of offence thus to execute and spend, yea, to exceid all tormentis dew to all offencis, in quhat degre of crueltie sall we accompt it? Bot let thir thingis availl in uther personnis to rais haitrent, to bring punischment, and to mak exempillis to posteritie. Bot in this cace let us beir mekle with hir youth, mekle with hir nobilitie, mekle with the name of ane prince. As for myne awin part, I am not ane that think it alway gude to use extreme straitnes of law—na, not in private, meane, and commoun personnis. Bot in ane maist haynous misdeid, to dissolve all force of law, and quhair is na measure of ill-doing, thair to discend beneth all measure in punisching, wer the way to the undoing of all lawis, and the overthraw of all humane societie. Bot in this ane horribill act is sic ane hotch-potch of all abhominabil doingis, sic ane egernes of all outragious crueltie, sic ane forgetfulness of all naturall affectioun, as nathing mair can be fengeit or imaginit."—Anderson's Collection, ii. 85-88.

This is the work of a mind saturated with the spirit which comes to its perfection in the oration against Verres : " Quod si hæc non ad cives Romanos, non ad aliquos amicos nostræ civitatis, non ad eos qui populi Romani nomen audissent ; denique si non ad homines verum ad bestias ; aut etiam ut longius progrediar, si in aliqua desertissima solitudine, ad saxa et ad scopulos hæc conqueri et deplorare vellem, tamen omnia muta atqua inanima, tanta et tam indigna rerum atrocitate commoverentur."

in Knox, because it is the echo of reaction. To Knox she was a Popish Jezebel from the beginning. But Buchanan, though a zealous Protestant, had a good deal of the catholic and sceptical spirit of Erasmus, and an admiring eye for everything that was great and beautiful. Like the rest of his countrymen, he bowed himself in presence of the lustre that surrounded the early career of his mistress. More than once he expressed his pride and reverence in the inspiration of a genius deemed by his learned contemporaries to be worthy of the theme. There is not, perhaps, to be found elsewhere in literature so solemn a memorial of shipwrecked hopes, of a sunny opening and a stormy end, as one finds in turning the leaves of the volume which contains the beautiful epigram 'Nympha Caledoniæ' in one part, the 'Detectio Mariæ Reginæ' in another; and this contrast is no doubt a faithful parallel of the reaction in the popular mind. This reaction seems to have been general, and not limited to the Protestant party; for the conditions under which it became almost a part of the creed of the Church of Rome to believe in her innocence had not arisen.

To come back to the contents of the casket, which were first made public along with the Detection. The question of their genuineness is surrounded by doubts and disputes; but about another matter there can be no doubt—namely, that the party in power resolved to treat them as genuine, and steer their policy accordingly. She was to be dealt with as a murderess. Whatever demands might be made on her were to be backed by the prospect of a public trial and the block. It was a tacit foreshadow of strong measures that both the English ambassador and a special envoy from the

THE ABDICATION. 453

Court of France were refused access to the queen. If she was still queen, this was a deadly affront to two great powers, and there could be no way out of the difficulty but a dethronement.

The secret counsels of the confederates were not long of coming out in action. On the 23d of July the Lord Lindsay and Robert Melville set off on a memorable mission to Lochleven. They presented to the queen two documents, which she must sign : the one, a renunciation of her crown in favour of her son ; the other, an appointment of Murray to the office of regent during the child's minority. Several stories got afloat about what passed at this interview. It was said that Melville, who had a preliminary private interview with her, carried, concealed in the sheath of his sword, a letter from a friend, recommending her to consent to everything, as all she did while under restraint might be revoked. Another account says that Lindsay, provoked by her obstinacy, lost his temper, and used violence. But Mary's was not the spirit to be broken by brute force. The influence that made her sign the deeds must have been crushing indeed. There is no doubt that the tenor of the casket letters was brought before her; indeed the first rumour of their existence was in a letter written two days afterwards by Throckmorton, stating that the confederates boasted of possessing sure evidence of her guilt. At all events, the deeds were signed. Of course documents of so much moment were drawn up in the perfection of formality. They do not contain a hint of guilt or a reference to Bothwell. Any one stumbling on them as they are recorded in the statute-book, without any explanation from the events of the age, might take them for the voluntary utterance of one weary of the cares of a throne, going, like the Emperor Charles V., to seek consolation in the calm of monastic life. She declares the act to be done of her own free will; and of her motive to it, that, "after long, great, and intolerable pains and labours taken by us since our arrival within our realm for government thereof, and keeping of the lieges of the same in quietness, we have not only been vexed in our spirit, body, and senses thereby, but also at length are altogether so wearied thereof that our ability and strength of body is not able to endure the same." The deed of demission appointed, as a commission of regency in Murray's absence, the head of the house of Hamilton, Lennox, Argyle, Athole, Morton, Glencairn, and Mar. The affixing of the privy seal was wanted for these documents, but the keeper refused so to use it. This little difficulty was got over by Lindsay, who took it from him by force. The documents were ratified in Parliament, with a declaration that the prince's title was as effectual as if his mother, at the time of his coronation, "had been departed out of this mortal life."

From the date of these documents Mary Stewart ceases to appear as sovereign in the public proceedings of the realm, and the reign of King James VI. begins.

An item remains in the winding-up of the tragic story, before we open a new chapter in history. The remorseless villain of the plot, who has bent a finer nature than his own to his evil purposes, has to be disposed of. It is an end quickly told. He escaped to his dukedom of Orkney—that one of his feudal estates which was farthest off from the avenging power. It was long believed that in his island principality he got a small fleet fitted out, with which he turned pirate captain in the north seas. This was a suitable end for such a career, according to the rules of the romances; but to a man so marked and pursued, for whom every sea would be swept, the attempt would be certain destruction. Grange was in pursuit of him, and in dire emergency he made vehement efforts to get the means of escape to the northern states of the Continent. It happened that he thus purchased the vessel of a troublesome pirate named David Wodt. When this craft was seen off the Danish coast, it was naturally under suspicion; and when it was taken in charge by a Danish ship, and Bothwell found in command, and in the broken-down condition of one fleeing from justice, there naturally followed an investigation when he was landed at Bergen. His story, that he was a king in difficulties, made the affair inexplicable and wonderful; but it was soon seen that he was not the pirate who had transacted business in the ship he sailed in.[1]

He seems to have become popular—to have been getting, as it were, into society—in this northern region, when trouble came upon him in a shape that, affect-

[1] We owe these revelations to a justly popular writer of travels in northern Europe, who, finding himself in the scenes of Bothwell's latter days, thought it worth while discovering what local records there were of his sojourn. He found in the record which he terms the Liber Bergensis, how, "September 2, A.D. 1568, came the king's ship David, upon which Christian of Aalborg was head man. He had taken prisoner a count from Scotland of the name of Jacob Hebroe of Botwile, who first was made Duke of the Orkneys and Shetland, and lately married the Queen of Scotland, and after he was suspected of having been in the counsel to blow up the king. They first accused the queen, and then the count; but he made his escape and came to Norway, and was afterwards taken to Denmark by the king's ship David."—Marryat's Jutland, chap. xxvii.

ing the final destiny of a life like his, has, by contrast, an air of the ludicrous. He was claimed by a certain Anna, daughter of Christopher Trandson, as her husband, who had deserted her; and it seems to have been on this charge, and not for any reason of state, that he was detained in the Castle of Malmoe.[1]

Strong demands were made for his extradition both by England and Scotland, but they were resisted. The Danish Government offered to put him on trial, under their own laws and before their own courts, for any crime he might be charged with, but would not give him up.

There was a rumour that he had died in 1573. It was received as conclusive in England and Scotland, and the name of Bothwell belonged only to the past. It would seem, however, that this rumour was propagated to save Denmark from the pursuit of the troublesome pressure to render him up. Bothwell, at all events, lived down to the year 1577, leaving, in a country not peculiarly temperate, records of hard drinking and wild carouses with those who would join him in his revels. He died in the Castle of Draxholm, and was buried in the church of Farveile.[2] Not many years ago there came to light a vindication of his

[1] On the 17th of September, "Mrs Anna, Christopher Trandson's daughter, brought a suit against the Earl of Bothwell for having taken her away from her native country, and refusing to treat her as his married wife, although he by hand, word of mouth, and by letters had promised her so to do, which letters she caused to be read before him. And inasmuch as he had three wives living—first, herself; then another in Scotland, of whom he had rid himself by purchase; last of all, the Queen Mary—Mrs Anna was of opinion that he was not at all a person to be depended on; he therefore promised her the yearly allowance of a hundred dollars from Scotland, and gave her a pink, with anchor, cable, and other appurtenances."—Marryat's Jutland, chap. xxvii.

[2] Marryat's Sweden, 16-18.

conduct, written at some length, and intended for a public state paper. It is valuable only as showing the shape which the lies of such a man put on. He maintains his own innocence and that of the queen, and both with pretty equal success, showing how he was the unconscious victim of the machinations of Murray, Lethington, and other his enemies. He left behind him a shorter paper in the shape of a confession. It is an example, added to countless others, of a phenomenon peculiar to the nature of criminals—a propensity to confess things not charged against them, while denying those as to which guilt is beyond possible question. With unseemly details, the murderer of Darnley confesses to sins and vices which nobody heard of and nobody cared about. Among other things equally credible, he said he owed his influence over Queen Mary to philters and sweet waters.[1]

[1] 'Les affaires du Conte de Boduel,' Bannatyne Club. These papers will also be found among the ' Documents relatifs au Meurtre de Darnley,' printed by M. Teulet, in his 'Supplément au Recueil du Prince Labanoff', 1859.'

END OF THE FOURTH VOLUME.